*The John Harvard Library*

*The History of the Province of New-York*
*Volume One*

*William Smith, Jr., in 1751*

The John Harvard Library

# The History of the Province of New-York

Volume One

## From the First Discovery to the Year 1732

by William Smith, Jr.

*Edited by Michael Kammen*

The Belknap Press of Harvard University Press
Cambridge, Massachusetts 1972

© Copyright 1972 by the President and Fellows of Harvard College
All rights reserved
Library of Congress Card Number 78-160028
SBN 674-40321-5
Printed in the United States of America

*For Jane and Wendell Garrett*
*Yorkers by adoption*
*and dear Friends*

# Acknowledgments

During the four years of intermittent effort and indulgence required by this project, I have received assistance and correspondence from many considerate people. I am indebted to James W. Henderson, Chief of the Research Libraries of the New York Public Library, for permission to use William Smith's original manuscript as the basic text for Volume Two of this edition. I am obliged to Clive E. Driver, Director of The Philip H. and A. S. W. Rosenbach Foundation, in Philadelphia, for permission to publish Smith's extensive marginalia interleaved in his personal copy of Volume One.

Bernard Bailyn, erstwhile Editor-in-Chief of the John Harvard Library, waited patiently for a work long overdue and responded thoughtfully to many inquiries along the way; once again I am deeply grateful to him. Bailyn, Hugh F. Bell, Michael J. Colacurcio, Jane Garrett, Douglas S. Greenberg, Milton M. Klein, Marc Kruman, and Richard Polenberg gave my introductory essay the benefit of their constructive scrutiny. I would recite to them two lines from *The Seasons* by James Thomson: "An elegant sufficiency, content,/Retirement, rural quiet, friendship, books," and thank them especially for their friendship.

Carol Koyen Kammen, Douglas Greenberg, Langdon Wright, and Joseph Los have helped in many ways: research, collating texts, and proof-reading. I must also thank Dean Alfred E. Kahn and the Humanities Faculty Research Fund of Cornell University for a vital grant to support research time in New York City and preparation of the manuscript.

Several members of the Manuscript Division and staff of the

New York Public Library have been most courteous and helpful, notably Paul Rugen, now Acting Keeper of Manuscripts, the late Robert W. Hill and Gerald T. McDonald, and Joseph T. Rankin, Chief of the Art and Architecture Division. James J. Heslin, Director of The New-York Historical Society, and Arthur J. Breton of the manuscript section there assisted in essential ways.

Archivists and librarians at many institutions took considerable time and patience to make searches and respond to my inquiries, especially Doris E. Cook, Manuscript Cataloger at The Connecticut Historical Society; Suzanne Flandreau, The Houghton Library, Harvard University; William E. Ewing, Curator of Manuscripts at The William L. Clements Library, Ann Arbor; and Isabel Pridmore, Archivist of The United Society for the Propagation of the Gospel, London. Also, the staffs of the Museum of the City of New York; The New York State Library, Albany; The New York Society Library; the Franklin D. Roosevelt Library, Hyde Park; the Museum, Manor of St. George, Center Moriches, New York; Division of Special Collections, New York University Libraries; The Butler Library, Columbia University; the libraries of Princeton, Yale, Dartmouth, Brown, and Cornell universities; The Connecticut State Library in Hartford; the American Philosophical Society, Philadelphia; the Henry E. Huntington Library and Art Gallery, San Marino; The Library of Congress; the historical societies of Pennsylvania, New Jersey, The New Haven Colony, and Massachusetts; the Manuscript Division, Public Archives of Canada, Ottawa; the Public Record Office, British Museum, Lambeth Palace Library, Guildhall Library, Dr. Williams's Library, and Francis Edwards, Ltd., in London; The National Library of Scotland and the Scottish Record Office in Edinburgh.

Finally, my thanks to Paula Cronin, Leslie F. S. Upton, John Shy, and John White Delafield for their help. Harry Caplan of Cornell University, Goldwin Smith Professor of the Classical Languages and Literatures, Emeritus, was kind enough to translate and identify the Latin passages for me, and I am very grateful to him. J. S. Bernstein helped to make the French translations more felicitous. Sandy Huttleston did a splendid job of preparing the final manuscript, as she always does; and Ann Louise McLaughlin brought her sensitive editorial instincts to bear upon a complicated production and its attendant problems.

Ithaca, New York                                                    M.K.
January 20, 1971

# Contents

# Illustrations

*Volume Two*

*Introduction*

---

*I   A Character of William Smith, Jr.*

Even more than most men, William Smith, Jr., was torn between contrapuntal tendencies: between involvement in the hurly-burly of legal life and "retirement" to the country; between partisanship and detachment; between opposition to the political Establishment and participation in its highest councils; between visionary plans and mundane maneuvering for perquisites; between humane learning and politics; between urgency and serenity. In 1780 he became a Chief Justice without a court. He wrote letters and essays on friendship, but alienated many and became misanthropic. He was, in short, a complex man, yet not so inconsistent, perhaps, as these contradictory impulses might imply. There were in his make-up a number of qualities that help to explain the peculiar pattern of his personality and career.

Smith was not, however, *sui generis* or especially atypical of educated, ambitious men among the eighteenth-century colonial elite. Like his contemporary, Daniel Dulany of Maryland (1722–1797), for example, he was born in his provincial capital, New York City, the son of a lawyer and politician who had emigrated from England. Like Dulany he was trained in the law, married into an influential family in the province, held minor offices at an early age, and was appointed to the colonial council as recognition of his abilities and potential influence. Also like Dulany he became one of the most respected men in his bailiwick, wrote legal opinions of importance, engaged in political pamphleteering, suffered from intermittent ill health, and lost favor steadily as the revolutionary crisis became more acute. Finally, with Dulany and others, when Independence became a reality he retired to the country as a "neutral-Loyal-Whig," waited out the war, and endured the confiscation of his property. Smith's intelligence and personal complexities may have been exceptional, but his career line and series of crises were not. He was very much of his age.[1]

He was born in 1728, a year after the accession of King George II, a year after John Wilkes was born, the same year as Oliver Goldsmith, a year before Edmund Burke, and four years before George Washington. He died in 1793, four years before Wilkes and Burke, six years before the heroic General George. His major work, the *History of New York,* was published in London in 1757, the same year as Tobias Smollett's *Compleat History of England,* two years before William Robertson's *History of Scotland,* Dr. Johnson's *Rasselas,* Voltaire's *Candide,* and Laurence Sterne's *Tristram Shandy.* When William Smith's *History* appeared he was only twenty-nine, which makes him almost as precocious as Washington Irving, who published his *Knickerbocker History of New York* in 1809 at the age of twenty-six.

Smith owed his precociousness—in part at least—to the example and encouragement of his father, a man of strong convictions and considerable ability. William Smith, the elder, was born in England in 1697. His father, a substantial tallow chandler in Newport Pagnell, Buckinghamshire, brought his family to New York City in May 1715, "where they hoped to fare better." Thomas Smith sent young William to Yale, where he studied Hebrew, classics, and theology, receiving the A.B. in 1719. For a few years Smith tutored at Yale and read law, being admitted to the New York bar in 1724. Thereupon, reversing the customary order, he went to London to study law intensively for several years. He returned to New York in 1727, established a lucrative and prestigious practice, became prominent in the "Presbyterian faction" in opposition to the governor's prerogative, and allied himself with Lewis Morris and James Alexander

---

[1] See Aubrey C. Land, *The Dulanys of Maryland: A Biographical Study of Daniel Dulany, The Elder (1685–1753) and Daniel Dulany, the Younger (1722–1797)* (Baltimore, The Maryland Historical Society, 1955; Johns Hopkins University Press, 1968), esp. pp. 213–331; William A. Benton, *Whig-Loyalism: An Aspect of Political Ideology in the American Revolutionary Era* (Rutherford, N.J., Fairleigh Dickinson University Press, 1969).

against the Cosby-DeLancey-Philipse interest. In 1751 he was made Attorney General of New York, and two years later received his appointment to the provincial Council, which he held until 1767. In 1760 he declined the position of Chief Justice of New York's Supreme Court because the position would have been conditional: at pleasure rather than during good behavior. Nevertheless, in 1763, paradoxically, he accepted the rank of Associate Justice at pleasure, and retained that office until his death in 1769.[2]

His son, the historian, inherited many of his attitudes, political alignments, and causes, including the elder Smith's emphasis upon education and thorough professionalism. Just as William Smith, Sr., was the foremost teacher of law in New York City during the 1740's and 1750's—training, among others, William Livingston, John Morin Scott, and his own son—William Smith, Jr., became the pre-eminent legal scholar and teacher in the province during the 1760's and 1770's.

The elder Smith is mentioned infrequently in the first volume of Smith's *History;* but in the second he becomes a prominent participant and receives an unusual biographical sketch with warm praise as an orator and jurist and for his role in the Albany Congress. His involvement in so many of the political circumstances of the 1730's, 1740's, and 1750's clearly affected his son's treatment of those events and their principal actors. One has the feeling that the historian does not particularly admire Governor George Clinton, yet muffles his criticisms because Clinton was generous to Smith's father. The latter had been a strong proponent of colonial unity at Albany in 1754, and his son would pursue such a tack vigorously during the French and Indian War, again at the time of the Stamp Act crisis, and ultimately—as an advocate of imperial unity—during the revolutionary combustion.

In many respects the Smiths, père et fils, were at the heart of the "country party" in New York during the fifth and sixth decades of the eighteenth century. Their adherence to the country party ideology goes far toward explaining apparent inconsistencies in the son's career: his youthful "radicalism" in the

[2] See L. F. S. Upton, *The Loyal Whig: William Smith of New York & Quebec* (Toronto, University of Toronto Press, 1969), pp. 3–4; "William Smith," *Dictionary of American Biography;* George Clinton to the Duke of Bedford, August 31, 1751, in Edmund B. O'Callaghan, ed., *Documents Relative to the Colonial History of the State of New York,* VI (Albany, 1855), 737.

1750's and his middle-aged "conservatism" from the 1770's on. Smith did not change as much as the issues changed, although, to be sure, his increasing access to powerful persons made him more sympathetic to the manipulation of executive power for partisan goals. In any case, an appraisal of his early career must necessarily distinguish between radicalism and opposition. Though Smith often found himself in opposition, he was not really a radical in the sense of seeking remarkable or rapid change. He was a partisan by nature, opposed to what he re-garded as abuses of authority by the DeLancey party and the Anglican interest; but he was never quite comfortable as a radi-cal in the 1750's. Membership in the country party brought him together with other men of professional skill who hoped to de-rive prestige and economic advancement from their technical competence. They were largely merchants and lawyers, often dissenters, relatively well educated, had access to a printer, kept active in the legislature, and shared a cluster of political as-sumptions: that they were men on the periphery of political power; that their independence must be protected; that the Eng-lish gentry were an appropriate object of emulation; and that executive power must be watched jealously.[3]

All of "Billy" Smith's education and intellectual inclinations during the 1740's prepared him for and directed him toward the country party ideology. He graduated from Yale College in 1745, studied law in his father's office, and was admitted to the New York bar in 1750. With William Livingston as his partner, he rapidly became established as a practitioner in the Mayor's Court, Supreme Court, and Court of Vice-admiralty. As impor-tant as his classical and legal training was the longing he shared with Livingston for the quiet, pastoral life of the lettered gentry. The theme of retreat and "retirement," so prevalent among the English Augustans, had become fashionable among educated colonists after the 1720's.[4] "He loves retirement," Wil-

[3] See J. G. A. Pocock, "Machiavelli, Harrington, and English Politi-cal Ideologies in the Eighteenth Century," *William and Mary Quar-terly*, 3d series, XXII (1965), 549–583; Robert M. Weir, " 'The Har-mony We Were Famous For': An Interpretation of Pre-Revolutionary South Carolina Politics," *ibid.*, XXVI (1969), 473–475, 484–485. Smith explicitly identifies his father's faction as "the country party."

[4] See Maynard Mack, "*Secretum Iter:* Some Uses of Retirement Literature in the Poetry of Pope," in Earl R. Wasserman, ed., *Aspects of the Eighteenth Century* (Baltimore, Johns Hopkins University Press, 1965), pp. 207–243; Howard Mumford Jones, *O Strange New World: American Culture: The Formative Years* (New York, Viking, 1964), pp. 245–246.

liam Byrd of Virginia wrote autobiographically, "that while he is acquainted with the world, he may not be a stranger to himself." And in 1747, at the age of twenty-five, Livingston wrote his essay on *Philosophic Solitude*.[5]

Smith's early obsession with "retirement" was so strong, however, and became such a determinative force during the revolutionary years, that it must be regarded as something more than mere self-indulgence with a literary trope. His regular correspondence with William Samuel Johnson of Connecticut, maintained between Smith's sixteenth and twenty-first years, was dominated by his yearning to escape the world of cares and affairs. In 1744 he wrote an epistolary essay on "retirement," and in 1746 relished "a solitary Hermetical retreat" and longed for the contemplative life. In 1748 he pleaded for "detachment" and "disengagement" from the busy-ness of the city. He associated "tranquillity" with the countryside and yearned to devote himself fully to his books, complaining in 1750 that the constant routine of work in a law office "imbitters my Life in every part of it."[6] The irony is that only twice in his sixty-five years would Smith actually achieve "retirement"—and then by inadvertence: at Livingston Manor during the War of Independence, and in London during the 1780's while waiting for his political future in Quebec to be resolved.

Smith's youthful correspondence—important because he wrote the first volume of his *History* at age twenty-seven to twenty-eight—reveals him as a very serious person indeed. He was preoccupied with the proper modes of becoming a cultivated gentleman, and ambitious for fame. He called his conscience—one of his constant concerns—"that little Court of Equity," and commonly referred to "that thick gloom that overshadows my Life."[7] Again, we must remember the modish convention of gloom among the Tory satirists of Augustan England. Pope, Swift, and their contemporaries brooded endlessly over their sense of luxuriousness, corruption, and degeneracy in

[5] Maude H. Woodfin, ed., *Another Secret Diary of William Byrd of Westover, 1739–1741, With Letters & Literary Exercises, 1696–1726* (Richmond, The Dietz Press, 1942), p. 281; [Livingston], *Philosophic Solitude; or, The Choice of a Rural Life. A Poem* (New York, 1747; Boston, 1762; New York [1769?]).

[6] See especially Smith's letters to Johnson of July 29, 1744, June 18, 1746, July 12, 1746, September 28, 1748, May 25, 1749, May 29, 1750, November 28, 1750, William Samuel Johnson Papers, Connecticut Historical Society, Hartford.

[7] See Smith to Johnson, June 18, 1746, May 2, 1748, November 5, 1748, May 25, 1749, May 29, 1750, *ibid.*

Georgian life.[8] Although most of these symptoms were missing from the raw life of Governor Clinton's New York, Smith managed to agonize over his ill health, family deaths, clients, noise, and the "Damned Hurly burly of the town." "A Combination of black Ideas brood over my Soul," he wrote, "and dispel every bright and agreeable thought."[9]

Only occasionally was Smith capable of frivolity. In 1748, when Johnson informed him that he had found a girl friend, the young historian wished his college chum "happy Conjunctions, an easy Preposition, and a thousand soft Interjections." More often Smith complained that "a wife to me would double all my miseries."[10] Somehow he managed to overcome his doubts, for in November 1752 he married Janet Livingston, the twenty-two-year-old daughter of James and Maria Livingston, and between the years 1753 and 1776 he sired ten children. This match connected Smith formally with the politically prominent Livingston clan, a connection he had already made informally through his close friend William Livingston.

Despite Smith's misanthropic moods and despondent tendencies—and his capacity for bitter enmities—he was capable of sustained cerebral friendships. Between 1750 and 1756, Livingston and he collaborated on various literary and legal ventures. At the request of the New York Assembly, they brought together the first digest of the colony's statutes, *Laws of New York from the Year 1691 to 1751, Inclusive* (New York, 1752), a project that gave Smith his first taste of historical explorations, a taste he would savor and cultivate in years to come.[11] His work on this codification hardly qualified him as a Gratian undertaking elaborate systematization of the law; but it was a major effort for a youth of twenty-three, an enormous contribution to the provincial bench and bar, and, more than any other activity, steered him in the direction of writing a history of his native province.

[8] See Louis I. Bredvold, "The Gloom of the Tory Satirists," in James L. Clifford and Louis A. Landa, eds., *Pope and His Contemporaries: Essays Presented to George Sherburn* (Oxford, Oxford University Press, 1949), pp. 1–17.

[9] Smith to Johnson, May 25, 1749, May 29, 1750, November 28, 1750, Johnson Papers, Connecticut Historical Society.

[10] Smith to Johnson, July 18, 1748, May 29, 1750, *ibid.*

[11] Ten years later they produced a continuation, *Laws of New York . . . 1752–1762* (New York, 1762). See Theodore Sedgwick, A *Memoir of the Life of William Livingston . . .* (New York, 1833), pp. 58, 66–68, 72, 114, 117, 120, 151–152.

By the later 1750's, Smith, Livingston, and John Morin Scott —known as "the New York Triumvirate"—had reached the forefront of the provincial bar. Scott had graduated from Yale in 1746, and studied law with Smith's father. In 1748 the Triumvirate, along with William Alexander, Philip and Peter Livingston, their cousin Robert R. Livingston, David Van Horne, and Thomas Jones, organized their informal evening discussions into a club called The Society for the Promotion of Usefull Knowledge. The group kept its existence secret until 1749, when it was attacked in local newspaper essays. It could not have been so clandestine as its members desired, for there was obviously an informer. In 1752 the same men formed the Whig Club—perhaps the first political caucus in New York—and in 1754 they established the New York Society Library, an institution which survives to this day. In every case Smith played a major part, thereby deepening his involvement in the cultural and political life of New York City—all the while, of course, yearning eloquently for "retirement."[12]

In addition to his very close relationship with Scott and William Livingston, "Billy" Smith enjoyed the friendship of Robert Ogden (1716–1787) from Elizabethtown, New Jersey, a member of that colony's Assembly and in 1763 its Speaker; of Aaron Burr (1715–1757), the Yale graduate and Presbyterian cleric who helped to establish Princeton and in 1748 became its second president; of Staats Long Morris (1728–1800), a son of Judge Lewis Morris, Smith's classmate at Yale, and a commissioned officer during the French and Indian War;[13] and of William Alexander (1726–1783), the son of attorney James Alexander (who provided considerable information for the *History*), aide to Governor Shirley during the French and Indian War, and claimant to the ancient title of Earl of Stirling.

In 1756 and 1757 Smith maintained a covert correspondence with Alexander, who supplied him with invaluable information for *A Review of the Military Operations in North America* which

[12] Dorothy Rita Dillon, *The New York Triumvirate: A Study of the Legal and Political Careers of William Livingston, John Morin Scott, William Smith, Jr.* (New York, Columbia University Press, 1949), pp. 13–30; Harry M. Dunkak, "John Morin Scott and Whig Politics in New York, 1752–1769" (unpublished Ph.D. dissertation, St. John's University, 1968), pp. 29, 39, 120; Austin B. Keep, *History of the New York Society Library* . . . (New York, The De Vinne Press, 1908), pp. 130–131, 134, 159, 180.

[13] William Smith, Jr., to Robert Ogden, August 26, 1756, Ogden-Kennedy Papers, Princeton University Library, Special Collections.

Smith and Livingston prepared as an apologia for Governor
Shirley and as an attack upon the policies of James DeLancey
and Sir William Johnson.[14] There survives among Alexander's
papers the draft of a letter to Smith, dated March 23, 1756:

> I shall inclose to you Copys of the two Councils of War
> held at Oswego, and also a copy of that lately held at New
> York, but remember my dear Smith of what a nature these
> minutes are; no person must even know that you [have] them
> but yourself and Wm. Livingston. What I write you for the
> future I intend for you both, and I hope the Boss [Livingston]
> will take that for a sufficient apology if I don't write to
> him. . . . What leisure moments I have, I shall employ in
> stating the [truth?] of facts, a Copy of which you shall have.[15]

And among Smith's papers is the draft of an intimate letter
from him to a close associate going to London on a political
mission in 1756–1757. That associate could only have been Alexander. The historian instructed his friend to work with John
Pownall at the Board of Trade and with the New Jersey agent
Richard Partridge in transacting business concerning that colony: "In a word you are to be all Things to all men, for there
are certain uses to be made of every man & according to their
Dispositions must be your Conduct." (He who longed for rustic
retreats was also capable of Machiavellian instincts.) "No stone
should be left unturned to bring Mr. Smith [Senior] into the
Council [of New Jersey]." As for his own affairs, Smith remarked that Lord Halifax at the Board of Trade seemed favor-
ably inclined, and that "Dr. Avery[16] is my Friend."[17]

[14] *A Review of the Military Operations in North America, from
the commencement of the French hostilities on the frontiers of Virginia in 1753 to the surrender of Oswego, on the 14th of August,
1756; in a Letter to a Nobleman* (London, 1757; New Haven, 1758).
Reprinted in *Collections of the Massachusetts Historical Society for
the Year 1800* (Boston, 1801), pp. 67–163.

[15] [Alexander] to William Smith, Jr., from Boston, March 23,
1756, Alexander Papers, II, 11, New York Historical Society.

[16] Benjamin Avery (d. 1764) was a physician and Presbyterian
minister in London, a political and theological liberal, a leader
among the Protestant Dissenting Deputies, and a man much admired
by Smith. It was Avery who actually expedited the printing and publishing of Smith's *History* in London; and it may very well have
been William Alexander who transmitted the manuscript from Smith
to Dr. Avery. See William Smith, Jr., to ?, New York, February 15,
1757, Princeton University Library, Special Collections; Carl Bridenbaugh, *Mitre and Sceptre: Transatlantic Faiths, Ideas, Personalities,*

It would be fair to say, on the basis of Smith's clandestine correspondence and various actions he took, that he was a secretive, suspicious man. He kept his own counsel and consulted few others. The words "subtle" and "cool" recur constantly in evaluations by his contemporaries; often their appraisals expressed admiration for his intelligence mingled with mistrust for his intentions.[18] Even Livingston alluded to Smith's "ministerial Severity" and reserved "compunction of Conscience" about tavern tippling with the boys. Smith had ascetic instincts: he frowned on "debauchery" and regarded even his own chums on occasion as "a set of noisy fops."[19]

Like many of his contemporaries of comparable birth and education, Smith was socially and intellectually snobbish. He disdained the mercenary commercial types in New York (though he himself speculated greedily in frontier lands), looked down upon most assemblymen for their lack of learning and taste, and believed that public office should be held by "the better Class of People," for only then would they be able to introduce that "Spirit of Subordination essential to good Government."[20] This elitism was accompanied by a powerful sense of professionalism—in law, medicine, and politics. Smith complained bitterly when colonial governors issued law licenses to unqualified applicants, lamented the lack of lawyers in New York with college degrees, and wrote a comprehensive curriculum in 1756 for the edification of law students. In his view a competent lawyer ought to know Latin, French, arithmetic, geometry, surveying, merchant accounts, bookkeeping, geography, chronology, history, logic, rhetoric, divinity, Laws of Nature and of Nations, the law of England, Hebrew, astronomy, and philosophy. "Cronology he may learn enough of by inspecting and

and Politics, 1689–1775 (New York, Oxford University Press, 1962), esp. pp. 43, 106, 183.

[17] Smith to [Alexander ?], [1756–57], Smith Mss, Miscellaneous documents box, New York Public Library.

[18] See his diary, entry for April 14, 1780, New York Public Library; Upton, *Loyal Whig,* pp. 116, 121.

[19] See Milton M. Klein, ed., *The Independent Reflector, or Weekly Essays on Sundry Important Subjects More Particularly Adapted to the Province of New York by William Livingston and Others* (Cambridge, Mass., Harvard University Press, 1963), p. 16; Smith to William Samuel Johnson, September 28, 1748, May 25, 1749, Johnson Papers, Connecticut Historical Society.

[20] Smith to Johnson, March 2, 1747, *ibid.; Journal of the Legislative Council of the Colony of New York . . . 1743 . . . 1775* (Albany, 1861), pp. 1677–1678 (December 30, 1768).

perusing Talent's Cronological Tables which exhibit in a general view the Dates of the Grand Events of past times. In History our student must take a longer scope. Here I would recommend Bossuet's View of Universal History, Rollins' antient History of the Egyptians, Abyssinians, Medes, [Syrians], Macedonians, and Greeks and his Roman History. As for English history, Rapin is the best."[21]

Smith's abiding sense of professionalism was fully congruent with his primary motives for writing history: personal ambition in tandem with a desire to improve the quality of life in New York and to overcome provincialism, raise local standards, and gain recognition and understanding for the colony in Whitehall. Late in 1756, shortly after he had completed the manuscript of his *History*, Smith and fourteen other lawyers established an organization to elevate the quality of bench and bar in New York. They agreed to hold quarterly meetings, and made a restrictive agreement to limit the number of men trained and admitted as practicing attornies. Obviously, self-interest was intermingled with their altruistic desire to improve the quality of juridical administration. During the later 1750's and throughout the next decade, Smith and his cohorts would argue vigorously that judges ought to be appointed to indefinite terms during good behavior, and not at the pleasure of the King and his councilors. Unconditional tenure was the only status consistent with truly professional criteria, they believed, and both William Smiths would return to this battlefield repeatedly in the decades to come.[22]

In 1767, when Governor Henry Moore submitted to the Earl of Shelburne a recommendation for the younger Smith's appointment to the Council, he said the candidate was "now at the head of the Profession of the Law, and will be of great Service in the Council as his opinions may always be depended on, not only from his knowledge of the Law but his integrity. He is connected with the best families in this Province, is of unblemished Character and high in the estimation of every one here."[23] When John Adams met Smith in August 1774, he noted

[21] Paul M. Hamlin, *Legal Education in Colonial New York* (New York, New York University Press, 1939), pp. 61–62, 197–200.
[22] Dunkak, "John Morin Scott and Whig Politics," pp. 57–58; Upton, *Loyal Whig*, p. 25; Milton M. Klein, "Prelude to Revolution in New York: Jury Trials and Judicial Tenure," *William and Mary Quarterly*, 3d series, XVII (1960), 439–462.
[23] February 23, 1767, in O'Callaghan, ed., *Documents Relative to the Colonial History of the State of New York*, VII, 909–910.

in his diary that this new acquaintance—unlike Scott and Livingston, who were lazy—"improves every Moment of his Time." A few days later Adams made a formal call upon Smith, and afterward observed, "This Gentleman has the Character of a great Lawyer, a sensible and learned Man and yet a consistent unshaken Friend to his Country and her Liberties." During this same interview Smith insisted that he would never become an imperial placeman: "Mr. Smith said that he would not do the dirty Jobbs of Government—He would not hold any Thing under the Crown upon such Terms." The historian expressed his contempt for anyone who would "dwindle down into a mere Scribbling Governor, a mere Bernard, or Hutchinson."[24] But, within a few years Smith—always a scribbler—would himself "dwindle" into an imperial placeholder—as Chief Justice of New York (1780) and of Quebec (1786).

Evaluations of Smith by his contemporaries are important for their insights into his character. But perhaps equally valuable in this respect are Smith's appraisals of others, such as the lengthy estimate of James DeLancey, Lieutenant Governor and Chief Justice of New York, written by Smith in the *Continuation* of his *History*.[25] Smith's characterization of DeLancey is in fact the mirror image, or obverse, of the historian himself. DeLancey was lively in conversation, jovial and casual; Smith was studied and serious. DeLancey loved company; Smith usually preferred the solitary of his library or his country home at Haverstraw on the Hudson. DeLancey was not erudite, and was too indolent for detailed research; Smith was erudite, if anything, and loved legal and historical explorations. DeLancey disliked writing, especially legal opinions; Smith was a prolix writer, always compelled by a *furor scribendi*. A non-contemplative man, DeLancey's initial response was usually his best; whereas Smith was excessively reflective, too often and too long, like Hamlet, "sicklied o'er with the pale cast of thought." DeLancey was not a conscious aesthete; Smith was extremely sensitive to language and literary style. Finally, and perhaps most important, DeLancey "had rather be the head of a dog than the tail of a lion"; whereas Smith came to realize that he was attached to a larger political entity—an empire—and acted accordingly when the great breach occurred.

[24] L. H. Butterfield, ed., *Diary and Autobiography of John Adams* (Cambridge, Mass.: Harvard University Press, 1961), II, 105, 110, 113, 312 n.
[25] See Volume Two, pp. 245–247.

What sort of man was this who combined visionary plans of statesmanlike quality with crafty political maneuvering?[26] Smith's enduring interests were the law, politics, and history. He worked at all three with compulsive diligence and combative intelligence. The words "importunity," "zeal," and "ardor," which recur so often in the second volume of his *History,* must have been in the forefront of his consciousness because they are essential to an understanding of his character. He was a pious Presbyterian, hostile to the Church of England (ironically he was buried in an Anglican cemetery), an advocate of toleration and secularization. He remained, almost consistently throughout his career, the disgruntled dissenter—uncomfortable with the Establishment even while a part of it. He was an uneasy person—with others and with himself—and suffered through all the years of his middle life from intestinal disorders.[27]

This man of "tenacious memory" had a profound awareness of history and posterity.[28] Often he seems to be writing with an eye to the ultimate evaluation of his own conduct and the events of his own tumultuous time. Above all, he was what I must call a constitutional legitimist, fully devoted to institutional precedents. More than any other factor, this consideration provides a line of consistency through his long and erratic career. In 1751–1752 he helped to codify the laws of New York. In 1756 he wrote the provincial history in order to legitimize New York's tenuous status in Whitehall and at Westminster. Early in the 1760's he insisted that judicial tenure be predicated upon good behavior, and that the traditional right of jury trial be protected. In 1765–1766 he could not bring himself to support an illegal resumption of business in response to the Stamp Act—in spite of his strong personal opposition to that law.[29] In 1768 he urged the necessity of "a regular American Constitution."[30] During the years between 1775 and 1778, despite his

[26] See Upton, *Loyal Whig,* p. 202; Robert M. Calhoon, ed., "William Smith Jr's. Alternative to the American Revolution," *William and Mary Quarterly,* 3d series, XXII (1965), 105–118:

[27] L. H. Butterfield, ed., *Letters of Benjamin Rush* (Princeton, Princeton University Press, 1951) II, 858; for the London years of anxious waiting, see L. F. S. Upton, ed., *The Diary and Selected Papers of Chief Justice William Smith, 1784–1793* in *The Publications of the Champlain Society,* XLI–XLII (Toronto, The Champlain Society, 1963–65), 2 vols.

[28] See the obituary in the *Quebec Gazette,* December 12, 1793.

[29] See Upton, *Loyal Whig,* p. 54.

[30] See Calhoon, "William Smith Jr's. Alternative to the American Revolution," p. 109.

deeply felt Whiggery, he could not participate in an illegitimate rebellion, and he did not. Nevertheless, in 1777 he was willing to help the rebels draft a new constitution for the independent state of New York! Insofar as Smith's character and career may be said to have had a gyrostabilizer, its components were legitimacy and constitutionality.

Just as the elder Smith had rejected the Chief Justice's seat in 1760 because he could not have it with unconditional tenure, William Smith, Jr., rejected an identical invitation in 1763—but for more complex reasons: the salary of £500 per annum was less than half of what he could make in private practice; he feared the jealousy and controversy his appointment would arouse; and he was motivated by his father's earlier anxiety about tenure. Again he had to choose between power with travail or disengagement with relative tranquillity. He pursued the latter path, of less resistance.[31]

Although Smith remained active in politics during the 1760's —he took his father's seat on the Council in 1767—his law practice and teaching absorbed a great deal of his time. Nearly every prominent lawyer active in revolutionary New York took his training under Smith's aegis: Robert R. Livingston, Gouverneur Morris, George Clinton, and Peter Van Schaack are just a few examples. There was a great deal of drudgery to be done by Smith's clerks, because his practice was extensive and all documents had to be copied by hand.[32]

Meanwhile he kept a watchful eye upon imperial problems, and maintained an active interest in colonial patronage. "We are a great Garden," he wrote in 1764, "constant Cultivation will keep down the weeds—remember they were planted by Liberty and Religion near a hundred years ago. There are strong Roots, that will soon despise the gardener's utmost strength." Such proleptic statements usually occurred in the context of appealing for governors and judges of greater ability, and then asking that they be suitably supported. In 1769 he hoped that he might become the American colonies' representative in London—a kind of super-agent—but that expectation too was frustrated.[33] All the while Smith found himself distrusted by enemies

[31] Dunkak, "John Morin Scott and Whig Politics," p. 64; Upton, *Loyal Whig,* p. 48.

[32] Henry C. Van Schaack, *The Life of Peter Van Schaack, LL.D. . . .* (New York, 1842), p. 5; *Public Papers of George Clinton . . .* (New York, State of New York, 1900), II, 486 n.

[33] Smith to Major Horatio Gates, March 9, 1764, Gates Papers,

in the conservative camp—Lieutenant Governor Cadwallader Colden, Indian Superintendant Sir William Johnson, the De-Lancey party—and increasingly out of touch with the radical Whigs after 1770. The Triumvirate of happier days ran aground on ideological shoals.

By 1775, therefore, Smith's political isolation made the personal decision for or against independence even more difficult. Like his former student, Peter Van Schaack, he maintained his neutrality, retired to the woods, and chopped logic as his servants chopped firewood.[34] Now that he had finally achieved the "retirement" he had yearned for a quarter-century earlier, he complained about it bitterly to George Clinton. He hoped that his erstwhile student's "Compassions rise in favor of a sett of People moping under the melancholly change from a Life of Society to the profoundist solitude in an outcast corner of the Creation."[35] Smith's capacity for self-pity had not diminished over the decades.

In December 1775 Smith announced that he "would list on neither side during the present troubles"; and four months later he betook himself and his family from their handsome house at no. 5 Broadway (soon to become General Washington's headquarters) to his country seat at Haverstraw, thirty miles up the west bank of the Hudson. There, where the highlands begin, on a ridge overlooking a small bay, Smith had built in 1770 a square, white, two-story clapboard house. The eight large fireplaces were unadorned, built for maximum warmth rather than stylish design. The adzed beams were pinned together with wooden pegs, and they responded in sympathy to the squeak of the wide-board floors as Smith paced off his restless indecision.[36]

In isolation at Haverstraw, Smith began once more to con-

box 2, no. 2, New-York Historical Society; Smith to Robert R. Livingston, March 5, 1769, Livingston Miscellaneous MSS, New-York Historical Society.

[34] Carl Becker's brilliant essay on "John Jay and Peter Van Schaack" (1919) is by analogy one of the most useful guides to Smith's tormented state of mind in 1775–76. See *Everyman His Own Historian: Essays on History and Politics* (Chicago, Quadrangle, 1966), pp. 284–298.

[35] Smith to Clinton, June 7, 1775, *Public Papers of Clinton*, I, 197.

[36] Upton, *Loyal Whig*, pp. 99, 111; LeRoy Elwood Kimball, "The Smiths of Haverstraw: Some Notes on a Highland Family," *New York History*, XVI (1935), 392–404; Raymond T. B. Hand, "Old Manor House 'Discovered,'" *New York Sun*, October 12, 1940, clipping in The New-York Historical Society (10 Biog. Smith).

template continuing his history of New York beyond 1732 where the first volume had concluded. He had brought many of the necessary documents with him, for as long before as Christmas 1773, he had indicated in his diary a determination to extend the youthful narrative.[37] He scarcely had time to begin unpacking his papers, however, before he was ordered to Livingston Manor on parole for refusing to take the patriots' oath of allegiance. At the Manor, thirty miles south of Albany on the eastern bank, amidst many branches of the Livingston family tree, under the watchful eye of Robert L. Livingston, third Lord of the Manor and elder brother of Smith's old friend William, the forty-eight-year-old jurist and historian settled down to watch the progress of the war. Like the characters in Fenimore Cooper's classic, *The Spy,* they all waited in a wooded borderland, beyond the American and British armies. There, early in 1777, Smith began to draft the text of a history covering the years 1732–1762, "from Notes formerly collected, but great additions will be made when I again have Recourse to a Collection of Gazettes & other Papers left at Haverstraw."[38]

Returning to Haverstraw, however, proved to be infinitely complicated, and became the topic of prickly correspondence between Smith and Governor Clinton late in 1777. "I think both Sides wrong," Smith declared self-righteously, "but I find no Inclination to persecute those who are not of my mind; nor should if my little Party grew large and powerful, as I think it will in proportion to the growing miseries of our Country."[39]

Soon thereafter Smith began his steady drift from neutrality to open support for the Loyalist cause. In December 1777 he made the clearest, most concise statement of his constitutionalist position based upon historical legitimacy: "I am a Whigg of the old Stamp—No Roundhead—one of King Wm's Whiggs: for Liberty & the Constitution." Better than anyone else, the historian could appreciate the irony in his ambiguous situation: "To my old Whigg Friends of Rank I am represented as a Tory

---

[37] William H. W. Sabine, ed., *Historical Memoirs from 16 March 1763 to 9 July 1776 of William Smith . . .* (New York, Colbourn and Tegg, 1956), I, 165; Governor Tryon to Lord Germain, September 24, 1776, O'Callaghan, ed., *Documents Relative to the Colonial History of the State of New York,* VIII, 685.

[38] Harold D. Eberlein, *The Manors and Historic Homes of the Hudson Valley* (Philadelphia, Lippincott, 1924), pp. 66–79; Upton, *Loyal Whig,* p. 111.

[39] Smith to Clinton, October 28, 1777; Clinton to Smith, October 31, 1777, in *Public Papers of Clinton,* II, 484–485, 492.

—But to the Lower Sort as favoring the popular Measures." By 1778 Smith had convinced himself that American independence would fail, and in August he returned to New York City after an absence of twenty-nine months.⁴⁰

He remained there for five more years, serving as a kind of adviser to General Sir Henry Clinton and his staff, gathering more documentary materials, and writing an occasional pamphlet, legal opinions, and constant entries in his now voluminous diaries. In December 1783 he left for England with the British troops, never to see New York again. After two years of waiting and fawning in London, he finally received the appointment as Chief Justice of Canada, a position he held until his death in 1793. When he returned to Quebec late in 1786, his characteristic ambivalence became manifest in his relations with the Loyalists there, the second largest group in the community. Although he spoke warmly of them, he never identified with them. His references were never "we," always "they." His final seven years were not easy ones; once more—torn between conservatism and dissent—he found himself politically isolated.⁴¹

In the best of all possible worlds, Smith would have been a leisured man of letters writing impolite essays on polite subjects—in the manner of Addison and Steele. He began doing so in 1744 at the tender age of sixteen,⁴² and flourished happily in the 1750's as "Lover of Merit," "Philo-patriae," "A," "Publius," "Goose Adrianse, Jr.," "Layman," "F," and "Philo Reflector." Private letters often took the form of didactic little essays (on friendship, women, the law); and many readers will find the six appendixes to Volume One of his *History* the most readable and enduring portion precisely because they are tidy, discrete essays: A Geographical Description of the Country, Of the Inhabitants, Of Our Trade, Of Our Religious State, The Political State, Of Our Laws and Courts.

Smith especially respected the English poet James Thomson (1700–1748), particularly his "Britannia," a patriotic poem,

---

⁴⁰ William H. W. Sabine, ed., *Historical Memoirs from 12 July 1776 to 25 July 1778 of William Smith* . . . (New York, Colbourn and Tegg, 1958), II, 278, 183; Upton, *Loyal Whig*, pp. 118–119, 123.

⁴¹ *Ibid.*, pp. 159, 163–165; Frederick Bernays Wiener, *Civilians Under Military Justice: The British Practice Since 1689, Especially in North America* (Chicago, University of Chicago Press, 1967), pp. 117–119, 124–125, 127, 129–133, 275–276.

⁴² See Smith to William Samuel Johnson, July 29, 1744, Johnson Papers, Connecticut Historical Society.

*The Seasons,* and most of all *Liberty* (1735–36). Smith, Livingston, and Scott quoted extensively from *Liberty* in *The Independent Reflector,*[43] and the headquote they chose for the fifty-second and final issue in that series was the very same passage Smith would use on the title page of his *History* four years later.

> Lo! Swarming o'er the new discover'd World,
> Gay Colonies extend; the calm Retreat
> Of undeserv'd Distress. The better Home
> Of those whom Bigots chase from foreign Lands:
> Not built on Rapine, Servitude and Woe,
> And, in their Turn some petty Tyrant's Prey;
> But bound by social Freedom, firm they Rise;
> Of Britain's Empire the Support and Strength.[44]

As irony and posterity would have it, however, Smith's most enduring legacy—like Lord Clarendon's and Bishop Burnet's—would take the form of historical memoirs rather than literary essays. Between 1753 and 1787 he kept a diary as part of his daily routine. The amount of time he could devote to this autobiographical mistress varied with his circumstances and inclination. The diary is fullest for the two decades after 1767, but it is an invaluable source throughout. Smith went back over the diaries, especially for the 1750's, to make insertions and alterations because he hoped ultimately to use them as the basis for an expanded public history of his own time.[45] He fulfilled this wish only in part, and the result is the *Continuation* of his history from 1732 until 1762.

One of the greater frustrations of Smith's career must have been the inability to bring his diverse and little known historical explorations to fruition. He must have been born with the peculiar instincts of one who takes pleasure in reconstructing

[43] See Klein, ed., *Independent Reflector,* pp. 103, 221, 299, 305 n. 3, 336, 419, 433.

[44] For the historical significance of this passage to Smith and his contemporaries, see Michael Kammen, "The Meaning of Colonization in American Revolutionary Thought," *Journal of the History of Ideas,* XXXI (1970), 337–358, esp. p. 340; Alan D. McKillop, *The Background of Thomson's Liberty,* Rice Institute Pamphlet, XXXVIII (1951), no. 2.

[45] For the published portions of his forty-four-year diary, see notes 25, 35, and 38. The unpublished sections are spread through six closely written volumes in the New York Public Library.

and savoring times past. But if political motives were often a
stimulus to his historical investigations, political problems and
pressures frequently caused those same inquiries to be stifled
or stillborn. In 1757 and 1759 he wrote insistently to President
Clap of Yale, urging the need for a history of Connecticut:

> the better we are known by our Mother Country, the more
> we shall be respected.—The more I reflect upon this subject
> I am the more confirmed in the opinion, that such a work
> will be useful if not necessary. The present war draws
> us into public notice; and it is easy to foresee, that the long
> hand of the Prerogative, will be stretched over to us, more
> than ever, upon the conclusion of the next general peace. It
> is of the utmost importance that our true state should be
> known; and many things may be disclosed relative to
> the condition of the country, the principles, religion, loyalty
> and spirit of the people, which may prevent measures
> equally disagreeable and destructive.[46]

During the 1750's Smith read widely in James Alexander's library, gathering materials there concerning the history of New
Jersey. In 1767 he prepared a "Sketch of the Polity of the
Province of North Carolina, including the Powers and Jurisdiction of the Courts of Law" for Lord Shelburne, then Secretary of State for the Southern Department with jurisdiction
over the colonies. As preparatory background, Smith had made
extensive extracts and notes from Governor Tryon's letterbook;
and in 1768 he continued his research by investigating the
prologue to the Regulator controversy in Carolina.[47]

Late in 1770 Smith prepared for Governor Dunmore an interpretative version of the political narrative of New York since
1759, and called the historical memorandum "Thoughts on the
State of Things." It really had as its focus the rivalry between
Livingstons and DeLanceys for control of the provincial As-

[46] Clap did, in fact, contemplate writing a history of Connecticut,
but he never finished it. The headnotes, as he called them, are in the
Yale University Library. I am indebted to Dr. Louis L. Tucker, Assistant Commissioner for New York State History, who called this
to my attention.

[47] Henry Noble MacCracken, *Prologue to Independence: The Trials
of James Alexander, American, 1715–1756* (New York, J. H. Heine-
man, 1964), p. 132; Smith's letter to Shelburne, June 29, 1767, and
the various manuscripts concerning North Carolina are among his
miscellaneous papers in two folio volumes in the New York Public
Library.

sembly.[48] In 1773 he was again encouraging efforts toward a history of Connecticut. "I am so desirous that justice should be done to the History of the origin of this Country," he wrote Governor Trumbull, "that I cannot help reminding your Honor, of the Promise of certain MSS, which you was pleased to make me at Hartford." Smith planned to send the documents to William Robertson, the distinguished Scottish historian then at work on his *History of America*.[49] It seemed especially important not only to help Robertson avoid making "fabulous mixtures, but [also] to perpetuate the honorable Descent, and eminent merit of the bold and free spirits of the first Planters, especially in New England and Virginia." More than saving Robertson from professional embarrassment and the colonies from neglect, Smith again anticipated the political imperatives of historical research.

It is easy to foresee, that a Foundation is laid for a vast
Empire in this western World; and I cannot help thinking
that it will conduce to the Establishment of the common
Liberty and Felicity of America, to hold up to the View of
Posterity, the Principles upon which this great Fabric was
begun, and the indefatigable Pains of the Undertakers.
The Eastern Colonies have most to boast of in this Respect,
and yet to the shame of Connecticut, it has hidden its
Head as if descended from Convicts and Banditts; and thus
one of the fairest, best peopled and happiest of the Colonies,
is almost intirely unknown. I wrote to Mr. Clap in 1756,
urging him to take some measures to brighten this Part of
the American Picture, forseeing that there could be no
good History of the British Empire in General, till we
had distinct accounts of the several Plantations.

Trumbull complied immediately and fulsomely with duplicate copies of a pile of seventeenth-century documents; and Smith presumably passed them along promptly to his friend in Edinburgh.[50]

[48] Sabine, ed., *Historical Memoirs . . . of William Smith*, I, 94–97; Upton, *Loyal Whig*, p. 75.

[49] See William Robertson, *The History of America* (London, 1777), 2 vols. Books 1–8 cover the discovery of the New World and the Conquest of Mexico and Peru. Books 9–10 treat the history of Virginia (to 1688) and New England (to 1652), and first appeared separately in 1796, three years after the deaths of Robertson and William Smith.

[50] Smith to Jonathan Trumbull, June 12, 1773, and Trumbull to

Smith's diaries during the war years, especially the period 1780–1783 when he was closely in touch with the British high command in New York City, are very full and read like notes toward a history of the war. Military matters are reported in elaborate detail, and various strategies are analyzed. Early in 1781 Smith prepared for General Sir Henry Clinton "a full view of the history of Vermont" as a position paper on the possibilities of a separate government for the people living there and settlements to be made with speculators in Vermont lands (which number included William Smith, Jr.).[51]

Finally, in May 1784, after Smith had returned to England for comfort, recompense, and recreation, he turned to the history of his own family, visited ancestral homes and farms, made genealogical notes, and sketched diagrams of places where Smiths had dwelled in calmer days. At the Buckinghamshire home which his grandfather had left for New York in 1715, Smith performed all the usual pieties as well as visiting the local meetinghouse, church, and nearby villages. He was as thorough as ever, as concerned with the record of his family's past as with those of the colonies, the war, and himself.[52]

To William Smith, Jr., living in a time and place when precedents meant a great deal because they helped one judge the constitutionality of a cause, the past and the present were equally determinative of the future. He devoted a great deal of his life to researching the past and recording the present— more than most men would, but less than he would have liked. In part he was motivated by ego, like any other author. When persons of prominence asked for a copy of his *History*, Smith was delighted to oblige, even twenty-five years after its initial publication.[53] When he published (anonymously) *The Candid*

---

Smith, July 12, 1773, Trumbull Papers, Connecticut Colonial Official Papers, 1631–1784, volume 21, 24a–d, 34a–c, Connecticut State Library, Hartford. For the eventual fulfillment of Smith's exhortation, see Benjamin Trumbull, *A Complete History of Connecticut, Civil and Ecclesiastical . . .* (New Haven, 1818), 2 vols.

[51] Smith's diaries for this period are in manuscript in the New York Public Library. For his "history of Vermont," see the entries for January 4 and 5, 1781.

[52] Smith's notes on his family's English roots cover eight legal-sized sheets headed "Monday, 11th May 1784," Smith Papers, M.G. 23, G II 14, volume 6, Public Archives of Canada, Ottawa.

[53] On the front flyleaf of Smith's personal copy of the *History* he wrote: "Wedn: 10 July 1782 sent a copy of this History to Govr. Digby with a Note for his putting it into the hands of Prince William—He answered the next day that the Prince recd. it with Pleas-

*Retrospect or the American War Examined by Whig Principles* in 1780, Smith concerned himself greatly with the number of copies distributed by Rivington, and to whom.[54]

But politics and provincial pride were prime movers to an even greater extent than private gratification. *The Independent Reflector* of 1752–53 had been intended, like other essays of its day, to give persons "at a distance a just idea of the public state of these *American* colonies."[55] *The Review of the Military Operations in North-America,* prepared by Smith and Livingston in 1756, began and ended by pointing out that the colonies had been neglected for too long by Britain because they were not considered important. Smith's *History,* too, was stimulated by his belief that "the colonies were at home disregarded and despised, nor can any other reason be assigned for it, than that they were unknown. This is, in a great degree, to be imputed to ourselves" (Preface). The *History* is significant because it testifies to the Americans' growing self-consciousness and search for an identity during the middle years of the eighteenth century.[56]

Both *The Review of the Military Operations* and the *History* were published in 1757, and both were dedicated to George Montagu Dunk, second Earl of Halifax (1716–1771). The energetic Earl had become head of the Board of Trade in 1748 and was admitted to the cabinet in 1757. He was certainly the most influential man in England then concerned with colonial administration, and William Smith, Jr., understandably hoped to catch his attention and favor.[57] Thus personal ambition, provincial aspiration, and political action were intertwined as stimuli for Smith's *History.*

---

ure." See also Smith's diary for July 12, 1782, New York Public Library.

[54] *Ibid.,* February 3, 1781.

[55] Klein, ed., *Independent Reflector,* p. 2; See Upton, *Loyal Whig,* pp. 44–45. Smith wrote numbers 8, 12, 16, 18, 21, 28, 40, 44, and 50 of *The Independent Reflector,* and parts of numbers 10, 24, 27, 35, and 52.

[56] See Max Savelle, *Seeds of Liberty: The Genesis of the American Mind* (Seattle, University of Washington Press, 1965), pp. 308, 381–382.

[57] For other references to Halifax, see Smith to Robert Ogden, August 25, 1756, Princeton University Library, Special Collections; Smith's *Continuation,* Volume Two, pp. 132, 135, 249, 266. For Halifax, see the *Dictionary of National Biography.*

## II   William Smith, Jr., and Historical Writing
## in Anglo-America, 1660-1760

In 1630, when the Puritan migration to America began, Richard Brathwaite, author of *The English Gentleman,* called history "the sweetest recreation of the mind." He referred to the
reading of history. For several generations thereafter, the
writing of history in England and her colonies was often stimulated by political motives more bitter than sweet. During the
tumultuous middle years of the Stuart century, writers debated
the constitutional implications of the Norman conquest because
their conclusions buttressed diverse interpretations of the origin and powers of Parliament.[1]

In March 1646, Edward Hyde, later Lord Clarendon, found
the Royalist cause in dire straits and himself with nothing to
do. So he took himself to the Scilly Islands and began to write
his great *History of the Rebellion and Civil Wars in England,*
largely as a criticism of royalist actions for the King's benefit.
Like William Smith's work at Livingston Manor in 1777–78,
Clarendon's narrative was not intended for contemporary publication, merely for Charles II and a few of his counselors. But
like Smith's *Continuation,* it has proved to be an invaluable
account to subsequent historians.[2] In the Anglo-American world

[1] See Quentin Skinner, "History and Ideology in the English Revolution," *Historical Journal,* VIII (1965), 151–178.

[2] See B. H. G. Wormald, *Clarendon: Politics, History, and Religion,*
*1640–1660* (Cambridge, Cambridge University Press, 1951), p. 177;
Sir Charles Firth, *Essays Historical and Literary* (Oxford, Oxford
University Press, 1938), pp. 114–115. Clarendon's *History* was published posthumously in 1702–1704, as long after his death as Smith's
second volume after his.

of the seventeenth and eighteenth centuries, history writing was a common pursuit for politicians out of favor or power. Men often absorbed themselves in times past while awaiting future prospects. Thomas Jefferson, for example, brought his *Notes on Virginia* near completion in 1782 during weeks of enforced idleness at Poplar Forest. Thomas Hutchinson wrote the third and final volume of his *History of Massachusetts-Bay* during his English exile. Nostalgia for beloved and remote New England quickened his pen as well as his historical perspective.

During the final third of the seventeenth century, England's penchant for making political history the stuff of hysterical politics reached its peak; thereafter antiquarian arguments for partisan purposes were gradually discredited.[3] Much of the historical writing during the years between 1660 and 1730 concerned relations between church and state, or the status of dissenters, and was produced by such churchmen as William Wake, Archbishop of Canterbury, Edmund Gibson, Bishop of London, and White Kennett, Bishop of Peterborough. The Church of England remained the chief repository of English learning, and clerical endowments were regularly used to foster medieval scholarship.[4] In a very real sense, therefore, the absence of a strong Episcopacy in colonial America may have been one obstacle to historical efforts there.

During these same decades, however, many English historians had an impulse to bring their books not merely within living memory, but even up to the very year of writing.[5] Their example was not lost on colonial writers, who repeatedly offered "the history and present state of . . ." This was precisely

[3] See F. Smith Fussner, *The Historical Revolution: English Historical Writing and Thought, 1580–1640* (London, Routledge and Kegan Paul, 1962), pp. 112–113; J. G. A. Pocock, *The Ancient Constitution and the Feudal Law: A Study of English Historical Thought in the Seventeenth Century* (Cambridge, Cambridge University Press, 1957), pp. 229–251.

[4] David C. Douglas, *English Scholars, 1660–1730* (London, Eyre & Spottiswoode, 1951), p. 246.

[5] Bonamy Dobree, *English Literature in the Early Eighteenth Century, 1700–1740* (Oxford, Oxford University Press, 1959), p. 379. William Smith, Jr., had available to him, for example, the *History of My Own Time* by Gilbert Burnet, Bishop of Salisbury (1643–1715), published posthumously between 1723 and 1734. Burnet's work, like Smith's later, made no special attempt at style or eloquence, and was violently attacked for inaccuracy and prejudice. Like Smith's *History*, however, it was remarkably honest, filled with trenchant appraisals of men, and has become an invaluable historical source.

the nature of Smith's *History* in 1757. Current history was especially popular in the colonies because European news was so commonly published several months after the fact. And lacking adequate space in their newspapers, colonial editors frequently fell behind. In 1718 John Campbell, editor of the *Boston News Letter,* found himself an entire year in arrears in printing foreign news. The history of the recent past fascinated colonial Americans because so often it came to them literally as news.[6]

During the first half of the eighteenth century, more than a hundred historical works appeared in Britain: ecclesiastical and Biblical histories, chronologies, travels and voyages, works of heraldry and genealogy, family and local histories, editions of historical texts, biographies, and histories of recent events. Nevertheless, as late as 1742 this harshly critical indictment appeared in *A Collection of the State Letters of the First Earl of Orrery*:

> England, however productive of eminent writers in various kinds of literature, still remains defective in excellent historians . . . We have had a Locke, a Newton, and a Dryden, but we cannot boast a Livy, a Thucydides, or a Tacitus. If we enquire into the reasons why all other branches of learning have flourished and spread themselves auspiciously in our climate, and why history has brought forth little, or at least unrelishable fruit, and has remained uncultivated by such hands as were best able to bring it to perfection, we shall find this misfortune may be assigned to two causes. The first is, that persons best qualified for works of this nature are seldom sufficiently at leisure for the performance; and the second that the proper materials for a history of these kingdoms are either entirely lost or warily preserved in such secret repositories, that the treasure . . . can be of no use, not even to the owner.[7]

Before the age of Hume and Gibbon, British historical writing lacked profound insights into the minds of men or the peculiar characteristics of an age. Such writing was seduced by the lure

---

[6] See Gerald A. Danzner, "America's Roots in the Past: Historical Publication in America to 1860" (unpublished Ph.D. dissertation, Northwestern University 1967), p. 18.

[7] Quoted in M. A. Thomson, *Some Developments in English Historiography During the Eighteenth Century* (London, University of London Press, 1957), p. 11.

of the dramatic, so that subjects with intrinsic excitement were superficially successful as history. Even after mid-century—a pivotal point in many respects—the growing belief in an exact science of politics caused many men to regard the historical enterprise as a gathering of raw data ancillary to that "science." Their theories of causation were inadequate or nonexistent, and they fell back upon the composition of political narratives because they really did not know how to write in depth what they said they most wanted to: the history of intellect and society.[8]

By the 1740's, however, English poets, politicians, and clerics began to praise history as the primary source of knowledge, and as philosophy teaching by example. One had to know the past in order to anticipate the future, in order to understand the workings of Providence, the cyclical nature of history, and the life cycles of society.[9] "History prepares us for experience, and guides us in it," wrote Bolingbroke in 1735. "History serves to purge the mind of those national partialities and prejudices that we are apt to contract in our education." His theory of history as philosophy teaching by example, even though predicated upon a commonplace of classical and Renaissance thought, provided one of the earliest detailed statements of a doctrine previously mentioned only in passing or used as a prefatory slogan. If men could only grasp the whole sweeping panorama of humanity "in every age," their notions of conduct would be enriched. Bolingbroke combined an ethical concept of history with high standards of objectivity and a sense of development through time.[10]

Like his contemporaries Voltaire and Hume, Bolingbroke had a high regard for recent history. "Experience is doubly defective," he wrote in 1735. "We are born too late to see the beginning, and we die too soon to see the end, of many things. History supplies [i.e., remedies] both these defects. Modern history shews the causes, when experience presents the effects alone."

[8] See R. N. Stromberg, "History in the Eighteenth Century," *Journal of the History of Ideas*, XII (1951), 299–301, 303.

[9] James W. Johnson, *The Formation of English Neo-classical Thought* (Princeton, Princeton University Press, 1967), pp. 38–39.

[10] Bolingbroke [Henry St. John], *Letters on the Study and Use of History* (2nd ed., London, 1777), pp. 35–36, 51, 56–58; Dorothy A. Koch, "English Theories Concerning the Nature and Uses of History, 1735–1791" (unpublished Ph.D. dissertation, Yale University, 1946).

He iterated a reason for history writing that corresponded closely with Smith's boosterism on behalf of New York: "Tho' an early and proper application to the study of history will contribute extremely to keep our minds free from a ridiculous partiality in favour of our own country, and a vicious prejudice against others; yet the same study will create in us a preference of affection to our own country."[11]

Historical writing played an especially vital role in the English and Scottish Enlightenments of the middle eighteenth century. Politics, as Peter Gay has observed, gave Enlightenment histories their special flavor. "For the philosophes, history was a policy science as well, but it was also . . . something different; it was a discipline in which too much insistence on policy would compromise the science."[12] The dilemma for Enlightenment historical thought was somehow to reconcile their conception of human progress with their firm conviction that men in all times and places are universally the same. Englishmen from Dryden through Burke subscribed to the notion of "uniformitarianism" because their analytical inclination stressed similarity and constancy rather than change and flux in the treatment of historical phenomena.[13] Nevertheless the doctrine of unity did not preclude the possibility of historical heterogeneity. David Hume found that the study of history taught him nothing "new or strange" about human nature, yet the "revolutions of human kind, as represented in history," surprised him with their "prodigious changes" and offered a "spectacle full of pleasure and variety." The passions and instincts of men may have been universally the same, but customs, religions, institutions, and sorts of social organization were capable of infinite variety. For the Enlightenment, again in

11 *Letters on the Study and Use of History,* pp. 34, 42–43, 47.
12 See Ian Watt, "Two Historical Aspects of the Augustan Tradition," in R. F. Brissenden, ed., *Studies in the Eighteenth Century: Papers Presented at the David Nichol Smith Memorial Seminar, Canberra 1966* (Canberra, Australian National University Press, 1968), pp. 67–88; Peter Gay, *The Enlightenment: An Interpretation,* volume II, *The Science of Freedom* (New York, Knopf, 1969), p. 395; Eric J. Streiff, "The Politics of Enlightenment Historiography: Studies in the Development of Historical Thought in France, Scotland, and Germany During the Later 18th Century" (unpublished Ph.D. dissertation, Yale University, 1969).
13 See Ernst Cassirer, *The Philosophy of the Enlightenment* (Princeton, Princeton University Press, 1951), p. 226; James W. Johnson, "Swift's Historical Outlook," *Journal of British Studies,* III (1965), 56.

Gay's words, "the past was not a monochrome."[14] William Smith and his younger contemporaries—such men as Madison, Hamilton, and Jay—would celebrate the variety of human conduct while insisting upon the uniformity of human nature.

If Smith shared some of the major assumptions of Enlightenment thought, he related even more particularly to that local renaissance called the Scottish Enlightenment. The works of Hume and Adam Ferguson were known to him, and he corresponded enthusiastically with Lord Kames, author of *The Historical Law of Tracts* (1758), and William Robertson, the cleric, Historiographer Royal of Scotland, and principal of the University of Edinburgh. Like Smith, Robertson was a staunch Presbyterian, began work on his *History of Scotland* in 1753, became deeply involved in ecclesiastical politics, and during the 1760's was drawn ever more fully into public affairs. Smith provided his colleague with goodly amounts of source material concerning the English colonies; and in his popular *History of America* (1777) Robertson expressed warm gratitude to "the ingenious historian of New York."[15]

Smith and Robertson shared a strong admiration for David Hume's historical abilities. In 1752, at the age of forty-one, Hume became librarian to the Advocates' Library in Edinburgh, and thereby gained access to one of the finest book collections in Britain. Within four years he produced a history of Stuart England in two volumes, followed in 1759 by two more volumes on the Tudors. In 1762 he completed his *History* by covering the long centuries from Julius Caesar to Henry VII. Hume undertook his initial inquiry into the Stuarts because he held a low opinion of the educational value of ancient and barbarian history. The seventeenth century appealed to him as "the most curious, interesting, and instructive part of our history," the richest in lessons for statesmen and citizens, and the epoch in which the public liberty of Englishmen was firmly established. He was also impelled by the belief—exactly the same as Smith's about New York—that "the history of England has

[14] Hume, "Of the Study of History," in David F. Norton, ed., *David Hume: Philosophical Historian* (Indianapolis, Bobbs-Merrill, 1965), pp. 35–39; Gay, *The Science of Freedom*, pp. 380–381, 565.

[15] A. Skinner, "Economics and History—The Scottish Enlightenment," *Scottish Journal of Political Economy*, XII (1965), 1–22; Smith to Jonathan Trumbull, June 12, 1773, Connecticut State Library, Hartford; Robertson, *The History of America* (Albany, 1822), I, xiii.

never yet been written; not only for style . . . but also for matter; such is the ignorance and partiality of all our historians."[16]

Hume strongly distrusted revolutions, believing that the ultimate test of all political movements, institutions, and policies lay in the utility they provided the nation. He was concerned that writers be more historically accurate when discussing the origins of government, a favorite topic in the eighteenth century. His *History of England,* like Smith's *History of New York* published eighteen months earlier, narrates relentlessly the dynasties, decrees, and campaigns of yore in strict chronological fashion. What we would regard as the cultural history of seventeenth-century England was relegated to four brief appendixes—comparable to Smith's six—scattered through the work. Moreover, Hume the essayist, like Smith in *The Independent Reflector* and other journals, ignored kings, battles, and dates in favor of manners, customs, ideas, and institutions discussed in the most sophisticated fashion.[17] It seems clear, in short, that the most advanced writers in the enlightened Anglo-American world shared similar views regarding the proper content and structure of historical writing. Political, military, and diplomatic history ought to be treated chronologically in an extended, factual narrative. The history of culture and society were the proper province of briefer essays.

During the third quarter of the eighteenth century, a major transformation occurred in Anglo-American historical writing; and the critical thrust of that transformation came in the 1750's. "You know that there is no post of honour in the English Parnassus more vacant than that of History," Hume wrote in 1753. "Style, judgement, impartiality, care—everything is

---

16 J. B. Black, *The Art of History* (New York, F. S. Crofts, 1926), pp. 82--83; Hume to Adam Smith, September 24, 1752, and to James Oswald, June 28, 1753, in J. Y. T. Greig, ed., *The Letters of David Hume* (Oxford, Oxford University Press, 1932), I, 167–168, 178–179.

17 Black, *Art of History,* p. 110; Hume, "Of the Origin of Government," in T. H. Green, ed., *Essays Moral, Political, and Literary* (London, 1889), I, 113–117; [George Frere], *A Short History of Barbados, from its first discovery and settlement, to the end of the year 1767* (London, 1768), pp. 90–121. Like Hume dealing with the delicate constitutional problem of the legacy of 1066, Smith had a major conquest to handle: that of New York in 1664 by the English —also a source of constitutional ambiguities. See Michael Kammen, "The Meaning of Colonization in American Revolutionary Thought," *Journal of the History of Ideas,* XXXI (1970), 346–348, 354 n. 45.

wanting to our historians." By 1770, however, his tune had changed immeasurably: "I believe this is the historical Age and this the historical Nation: I know no less than eight Histories upon the Stocks [being prepared] in this Country."[18]

What had happened? Several things. In Scotland during the 1740's and 1750's the intelligentsia became intrigued with tracing the primitive origins of human society and modern peoples. Their interest served as one major stimulus.[19] Even more important, perhaps, were the publication in 1748 of Montesquieu's *De l'esprit des lois* and in 1750 of Turgot's *Discours* on the benefits of Christianity and the progress of the human spirit in history. These major works inspired a new wave of historical inquiry in general and philosophical history in particular. By 1749 Montesquieu had already influenced Hume; he would reach Dr. Robertson soon after. In effect, Montesquieu declared the principles on which historians should work, while Turgot determined the thread they ought to pursue. The former demonstrated the utility of law as a means of understanding the history of government; the latter led the way toward a history of political society and civil change.[20]

So began an extraordinary outpouring in the later 1750's, of which William Smith's *History* was a part. *The Parliamentary or Constitutional History of England* appeared in twenty-four volumes between 1751 and 1761, a vast collection of source materials prepared by many hands. Richard Rolt wrote *A New and Accurate History of South-America* (London, 1756). *An Account of the European Settlements in America*, by William and Edmund Burke, published in 1757 in two volumes, covered the discoveries, "the manners and customs of the original inhabitants," the patterns of Spanish, Portuguese, French, Dutch, Danish, and English colonization. Then came Tobias Smollett's *Compleat History of England* (1757–58), Hume's

[18] Hume to John Clephane, January 5, 1753; Hume to William Strahan, [August 1770], in Greig, *Letters of David Hume*, I, 170; II, 230.

[19] See Lois Whitney, "English Primitivistic Theories of Epic Origins," *Modern Philology*, XXI (1924), 337–378.

[20] Hugh Trevor-Roper, "The Historical Philosophy of the Enlightenment," in *Studies on Voltaire and the Eighteenth Century*, XXVII (1963), 1671, 1675. There is more than a touch of irony in the fact that Montesquieu had a much greater impact in England than in France, whereas Bolingbroke, who wrote his *Letters on the Study and Use of History* in France, may have had greater appeal to the French philosophes than to his own countrymen.

(1758–59), Robertson's *Scotland* (1759), and in 1759–1761 *The World Displayed; or, A Curious Collection of Voyages and Travels,* a pretentious collection of sources in twenty volumes. In 1759 some earlier works were made available for the first time in English translation: among them were *A Relation of the Missions of Paraguay* by Ludovico Antonio Muratori (Venice, 1743–1749), and the *Noticia de la California* by Miguel Venegas (Madrid, 1757), an excellent account of the temporal and spiritual conquest of California to the middle of the eighteenth century.

Colonial historiography took a new turn in 1749–1751 with the publication of Dr. William Douglass' *A Summary, Historical and Political, of the First Planting, Progressive Improvements, and Present State of the British Settlements in North America* in two volumes. Many colonials—including William Smith, Jr.—would snipe at Dr. Douglass' findings and interpretations; but here at last was an attempt at a comprehensive view of the English colonies in historical perspective. In 1754–55 Thomas Prince published his second volume with a new title: *Annals of New England.* Then came the banner year of 1755: John Huske wrote *The Present State of North America;* Provost William Smith, Anglican cleric in Philadelphia, wrote *A Brief State of the Province of Pennsylvania;* Cadwallader Colden's *History of the Five Indian Nations* had its third edition in London; and there were others.[21] In 1758 Israel Acrelius published *A History of New Sweden; Or, the Settlements on the River Delaware,* covering the years 1638–1753. Between 1758 and 1760 Samuel Nevill compiled *The History of the Continent of America* as a supplement to his *New American Magazine.* And in 1759 Richard Jackson, with assistance from Benjamin Franklin, put together *An Historical Review of the Constitution and Government of Pennsylvania.* The appendixes in that volume, like those in William Smith's *History of New York,* treated contemporary issues of the 1750's.[22]

After the 1750's, then, in both England and her American colonies, the writing and reading of history became steadily more popular. The cost of bookmaking began to decline, and

[21] See Lawrence C. Wroth, *An American Bookshelf: 1755* (Philadelphia, University of Pennsylvania Press, 1934).

[22] The most complete guide to historical literature in colonial America is Giorgio Spini, *Autobiografia della giovane America: La Storiografia American dai Padri Pellegrini All'Indipendenza* (Turin, Giulio Einaudi, 1968).

the size of various printings increased. The colonists, nevertheless, ever conscious of their provincialism, seemed to prefer the best European historians—Voltaire, Hume, and Robertson—to indigenous authors. Good writing and a wide canvas usually had more appeal than native themes. These attitudes prevailed right down to the eve of Independence.[23] Even so, the uses, development, nature, and meaning of historical thought in colonial America constitute an important configuration of ideas —for William Smith and for us. Seventeenth-century English historians used the past to buttress political particulars, whereas eighteenth-century British historians were fascinated by their subject matter as a window to universal laws. Why did Englishmen overseas write history?

In the seventeenth century, when most colonial historians were New England divines, they especially concerned themselves with providential history, as a moral lesson, with the unique American mission as a stage in the unfolding of God's purpose in history. In the eighteenth century, by contrast, history came to serve more secular needs: the quest for constitutional legitimacy, or for provincial identity, or for partisan political purposes, or to guard against misconceptions abroad, or to promote emigration to a particular colony. Colonial history began as a kind of moral injunction and hagiography written by ministers, and often ended as a tactical maneuver by provincial politicians. Some volumes were designed as apologies for particular colonial administrations; others, like Colden's *History of the Five Indian Nations*, were intended to influence public policy where the legislature regulated the vital Indian trade; and various narratives of the Indian wars were simply regarded as good—albeit gory—entertainment.[24]

Many early American histories, the best ones especially, were directed primarily at a European audience, either to answer

[23] Danzner, "Historical Publication in America to 1860," p. 74; Black, *Art of History*, p. 41; James T. Flexner, *Mohawk Baronet: Sir William Johnson of New York* (New York, Harper & Row, 1959), p. 332.

[24] See Richard S. Dunn, "Seventeenth-Century English Historians of America," in James M. Smith, ed., *Seventeenth-Century America: Essays on Colonial History* (Chapel Hill, University of North Carolina Press, 1959), pp. 195–225; Peter Gay, *A Loss of Mastery: Puritan Historians in Colonial America* (New York, Vintage, 1968); Ralph N. Miller, "The Historians Discover America: A Study of American Historical Writing in the Eighteenth Century (unpublished Ph.D. dissertation, Northwestern University, 1946).

or to forestall criticism, to attract attention, or to defend the legitimacy of the colonies. Robert Beverley's *History and Present State of Virginia* (1705), John Lawson's *New Voyage to Carolina* (1709), and Smith's *History of New-York* were certainly written with English readers uppermost in the authors' minds. The more antiquarian and parochial endeavors as a rule were directed primarily at colonials: Thomas Prince's *Chronological History* (1736), John Callender's *Historical Discourse on . . . Rhode Island* (1738), and William Stith's *History of the First Discovery and Settlement of Virginia* (1747), for example.

The uses and applications of historical information were manifold. All of William Penn's writings were heavily laden with historical materials, for he constantly cited past events to illustrate conclusions drawn about the present; the illustrations, arranged chronologically, comprised an integral part of his theories. In 1749, when Benjamin Franklin published *Proposals Relating to the Education of Youth in Pennsylvania,* he urged that "HISTORY be made a constant Part of their Reading." He pointed out that "as nothing *teaches* (saith Mr. Locke) so nothing *delights* more than HISTORY. The first of these recommends it to the Study of grown Men, the latter makes me think it the *fittest* for a young Lad, who as soon as he is instructed in Chronology, and acquainted with the several Epochas in Use in this Part of the World . . . should then have some History put into his Hand." Franklin proceeded to devote thirteen paragraphs to justifying the value of historical studies, including geography, chronology, "antient customs," "Universal History," natural history, and the history of commerce. The study of history would demonstrate, among other things, the political impact of oratory, the necessity of a *"Publick Religion,"* and the "Advantage of Civil Orders and Constitutions, how Men and their Properties are protected by joining in Societies and establishing Government."[25]

This last point of Franklin's meant a great deal to colonial minds because they were particularly sensitive about the legitimacy of their constitutional arrangements. In addition, one of the most important modes of investigating the past in seven-

[25] Mary Maples Dunn, *William Penn: Politics and Conscience* (Princeton, Princeton University Press, 1967), pp. 48–50; Leonard W. Labaree, ed., *The Papers of Benjamin Franklin,* III (New Haven, Yale University Press, 1961), 410–418.

teenth-century Europe had been the study of law. Many Europeans obtained knowledge of their origins by reflecting upon
the evolution of their legal systems.[26] This was precisely the
path that William Smith, Jr., would follow in the 1750's. In-
tensive study of the law led him into historical explorations. He
came to believe that a fuller public knowledge of New York's
development would help to legitimize the product of that development. Wherefore history became a source both of provincial identity and integrity.

In the eighteenth-century colonies, as in England, political
problems were commonly looked at in historical terms. Men
believed that by examining the country's past, and especially
its law, they would be able to "unravel those mysteries of
authority and obligation which so baffled them." History came
increasingly to be valued as an arsenal of useful precedents.
Thus, in 1735, in the case of John Peter Zenger, James Alexander (a close friend of the the William Smiths), looked to history
to prove his argument that free speech is a constitutional
method of keeping a popular government in harmony with the
aspirations of the populace. He described the repressive effects
of restricted speech in ancient Rome, a lesson the Tudor and
Stuart kings supposedly had learned. Similarly, in 1737 Andrew Hamilton replied to his critics in the Zenger case with
extensive citations from history and law.[27]

By the 1750's, when William Smith started work on his
*History*, colonial historiography had passed through several
discernible phases. The earliest Puritans and chroniclers read
history as a record of divine providences. Their successors in
the later seventeenth century felt a morbid fascination for the
decline and hopeful recovery of society in the New Jerusalem.
For both Increase and Cotton Mather, with their emotions con-
centrated upon the destiny of a society, this thesis controlled
their respective compositions.[28] During the first decades of the

[26] See Pocock, *Ancient Constitution and the Feudal Law*, pp. vii–
viii; Javier Malagon-Barcelo, "The Role of the *Letrado* in the Colonization of America," *The Americas*, XVIII (1961), 1–17.

[27] J. H. Plumb, *Sir Robert Walpole: The Making of a Statesman*
(London, Cresset Press, 1956), pp. 21–22; Stanley N. Katz, ed., *A
Brief Narrative of the Case and Trial of John Peter Zenger, Printer
of the New York Weekly Journal, by James Alexander* (Cambridge,
Mass., Harvard University Press, 1963), pp. 27–28, 95, 181–202,
219 n. 50.

[28] See Kenneth B. Murdock, *Literature & Theology in Colonial
New England* (Cambridge, Mass., Harvard University Press, 1949),

eighteenth century, secularization and revisionism began to appear. Historians wrote less about Man's struggle to do Good and more about men's battle to survive in the wilderness. They also wrote to set the record straight. Robert Beverley's account of the Virginia Indians was composed, in part, to correct erroneous materials in John Oldmixon's *British Empire in America* (1708), which Beverley had seen in manuscript.[29] By the end of the 1740's colonial history writing had become fully disengaged from theology, more concerned with causation and explanation, and intimately tied to the cultural self-consciousness of the colonists. Franklin urged students to read histories "of these colonies; which should be accompanied with Observations on their Rise, Encrease, Use to Great-Britain, Encouragements, Discouragements, & the Means to make them flourish, secure their liberties, &c."[30]

Judging by the sequential newspaper advertisements of Hugh Gaine, importer and bookseller in New York City, the market for histories expanded steadily throughout the 1750's and even more in the 1760's.[31] The New York Society Library, established by William Smith and others in 1754, shortly secured a number of historical titles, many of which Smith must at least have browsed through: histories of England by Guthrie, Rapin, Tyrrel, and Smollett, plus Rollins' *Roman History*, a Tacitus, Bishop Burnet's *History of My Own Time*, all of Bolingbroke's works, Rushworth's *Historical Collections,* and Buchanan's *Scotland.*[32]

The greater availability of these admired tomes made colonials more readily discontented with their own pale efforts. Listen to John Huske's complaint in 1755, just when William Smith's research was fully under way.

---

chapter 3; Murdock, "Clio in the Wilderness: History and Biography in Puritan New England," *Church History,* XXIV (1955), 221–238.

[29] Louis B. Wright, ed., *The History and Present State of Virginia* (Chapel Hill, University of North Carolina Press, 1947), pp. xvii, 349 n. 8.

[30] See Max Savelle, *Seeds of Liberty: The Genesis of the American Mind* (Seattle, University of Washington Press, 1965), pp. 567, 569–570; Labaree, *Papers of Benjamin Franklin,* III, 415.

[31] See Paul L. Ford, ed., *The Journals of Hugh Gaine, Printer* (New York, Dodd, Mead, 1902), I, 188–202.

[32] See H. Trevor Colbourn, *The Lamp of Experience: Whig History and the Intellectual Origins of the American Revolution* (Chapel Hill, University of North Carolina Press, 1965), p. 205; Danzner, "America's Roots in the Past," p. 58.

Every Person that knows any thing of *North-America* in
general, or of any one Province in Particular, must be
sensible that the Histories or Works of *Mather, Oldmixon,
Neal, Salmon,* etc. who have chiefly copied each other . . .
might almost as properly have called their Works Histories
of Prester John's or the *Hottentots* Country . . . as Histories
of *North-America* . . . . In short, there is not one work
yet published to the World in our language that in any
degree deserves the title of a *History of North-America,*
but [John] Smith's *History of Virginia,* and Douglas's *Summary* . . . . And this last is only valuable for being the
best Collection of Facts in general, for a future Historian
. . . . As to the Histories of the Indians . . . not one
. . . [is] worth reading, but that of Colden.[33]

Smith's *History* in 1757, Richard Jackson's *Historical Review of
the Constitution and Government of Pennsylvania* (1759), and
Thomas Hutchinson's *History of the Colony and Province of
Massachusetts-Bay* (1764–1767) finally began to supply a remedy for Huske's lament.

Like William Smith in New York, Hutchinson emerged rapidly as a leading figure in Massachusetts' political and judicial
life. He read widely in English and colonial history, and his
work on New England boundary disputes led him into historical research which he found quite congenial. Enforced political
inactivity in 1763 gave him the leisure to complete a volume
on Massachusetts through 1691. At first he felt reluctant to
publish it in his own lifetime; but early in 1764 he changed
his mind and had it produced in Boston immediately and in
London a year later. By 1765 he had completed a second volume, carrying the story to 1750. The manuscript was nearly
destroyed by Stamp Act rioters, recovered by a friend, transcribed laboriously a second time, and finally published in
1767. Even more than Smith, perhaps, Hutchinson was fair
and courteous to political opponents in his *History,* and, the
work, though dull, remains a judicious and indispensable
source.[34]

---

[33] Huske, *The Present State of North America* (London, 1755),
pp. 41–42.

[34] The most recent edition is by Lawrence Shaw Mayo (Cambridge,
Mass., Harvard University Press, 1936), 3 vols.; see Clifford K.
Shipton, "Thomas Hutchinson," in *Biographical Sketches of Those
Who Attended Harvard College in the Classes 1726–1730* (Boston,
Massachusetts Historical Society, 1951), pp. 168–170.

There is a sense in which most histories written in early America will seem dull to us simply because they were usually organized by gubernatorial administrations and proceeded chronologically with numbing regularity. This was the case, for example, with Charles Leslie's *New History of Jamaica* (1740), Stith's *History of . . . Virginia* (1747), Smith's *New-York* (1757), and Frere's *History of Barbados* (1768). They also suffered from a penchant to incorporate large chunks of original documents directly into the text. As William Bradford had written during the first generation, "because letters are by some wise men counted the best parte of histories, I shall shew their [the Pilgrims] greevances hereaboute by their owne letters, in which the passages of things will be more truly discerned."[35]

The colonial historian faced still other temptations and difficulties. Too often he was dependent upon the prerogative for access to documentary sources, and therefore required unusual tact both at the research stage and in writing. One false step and he might be denied access a second time or, worse, lose political patronage altogether.[36] In addition, he rarely had a clear sense of the relation between the history of his colony and that of the others, thereby creating a problem of proportion and perspective. In this respect he shared the dilemma of the sixteenth-century chorographers of Europe, a group whose work and function suggest striking parallels with early American historiography. Since the analogy has never before been made, let us examine for a moment the character of historical chorography.[37]

The sixteenth-century German topographers wished to "illustrate" the German past and its passage into the present, as well as to "display" the land and its inhabitants in their own time. To accomplish this purpose they blended together descriptive geography with narrative history; and the resulting volumes were known as topographies or chorographies. Their leisurely style and loose structure offered many opportunities for

[35] William T. Davis, ed., *Bradford's History of Plymouth Plantation, 1606–1646* (New York, C. Scribner's Sons, 1908), p. 68.

[36] See, e.g., Cadwallader Colden, *The History of the Five Indian Nations Depending on the Province of New York in America* (Ithaca, N.Y., Cornell University Press, 1958), p. 78.

[37] See Gerald Strauss, *Sixteenth-Century Germany: Its Topography and Topographers* (Madison, University of Wisconsin Press, 1959), p. 111; F. J. Levy, *Tudor Historical Thought* (San Marino, Calif., Huntington Library, 1967), p. 140.

comparison and generalization. Chorography differed from traditional geography in selecting only certain places for special attention to all their particulars: harbors, farms, villages, and river courses. Whereas geography aimed at a synoptic view of lands in their entirety, chorography was restricted to individual localities described in the manner of a painting. The author aimed at intertwining *"locus, tempus, & historia."* During the 1570's local history and topography began to be fused by Elizabethan writers, such as William Lambarde in his *Perambulation of Kent* (1576) and Richard Carew in his *Survey of Cornwall. Views* and *Surveys* were regarded as historical titles in Stuart England, where there was an extraordinary growth in the production of local chorographies. Many were published, but numerous ones remain in manuscript to this day.[38]

The chorographer assumed that there were certain categories of information which were peculiarly relevant to the character of a given region; that there were parameters of description appropriate to understanding each locality; that the variability of these parameters differentiated one region from another; that the most important of these parameters were the human inhabitants and their mode of existence, topography, climate, mineral resources, animals, and vegetables. The great age of discovery in the sixteenth century had done much to stimulate cartography and geographic description, and they in turn caused chorography to flourish. But it also flourished in sixteenth-century Germany and England for the very same reasons that made it so popular in colonial America. Chorography developed in response to the emergence of a certain type of German and English regionalism, to the particular sense of pride in place peculiar to a people just coming of age and seeking recognition. This chauvinism was especially prevalent in the German territories because the allegiances of the German humanists were intensely regional and even local. For most Teutons "Germany"—like "America"—was an amorphous designation, too large and vague to be the focal point of emotional attachment or scholarly commitment. In the absence of a national consciousness in the modern sense, men looked to smaller geopolitical units for their fulfillment.[39]

Much of what passed for history, geography, or natural his-

[38] Strauss, *Sixteenth-Century Germany,* pp. vii, 6, 55–58; Fussner, *The Historical Revolution,* pp. 156–157, 180.

[39] Gerald Strauss, "Topographical-Historical Method in Sixteenth-Century German Scholarship," *Studies in the Renaissance,* V (1958), 87–101.

tory in colonial America was really chorography, this very special composite of all three. The illustrations are almost limitless: Adriaen Van Der Donck's *Description of the New Netherlands* (1656), John Ogilby's *America* (1671), Thomas Gabriel's *Historical and Geographical Account of Pennsylvania and of West-New-Jersey* (1698), the first six chapters of William Hubbard's *General History of New England* (1680), John Lawson's *New Voyage to Carolina* (1710), and Hugh Jones's *Present State of Virginia* (1724) provide a few examples. It may fairly be said that the apogee of colonial chorography was achieved in Jefferson's *Notes on the State of Virginia* (1785) and William Bartram's *Travels*.[40]

All of these American volumes shared a deep interest in environment, climate, species of flora and fauna, natural barriers, indigenous inhabitants, and local awareness. "In every order of nature," wrote Bartram, "we perceive a variety of qualities distributed amongst individuals, designed for different purposes and uses." It may be important to note that the belief in climate as a powerful historical determinant, so strongly adhered to in Augustan England but dismissed thereafter by David Hume and Dr. Johnson, remained influential in America during the second half of the eighteenth century and helped to keep up the popularity of chorographical writing. "God made all countries to be inhabited," wrote George Frere, "and probably he has bestowed some advantages upon these climates between the tropicks, which colder regions want."[41]

Just as the colonists of Smith's generation were intrigued by the historical influence of climate, an Augustan notion discarded in the reign of George II, they were also fascinated by the idea of historical analogy, so popular in Sir Robert Walpole's day, especially the 1730's. Classical conceptions of citizenship were revived in prerevolutionary America, and the

[40] Allen Tate has remarked that the Southerner's sense of place is his most fundamental instinct; and Clarence Ver Steeg has suggested that environmental factors shaped the Southern mind more than anywhere else in the English colonies. (See "Historians and the Southern Colonies," in Ray A. Billington, ed., *The Reinterpretation of Early American History: Essays in Honor of John Edwin Pomfret* [New York, Norton, 1968], p. 82.) There is obviously a connection between these two phenomena, and I would hazard the guess that chorography had a very special appeal in the Southern colonies.

[41] Bartram, *Travels*, ed. by Francis Harper (New Haven, Yale University Press, 1958), p. lii; [Frere], *Short History of Barbados*, pp. 104–121.

corruptness of imperial Rome in her declining days was invoked as a prophetic warning to Grenville, Townshend, Lord North, and their myrmidons. Paradoxically, however, where the Augustans tended to be fatalistic about the lessons of history, the colonists during the third quarter of the eighteenth century began to believe that they would be able to transcend history. The American Calvinists persuaded themselves that the Great Awakening had reversed the apparent course of history. Regeneration was easily within reach. More secular types, however, at first groped only tentatively in this direction. Charles Carroll of Carrollton informed his father from London that he was studying "the profitable and faithful lessons of History; here I learn to be wise at the expense of others and to attain to true glory by the example of the great, good & just."[42]

But, with the coming of independence, republicanism, and a multitude of innovations, historical limitations had to be fully reconceived. In consequence, the historical philosophy of the founding fathers would help to distinguish the American Enlightenment from its European counterpart. John Adams, like the *philosophes*, regarded history as retrospective; but Thomas Jefferson saw it as prospective. Where Adams assumed that Americans were doomed to repeat the errors of the past, Jefferson believed that they would transcend history, that human nature changed in a new environment. Jefferson and his like-minded Americans were optimists. They took the idea of progress, an elitist concept in Europe, and Americanized it by democratizing it. Progress would mean a new day in the welfare of ordinary Americans.[43]

The optimistic Jeffersonians thought about history philosophi-

[42] Herbert Davis, "The Augustan Conception of History," in J. A. Mazzeo, ed., *Reason and the Imagination: Studies in the History of Ideas, 1600–1800* (New York, Columbia University Press, 1962), pp. 213–229; Alan Heimert, *Religion and the American Mind from the Great Awakening to the Revolution* (Cambridge, Mass.: Harvard University Press, 1966), pp. 62–63; *Maryland Historical Magazine*, XXXVII (1942), 302.

[43] See Henry Steele Commager, "The Past as an Extension of the Present," *Proceedings of the American Antiquarian Society*, LXXIX, part 1 (1969), 17–27. Spanish Americans, as soon as they had justified their newly won independence, were led to investigate the meaning that "America" would hold for them, not as tradition but as a future to be achieved. See Richard M. Morse, "Crosscurrents in New World History," in Joseph Maier, ed., *Politics of Change in Latin America* (New York, Praeger, 1964), p. 45.

cally—about time, and human nature, and environmental de-
terminism—but they did not write formal histories as extended
narratives. Those colonials who did, such as William Douglass,
Cadwallader Colden, William Smith, Jr., and Thomas Hutchinson, uniformly became Loyalists. Their sense of past realities
ran deeper and firmer, so that, despite their warm attachment
to Whig principles, they could not become rebels. Revolutionaries may subsequently write history; but historians rarely
turn into revolutionaries. A revolutionary may seek to invoke
history to legitimize his actions, but revolutions, regardless of
their rhetoric, loom up as a repudiation of history.[44]

[44] Cf. Stow Persons, "The Cyclical Theory of History in Eighteenth
Century America," *American Quarterly*, VI (1954), 147–163; Douglass Adair, " 'Experience Must Be Our Only Guide': History, Demo-
cratic Theory, and the United States Constitution," in Billington,
ed., *Reinterpretation of Early American History*, pp. 129–148.

## III  *William Smith's* History of New York: *Its Qualities, Sources, and Critics*

### Qualities

Chronicles and chronological charts enjoyed enormous popularity in eighteenth-century America. *The Chronicle of the Kings of England,* for example, a curious work often attributed to Robert Dodsley, was reprinted in Boston in 1758 and went through seven more American editions before 1800. Most early American magazines devoted a section to "historical chronicles," which normally listed current events and occasionally included historical essays. The *First Book of the American Chronicles of the Times* (1774) provided a parody in scriptural language of events preceding the Revolution.

It is not surprising, therefore, that Smith's *History* was chronologically organized by gubernatorial administrations. Like many of its contemporaries, it devoted a few additional chapters to topical matters of contemporary interest—but Smith's at least were in no way perfunctory. Although William Smith, Jr., was many light years removed from Erik Erikson's appeal for a new sort of narrative history—"maybe it is time to study political sequences as psychological continuities rather than as accidental fatalities"—he did not lack for sophistication and he knew precisely what he was doing.[1] He tried to portray each administration by noting the personality and character of its

[1] Erik Erikson, *Insight and Responsibility: Lectures on the Ethical Implications of Psychoanalytic Thought* (New York, Norton, 1964), p. 205; Leo Braudy, *Narrative Form in History and Fiction: Hume, Fielding, and Gibbon* (Princeton, Princeton University Press, 1970).

governor, and by reporting the major events during the tenure of each. As Nathaniel Hawthorne would call his works romances rather than novels, so Smith deprecated the scope and structure of his *History,* preferring to call it a "narrative." "He who delights only in pages shining with illustrious characters, the contentions of armies, the rise and fall of empires, and other grand events, must have recourse to the great authours of antiquity. A detail of the little transactions, which concern a colony, scant in its jurisdiction, and still struggling with the difficulties naturally attending its infant state, to gentlemen of this taste can furnish no entertainment. The ensuing narrative (for it deserves not the name of a history, though for brevity's sake I have given it that title) presents us only a regular thread of simple facts." Actually, given both the paucity of reliable predecessors and his chronological scope, Smith had undertaken an extremely ambitious task.

The disadvantage in Smith's emphasis upon gubernatorial administrations is that his *History,* especially the *Continuation,* becomes primarily a public account of Indian relations, of constitutional relations between the governors and their assemblies, and of judicial arrangements. It is quite good on the English dimension of New York politics, on the composition and internal alignments of the Assembly, and on boundary problems. It is extraordinarily inadequate, however, in the areas of social and economic history and in the government and politics of localities. Despite the fact that George Whitefield was once a guest in Smith's home, the historian never even mentions the Great Awakening of the 1740's. Smith's apparent obliviousness to social history must have been the result of convention rather than insensitivity, for he demonstrates every so often his awareness of such phenomena as social structure, the effects of affluence, and cultural lag. "We follow the London fashions," he wrote, "though, by the time we adopt them, they become disused in England." The first appended chapter in Volume One required him to do a bit of demographic research; and he does remark upon the origins (in the 1720's) of the family orientation of politics in eighteenth-century New York—a favorite subject of modern historians.

Smith's professional interest in the bench and bar of New York account for the very considerable attention he devoted to laws, the various courts, and the administration of justice under the Dutch, the English, and even among the Iroquois. Moreover, his fascination with politics also extended to the Indians. He fully understood that conflicts of interest within the great federation had a profound impact upon Anglo-French diplomacy. Above all, Smith brought a spirit of boosterism to his *History*. New York was a good place to live, in his view, and his six appendixes lovingly described the natural advantages of the Province, just as he had in the eighth number of *The Independent Reflector* in 1753: "A brief Consideration of NEW-YORK, with respect to its natural Advantages: Its Superiority in several Instances, over some of the neighboring Colonies."

In addition to his special emphases, Smith had very real prejudices. He was hostile to Catholicism and Anglicanism. He had his political partialities, and he slipped into the appendixes to Volume One controversial views on matters pertaining to the later 1730's and 1740's, despite his virtuous statement to the contrary at the end of the narrative: "the history of those times will be better received from a more disinterested pen. To suppress truth on the one hand, or exaggerate it on the other, are both inexcusable faults, and perhaps it would be difficult for me to avoid those extremes."

Historical objectivity and impartiality did not carry quite the same meaning two centuries ago that they have today. The quality of impartiality simply denoted not being formally associated with a particular cause or organization. "As the writer is independent," wrote William Douglass of himself in 1755, "being in no publick office, no ringleader of any party, or faction; what he writes may be deemed impartial."[2] Men would inevitably hold opinions, even strong opinions; but objective history was possible so long as it was not patent propaganda in service to a particular cause.

Judged by the standards of his own day, William Smith's detachment is impressive. He was very generous to Burnet's administration during the 1720's despite the fact that the Governor had overruled Smith's father in a major court case. The elder Smith had also played an unfortunate part in the so-called "Negro Plot" of 1741, for he had conducted the prosecution and made an impassioned speech condemning the blacks of

[2] Douglass, *A Summary, Historical and Political . . . of the British Settlements in North America* (Boston, 1755), II, 1; see also Thomas Hutchinson, *The History of the Colony and Province of Massachusetts Bay* (Cambridge, Mass., Harvard University Press, 1936), I, xxix; William Livingston to Noah Welles, August 18, 176?, Livingston-Welles MSS, Johnson Collection, Yale University Library.

New York for their ingratitude. Nevertheless, the historian made no attempt to whitewash his father, and took a fairly liberal view of the whole sordid affair. Despite the younger Smith's deep involvement in New York politics during the 1750's, the fewer than a dozen references to himself in the *Continuation* are reasonably innocuous.

On the whole, Smith set a high standard for accuracy, though one can find errors easily enough. He stated that Peter Zenger's bail was £800 when in fact it was about half that amount. He argued that land conveyances need not be written and registered when they had been, in fact, for years.[3] Despite such slips as these, however, Smith was extremely conscientious. Early in his career he gained access to *A Treatise On Evidence* and copied it out entirely. Although it dealt with evidence in the legal sense, it certainly had applicability for the historian: "The first therefore and most Signal Rule in Relation to Evidence is this: That a Man must have the utmost Evidence that the Nature of the Fact is Capeable of."

Smith took one liberty which contravened the wisdom of his *Treatise On Evidence,* but for which there were precedents going all the way back to Thucydides. He included speeches, most of dubious accuracy, such as Governor Dongan's long address to the Iroquois. Smith's first volume incorporated many more documents directly into the text than did his second; but the latter, which rarely revealed sources of information, paraphrased many primary sources in the most tedious, unliterary manner. In general, the second volume lacks the smooth continuity of the first. Too often paragraphs jump from one matter to another without transitional connections.

On balance Smith's *History* deserves our respect and close attention. It is neither as poignant as Bradford's *Plymouth Plantation* nor as lively as Beverley's *Virginia;* but along with them and Hutchinson's *Massachusetts-Bay* it stands as one of the four finest histories written in colonial times. In 1777, during Smith's difficult exile at Livingston Manor, he expressed

---

[3] See Stanley N. Katz, ed., *A Brief Narrative of the Case and Trial of John Peter Zenger, Printer of the New York Weekly Journal, by James Alexander* (Cambridge, Mass., Harvard University Press, 1963), p. 209 n. 51; Irving Mark, *Agrarian Conflicts in Colonial New York, 1711–1775* (Port Washington, N.Y., Ira J. Friedman, 1965), p. 80 n. 125; and see Beverly McAnear, "Politics in Provincial New York, 1689–1761" (unpublished PhD dissertation, Stanford University, 1935), p. 569 and n. 24.

the hope that "it may however at some distant Day be of use."[4] That hope has been amply fulfilled, for unlike many historians of their own times, Smith was not a blind voyeur. His accounts and interpretations of major events, such as Leisler's Rebellion or Governor Hunter's administration, seem very familiar and remarkably modern. The characters of many colonial New Yorkers sketched in the *Dictionary of American Biography* are taken directly from Smith and reinforced by other evidence. To an extraordinary degree, William Smith, Jr., shaped our contemporary understanding of colonial New York.

## Sources

Even before Smith began to research and write his own *History,* he had developed a strong appetite for historical studies. He especially valued six works, three by English authors and three by French. The first was *A View of Universal History* (London, 1685) by Francis Tallents (1619–1708), really a series of chronological tables which the author had engraved on sixteen copperplates in his own home. Smith also admired the *Discours sur l'histoire universelle* of Bossuet (1627–1704) and Charles Rollin's *The Ancient History of the Egyptians, Carthaginians, Assyrians, Babylonians, Medes and Persians, Macedonians and Grecians . . .* (London, 1738–40), translated from the French in ten volumes. For the history of England he enjoyed the folio edition of the *Works* of Sir Francis Bacon, Bishop Burnet's *History of His Own Time,* and most of all *The History of England* (London, 1725–31) by Paul de Rapin-Thoyras (1661–1725). Smith, William Livingston, and their circle of friends had the greatest admiration—paradoxically it now seems—both for Rapin's impartiality and for his whiggery. "In my opinion," Livingston wrote, "[Rapin] still carries the Palm among the writers of our story; and wants nothing but a reduction of His Enormous Bulk to about half his Present Size."[5] Thus, when Smith first set about his own project he had clearly in his mind the example of various masters who had worked at chronology, ancient history, national history, historical essays, and contemporary history.

---

[4] William H. W. Sabine, ed., *Historical Memoirs from 12 July 1776 to 25 July 1778 of William Smith . . .* (New York, Colbourn and Tegg, 1958), II, 93–94.

[5] Livingston to Noah Welles, August 18, 176?, Livingston-Welles MSS, Johnson Collection, Yale University Library.

Research on the Dutch period of New York history must have been frustrating because New Netherland had been administered from Amsterdam. All daybooks, apologias, and literary efforts by provincial officers were sent there. Governor Kieft's historical essay had been lost at sea with him (and, incidentally, most documents which did reach the archives of the West India Company were eventually sold in 1821 to dealers in waste paper!).[6] "We have no Books among our *Dutch* Records remaining in the Secretary's Office," Smith complained, "relating to State Matters before Kieft's Time, nor any Enrolment of Patents, till a Year after *Van Twiller* arrived here [1634]. Mr. Jacob Goelet supplied us with several Extracts from the Dutch Records." Smith also used John de Laet's *Nieuwe Wereldt ofte Beschrijvinghe van West-Indien, wt veelerhande Schriften ende Aen-teekeningen van verscheyden Natien* (Leyden, 1625), and the same author's *Historie Ofte Iaerlijck Verhael Van de Verrichtinghen der Geoctroyeerde West-Indische Compagnie . . .* (Leyden, 1644),[7] as well as a chorographical view of New Netherland written in 1649. There remain among Smith's manuscripts in the New York Public Library 161 pages of translations, notes, and extracts taken from Dutch records (1630–1663) in 1753.

For the English period, Smith had access to various unpublished materials. James Alexander, his father's close associate in the law, had accumulated a considerable collection of historical manuscripts, especially for the 1730's, and made that collection available to the young historian. Smith very much regretted Alexander's death in April 1756, just a few months before he completed the *History*, because he had hoped the shrewd master would give his manuscript a close, critical reading. The minutes of the commissioners of Indian affairs from 1675 onward had been kept in separate quires until 1751 when Alexander had them bound up into four large folio volumes. They contained, among other things, all of the Indian treaties made by the governments of New York on behalf of the Crown. In Smith's Preface he explains that he used minutes of the Governor's Council, journals of the Assembly, and records found in the office of the secretary of the Province. Among his manu-

[6] See Ellis L. Raesly, *Portrait of New Netherland* (Port Washington, N.Y., Ira J. Friedman, 1965), p. 254.
[7] *New World, or the Description of the West Indies from many publications and notes of various nations;* and *History, or Annual Relation of the Achievements of the West India Company.*

scripts are quantities of documents relating to Jacob Leisler and Albany in 1689–90, the Oneida Indians in the eighteenth century, King's College (later Columbia), the Presbyterian Church in New York (1718–1732), the correspondence of New York's agent, Robert Charles (1748–1760), "sundries" pertaining especially to 1683 and 1735, William Burnet's commission as Governor, and Governor Montgomerie's royal instructions. From the text of Volume One itself we know that Smith had access to reports concerning New York sent from the Board of Trade to the Crown, as well as personal correspondence concerning the Iroquois language from a missionary who lived among them in 1748.

Various published sources were utilized by Smith, such as printed abstracts of the accounts written by missionaries of the Society for the Propagation of the Gospel, *The Account of the Scotch Mission at Stockbridge,* Noah Hobart's various *Addresses to the Members of the Episcopal Separation in New-England* (1748–51), Francis Makemie's *Narrative of a New and Unusual American Imprisonment of Two Presbyterian Ministers* (1755), English and colonial legal opinions, and the *State Trials at Large.* In addition, of course, Smith had access to his own earliest writings: *Laws of New York from the Year 1691 to 1751, Inclusive* (1752), *The Independent Reflector* (1753), *The Occasional Reverberator* (1753), and *The Watch Tower* (1754–55), all of which contained a fair amount of historical material.

Among secondary sources published in English, Smith relied upon various works by New England historians. In several cases, such as Cotton Mather's *Life of His Excellency Sir William Phips* (1697), he challenged Mather's judgments on major issues. Smith generally used the writings of other colonials critically and cautiously. He respected the reliability of Stith's *History of the First Discovery and Settlement of Virginia* (1747), mistrusted John Oldmixon's *British Empire in America* (1708), and had severe strictures upon William Douglass' *Summary, Historical and Political . . . of the British Settlements in North America* (1751): "a sensible, immethodical, Writer, often incorrect." He relied a great deal upon Colden's *History of the Five Indian Nations,* found some passages accurate and others incorrect, and noted carefully where Colden and Charlevoix, the French Jesuit, contradicted each other.

The French influence upon historical writing in the English

colonies was quite significant and has never been adequately appreciated. Both as sources of substantive information and as interpretative touchstones to react against, the Gallic impact was considerable. Colden's *Five Indian Nations* drew heavily upon French sources; Douglass' *Summary* opened with a fold-out map of North America taken from the Duke D'Anville; and Smith's *History* provides a running commentary upon the *History and General Description of New France* (Paris, 1743–44), of Pierre de Charlevoix (1682–1761), the *New Voyages to North-America, Containing an Account of the Several Nations of that Vast Continent* (London, 1703, 1735) of Baron de la Hontan (1666–1715?), the *Histoire de l'Amérique septentrionale* (Paris, 1722, 1753) of Claude Charles Le Roy Bacqueville de la Potherie (c. 1668–c. 1738), which was a history of New France and the North American Indians,[8] and the *Nouvelles cartes des découvertes de l'Amiral DeFonte, et autres navigateurs . . . dans les mers septentrionales. . . .* of De L'Isle (Paris, 1753).

Smith had great admiration for Montesquieu's *L'Esprit des lois* and Voltaire's *Age of Louis XIV*. He must have agreed with Voltaire's pronouncement that Jesuits could not write sound history,[9] for his continuous criticism of Charlevoix provides one of the steadiest themes in Volume One. Smith admitted that he did not trust the Jesuit, faulted his partiality to the French in discussing North American diplomacy, contradicted his cartographic data, and disliked his judgment, his use of documents, and his inconsistencies. Actually, the Jesuit scholar and teacher, who first visited New France from 1705 to 1709, was probably no more partisan than Smith himself. When the Regent of France wished to send an agent to New France for secret reconnaissance purposes involving boundaries and routes to the west, he selected Charlevoix. The Jesuit disguised the real purpose of his errand by visiting Catholic missions in North America. His *Journal of a Voyage*, published in 1744 as an appendix to his *History of New France*, proved so popular that it was reprinted separately and translated into English in 1761. The accuracy and maturity of his observations have made his

[8] See Emma H. Blair, ed., *The Indian Tribes of the Upper Mississippi Valley and Region of the Great Lakes as Described by . . . Bacqueville de la Potherie, French Royal Commissioner to Canada . . .* (Cleveland, Arthur H. Clark, 1911), I, 275–372; II, 13–136.

[9] See Peter Gay, *The Enlightenment: An Interpretation*, volume II, *The Science of Freedom* (New York, Knopf, 1969), p. 377.

journal an invaluable source ever since.[10] In 1756–57 Charlevoix published a *Histoire du Paraguay* in three volumes, which were printed in English translation in London and Dublin in 1769. Despite Smith's strictures, Charlevoix was his equal as a historian, and perhaps even his superior.

Cartographic sources were as important to eighteenth-century historians as literary documents, and Smith examined and compared maps with the same critical attention he devoted to primary sources and contemporary histories. He relied especially upon the maps of Jacques Nicholas Bellin (1703–1772), an engineer and geographer with the French navy. Between 1744 and 1757 Bellin produced a fine set of maps of North American regions, remarkable for their detail, including one of northern New York and the Saint Lawrence River and another of New England, New York, and Pennsylvania. Smith most admired *A Map of the British and French Dominions in North America* (1755) by Dr. John Mitchell of Urbanna, Virginia, a fellow of the Royal Society; and he was quite critical of Lewis Evans' *Geographical, Historical, Political, Philosophical, and Mechanical Essays . . . wherein the author sets forth an analysis of a* GENERAL MAP *of the Middle British Colonies* (1755) and Evans' pamphlet defending his map in 1756.[11]

It is more difficult to inventory the sources Smith used for his *Continuation* because he was less explicit about them and because they were often not the sort that have survived. In this sense, the very virtues of these personal sources were also their disadvantage, for we cannot always examine them ourselves or, in some cases, even reconstruct them. Smith engaged in what we would now call "oral history": he knew many of the participants, and can be said to have "interviewed" or conversed with them. He actually attended many of the events he describes, kept his own journal beginning in 1753, and read his father's secret diary (which has not been found), even quot-

[10] There is a brief sketch of Charlevoix in John H. Kennedy's, *Jesuit and Savage in New France* (New Haven, Yale University Press, 1950), p. 59. The best modern edition of Charlevoix's *History*, translated by John G. Shea, was published in New York, 1866–1872, in six volumes. Charlevoix's *Journal of a Voyage to North America* [1720–22] has had a recent printing in the *March of America Facsimile Series*, no. 36 (Ann Arbor, Xerox Corp., 1966).

[11] See Lawrence H. Gipson, *Lewis Evans* (Philadelphia, University of Pennsylvania Press, 1939), p. 14; L. F. S. Upton, *The Loyal Whig: William Smith of New York & Quebec* (Toronto, University of Toronto Press, 1969), p. 37 n.

ing from it. He had access to the correspondence of David Jones, Speaker of the Assembly, notably Jones's communications with New York's London agent. In the course of Volume Two Smith mentions newspapers, journals of the Council and Assembly, journals of the Board of Trade, unpublished official papers, printed pamphlets, and broadsides. Among his manuscripts in the New York Public Library, there are papers concerning the establishment of King's College in the 1750's, the New York—New Jersey and New York—Massachusetts boundary controversies, opinions written by Lewis Morris, extracts from wartime accounts, materials toward a history of the administrations of Clarke and Clinton (1736–1746), and a commonplace book for the years 1753–1764.

In brief, Smith used the same sorts of sources a modern historian would, and in much the same way. His efforts were of a pioneering nature, and have endured remarkably well despite the subsequent availability of evidence he could not have seen.

## Critics

Publication of Smith's *History* in the spring of 1757 caused a few ripples but no great splash. It received a rather condescending notice in the English *Monthly Review* (see Editor's Appendix A), an anonymous review which may have been written by Oliver Goldsmith. The *Gentleman's Magazine* and the *London Magazine* merely listed it among books recently published. Colonial newspapers devoted about as much attention as the London press. Garrat Noel advertised it in the *New York Mercury*, March 27, 1758, and a few other advertisements appeared subsequently; but it was hardly a "hot" item. New Yorkers, especially clergymen and lawyers, cheerfully paid an even pound for their copies, but the public response was on the whole a quiet one.

The private response, at least on the part of interested individuals, was less quiet. Jacob Leisler's granddaughter wrote Smith a stormy letter of protest which has not survived, although we have the draft of the author's reply:

> I am very sorry my account of Leisler's times has given
> you the least offense, more especially because few Persons
> so sincerely compassionate the Troubles which his unjust fall
> brought upon his Family or were more tenderly concerned
> for you in particular who have been uncommonly afflicted of
> late by a [more?] interesting Circumstances.

I don't propose a long vindication of myself from the Charge of Partiality. [?] would suit your Taste or moderate your grief, and therefore I shall only say that what I wrote was collected from the most authentic materials—I mean the original Letters and Papers of Mr. Leisler and Mr. Milbourne most of which are still in my custody. The facts asserted are indisputable and if my observations upon them are not well founded I am sure they were not owing to any Bias in Favour of Mr. Leisler's opponents for I had always a good opinion of his Heart and Designs in setting up for the Prince of Orange, and if there was not the greatest Prudence used by that Party it must be ascribed in a great Degree to the Confusion & Heat of the Times. This is my opinion & must appear to be so to every Reader of the History of those Transactions.

I don't think I have need to add any thing more than my Promise to peruse the Paper you inclosed & that if I find I have fallen into an error it shall be publicly corrected when a proper opportunity presents—I take your letter in very good [?]. . . .[12]

At the same time Anglican advocates in New York were provoked by Smith's apparent bias against the Church, the Society for the Propagation of the Gospel, and its missionaries. The Reverend Samuel Johnson, president of King's College and father of Smith's college friend, William Samuel Johnson, wrote to Archbishop Secker in March 1759 warning him of the historian's malice (see Editor's Appendix B, no. 7). Once again in 1763 Johnson urged the Archbishop of Canterbury to publish a critique of Smith's strictures written by the Reverend Henry Barclay, sometime missionary to the Mohawks and Rector of Trinity Church in New York City (see the Biographical Directory in Volume Two).[13]

The biggest fuss, however, arose in 1759–60 between Cadwallader Colden and Smith concerning many points of factual detail and interpretation. Colden's heated correspondence with both Smiths and with his own son, Alexander Colden, is printed below (see Editor's Appendix B, nos. 1–6, 8–17). Colden's ten lengthy letters to his son, over which he labored long and hard, ostensibly comprise a running commentary upon Smith's *History*, with each "letter" treating a separate episode or guber-

[12] Smith to Mrs. Farmer, July 7, 1759, Smith MSS, lot 208 (3), New York Public Library.
[13] Hugh Hastings, ed., *Ecclesiastical Records: State of New York* (Albany, James B. Lyon, 1901–16), VI, 3887–3890.

natorial administration. Actually the letters were written for posterity—or at least for the benefit of future historians—and constitute a kind of political history of colonial New York writ small.[14] Although there certainly were legitimate differences of opinion between Smith and Colden, it must be borne in mind that in 1751 Colden had approached Smith and Livingston to ask them to omit from their compilation of the colony's laws a reference that might conceivably cast doubt upon the legality of a land grant in which he held an interest. The two young lawyers, with all of the confidence and righteousness of youth, promptly told Colden to "go to the Devil," and the Scot never forgave them.[15]

Colden's criticisms of Smith's *History* were manifold: some well taken, others not. He found Smith uninformed or misinformed on some matters, and willfully misrepresenting still others. He complained that the historian gave the Dutch arguments supporting their constitutional claim to New York, but not the English side; that he followed Dutch historians in overlooking Dutch acts of cruelty; that the account of the English surrender of New York in 1673 was wrong and unfair to the English; and that Smith failed to understand the legal issues involved in reclaiming conquered land.

Colden differed strongly with Smith's evaluation of various governors. He believed the cheeky young historian was too kind to certain governors who had ruled arbitrarily, and was too severe with others whom Colden admired—namely, Andros, Sloughter, Fletcher, Hunter, and Burnet. He felt that Smith overrated Colonel Peter Schuyler and the first Robert Livingston, and faulted his treatment of various questions concerning Burnet's administration in the 1720's. Colden's steadfast devotion to executive prerogative caused him to believe that Smith was too partial to the Assembly, that he failed to reveal how extravagant that body had been with public money, and that he tended to overlook the Assembly's failures.

[14] In addition to his *History of the Five Indian Nations* (1727–47), Colden also wrote a "History of Gov. William Cosby's Administration and of Lt.-Gov. George Clarke's Administration Through 1737," published in the *New-York Historical Society Collections*, LXVIII (1935), 283–355. This partisan essay, poorly written and hostile to Cosby, must have been written by Colden only as a memoir for his own use.

[15] See Milton M. Klein, "Prelude to Revolution in New York: Jury Trials and Judicial Tenure," *William and Mary Quarterly*, 3rd series, XVII (1960), 445–446.

Colden wondered why Smith failed to respect the legitimacy of laws passed under Governor Dongan, and accepted only legislation passed after 1691. He criticized Smith for not being more severe in his treatment of Leisler's Rebellion. Essentially, Smith seemed to believe that each faction had some merit to its arguments in 1689, whereas Colden believed that they were all sadly in error. If anything, Colden was even more of a legitimist than Smith. He complained that Smith's account of the Anglo-French confrontation in New York in 1689 was not sufficiently damaging to the French. One might fairly say that Colden was most often upset at the moderation of Smith's positions.

Colden was most especially enraged because Smith gratuitously overreached his terminal date of 1732 in Volume One in order to cast a dark shadow upon Colden's role as Surveyor-General in 1740 in the case of Captain Laughlin Campbell and his dealings in lands to be settled by Scottish immigrants. In 1734 Governor Cosby had issued a proclamation offering 100,-000 acres of land near Lake George to Protestant families who would come to settle. This offer induced Campbell, a Scottish gentleman, to import some five hundred Highland immigrants between 1737 and 1740. According to Smith's version, because of the greed and treachery of colonial officials, Campbell was then unable to obtain the 50,000 acres promised him. Colden insisted that most of the Highland families had paid their own passage across and did not want to be Campbell's tenants, that Campbell did not have the capacity to settle and improve such a huge grant as he demanded, and that such a large grant would have been a permanent obstruction to settlement of the frontier.[16]

In actual fact, Campbell's petitions and the actions of the Council's subcommittee appear to confirm Colden's view. Campbell must have known that the 100,000 acres mentioned in Cosby's proclamation had already been allocated to others before he made his own application. He had simply been promised "sufficient land" for as many settlers as he brought at three pounds per hundred acres and the annual quitrent to

[16] See Alice M. Keys, *Cadwallader Colden: A Representative Eighteenth Century Official* (New York, Macmillan, 1906), pp. 270–271; Memorial of Lt. Donald Campbell to the Board of Trade, May 1764, in E. B. O'Callaghan, ed., *Documents Relative to the Colonial History of the State of New York*, VII (Albany, 1856), 629–631; *New-York Historical Society Collections*, 2d series, II (1848), 207–214.

the Crown. He was offered 19,000 acres but refused them, and he included in his list of settlers several people known to have been in New York before he ever arrived there. In short, Campbell could have obtained a generous amount of land had it not been for his determination to make tenants of his settlers and his greed for excessive land. His prospective tenants—scattered throughout the colony—had no complaints, despite William Smith's touching lament for them. Smith should have known all of these circumstances from the contemporary records.[17]

It is ironic, however, that Colden, who despised lawyers in general and Smith's claque in particular, should have expected Smith's *History* to be more thoughtful simply because the author was bred to the law (see Editor's Appendix B, letter no. 9). Colden grossly overstated his case when he wrote that Smith's *History*, "was written to serve the purposes of a Faction then in this Province, & with a view to asperse and weaken the administration." Smith wrote many things to serve the purposes of his faction; but the *History*, as it happened, he most intended to further his personal development and the interests of New York generally in the imperial market place.[18]

For the rest of Colden's life, Smith's version of New York's history nagged at his notion of historical integrity, his sense of legitimacy, and his bruised ego. Colden's correspondence with Whitehall during the 1760's, particularly with Hillsborough, Mansfield, Halifax, and Grenville, never neglected an opportunity to denigrate Smith and his writings. The historian, in turn, behaved in much the same manner; so that each became obsessed with the other as a political Mephistopheles meddling in the affairs of New York.[19] In 1770 Smith even filed a document with Governor Dunmore designed to have Colden's salary as Lieutenant Governor reduced. When Colden died in 1776, Smith filled his diary with eleven paragraphs elaborating his

[17] See Ruth L. Higgins, *Expansion in New York, With Especial Reference to the Eighteenth Century* (Columbus, Ohio, Ohio State University Press, 1931), pp. 88–89; Ian C. C. Graham, *Colonists from Scotland: Emigration to North America, 1707–1783* (Ithaca, Cornell University Press, 1956), pp. 77–80.

[18] See Paul M. Hamlin, " 'He Is Gone and Peace to His Shade': William Smith, Historian, Posthumously Boils Lieutenant Governor Cadwallader Colden in Oil," *New-York Historical Society Quarterly,* XXXVI (1952), 161–174.

[19] See *The Colden Letter Books, Collections of the New-York Historical Society for the Years 1876 and 1877* (1877–78), pp. 137–138, 187–188, 346, 71, 150, 159–160, 165, 240–248, 323; O'Callaghan, ed., *Documents Relative to the Colonial History of the State of New York,* VIII, 62, 257.

enemy's "Duplicity, Pride, Craft, Obstinacy, Vanity, Petulance, Ambition, vindictive Spirit and Avarice. . . . He was quick and subtle, conceited and fond of Disputation, easily flattered, and anxious for preheminence on all Topics of Conversation, and rather disgustful than insinuating for he was hot, coarse, & assuming." Death did nothing to assuage the most passionate hatred of Smith's tumultuous lifetime. Late in 1777, fourteen months after his enemy had gone to his rest, Smith recopied the drafts of his own fading rejoinders to Colden's letters of 1759 concerning the *History*. He seemed determined that, if his shouting match with Colden should reverberate through the chambers of time, his would be the last voice heard.[20]

In his own time Smith's *History* cannot be regarded as a "popular" success. But it did arouse the interest of men and women concerned about the history and politics of North America. Governor Henry Ellis of Georgia cited the work in 1760–61, as did Thomas Pownall in writing his *Administration of the Colonies* (London, 1764), not to mention various pamphleteers of the prerevolutionary era. More than a quarter-century after its publication, Smith still proudly presented copies of his *History* to interested and influential friends.[21]

The passage of time played strange tricks upon the relations between Smith, his circle, and his critics. During the 1730's and 1740's, Smith's father and Cadwallader Colden had been good friends and political allies; both had opposed the De-Lancey-Philipse coalition on the issue of regulating the fur trade. In the 1750's and 1760's the Colden-Smith connection turned to bitter hatred. During the 1740's William Smith, Jr., and William Samuel Johnson became close friends. In 1759 Johnson's father became one of Smith's harsher critics; and in 1771 Cadwallader Colden established a friendly correspondence with the younger Johnson in which the Lieutenant Governor roundly denounced Smith.[22] Then there was the case of Thomas Jones (1731–1792), the jurist and Loyalist from Long

[20] Sabine, ed., *Historical Memoirs . . . of William Smith*, II, 29–33; Smith to Colden, February 1, 1759, recopied December 12, 1777, Miscellaneous documents box, Smith MSS, New York Public Library. This letter is the same as no. 4 of Editor's Appendix B.

[21] Sabine, ed., *Historical Memoirs . . . of William Smith*, II, 32; *Collections of The New-York Historical Society for the Year 1877*, p. 451. The New York Public Library has a presentation copy of the 1757 edition, inscribed "To Robert Barclay from the Author—1774".

[22] See Milton M. Klein, "Politics and Personalities in Colonial New York," *New York History*, XLVII (1966), 6; *Collections of The New-York Historical Society for the Year 1877*, pp. 322–323.

Island. Jones was the son of David Jones, the influential assemblyman and judge who gave Smith access to various unpublished documents of the 1740's and 1750's. Thomas Jones and the younger Smith quarreled rancorously in 1753 over the clerkship in Queens County; and when Jones subsequently wrote his *History of New York During the Revolutionary War*, he excoriated Smith wherever he could. Despite many parallels in their careers, despite their common Loyalism and exodus to England at the end of the war, and despite their shared interest in New York history, they remained political rivals and personal enemies.[23]

Finally there is the case of Samuel Jones (1734–1819), lawyer and Whig patriot, member of the New York Assembly and Senate, recorder of New York City, and a man of vast learning. In 1782 he and Richard Varick made an authoritative digest of the laws of New York—precisely the same job Smith and Livingston had done in 1752 and 1762. In fact, Jones had even studied law with Smith in the 1750's and inherited his mentor's mantle after independence as the premier legal scholar in New York. Nonetheless, at the age of eighty-three Samuel Jones sat down to compose long epistolary critiques of his erstwhile teacher's *History*. The printing of these letters in 1821 (see Editor's Appendix B, nos. 18–21) provided Smith's son with one stimulus to publish the *Continuation* of his father's *History*—as a vindication of the historian's judgment and as a partial embarrassment to the gangliated Jones family of New York.[24]

Thus history (as change through time) and History (as man's record of the past) turn in upon themselves both literally and figuratively. Writing about the age of Jefferson, Henry Adams observed that "the quarrel between law and history is old, and its sources lie deep. Perhaps no good historian was ever a good lawyer: whether any lawyer could be a good historian might be equally doubted. The lawyer is required to give facts the

[23] Paul M. Hamlin, *Legal Education in Colonial New York* (New York University Press, 1939), p. 102 n. 2; "Thomas Jones," *Dictionary of American Biography;* Edward F. DeLancey, ed., *History of New York During the Revolutionary War . . . by Thomas Jones* (New York, 1879), esp. I, 41 n, 59, 147–149, 167–168, 642, 644; II, 209, 212.

[24] "Samuel Jones," *Dictionary of American Biography;* John H. Jones, *The Jones Family of Long Island* (New York , Privately printed, 1907).

mold of a theory; the historian need only state facts in their sequence."[25] There is surely a touch of playfulness and irony in Adams' final phrase; nonetheless, he lucidly put one of the central problems in the career of our subject. William Smith, Jr., regarded himself first as a jurist, and secondarily as a historian. As a historian, for the most part, he simply tried to present a narrative. But occasionally he did "give facts the mold of a theory," and in doing so aroused the ire of his critics. On balance Smith must be rated an excellent lawyer and a very good historian. The two interlocked in his life's work; but significantly, his most enduring contribution rests not in his work at the bar or on the bench, but in his *History of the Province of New-York* and in his *Historical Memoirs.*

[25] Herbert Agar, ed., *The Formative Years: A History of the United States During the Administrations of Jefferson and Madison* by Henry Adams (Boston, Houghton Mifflin, 1947), I, 302.

## A Note on the Text

Between 1757, when the first edition of Smith's *History* appeared in London, and 1830, when the last was published in New York, various printings and editions became available. They may be cited as follows:

1. *The History of the Province of New-York, from the First Discovery to the Year MDCCXXXII. To which is annexed, A Description of the Country, with a short Account of the Inhabitants, their Trade, Religious and Political State, and the Constitution of the Courts of Justice in that Colony* (London: Printed for Thomas Wilcox, 1757), 4to, pp. xii, 255. It included a folded engraving entitled "The South View of Oswego on Lake Ontario." Most copies had a leaf measurement of 11 by 8½ inches, with an inner margin ⅞ of an inch in width. A few copies were printed on larger and thicker paper, with wider inner margins. Examples of the latter will be found in the Yale University Library and in the Huntington Library, San Marino, California.

2. *Histoire de la Nouvelle-York, depuis la découverte de cette province jusqu'a notre siécle, dans laquelle on rapporte les démêlés qu'elle a eus avec les Canadiens & les Indiens; les guerres qu'elle a soutenues contre ces peuples; les traités & les alliances qu'elle a faits avec eux, &c. On y a joint une description géographique du pays, & une histoire abrégée de ses habitans, de leur religion, de leur gouvernement civil & ecclésiastique, &c . . . traduite de l'Anglois par M. E.* [Marc-Antoine Eidous], (London, 1767), 12 mo., pp. vii-xvi, 415.

3. A printing with essentially the same title as the first (London: John Almon, 1776), 8vo, pp. viii, 334.

4. A printing, called the second edition, with essentially the same title as the first (Philadelphia: Mathew Carey, 1792), 8vo, pp. 276.

5. An edition with essentially the same title as the first, to which is added: *With a Continuation, From the Year 1732, to the Commencement of the Year 1814* (Albany: Ryer Schermerhorn, 1814), 8vo, pp. 511. The "Continuation" covers the years 1732–1747, and was prepared by John Van Ness Yates (1779–1839).

6. *Continuation of the History of New-York. Collections of the New-York Historical Society, for the Year 1826*. Vol. IV (New York: J. Seymour, 1826), 8vo, pp. 308. This is the first full printing of the continuation (1732–1762) prepared by Smith's son from his father's manuscript.

7. *The History of the late Province of New-York, from Its Discovery, to the Appointment of Governor Colden in 1762* (New York: New-York Historical Society, 1829), 2 vols., 8vo, pp. xvi, 320, 308. [*Collections of the New-York Historical Society for the Year 1829* (1830), vols. IV-V.] Volume I of this set is based upon the 1757 first edition, but has interpolated into the text and notes about two-thirds of Smith's marginalia from his own interleaved copy of the first edition. Many of Smith's marginal comments were not printed, especially in the latter part of the book where whole passages were ignored.

8. A printing with the same title as the last previous (New York: New-York Historical Society, 1829 [1830], 2 vols., 8vo, pp. xvi, 390; (8), 390. These are printed from a larger size of type than the preceding edition. Many of the longer footnotes have been taken from the text and placed at the end. In most cases the paper of both volumes is thicker than in any previous edition.

The text of Volume One in this edition follows that of the first edition, except that capitalization, swash s's, excessive use of italics, and use of quotation marks at the beginning of every quoted line have been brought into accordance with modern usage. Obvious typographical errors in the original have been corrected.

Smith's personal, annotated copy of Volume One survives, and is located in the Philip H. and A. S. W. Rosenbach Foundation in Philadelphia. In the endpapers of that copy Smith inscribed the following note.

> Manor of Livingston    6 Dec. 1777
>     Twenty years are elapsed since this work was published; in all which time I have had no leisure to read it. Some years ago I had this volume interleaved, with a view of correcting the impression, and making additions. When the MSS was sent home in 1756, I trusted the examination of the proofs, to my friend Doctor Avery of Guy's Hospital, London, who changed the orthography to his own taste. In running over it within two days past, I have corrected it in some places. If there is a Continuation of the History, it should precede the chapters beginning at page 183 [where the descriptive supplementary chapters commence]; but I am surprised at the great alterations, which the changes since the publication will render necessary. I have materials for a detail of our transactions to the present time; and last winter put it into form from 1731 to 1762. From that period, I have the materials in two books of memoirs, and letters of correspondence, with a collection of political MSS. What is prior to 1762, I propose to finish in draft this winter for a fair copy. The subsequent matters would carry me into a prodigious extent, and I do not mean to reduce them to the form of a narrative like the former published and unpublished part of the History.

Rosenbach purchased the volume at auction (The Anderson Galleries, 489 Park Avenue, New York; sale no. 1490) in 1920. It had been in the library of Henry F. DePuy, and before that owned by a descendant of Smith's in Warwickshire, England. Among the extra leaves, 41 have neatly written notes and additions; 42 pages of the printed text have marginal notes for interlineations.

Because the annotations in Smith's copy are extensive, they presented a problem in preparing this edition. Should they be integrated into the text, appear as footnotes to the text, or be set as endnotes along with my own annotations? I rejected the first alternative because the marginalia are often discursive and quote at length from documentary sources, and also because Smith was often second-guessing himself or his critics.

I rejected the second alternative because the original work had footnotes of its own—two simultaneous sets of footnotes seemed burdensome to me—and because of the extreme length of many of Smith's annotations. I have, therefore, adopted the third alternative, with the result that in the endnotes to Volume One my own comments, citations, references, and translations are set in square brackets; all other endnotes are Smith's 1777 marginalia from his own copy.

In transcribing Smith's marginalia I have tried to make them consistent in spelling and capitalization (but not always punctuation) with the text of Volume One. I have expanded abbreviations, changed many dashes to periods, and eliminated dashes following periods. Where Smith changed or added a word in the text proper, I have made the replacement or insertion silently. Beginning with p. 229 of the original, Smith started to make a brief, marginal index to the text; I have omitted these running references. (I have also omitted Smith's brief references to the dates and locations of commissions of high officials (see pp. 2, 28, 46, 65, 95, 129, 168 in Smith's copy). Some of Smith's secondary and tertiary observations (his comments on the commentary) have been placed in parentheses. Chapter V of the descriptive appendixes—"The Political State" —has especially heavy annotations. Smith obviously wished to do a considerable amount of updating. On the whole it is clear that he combed through the entire volume with scrupulous care, even rechecking his statistics.

Preparation of Volume Two for this edition also presented numerous challenges. Smith's son, William, who himself wrote a *History of Canada* (1815), prepared the *Continuation* in 1824 from his father's manuscript. That manuscript survives as an atlas folio volume in the Manuscript Division of the New York Public Library.[1] A close comparison of Smith's manuscript with the son's published version (1826, 1829, 1830) revealed a great many discrepancies and changes.[2] The son italicized

[1] The elephantine volume covers the years between 1732 and 1758. The years from 1759 through 1762 are continued in Volume Two of Smith's MSS, pp. 421–475, New York Public Library.

[2] Cf. the totally erroneous comments in Joseph Sabin, Wilberforce Eames, and R. W. G. Vail, *Bibliotheca Americana: A Dictionary of Books Relating to America, from Its Discovery to the Present Time* (New York, William E. Rudge, 1929–31), XXI, 110: "The

many words for emphasis; changed "I" to "the author" throughout; substituted words (for example, "request" for "instances"); inserted pronouns where they did not appear; altered phrasing (from "for that object" to "to promote the design"); inserted a surfeit of commas; misread words ("divided" for "delivered") often in ways subversive to his father's meaning ("require" for "acquire"); changed the wording in primary sources quoted by his father; reversed footnotes carelessly so that each explained the wrong subject; omitted negatives such as "not"—thereby reversing the meaning of a passage; misread dates; and, worst of all, omitted various passages often running to four or five sentences. The majority of these aberrations occur in the last 70 pages of Volume Two.

The son's errors and bowdlerizations may be partially explained by the fact that his father's manuscript was not left in a condition suitable for publication. It is written in a tiny hand, often virtually unreadable. Except for occasional periods and dashes, there is very little punctuation. Numerous sentences and even paragraphs of substantive import are scratched out. Titles are. consistently abbreviated. Much too often Smith summarized lengthy documents without quoting directly. Consequently, there are many sentences and even paragraphs with overlong series of clauses: "that . . . , that . . . , that . . ." On the one hand Smith was working closely with primary sources; but on the other his sense of writing gracefully for an audience seems to have been sadly diminished. Perhaps he who literally writes in isolation, as Smith did in 1776–77 at Haverstraw and Livingston Manor, also writes figuratively in isolation: for himself rather than for others.

I have prepared Volume Two of this edition directly from Smith's own manuscript. Those sentences which the author himself deleted have been omitted. I have occasionally combined sentences in order to make a proper paragraph. Punctuation and capitalization have for the most part been made consistent with Volume One. Ampersands are written "and," and abbreviated titles expanded. Occasionally Smith slips into the present tense, even when writing about the 1730's; I have con-

---

printed text is, almost without exception, a verbatim copy of that in the original manuscript as corrected, only a very few verbal changes having been made. Nothing is omitted or added except the five paragraphs omitted at the end." Those five paragraphs *merely* discuss Smith's very conception of himself as a historian!

sistently changed these to the past tense. All of the footnotes in Volume Two are Smith's own; my own comments and references appear as endnotes.

The original manuscript of Volume Two has no internal organization. It runs continuously with occasional small space breaks. Smith's son divided the *Continuation* arbitrarily into seven long chapters. On pp. 67–68 of the 1826 edition, for example, the son decided to end chapter I and begin chapter II. There is nothing in the manuscript, however, to indicate that Smith regarded this as a breaking point. Moreover, the son's descriptive table of contents for the seven chapters is misleading—if not positively confusing. The "contents" give the reader no clear notion whatever of what is included in each chapter.

I have, therefore, restructured the *Continuation* into eleven somewhat briefer chapters. My divisions are often equally arbitrary, but I have tried to follow Smith's space breaks and have tried to stop and start at logical points of division. Essentially I have organized these eleven chapters by gubernatorial administrations, or phases thereof in the cases of longer administrations, because Volume Two is very much a political history which emphasizes relations between governors and assemblies, between governors and their English connections, and the prosecution of wars against the French.[3]

I have not been faithful to one of Smith's desires. He left instructions on the endpapers of his copy of Volume One that, "if there is a continuation of the History, it should precede" the appendixes descriptive of New York in 1756. It seems to me that the original edition, running to 1732 and including these invaluable appendixes, stands as a unit, prepared for publication by the author, revised by him at one long "sitting," and eliciting an important response from Smith's contemporaries. Volume Two, on the other hand, was not prepared for publication by the author, lacks the grace, pace, and cohesion of Volume One, and in fact caused the author considerable anxiety because it treated controversial events in which he and his father had been participants. It is a less judicious volume than the first, and appeared fully seventy years after it. For these reasons I have decided not to honor Smith's request to insert

---

[3] I have also prepared for the reader's convenience two appendixes placed at the end of Volume Two: "The Governors of Colonial New York to 1762: A Chronology of Their Administrations" and "A Biographical Directory to William Smith's New-York."

the *Continuation* directly following Part V of Volume One. I have kept the two volumes separate because each was composed separately and has a discrete identity.

In summary, neither of the 1829–30 volumes bears a close resemblance to what Smith originally wrote. I therefore have prepared a new Volume One from the first edition (1757) and Smith's marginalia in his personal copy, and a new Volume Two from Smith's original manuscript of the *Continuation*.

# THE
# HISTORY

### Of the PROVINCE of

# NEW-YORK,

### FROM THE

## First Difcovery to the Year M.DCC.XXXII.

To which is annexed,

A Defcription of the Country, with a fhort Account of the
Inhabitants, their Trade, Religious and Political State, and the
Conftitution of the Courts of Juftice in that Colony.

---

*Lo ! fwarming o'er the new difcover'd World,*
*Gay Colonies extend ; the calm Retreat*
*Of undeferv'd Diftrefs. ———*
*——— Bound by focial Freedom, firm they rife ;*
*Of* Britain's *Empire the Support and Strength.* THOMSON,

*Nec minor eft Virtus, quàm quærere, parta tueri.*

---

## By WILLIAM SMITH, A.M.

===

### LONDON:

Printed for THOMAS WILCOX, Bookfeller at *Virgil's Head,* oppofite the
*New Church* in the *Strand.*
M.DCC.LVII.

To the Right Honourable
GEORGE
Earl of Hallifax,
Viscount SUNBURY,
First Lord Commissioner of Trade and Plantations,
&c. &c.

My Lord,

I beg your favourable acceptance of this short account of the ancient and present state of the Province of New-York.

It is not presented for your Lordship's information.—All the world knows, that the affairs of the British colonies, have been, for several years past, under your principal direction; and the wisdom of the measures pursued for their prosperity and defence, are indisputable arguments of your acquaintance with their condition.

Nor am I induced to inscribe these pages to your Lordship, by interest, the common motive to addresses of this kind.— Being therefore uninfluenced by the principle, I shall not follow the example of dedicators; but suppress those sentiments concerning your Lordship, which would, nevertheless, give offence only to yourself, and to those who envy your talents and your virtues, and are enemies to their effects, your reputation and your power.

My Lord, your ardent attention to the American plantations, and assiduous labours for their protection and growth, have laid us under the most indispensible obligations to gratitude.

Your Lordship will therefore excuse me for embracing this opportunity to make a publick declaration of the deep sense I have of your kind offices to my country, and to do myself the honour of testifying, that

    I am,
        My Lord,
            Your Lordship's,
                most obedient, and
                    most humble Servant,

                          William Smith.

New-York
15 June, 1756.

# The Preface

Whoever considers the number and extent of the British colonies, on this continent; their climates, soil, ports, rivers, riches, and numberless advantages, must be convinced of their vast importance to Great-Britain; and be at a loss to account for the ignorance concerning them, which prevails in those kingdoms, whence their inhabitants originally sprang. The merchants indeed, by profitable experience, have not been altogether unacquainted with our trade and our growth; and some gentlemen of an inquisitive turn, by the help of their correspondents, have obtained the knowledge of many other particulars equally important. But the main body of the people conceive of these plantations, under the idea of wild, boundless, inhospitable, uncultivated deserts; and hence the punishment of a transportation hither, in the judgement of most, is thought not much less severe, than an infamous death. Nay, appealing to facts, we may safely assert, that even the publick boards, to whose care these extensive dominions have been more especially commited, attained, but lately, any tolerable acquaintance with their condition. This is the more to be wondered at, as it is natural to imagine, that the King's Governours have statedly transmited full accounts of their respective provinces. The case has been quite otherwise. Governments were heretofore too often bestowed upon men of mean parts, and indigent circumstances. The former were incapable of the task, and the latter too deeply engrossed by the sordid views of private interest, either to pursue or study our common weal. The worst consequences have resulted from these measures. Perpetual animosities being engendered between the governours, and the people subjected to their authority; all attempts for conciliating the friendship of the Indians, promoting the fur trade, securing the command of the lakes, protecting the frontiers, and extending our possessions far into the inland country, have too often given place to party projects and contracted schemes, equally useless and shameful. The conduct of the French has been just the reverse: in spite of all the disadvantages of a cold climate, a long and dangerous navigation up the River of St. Lawrence, a rough, barren, unsettled* country, locked up from all communication with the ocean, the greatest part of the year; I say, notwithstanding these difficulties, they have seized all the advantages, which we have neglected. The continent, for many hundred leagues, has been thoroughly explored, the main passes fortified, innumerable tribes of Indians, either won over to their interest,† subdued or bridled, the fur trade engrossed, a communication maintained between the extremes of New-France, the British colonies restricted to scant limits along the sea shore, and nothing left remaining for the establishment of a vast empire, but to open a free water passage to the ocean, by the conquest of the province of New-York.

If the governours of these plantations had formerly been animated by the same generous and extensive views, which inspired Mr. Burnet;[1] the long projected designs of our common enemy might, with the aid of Great-Britain, have been many years ago supplanted, or at least defeated, at a trifling expence. But alas! little, too little, attention has been had to these important affairs, till the late encroachments on the River Ohio, in the Province of Pennsylvania, gave the alarm, and the ministry were apprised of the French machinations, by the seasonable representations of General Shirley; and if the colonies have now attracted the notice of his Majesty and his Parliament, their grateful acknowledgements are due principally to the noble Lord, to whom these sheets are dedicated, for his laudable enquiries into their state, and his indefatigable zeal and industry for their defence and prosperity.

At present our affairs begin to wear a more smiling aspect. We are under the guardianship of a sovereign, who delights in

---

* "Encore moins peuplé." Charlevoix.

† "Nôtre nation, la seule, qui ait eu le secret de gagner l'affection des Amériquains." Charlevoix.

the welfare of his people; are respected by a Parliament, affected with a generous sympathy for the distresses of their fellow subjects, in all their dispersions; and by a wise improvement of the British aids, it is hoped, we shall be able, to retrieve the ill consequences of our long, reproachful, and insensible, security.

Formerly the colonies were at home disregarded and despised, nor can any other reason be assigned for it, than that they were unknown. This is, in a great degree, to be imputed to ourselves. If our governours withheld those informations, which their duty required them to have given, persons of private characters ought to have undertaken that useful and necessary task. But, except some accounts of the settlements in the Massachusets Bay and Virginia, all the other histories of our plantations upon the continent are little else than collections of falsehoods, and worse than none. That this charge against those published concerning this Province, in particular, can be fully supported, I persuade myself, will incontestably appear from the following summary, concerning which I shall say a few words.

Having been formerly concerned, according to an appointment by Act of Assembly, in a review and digest of our provincial laws, it was the duty of myself, and my partner in that service, to peruse the minutes of the Council, and the journals of the general Assembly, from the glorious Revolution, at the accession of King William, to the year 1751: and as an acquaintance with our publick transactions, was a branch of instruction, of which a student for the profession of the law ought not to be ignorant, I have since reexamined those entries, beginning with the first minutes of Council, and read over many of the records in the Secretary's office. From these authentick materials, the following pages were, in a great measure, compiled. For many of those parts, which concern our affairs with the French and the Indians, antecedent to the Peace of Ryswick in 1697, I am bound to make liberal acknowledgements to Dr. Colden, the authour of the History of the Five Nations.

Mr. Alexander, a gentleman eminent in the law, and equally distinguished for his humanity, generosity, great abilities, and honourable stations, supplied me with some useful papers; and has left behind him a collection, that will be very serviceable to any gentleman, who may hereafter incline to continue this narrative, through the administrations of Mr. Cosby, and Lieutenant Governour Clarke. The draught of this work was unfinished, at the time of Mr. Alexander's decease;* and therefore, as it never passed under his examination, many important additions are lost, which his long and intimate acquaintance with the affairs of this Province would have enabled him to supply.

When I began to frame this digest, it was only intended for private use; and the motives which now induce me to publish it, are the gratification of the present thirst in Great-Britain after American intelligences: contributing, as far as this Province is concerned, to an accurate history of the British Empire,† in this quarter of the world; and the prospect of doing some small service to my country, by laying before the publick a summary account of its first rise and present state.

Influenced by these views, I am not so regardless of the judgement of others, as not to wish it may be, in some measure, acceptable. To please all sorts of readers I know is impossible: he who writes with such hopes, is a stranger to human nature, and will be infallibly disappointed. My design is rather to inform than please. He who delights only in pages shining with illustrious characters, the contentions of armies, the rise and fall of empires, and other grand events, must have recourse to the great authours of antiquity. A detail of the little transactions, which concern a colony, scant in its jurisdiction, and still struggling with the difficulties naturally attending its infant state, to gentlemen of this taste can furnish no entertainment. The ensuing narrative (for it deserves not the name of a history, though for brevity's sake I have given it that title) presents us only a regular thread of simple facts; and even those unembellished with reflections, because they themselves suggest the proper remarks, and most readers will doubtless be best pleased with their own. The sacred laws of truth have been infringed neither by positive assertions, oblique, insidious, hints, wilful suppressions, or corrupt misrepresentation. To avoid any censures of this kind, no reins have been given to a wanton imagination, for the invention of plausible tales, supported only by light probabilities; but choosing rather to be honest and

* He died on the 2d of April, 1756.

† As the provinces are different in their Constitutions, and with respect to government, independent of each other; no general history of America can be expected, till gentlemen of leisure, will draw up particular accounts, of the respective colonies, with which they are acquainted.

dull, than agreeable and false, the true import of my vouchers hath been strictly adhered to and regarded.

With respect to its style, the criticks, in that branch of literature, are at full liberty to condemn at their pleasure. The main use of language is to express our ideas. To write in the gay, pleasing, pomp of diction is above my capacity. If any are disposed to blame me for being too verbose, let it be remembered that this is the indefeasible right of my profession, founded upon immemorial prescription. Perspicuity is all I have endeavoured to maintain, nor am I at leisure to study any higher attainments in language. The errours of the press will doubtless be many, but for these I shall hardly be thought accountable, as my remote distance deprives me of all opportunities of examining the proofs.

# Part I

## From the Discovery of the Colony to the Surrender in 1664

Christopher Columbus, a Genoese, employed by Ferdinand and Isabel, King and Queen of Castile, was the first discoverer of America.* He sailed from St. Lucar in August 1492, and made sight of one of the Bahama Islands, on the eleventh of October following. Newfoundland, and the main continent, were discovered five years after, by Sebastian Cabato, a Venetian, in the service of Henry VII of England, from the 38th to the 68th degree of North Latitude.

On the tenth of April 1606, King James I for planting two colonies, passed the great North and South Virginia Patent. To Sir Thomas Gates and others, leave was given to begin a plantation, at any place on the continent, they should think convenient, between the 34th and 41st degrees of latitude: and all the lands extending 50 miles, on each side, along the coast, 100 miles into the country, and all the islands within 100 miles, opposite to their plantations, were granted in fee, to be called the First Colony. By the same Patent, a like quantity was granted to Thomas Henham, Esq; and others, for a plantation between 38 and 45 degrees of latitude, under the name of the Second Colony. The first began a settlement in the great Bay

* Some authours alledge, that Columbus first offered his Services to the Republick of Genoa; then to John II. of Portugal, and afterwards to our King Henry VII; but this disagrees with Lord Bacon's Account, who informs us, that Christopher Columbus failed, before his Brother Bartholomew had laid the Project before the King, which was owing to his falling into the hands of pirates on his way to England.

(Cheasapeak) in 1607. The latter was planted at Plymouth in New-England, 1620.

Henry Hudson, an Englishman, according to our authors, in the year 1608,* under a Commission from the King his master, discovered Long Island, New-York, and the river which still bears his name; and afterwards sold the country, or rather his right, to the Dutch. Their writers contend, that Hudson was sent out by the East-India Company in 1609, to discover a North-west passage to China; and that having first discovered Delaware Bay, he came hither, and penetrated up Hudson's River, as far North as the latitude of 43°. It is said, however, that there was a sale, and that the English objected to it, though they for some time neglected to oppose the Dutch settlement of the country.

In 1610, Hudson sailed again from Holland to this country, called by the Dutch, New-Netherlands; and four years after, the States General granted a Patent to sundry merchants, for an exclusive trade on the North River, who in 1614 built a fort, on the west side, near Albany, which was first commanded by Henry Christiaens. Captain Argal was sent out by Sir Thomas Dale, Governour of Virginia, in the same year, to dispossess the French of the two towns of Port-Royal and St. Croix, lying on each side of the Bay of Fundy in Acadia, then claimed as part of Virginia.† In his return, he visited the Dutch on Hudson's River, who being unable to resist him, prudently submited for the present to the King of England, and under him to the Governour of Virginia. The very next year, they erected a Fort on the South-west point of the island Manhattans, and two others in 1623: one called Good-Hope, on Connecticut River, and the other Nassau, on the East side of Delaware Bay. The authour of the Account of New-Netherland‡ asserts, that the Dutch pur-

---

* Charlevoix, a French Jesuit, author of the General History of New France, thinks this discovery was in 1609, vol. I 12° edition, p. 221. But Stith, Douglass, Oldmixon, and other English writers agree, that Hudson's first voyage was in the preceding year.

† Charlevoix places this transaction in 1613. vol I. *Hist. of N. France* in 12°, p. 210. But Stith, whom I follow, being a clergyman in Virginia, had greater advantages of knowing the truth than the French Jesuit.

‡ The Pamphlet is entitled, "Beschryvinghe van Virginia, Neiuw Nederland," &c. and was printed at Amsterdam in 1651. It contains two descriptions of the Dutch Possessions. The first is a copy of that published by John De Laet at Leyden. The second gives a view of this country several years after, in 1649. A short representation of the country of the Mahakuase Indians, written in 1644, by John

*t' Fort nieuw Amsterdam op de Manhatans*

*New Amsterdam in 1626–1627*

chased the lands on both sides of that river in 1632, before the
English were settled in those parts; and that they discovered a
little fresh river, farther to the East, called Varsche Riviertie, to
distinguish it from Connecticut River, known among them, by
the name of Varsche Rivier, which Vanderdonk also claims for
the Dutch.[2]

Determined upon the settlement of a colony, the States General made a grant of the country, in 1621, to the West-India
Company. Wouter Van Twiller, arrived at Fort-Amsterdam, now
New-York, and took upon himself the government in June 1629.
His style, in the Patents granted by him, was thus, "We Director
and Council, residing in New-Netherland on the Island Manhattans, under the Government of their High Mightinesses, the
Lords States General of the United Netherlands, and the Privileged West-India Company." In his time the New-England planters extended their possession westward as far as Connecticut
River. Jacob Van Curler, the Commissary there, protested against
it, and in the second year of the succeeding administration,
under William Kieft,* who appears first in 1638, a prohibition
was issued, forbidding the English Trade at Fort Good-Hope;
and shortly after, on complaint of the insolence of the English,
an Order of Council was made for sending more forces there, to
maintain the Dutch territories. Dr. Mather confesses, that the
New-England men first formed their design of settling Connecticut River in 1635, before which time, they esteemed that river,
at least 100 miles from any English settlement; and that they
first seated themselves there in 1636, at Hartford, near Fort
Good-Hope, at Weathersfield, Windsor, and Springfield. Four
years after, they seized the Dutch garrison, and drove them
from the banks of the river, having first settled New Haven in
1638, regardless of Kieft's protest against it.[3]

The extent of New-Netherland was to Delaware, then called
South River, and beyond it; for I find, in the Dutch records, a
copy of a letter from William Kieft, May 6, 1638, directed to
Peter Minuit,† who seems, by the tenour of it, to be the Swedish

---

Megapolensis, jun. a Dutch Minister residing here, is annexed to that
part of the pamphlet concerning New-Netherland.

* We have no books among our Dutch records remaining in the
Secretary's office, relating to state matters, before Kieft's time, nor
any enrolment of Patents, till a year after Van Twiller arrived here.
Mr. Jacob Goelet supplied us with several extracts from the Dutch
records.

† The anonymous Dutch author of the Description of New-

Governour of New-Sweden, asserting, "that the whole South River of New-Netherlands, had been in the Dutch possession many years above and below, beset with Forts, and sealed with their blood." Which Kieft adds, has happened even during your administration "in New-Netherland, and so well known to you."

The Dutch writers are not agreed in the extent of Nova Belgia, or New-Netherland; some describe it to be from Virginia to Canada; and others inform us, that the arms of the States General were erected at Cape Cod, Connecticut, and Hudson's River, and on the West side of the entrance into Delaware Bay. The authour of the pamphlet mentioned in the notes gives Canada River for a boundary on the North, and calls the country, North-west from Albany, *Terra Incognita.*

In 1640, the English, who had overspread the Eastern part of Long Island, advanced to Oysterbay. Kieft broke up their settlement in 1642, and fitted out two sloops to drive the English out of Schuylkill, of which the Marylanders had lately possessed themselves. The instructions, dated May 22, to Jan Jansen Alpendam, who commanded in that enterprise, are upon record, and strongly assert the right of the Dutch, both to the soil and trade there. The English from the eastward shortly after sent deputies to New-Amsterdam, for the accommodation of their disputes about limits, to whom the Dutch offered the following conditions, entered in their books exactly in these words:

> Conditiones à D. Directore Gen. senatuys Novi Belgii, Dominis Weytingh atque Hill, Delegatis a nobili Senatu Hartfordiensi, oblatae:
> Pro Agro nostro Hartfordiensi, annuo persolvent Praepotentiss. D. D. Ordinibus Foed. Provinciarum Belgicarum aut eorum Vicariis, decimam Partem *Reventûs* Agrorum, tum Aratro, tum Ligone, aliove Cultorum medio; Pomariis, Hortisq; Oleribus dicatis, Jugerum Hollandium non excedentibus

---

Netherland in 1649, calls him Minnewits; and adds, that in 1638 he arrived at Delaware with two vessels, pretending that he touched for refreshment in his way to the West-Indies; but that he soon threw off the disguise, by employing his men in erecting a fort. The same historian informs us, of the murder of several Dutch men, at South River, by the Indians, occasioned by a quarrel, concerning the taking away the States Arms, which the former had erected at the first discovery of that country; in resenting which, an Indian had been killed. If Kieft's letter alludes to this affair, then Minuit preceded Van Twiller, in the chief command here; and being perhaps disobliged by the Dutch, entered into the service of the Queen of Sweden.

exceptis; aut Decimarum Loco, Pretium nobile postea con-
stituendum, tam diu quàm diu possessores ejusdem Agri
futuri erunt. Actum in Arce Amstelodamensi in novo Belgio
Die Julii 9 Anno Christi 1642.[4]

We have no account that the English acceded to these proposals, nor is it probable, considering their superior strength,
that they ever did: on the contrary, they daily extended their
possessions, and in 1643 the colonies of the Massachuset's Bay,
Plymouth, Connecticut, and New-Haven, entered into a League
both against the Dutch and Indians, and grew so powerful as to
meet shortly after, upon a design of extirpating the former. The
Massachuset's Bay declined this enterprise, which occasioned a
letter to Oliver Cromwell from William Hooke, dated at New-
Haven, November 3, 1653, in which he complains of the Dutch,
for supplying the natives with arms and ammunition, begs his
assistance with two or three frigates, and that letters might be
sent to the Eastern colonies, commanding them to join in an
expedition against the Dutch colony. Oliver's affairs would not
admit of so distant an attempt,* but Richard Cromwell afterwards drew up instructions to his commanders for subduing the
Dutch here, and wrote letters to the English American governments for their aid; copies of which are preserved in Thurloe's
Collection, vol. I. p. 721, &c.

Peter Stuyvesant was the last Dutch Governour, and tho' he
had a Commission in 1646, he did not begin his administration
till May 27, 1647. The inroads and claims upon his government,
kept him constantly employed. New-England on the East, and

* The war between him and the States, which began in July
1652, was concluded by a peace on the fifth of April 1654. The
Treaty makes no particular mention of this country. If any part of
it can be considered as relating to the American possessions, it is
to be found in the two first articles, which are in these words:
*Imprimis,* It is agreed and concluded, that, from this Day forwards,
there be a true, firm, and inviolable Peace, a sincere, intimate and
close Friendship, Affinity, Confederacy, and Union, betwixt the
Republic of *England* and the States General of the United Provinces
of the Netherlands, and the Lands, Countries, Cities, and Towns,
under the Dominions of each, without Destinction of Places, together with their People and Inhabitants of whatsoever Degree."
"II. That hereafter all Enmity, Hostility, Discord, and Contention,
betwixt the said Republics, and their People and Subjects, shall
cease, and both Parties shall henceforwards abstain from the commiting all Manner of Mischief, Plunder, and Injuries, by Land, by
Sea, and on the fresh Waters, in all their Lands, Countries, Dominions, Places, and Governments whatsoever."

*New Amsterdam in 1643*

Maryland on the West, alarmed his fears by their daily increase; and about the same time Captain Forrester, a Scotchman, claimed Long Island for the Dowager of Stirling.[5] The Swedes too were perpetually incroaching upon Delaware. Through the unskilfulness of the mate, one Deswyck, a Swedish captain and supercargo arrived in Raritan River. The ship was seized, and himself made a prisoner at New-Amsterdam. Stuyvesant's reasons were these. In 1651, the Dutch built Fort Casimir, now called Newcastle, on Delaware. The Swedes, indeed, claimed the country, and Printz, their Governour, formally protested against the works. Resingh, his successor, under the disguise of friendship, came before the fortress, fired two salutes, and landed 30 men, who were entertained by the commandant as friends; but he had no sooner discovered the weakness of the garrison, than he made himself master of it, seizing also upon all the ammunition, houses, and other effects of the West-India Company, and compelling several of the people to swear allegiance to Christina Queen of Sweden. The Dutch, in 1655, prepared to retake Fort Casimir. Stuyvesant commanded the forces in person, and arrived with them in Delaware the 9th of September. A few days after, he anchored before the garrison, and landed his troops. The fortress was immediately demanded as Dutch property: Suen Scutz, the commandant, desired leave to consult Risingh, which being refused, he surrendered the 16th of September on Articles of Capitulation. The whole strength of the place consisted of four cannon fourteen pounders, five swivels, and a parcel of small arms, which were all delivered to the conquered. Fort Christina was commanded by Risingh. Stuyvesant came before it, and Risingh surrendered it upon terms the 25th of September. The country being thus subdued, the Dutch governour issued a proclamation, in favour of such of the inhabitants, as would submit to the new government, and about 30 Swedes swore, "Fidelity and Obedience to the States General, the Lords Directors of the West-India Company, their Subalterns of the Province of New-Netherlands, and the Director General then, or thereafter, to be established." Risingh and one Elswych, a trader of note, were ordered to France, or England, and the rest of the Swedish inhabitants to Holland, and from thence to Gottenberg. The Swedes being thus extirpated, the Dutch become possessed of the West side of Delaware Bay, now called The three lower Counties.

This country was afterwards under the command of lieutenant-governours, subject to the controul of, and commissioned by, the Director General at New-Amsterdam. Johan Paul Jaquet was the first Vice-Director, or Lieutenant-Governour, of South River. His successors were Alricks, Hinojossa, and William Beekman. The posterity of the last remains amongst us to this day. These lieutenants had power to grant lands, and their patents make a part of the ancient titles of the present possessors. Alrick's Commission, of the 12th of April 1657, shews the extent of the Dutch claim on the West side of Delaware at that time. He was appointed

> Director General of the Colony of the *South River* of *New-Netherlands,* and the Fortress of *Casimir,* now called *Niewer Amstel,* with all the lands depending thereon, according to the first Purchase and Deed of Release of the Natives, dated *July* 19, 1651, beginning at the West side of the *Minquaa,* or *Christina Kill,* in the *Indian* language named *Suspecough,* to the Mouth of the Bay, or River called *Bompt-Hook,* in the *Indian* language *Cannaresse;* and so far inland as the Bounds and Limits of the *Minquaas* Land, with all the streams, &c. Appurtenances, and Dependencies.

Of the country Northward of the Kill, no mention is made. Orders in 1658 were given to William Beekman to purchase Cape Hinlopen from the natives, and to settle and fortify it, which, for want of goods was not done till the succeeding year.

In the year 1659, fresh troubles arose from the Maryland claim to the lands on South River; and in September Colonel Nathaniel Utie, as Commissioner from Fendal, Lord Baltimore's Governour, arrived at Niewer Amstel from Maryland. The country was ordered to be evacuated, Lord Baltimore claiming all the land, between 38 and 40 degrees of latitude, from sea to sea. Beekman and his council demanded evidence of his Lordship's right, and offered to prove the States General's grant to the West-India Company, theirs to them, payment for the land and possession; and upon the whole proposed to refer the controversy to the republicks of England and Holland, praying at the same time, three weeks to consult Stuyvesant, the General. The commissioner, notwithstanding, a few days after, warned him to draw off, beyond the latitude of 40°: but Beekman disregarded the threat. Colonel Utie thereupon returned to Maryland, and an immediate invasion was expected.

Early in the spring of the year 1660, Nicholas Varleth, and

Brian Newton, were dispatched from Fort Amsterdam to Virginia, in quality of ambassadors, with full power to open a trade, and conclude a league, offensive and defensive against the barbarians. William Berckley, the Governour, gave them a kind reception, and approved their proposal of peace and commerce, which Sir Henry Moody was sent here to agree upon and perfect. Four Articles, to that purpose, were drawn up, and sent to the Governour for confirmation. Stuyvesant artfully endeavoured, at this treaty, to procure an acknowledgement of the Dutch title to the country, which Berckley as carefully avoided. This was his answer.

> SIR,
>
> I have received the Letter, you were pleased to send me, by Mr. *Mills* his Vessel, and shall be ever ready to comply with you, in all Acts of neighbourly Friendship and Amity. But truly, Sir, you desire me to do that, concerning your Titles, and Claims to Land, in this Northern Part of *America*, which I am in no Capacity to do; for I am but a Servant of the assembly's: neither do they arrogate any Power to themselves, farther than the miserable Distractions of *England* force them to. For when God shall be pleased in his Mercy, to take away and dissipate the unnatural Divisions of their native Country, they will immediately return to their own professed Obedience. What then they should do in Matters of Contract, Donation, or Confession of Right, would have little Strength or Signification; much more presumptive and impertinent, would it be in me to do it, without their Knowledge or Assent. We shall very shortly meet again, and then, if to them you signify your Desires, I shall labour all I can, to get you a satisfactory Answer.
>
> > I am, Sir,
> > > Your humble Servant,
> > > William Berckly.
>
> *Virginia,*
> *August* 20, 1660.

Governour Stuyvesant was a faithful servant of the West-India Company: this is abundantly proved by his letters to them, exciting their care of the colony. In one, dated April 20, 1660, which is very long and pathetic, representing the desperate situation of affairs on both sides of the New-Netherland, he writes, "Your Honours imagine, that the Troubles in England will prevent any Attempt on these Parts: alas! they are

*New Amsterdam in 1660*

Ten to One in Number to us, and are able without any Assistance, to deprive us of the Country when they please." On the
25th of June, the same year, he informs them, "that the Demands, Encroachments, and Usurpations, of the English, gave
the People here great Concern. The Right to both Rivers, says
he, by Purchase and Possession is our own, without Dispute.
We apprehend, that they, our more powerful Neighbours, lay
their Claims under a Royal Patent, which we are unable
hitherto to do in your Name."* Colonel Utie being unsuccessful
the last year, in his embassy for the evacuation of the Dutch
possessions on Delaware, Lord Baltimore, in Autumn 1660,
applied, by Captain Neal, his agent to the West-India Company, in Holland, for an order on the inhabitants of South
River to submit to his authority, which they absolutely refused,
asserting their right to that part of their colony.

The English, from New-England, were every day incroaching upon the Dutch. The following letter, from Stuyvesant to
the West-India Company, dated July 21, 1661, shews the state
of the colony at that time, on both sides.

> We have not yet begun the Fort on *Long Island*, near
> *Oysterbay*, because our Neighbours lay the Boundaries a Mile
> and an half more Westerly, than we do, and the more as
> your Honours, by your Advice of *December* 24, are not
> inclined to stand by the Treaty of *Hartford*,[6] and propose to
> sue for Redress on *Long Island* and the *Fresh Water
> River*, by Means of the States Ambassador. Lord *Sterling* is
> said to sollicit a Confirmation of his Right to all *Long
> Island*, and importunes the present King, to confirm the
> Grant made by his Royal Father, which is affirmed to be
> already obtained. But more probable, and material, is the
> Advice from *Maryland*, that Lord *Baltimore's* Patent,
> which contains the Southpart of *South River*, is confirmed by
> the King, and published in Print: that Lord *Baltimore's*
> natural Brother, who is a rigid Papist, being made Governour
> there, has received Lord *Baltimore's* Claim, and Protest

* If we should argue, from this letter, that the West-India Company had no grants of the New-Netherlands, from the States General, as some suppose, we discredit De Laet's History, dedicated to
the States in 1624, as well as all the Dutch writers, and even
Stuyvesant himself, who in his letter to Richard Nicolls, at the surrender, asserts that they had a grant, and shewed it under Seal to
the English deputies. But the genuine construction of the Dutch
Governour's letter, is this, that in 1660, he had not the Patent to
the West-India Company, to lay before the English in America, who
disputed the Dutch right to this county.

to your Honours in Council, (wherewith he seems but little satisfied) and has now more Hopes of Success. We have Advice from *England*, that there is an Invasion intended against these Parts, and the Country sollicited of the King, the Duke, and the Parliament, is to be annexed to their Dominions; and for that Purpose, they desire three or four Frigates, persuading the King, that the Company possessed and held this Country under an unlawful Title, having only obtained of King *James* Leave for a watering Place on *Staten Island*, in 1623.

In August 1663, a ship arrived from Holland at South River, with new planters, ammunition, and implements of husbandry. Lord Baltimore's son landed a little after, and was entertained by Beekman[7] at Niewer Amstel. This was Charles, the son of Cecilius, who in 1661, had procured a grant and confirmation of the Patent, passed in favour of his father in 1632. The papistical principles of the Baltimore family, the charge of colonizing, the parliamentary war with Charles I, and Oliver's usurpation, all conspired to impede the settlement of Maryland, till the Year 1661. And these considerations account for the extension of the Dutch limits, on the West-side of Delaware Bay.

While the Dutch were contending with their European neighbours, they had the art always to maintain a friendship with the natives, until the war which broke out this year with the Indians at Esopus, now Ulster County. It continued, however, but a short season. The Five Nations never gave them any disturbance, which was owing to their continual wars with the French, who settled at Canada in 1603. I have before observed, that Oliver Cromwell was applied to, for his aid in the reduction of this country, and that his son Richard took some steps towards accomplishing the scheme; the work was however reserved for the reign of Charles II, an indolent prince, and entirely given up to pleasure, who was driven to it, more perhaps, by the differences then subsisting between England and Holland, than by any motive that might reflect honour upon his prudence, activity, and public-spirit. Before this expedition, the King granted a Patent on the 12th of March 1664, to his brother, the Duke of York and Albany, for sundry tracts of land in America, the boundaries of which, because they have given rise to important and animated debates, it may not be improper to transcribe.

All that Part of the main Land of *New-England,* beginning
at a certain Place, called or known by the Name of *St.
Croix,* next adjoining to *New-Scotland* in *America,* and from
thence extending along the Sea-coast, unto a certain Place
called *Pemaquie,* or *Pemequid,* and so up the River
thereof, to the furthest Head of the same, as it tendeth
Northward; and extending from thence, to the River of
*Kimbequin,* and so upwards, by the shortest Course, to the
River *Canada* Northward: and also all that Island, or
Islands, commonly called by the several Name or Names of
*Meitowacks,* or *Long Island,* situate and being towards
the West of Cape *Cod,* and the narrow *Higansetts,* abutting
upon the main Land, between the two Rivers, there called
or known by the several Names of *Connecticut* and *Hudson's*
River, together also with the said River, called *Hudson's*
River, and all the Land from the West-side of *Connecticut*
River, to the East-side of *Delaware* Bay, and also, all
those several Islands, called or known by the Names of
*Martin's Vineyard,* or *Nantuck's,* otherwise *Nantucket:* together, &c.

Part of this tract was conveyed by the Duke, to John Lord
Berkley, Baron of Stratton, and Sir George Carteret of Saltrum
in Devon, who were then members of the King's Council. The
lease was for the consideration of ten shillings, and dated the
23rd of June 1664. The release, dated the next Day, mentions
no particular sum of money, as a consideration for the grant
of the lands, which have the following description.

All that Tract of Land, adjacent to *New-England,* and lying
and being to the Westward of *Long Island,* and bounded
on the East-part by the main Sea, and partly by *Hudson's*
River; and hath upon the West, *Delaware* Bay, or River,
and extendeth Southward, to the main Ocean as far
as *Cape May,* at the Mouth of *Delaware* Bay: and to the
Northward, as far as the northermost Branch of the said Bay
or River of *Delaware,* which is forty-one Degrees and
forty Minutes of Latitude: [and crosseth over thence in a
straight line to Hudson's River in forty-one Degrees of
Latitude]* which said Tract of Land is hereafter to be called
by the Name, or Names of *Nova Caesarea,* or *New Jersey.*

Thus the New-Netherlands became divided into New Jersey,
so called after the Isle of Jersey, in compliment to Sir George

* [See letter No. 20 in Appendix B.]

Carteret, whose family came from thence; and New-York, which took its name in honour of the Duke of York.

The Dutch Inhabitants, by the vigilance of their governour, were not unapprised of the designs of the English Court against them, for their records testify, that on the 8th of July, "The General received Intelligence, from one Thomas Willet, an Englishman, that an Expedition was preparing in England, against this Place, consisting of two Frigates of 40 and 50 Guns, and a Fly Boat of 40 Guns, having on board three hundred Soldiers, and each Frigate 150 Men, and that they then lay at Portsmouth, waiting for a Wind." News arrived also from Boston, that they had already set sail. The Burgomasters[8] were thereupon called into Council. The fortress ordered to be put into a posture of defence, and spies sent to Milford and West-chester for intelligence. Boston was in the secret of the expedition, for the General Court had in May preceding, passed a vote for a supply of provisions, towards refreshing the ships on their arrival. They were four in number, and resolved to rendezvous at Gardeners Island in the Sound, but parted in a fog about the 20th of July. Richard Nicolls and Sir George Carteret, two of the commissioners, were on board the *Guyny*, and fell in first with Cape Cod. The winds having blown from the South-west, the other ships, with Sir Robert Car, and Mr. Maverick, the remaining Commissioners, were rightly concluded, to be driven to the eastward. After dispatching a letter to Mr. Winthrop,[9] the Governour of Connecticut, requesting his assistance, Colonel Nicolls, proceeded to Nantasket, and thence to Boston. The other ships got into Piscataway. John Endicot, a very old man, was then Governour of Boston, and incapable of business. The Commissioners, therefore, had a conference with the Council, and earnestly implored the Assistance of that colony. Colonel Nicolls and Sir George Carteret, in their letter from Boston, to Sir H. Bennet, Secretary of State, complain much of the backwardness of that Province. The reasons urged in their excuse, were poverty and the season, it being the Time of harvest; but perhaps disaffection to the Stuart family, whose persecuting fury had driven them from their native country, was the true spring of their conduct. The King's success in the reduction of the Dutch, evidently opened him a door, to come at his enemies in New-England, who were far from being few;* and whether this consideration might not

* F. Dixwel, Esq; one of Charles I's Judges, and excepted out of the General Pardon, lived many years at New-Haven (incog.) in

have given rise to the project itself, I leave to the conjectures of others.

On the 27th of July, Nicolls and Carteret made a formal request in writing. "That the Government of Boston would pass an Act to furnish them with armed Men, who should begin their March to the Manhattans, on the 20th of August ensuing, and promised, that if they could get other Assistance, they would give them an Account of it." The governour and council answered, that they would assemble the General Court, and communicate the proposal to them.

From Boston, a second letter was written to Governour Winthrop in Connecticut, dated the 29th of July, in which he was informed, that the other ships were then arrived, and would sail with the first fair wind, and he was desired to meet them at the West-end of Long Island.

One of the ships entered the Bay of the North River, several days before the rest; and as soon as they were all come up, Stuyvesant sent a letter dated 19/30 of August at Fort Anill, directed to the Commanders of the English frigates, by John Declyer, one of the chief Council, the Reverend John Megapolensis Minister, Paul Lunder Vander Grift Major, and Mr. Samuel Megapolensis Doctor in Physic, with the utmost civility, to desire the reason of their approach, and continuing in the Harbour of Naijarlij, without giving notice to the Dutch, which (he writes) they ought to have done.

Colonel Nicolls answered the next day with a summons.

To the Honourable the Governors, and Chief Council at the *Manhattans.*

Right Worthy Sirs,
I received a Letter by some worthy Persons intrusted by
you, bearing Date the 19/30 of *August,* desiring to know the
Intent of the Approach of the *English* Frigates; in Return
of which, I think it fit to let you know, that his Majesty
of *Great Britain,* whose Right and Title to these Parts of
*America* is unquestionable, well knowing, how much it

---

quality of a country merchant: Sir Edmond Andross, in one of his tours through the Colony of Connecticut, saw him there at church, and strongly suspected him to be one of the regicides. In his last illness, he revealed himself to the minister of the town, and ordered a small stone to be set at the head of his grave, which I have often seen there, inscribed, *F.D. Esq.* While at New-Haven, he went under the name of John Davis.

derogates from his Crown and Dignity, to suffer any Foreigners, how near soever they be allied, to usurp a Dominion, and without his Majesty's Royal Consent, to inhabit in these, or any other of his Majesty's Territories, hath commanded me, in his Name, to require a Surrender of all such Forts, Towns, or Places of Strength, which are now possessed by the *Dutch,* under your Commands; and in his Majesty's Name, I do demand the Town, situate on the Island, commonly known by the Name of *Manhatoes,* with all the Forts thereunto belonging, to be rendered unto his Majesty's Obedience and Protection, into my Hands. I am further commanded to assure you, and every respective Inhabitant of the *Dutch* Nation, that his Majesty being tender of the Effusion of Christian Blood, doth by these Presents, confirm and secure to every Man his Estate, Life, and Liberty, who shall readily submit to his Government. And all those who shall oppose his Majesty's gracious Intention, must expect all the Miseries of a War, which they bring upon themselves. I shall expect your Answer by these Gentlemen, Colonel *George Carteret,* one of his Majesty's Commissioners in *America;* Captain *Robert Needham,* Captain *Edward Groves,* and Mr. *Thomas Delavall,* whom you will entertain with such Civility as is due to them, and yourselves and yours shall receive the same, from,

Worthy Sirs,

Your very humble Servant,<br>
*Richard Nicolls.*

Dated on board his
Majesty's Ship,
the *Guyny,* riding
before *Naych,* the
20/31 of *Aug.* 1664.

Mr. Stuyvesant promised an answer to the summons the next morning, and in the mean time convened the Council and Burgomasters. The Dutch Governour was a good soldier, and had lost a leg in the service of the States. He would willingly have made a defence; and refused a sight of the summons, both to the inhabitants and Burgomasters, lest the easy terms offered, might induce them to capitulate. The latter, however, insisted upon a copy, that they might communicate it, to the late magistrates and principal burghers. They called together the inhabitants at the Stadt-House, and acquainted them with the Governour's refusal. Governour Winthrop,[9] at the same time, wrote to the Director and his Council, strongly recommending a surrender. On the 22nd of August, the Burgomasters came again into Council, and desired to know the contents of the English message from Governour Winthrop, which Stuyvesant still refused. They continued their importunity; and he, in a fit of anger, tore it to pieces: upon which, they protested against the Act, and all its consequences. Determined upon a defence of the country, Stuyvesant wrote a letter in answer to the summons, which as it is historical of the Dutch claim, will doubtless be acceptable to the reader. The following is an exact transcript of the record.

My Lords,
Your first Letter, unsigned of the 20/31 *August,* together with that of this Day, signed according to Form, being the first of *September,* have been safely delivered into our Hands by your Deputies, unto which we shall say, That the Rights of his Majesty of *England,* unto any Part of *America* here about, amongst the rest, unto the Colonies of *Virginia, Maryland,* or others in *New-England,* whether disputable or not, is that which for the present, we have no Design to debate upon. But that his Majesty hath an indisputable Right, to all the Lands in the North Parts of *America,* is that, which the Kings of *France* and *Spain* will disallow, as we absolutely do, by Virtue of a Commission given to me, by my Lords, the High and Mighty States General, to be Governor General, over *New-Holland,* the Isles of *Curacoa, Bonaire, Aruba,* with their Appurtenances and Dependancies, bearing Date the 26th of *July,* 1646. As also by Virtue of a Grant and Commission, given by my said Lords, the High and Mighty States General, to the *West-India* Company, in the Year 1621, with as much Power and as authentic, as his said Majesty of *England* hath given, or can give, to any Colony in *America,* as more fully appears by the Patent and Commission of the said Lords the States General, by them signed, registered, and sealed with their Great Seal, which were shewed to your Deputies Colonel *George Carteret,* Captain *Robert Needham,* Captain *Edward Groves,* and Mr. *Thomas Delavall;* by which Commission and Patent, together (to deal frankly with you) and by divers Letters, signed and sealed by Our said Lords, the States General, directed to several Persons, both *English* and *Dutch,* inhabiting the Towns and Villages on *Long Island,* (which without doubt, have been produced before you, by those Inhabitants) by which they are declared and acknowledged to be their Subjects, with express Command, that they continue faithful

unto them, under Penalty of incuring their utmost Displeasure, which makes it appear more clear than the Sun at Noon-day, that your first Foundation, *viz.* (that the Right and Title of his Majesty of *Great Britain*, to these Parts of *America* is unquestionable) is absolutely to be denied. Moreover, it is without Dispute, and acknowledged by the World, that our Predecessors, by Virtue of the Commission and Patent of the said Lords, the States General, have without Controul and peaceably (the contrary never coming to our Knowledge) enjoyed *Fort Orange,* about 48 or 50 Years, the *Manhattans* about 41 or 42 Years, the *South River* 40 Years, and the *Fresh Water River* about 36 Years. Touching the second subject of your Letter, *viz.* His Majesty hath commanded me, in his Name, to require a Surrender of all such Forts, Towns, or Places of Strength, which now are possessed by the *Dutch,* under your Command. We shall answer, that we are so confident of the Discretion and Equity of his Majesty of *Great Britain,* that in case his Majesty were informed of the Truth, which is, that the *Dutch* came not into these Provinces, by any Violence, but by Virtue of Commissions from my Lords, the States General, first of all in the Years 1614, 1615, and 1616, up the *North River,* near *Fort Orange,* where, to hinder the Invasions and Massacres, commonly committed by the *Salvages,* they built a little Fort, and after, in the Year 1622, and even to this present Time, by Virtue of Commission and Grant, to the Governors of the *West-India* Company; and moreover, in the Year 1656, a Grant to the honourable the Burgomasters of *Amsterdam,* of the *South River;* insomuch that by Virtue of the abovesaid Commissions from the High and Mighty States General, given to the Persons interested as aforesaid, and others, these Provinces have been governed, and consequently enjoyed, as also in regard of their first Discovery, uninterrupted Possessions, and Purchase of the Lands of the Princes, Natives of the Country, and other private Persons (though Gentiles) we make no Doubt, that if his said Majesty of *Great Britain,* were well informed of these Passages, he would be too judicious to grant such an Order, principally in a Time when there is so straight a Friendship, and Confederacy, between our said Lords and Superiors, to trouble us in the demanding and Summons of the Places and Fortresses, which were put into our Hands, with Order to maintain them, in the Name of the said Lords, the States General, as was made appear to your Deputies, under the Names and Seal of the said High and Mighty States General, dated the 28th of *July,* 1646. Besides what had been mentioned, there is little Probability, that his said Majesty of *England* (in regard the Articles of Peace are printed, and were recommended to us to observe seriously and exactly, by a Letter written to us by our said Lords, the States General, and to cause them to be observed religiously in this Country) would give Order touching so dangerous a Design, being also so apparent, that none other than my said Lords, the States General, have any Right to these Provinces, and consequently, ought to command and maintain their Subjects, and in their Absence, We the Governor General are obliged to maintain their Rights, and to repel and take Revenge of all Threatenings, unjust Attempts, or any Force whatsoever, that shall be committed against their faithful Subjects and Inhabitants, it being a very considerable Thing, to affront so mighty a State, although it were not against an Ally and Confederate. Consequently, if his said Majesty (as it is fit) were well informed, of all that could be spoken upon this Subject, he would not approve of what Expressions were mentioned in your Letter; which are, that you are commanded by his Majesty, to demand in his Name, such Places and Fortresses as are in the Possession of the *Dutch* under my Government; which, as it appears by my Commission before mentioned, was given me by my Lords, the High and Mighty States General. And there is less Ground in the express Demand of my Government, since all the World knows, that about three Years ago, some *English* Frigotts being on the Coast of *Africa,* upon a pretended Commission, they did demand certain Places under the Government of our said Lords, the States General, as *Cape Vert,* River of *Gambo,* and all other Places in *Guyny,* to them belonging. Upon which, our said Lords, the States General, by Virtue of the Articles of Peace, having made appear the said Attempt to his Majesty of *England,* they received a favourable Answer, his said Majesty disallowing all such Acts of Hostility, as might have been done, and besides, gave Order, that Restitution should be made, to the *East-India* Company, of whatsoever had been pillaged, in the said River of *Gambo;* and likewise restored them to their Trade, which makes us think it necessary, that a more express Order, should appear unto us, as a sufficient Warrant for us, towards my Lords, the High and Mighty States General, since by Virtue of our said Commission, We do in these Provinces, represent them, as belonging to them, and not to the King of *Great Britain,* except his said Majesty, upon better Grounds, make it appear to our said Lords, the States General, against which they may defend themselves, as they shall think fit. To conclude: We cannot but declare unto you, though the Governors and Commissioners of his Majestie have divers Times quarrelled with us, about the Bounds of the Jurisdiction, of the High and Mighty the States General, in these Parts, yet they never questioned their Jurisdiction itself; on the contrary, in the Year 1650, at *Hartford,* and the last Year at *Boston,* they treated with us upon this Subject, which is a sufficient Proof, that his Majestie hath never been well informed, of the Equity of our Cause, insomuch as We cannot imagine, in regard of the Articles of Peace, between the Crown of *England* and the States General, (under whom there are so many Subjects in *America,* as well as *Europe*) that his said Majestie of *Great Britain* would give a Commission to molest and endamage the Subjects of my said Lords, the States General, especially such, as ever since 50, 40, and the latest 36 Years have quietly enjoyed their Lands, Countries, Forts, and Inheritances; and less, that his Subjects would attempt any Acts of Hostility, or Violence against them: and in case that you will act by Force of Arms, Wee protest and declare, in the Name of our said Lords, the States General, before GOD and MEN, that you will act an unjust Violence, and a Breach of the Articles of Peace, so solemnly sworn, agreed upon, and ratified by his Majesty of *England,* and my Lords, the States General, and the rather, for that to prevent the shedding of Blood, in the Month of *February* last, We treated with Captain *John Scott,* (who reported he had a Commission from his said Majestie) touching the Limits of *Long Island,* and concluded for the Space of a Year; that in the mean Time, the Business might be treated on between the King of *Great Britain,* and my Lords, the High and Mighty States General: and again, at present, for the Hindrance and Prevention of all Differences, and the Spilling of innocent Blood, not only in these Parts, but also in *Europe,* We offer unto you, a Treaty by our Deputyes, Mr. *Cornelius Van Ruyven,* Secretary, and Receiver of *New-Holland, Cornelius Steenwick,* Burgomaster, Mr. *Samuel Megapolensis,* Doctor of Physic, and Mr. *James Cousseau,* heretofore Sheriff. As touching the Threats in your Conclusion Wee have nothing to answer, only that Wee fear nothing, but what GOD (who is as just as merciful) shall lay upon us; all Things being in his gracious Disposall, and We may as well be preserved by him, with small Forces, as by a great Army, which makes us to wish you all Happiness and Prosperity, and recommend you to his Protection. My Lords, your thrice humble, and affectionate Servant and Friend, signed *P. Stuyvesant.*—At the Fort at *Amsterdam,* the second of *September,* New Stile, 1664.

While the Dutch Governour and Council were contending with the Burgomasters and people in the city, the English Com-

missioners published a proclamation* in the country, encouraging the inhabitants to submit, and promising them the King's
protection, and all the privileges of subjects; and as soon as
they discovered by Stuyvesant's letter, that he was averse to the
surrender, officers were sent to beat up for voluntiers in Middle-
borough, Ulissen, Jamaica, and Hempsted. A warrant was also
issued to Hugh Hide, who commanded the squadron, to prosecute the reduction of the fort; and an English ship then trading here, was pressed into the service. These preparations induced Stuyvesant to write another letter, on the 25th of August, old style, wherein, though he declares that he would stand
the storm, yet to prevent the spilling of blood, he had sent John
De Decker, Counsellor of State, Cornelius Van Riven, Secretary
and Receiver, Cornelius Steenwyck Major, and James Cousseau
Sheriff, to consult, if possible, an accommodation. Nicolls, who
knew the disposition of the people, answered immediately from
Gravesend, that he would treat about nothing but a surrender.
The Dutch Governour, the next day, agreed to a treaty and
surrender, on condition the English and Dutch limits in America, were settled by the Crown and the States General. The English deputies were Sir Robert Carr, George Carteret, John Winthrop, Governour of Connecticut, Samuel Wyllys, one of the
assistants or council of that colony, and Thomas Clarke, and
John Pynchon, Commissioners from the General Court of the
Massachuset's Bay, who, but a little before, brought an aid from
that province. What these persons agreed upon, Nicolls promised to ratify. At eight o'clock in the morning, of the 27th of
August, 1664, the Commissioners, on both sides, met at the

* It was in these words: "Forasmuch as his Majesty hath sent us
(by Commission under his Great Seal of England) amongst other
Things, to expell, or to reduce to his Majesty's Obedience, all such
Foreigners, as without his Majesty's Leave and Consent, have seated
themselves amongst any of his Dominions in America to the
Prejudice of his Majesty's Subjects, and Diminution of his Royal
Dignity; we his said Majesty's Commissioners, do declare and
promise, that whosoever, of what Nation soever, will, upon Knowledge of this Proclamation, acknowledge and testify themselves, to
submit to this his Majesty's Government, as his good Subjects,
shall be protected in his Majesty's Laws and Justice, and peaceably
injoy whatsoever GOD's Blessing, and their own honest Industry, have
furnished them with; and all other Privileges, with his Majesty's
English Subjects. We have caused this to be published, that we
might prevent all Inconveniences to others, if it were possible; however, to clear ourselves from the Charge of all those Miseries, that
may any way befall such as live here, and will acknowledge his
Majesty for their Sovereign, whom GOD preserve."

governour's farm, and there signed the following Articles of Capitulation.

These Articles following were consented to by the Persons here-under subscribed, at the Governour's *Bowery, August* the 27th Old Style, 1664.

I. We consent, That the States General, or the *West-India* Company, shall freely injoy all Farms and Houses (except such as are in the Forts) and that within six Months, they shall have free Liberty to transport all such Arms and Ammunition, as now does belong to them, or else they shall be paid for them.

II. All Publique Houses shall continue for the Uses which they are for.

III. All People shall still continue free Denizens, and shall enjoy their Lands, Houses, Goods, wheresoever they are within this Country, and dispose of them as they please.

IV. If any Inhabitant have a Mind to remove himself, he shall have a Year and six Weeks from this Day, to remove himself, Wife, Children, Servants, Goods, and to dispose of his Lands here.

V. If any Officer of State, or Publique Minister of State, have a Mind to go for *England*, they shall be transported Fraught free, in his Majesty's Frigotts, when these Frigotts shall return thither.

VI. It is consented to, that any People may freely come from the *Netherlands*, and plant in this Colony, and that *Dutch* Vessels may freely come hither, and any of the *Dutch* may freely return home, or send any Sort of Merchandize home, in Vessels of their own Country.

VII. All ships from the *Netherlands*, or any other Place, and Goods therein, shall be received here, and sent hence, after the manner which formerly they were before our coming hither, for six Months next ensuing.

VIII. The *Dutch* here shall injoy the Liberty of their Consciences in divine Worship and Church Discipline.

IX. No *Dutchman* here, or *Dutch* Ship here, shall upon any Occasion, be pressed to serve in War against any Nation whatsoever.

X. That the Townsmen of the *Manhattans*, shall not have any Soldiers quartered upon them, without being satisfied and paid for them by their Officers, and that at this present, if the Fort be not capable of lodging all the Soldiers, then the Burgomasters, by his Officers, shall appoint some Houses capable to receive them.

XI. The *Dutch* here shall injoy their own Customs concerning their Inheritances.

XII. All Publique Writings and Records, which concern the Inheritances of any People, or the Reglement of the Church or Poor, or Orphans, shall be carefully kept by those in whose Hands now they are, and such Writings as particularly concern the States General, may at any Time be sent to them.

XIII. No Judgment that has passed any Judicature here, shall be called in Question, but if any conceive that he hath not had Justice done him, if he apply himself to the States General, the other Party shall be bound to answer for the supposed Injury.

XIV. If any *Dutch*, living here shall at any Time desire to travaile or traffique into *England,* or any Place, or Plantation, in Obedience to his Majesty of *England,* or with the *Indians,* he shall have (upon his Request to the Governor) a Certificate that he is a free Denizen of this Place, and Liberty to do so.

XV. If it do appeare, that there is a publique Engagement of Debt, by the Town of the *Manhattoes,* and a Way agreed on for the Satisfying of that Engagement, it is agreed, that the same Way proposed shall go on, and that the Engagement shall be satisfied.

XVI. All inferior Civil Officers and Magistrates, shall continue as now they are, (if they please) till the customary Time of new Elections, and then new ones to be chosen by themselves, provided that such new chosen Magistrates shall take the Oath of Allegiance to his Majesty of *England,* before they enter upon their Office.

XVII. All Differences of Contracts and Bargains made before this Day, by any in this Country, shall be determined, according to the Manner of the *Dutch.*

XVIII. If it do appeare, that the *West-India* Company of *Amsterdam,* do really owe any Sums of Money to any Persons here, it is agreed that Recognition, and other Duties payable by Ships going for the *Netherlands,* be continued for six Months longer.

XIX. The Officers Military, and Soldiers, shall march out with their Arms, Drums beating, and Coulours flying, and lighted Matches; and if any of them will plant, they shall have fifty Acres of Land set out for them; if any of them will serve as Servants, they shall continue with all Safety, and become free Denizens afterwards.

XX. If at any Time hereafter, the King of *Great Britain,* and the States of the *Netherland* do agree that this Place and

Country be redelivered into the Hands of the said States, whensoever his Majestie will send his Commands to redeliver it, it shall immediately be done.

XXI. That the Town of *Manhattans* shall choose Deputyes, and those Deputyes shall have free Voyces in all publique Affairs, as much as any other Deputyes.

XXII. Those who have any Property in any Houses in the Fort of *Aurania*, shall (if they please) slight the Fortifications there, and then enjoy all their Houses, as all People do where there is no Fort.

XXIII. If there be any Soldiers that will go into *Holland*, and if the Company of *West-India* in *Amsterdam*, or any private Persons here, will transport them into *Holland*, then they shall have a safe Passport from Colonel *Richard Nicholls*, Deputy-Governor under his Royal Highness, and the other Commissioners, to defend the Ships that shall transport such Soldiers, and all the Goods in them, from any Surprizal or Acts of Hostility, to be done by any of his Majestie's Ships or Subjects. That the Copies of the King's Grant to his Royal Highness, and the Copy of his Royal Highness's Commission to Colonel *Richard Nicholls*, testified by two Commissioners more, and Mr. *Winthrop*, to be true Copies, shall be delivered to the honourable Mr. *Stuyvesant*, the present Governor, on *Munday* next, by Eight of the Clock in the Morning, at the *Old Miln*, and these Articles consented to, and signed by Colonel *Richard Nicolls*, Deputy-Governor to his Royal Highness, and that within two Hours after the Fort and Town called *New-Amsterdam*, upon the Isle of *Manhatoes*, shall be delivered into the Hands of the said Colonel *Richard Nicolls*, by the Service of such as shall be by him thereunto deputed, by his Hand and Seal.

| | |
|---|---|
| John De Decker, | Robert Carr, |
| Nich. Verleett, | Geo. Carteret, |
| Sam. Megapolensis, | John Winthrop, |
| Cornelius Steenwick, | Sam. Willys, |
| Oloffe Stevens Van Kortlant, | Thomas Clarke, |
| James Cousseau, | John Pinchon. |

I do consent to these Articles,

*Richard Nicolls.*

These Articles, favourable as they were to the inhabitants, were however very disagreeable to the Dutch Governour, and he therefore refused to ratify them, till two days after they were signed by the Commissioners.

The town of New-Amsterdam, upon the reduction of the

Island Manhattans, took the name of New-York. It consisted of several small streets, laid out in the year 1656, and was not inconsiderable for the number of its houses and inhabitants. The easy terms of the capitulation, promised their peaceable subjection to the new government; and hence we find, that in two days after the surrender, the Boston aid was dismissed, with the thanks of the Commissioners to the General Court. Hudson's and the South River were, however, still to be reduced. Sir Robert Carr commanded the expedition on Delaware, and Carteret was commissioned to subdue the Dutch at Fort-Orange. The garrison capitulated on the 24th of September, and he called it Albany, in honour of the Duke. While Carteret was here, he had an interview with the Indians of the Five Nations, and entered into a league of friendship with them, which remarkably continues to this day.* Sir Robert Carr was equally successful on South River, for he compelled both the Dutch and Swedes, to capitulate and deliver up their garrisons the first of October, 1664; and that was the day in which the whole New-Netherlands became subject to the English Crown. Very few of the inhabitants thought proper to remove out of the country.[10] Governour Stuyvesant himself, held his estate and died here. His remains were interred in a chapel, which he had erected on his own farm, at a small distance from the city, now possessed by his grandson Gerardus Stuyvesant, a man of probity, who has been elected into the magistracy, above thirty years successively. Justice obliges me to declare, that for loyalty to the present reigning family, and a pure attachment to the Protestant religion, the descendants of the Dutch planters, are perhaps exceeded by none of his Majesty's subjects.

---

* The Dutch were sensible of the importance of preserving an uninterrupted amity with those Indians, for they were both very numerous and warlike. The French pursued quite different measures, and the irruptions of those tribes, according to their own authours, have often reduced Canada to the brink of ruin.[11]

# Part II

*From the Surrender in 1664,*
*to the Settlement at the Revolution*

Richard Nicolls being now possessed of the country, took the government upon him, under the stile of "Deputy-Governor under his Royal Highness the Duke of York, of all his Territories in America." During his short continuance here, he passed a vast number of grants and confirmations of the ancient Dutch Patents, the profits of which must have been very considerable. Among these, no one has occasioned more animated contention, than that called the Elizabeth Town Grant in New-Jersey; which, as it relates to another colony, I should not have mentioned, but for the opportunity to caution the reader against the representation of that controversy contained in Douglass's Summary. I have sufficient reasons to justify my charging that account with partiality and mistakes; and for proofs, refer to the printed Answer in Chancery, published in the year 1751.

Besides the chief command of this Province, Nicolls had a joint Power* with Sir Robert Carr, Carteret, and Maverick, to settle the contested boundaries of certain great Patents. Hence we find, that three of them had a conference with several

---

* The Commission from King Charles II was dated the 26th of April, 1664. After a recital of disputes concerning limits in New-England, and that addresses had been sent home from the Indian natives, complaining of abuses received from the English subjects; the commissioners, or any three or two of them, of which Nicolls was to be one, were authorised to visit the New-England colonies, and determine all complaints military, civil, and criminal, according to their discretion, and such instructions, as they might receive from the Crown.

gentlemen from Connecticut, respecting the limits of this and that colony. The result was an adjudication, in these words:

By Virtue of his Majesty's Commission, we have heard the Difference, about the Bounds of the Patents granted to his Royal Highness the Duke of *York*, and his Majesty's Colony of *Connecticut*, and having deliberately considered, all the Reasons alledged by Mr. *Allyn*, sen. Mr. *Gold*, Mr. *Richards*, and Captain *Winthrop*, appointed by the Assembly held at *Hartford* the 13th of *October*, 1664, to accompany *John Winthrop*, Esq; the Governor of his Majesty's Colony of *Connecticut* to *New-York*, and to agree upon the Bounds of the said Colony, why the said *Long Island*, should be under the Government of *Connecticut*, which are too long here to be recited, we do declare and order, that the Southern Bounds of his Majesty's Colony of *Connecticut*, is the Sea, and that *Long Island* is to be under the Government of his Royal Highness the Duke of *York*, as is expressed by plain Words, in the said Patents, respectively, and also by Virtue of his Majesty's Commission, and the Consent of both the Governors and the Gentlemen above-named. We also order and declare, that the Creek, or River called *Mamaroneck*, which is reputed to be about thirteen Miles to the East of *West-chester*, and a Line drawn from the east Point or Side, where the fresh Water falls into the Salt, at high Water Mark, North-north-west to the Line of the *Massachuset's*, be the western Bounds of the said Colony of *Connecticut*, and all Plantations lying West-ward of that Creek and Line so drawn, to be under his Royal Highness's Government; and all Plantations lying Eastward of that Creek and Line, to be under the Government of *Connecticut*. Given under our Hands, at *James's* Fort in *New-York*, on the Island of *Manhattan*, this first Day of *December*, 1664.

*Richard Nicolls,*
*George Carteret,*
*S. Mavericke.*

We the Governour and Commissioners of the General Assembly of *Connecticut*, do give our Consent to the Limits and Bounds above-mentioned, as witness our Hands,

——— *Gold,*                                     *John Winthrop,*
*John Winthrop*, jun.                             *Allen*, sen.
                                                 *Richards.*

At the time of this determination, about two thirds of Long Island was possessed by people from New-England, who had gradually encroached upon the Dutch. As to the settlement between New-York and Connecticut on the main, it has always been considered by the former, as founded upon ignorance and fraud.* The station at Mamaroneck was about 30 miles from New-York, from Albany 150. The general course of the river is about North 12 or 15° East: and hence it is evident, that a North-north-west line will soon intersect the river, and consequently leave the Dutch Country, but a little before surrendered to Colonel Carteret, out of the Province of New-York. It has been generally esteemed, that the Connecticut Commissioners in this affair, took advantage of the Duke's agents, who were ignorant of the geography of the country.[1]

About the close of the year, the estate of the West-India Company was seized and confiscated, hostilities being actually commenced in Europe as well as America, though no declarations of war had yet been published by either of the contending parties. A great dispute between the inhabitants of Jamaica on Long Island, which was adjusted by Colonel Nicolls, on the second of January, 1665, gave rise to a salutary institution, which has in part obtained ever since. The controversy respected Indian deeds, and thenceforth it was ordained, that no purchase from the Indians, without the Governour's licence executed in his presence, should be valid. The strength and numbers of the natives rendered it necessary to purchase their rights; and to prevent their frequent selling the same tract, it was expedient, that the bargain should be attended with some considerable solemnity.[2]

Another instance of Colonel Nicolls's prudence, was his gradual introduction of the English methods of government. It was not till the 12th of June, this year, that he incorporated the inhabitants of New-York, under the care of a mayor, five aldermen, a sheriff. Till this time, the city was ruled by a schout, Burgomasters, and Schepens.[3]

In March preceding, there was a great Convention, before the Governour at Hempstead, of two deputies from every town on Long Island, empowered to bind their constituents. The design of their meeting was to adjust the limits of their townships for the preservation of the public peace.

The war being proclaimed at London on the fourth of this month, Nicolls received the account of it in June, with a letter

* The Town of Rye was settled under Connecticut, and the grant from that colony is bounded by this line of division.

from the Lord Chancellor, informing him, that De Ruyter, the Dutch Admiral, had orders to visit New-York. His Lordship was misinformed, or the Admiral was diverted from the enterprise, for the English peaceably held the possession of the country during the whole war, which was concluded on the 21st of July, 1667, by the Treaty of Breda.[4] Some are of opinion, that the exchange made with the Dutch for Surinam, which they had taken from us, was advantageous to the nation; but these judges do not consider, that it would have been impossible for the Dutch to have preserved this colony against the increasing strength of the people in New-England, Maryland, and Virginia.

After an administration of three years, Nicolls returned to England. The time during his short residence here, was almost wholly taken up in confirming the antient Dutch grants. He erected no courts of justice, but took upon himself the sole decision of all controversies whatsoever. Complaints came before him by petition; upon which he gave a day to the parties, and after a summary hearing, pronounced judgment. His determinations were called edicts, and executed by the sheriffs he had appointed. It is much to his honour, that notwithstanding all this plentitude of power, he governed the province with integrity and moderation. A representation from the inhabitants of Long Island, to the General Court of Connecticut, made about the time of the Revolution, commends him as a man of an easy and benevolent disposition; and this testimonial is the more to be relied upon, because the design of the writers, was by a detail of their grievances, to induce the colony of Connecticut to take them under its immediate protection.

Francis Lovelace, a Colonel, was appointed by the Duke, to succeed Nicolls in the government of the province, which he began to exercise in May, 1667. As he was a man of great moderation, the people lived very peaceably under him, till the re-surrender of the colony, which put an end to his power, and is the only event, that signalized his administration.

The ambitious designs of Louis XIV against the Dutch, gave rise to our war with the States General in 1672. Charles II a prince sunk in pleasures, profligate, and poor, was easily detached from his alliance with the Dutch, by the intrigues and pecuniary promises of the French King. The following passage from a fine writer,* shews that his pretences for entering into the war, were perfectly groundless and trifling.

* Voltaire's *Age of Lewis XIV*.

The King of *England,* on his Side, reproached them with Disrespect, in not directing their Fleet to lower the Flag before an *English* ship; and they were also accused in regard to a certain Picture, wherein *Cornelius de Witt,* Brother to the Pensionary, was painted with the Attributes of a Conqueror. Ships were represented in the Back-ground of the Piece, either taken or burnt. *Cornelius de Witt,* who had really had a great Share in the maritime Exploits against *England,* had permitted this trifling Memorial of his Glory: but the Picture, which was in a manner unknown, was deposited in a Chamber wherein scarce any body ever entered. The *English* Ministers, who presented the Complaints of their King against *Holland,* in Writing, therein mentioned certain *abusive Pictures.* The States, who always translated the Memorials of Ambassadors into *French,* having rendered *abusive,* by the Words *fautifs trompeurs,* they replied, that they did not know what these *rougish Pictures (ces tableau x trompeurs)* were. In reality, it never in the least entered into their Thoughts, that it concerned this Portrait of one of their Citizens, nor did they ever conceive this could be a Pretence for declaring War.

A few Dutch ships arrived the year after on the 30th of July, under Staten Island, at the distance of a few miles from the City of New-York. John Manning, a Captain of an independent company, had at that time the command of the Fort, and by a messenger sent down to the squadron, treacherously made his peace with the enemy. On that very day the Dutch ships came up, moored under the Fort, landed their men, and entered the garrison, without giving or receiving a shot. A Council of War was afterwards held at the Stadt-House, at which were present

| | |
|---|---|
| Cornelius Evertse, jun. <br> Jacob Benkes, | } Commodores. |
| Anthony Colve, <br> Nicholas Boes, <br> Abraham Ferd. Van Zyll, | } Captains. |

All the magistrates and constables from East Jersey, Long Island, Esopus, and Albany, were immediately summoned to New-York; and the major part of them swore allegiance to the States General, and the Prince of Orange. Colonel Lovelace was ordered to depart the province, but afterwards obtained leave to return to England with Commodore Benkes. It has often been insisted on, that this conquest did not extend to the whole Province of New Jersey; but upon what foundation I cannot discover. From the Dutch records, it appears, that deputies were sent by the people inhabiting the country, even so far westward as Delaware River, who in the name of their principals, made a Declaration of their submission; in return for which, certain privileges were granted to them, and three judicatories erected at Niewer, Amstel, Upland, and Hoer Kill. Colve's Commission to be Governour of this country is worth printing, because it shews the extent of the Dutch claims. The translation runs thus:

> The honourable and awful Council of War, for their High Mightinesses the States General of the United *Netherlands,* and his Serene Highness the Prince of *Orange,* over a Squadron of Ships, now at Anchor in *Hudson's* River in *New-Netherlands.* To all those who shall see or hear these, *Greeting.* As it is necessary, to appoint a fit and able Person, to carry the chief Command over this Conquest of *New-Netherlands,* with all its Appendencies and Dependencies from Cape *Hinlopen* on the South Side of the South or *Delaware,* Bay, and fifteen Miles more Southerly, with the said Bay and *South River* included; so as they were formerly possessed by the Directors of the City of *Amsterdam,* and after by the *English* Government, in the Name and Right of the Duke of *York;* and further from the said Cape of *Hinlopen,* along the *Great Ocean,* to the East End of *Long Island,* and *Shelter Island;* from thence Westward to the Middle of the *Sound,* to a Town called *Greenwich,* on the Main, and to run Landward in, Northerly; provided that such Line shall not come within ten Miles of *North River,* conformable to a provincial Treaty made in 1650, and ratified by the States General, *February* 22, 1656, and *January* 23, 1664; with all Lands, Islands, Rivers, Lakes, Kills, Creeks, fresh and salt Waters, Fortresses, Cities, Towns, and Plantations therein comprehended. So it is, that we being sufficiently assured, of the Capacity of *Anthony Colve,* Captain of a Company of Foot, in the Service of their High Mightinesses, the States General of the United *Netherlands,* and his Serene Highness the Prince of *Orange,* &c. By Virtue of our Commission, granted us by their before-mentioned High Mightinesses and his Highness, have appointed and qualified, as we do by these Presents appoint and qualify, the said Captain *Anthony Colve,* to govern and rule these Lands, with the Appendencies and Dependencies thereof, as Governor General; to protect them from all

Invasions of Enemies, as he shall judge most necessary; hereby charging all high and low Officers, Justices, and Magistrates, and Others in Authority, Soldiers, Burghers, and all the Inhabitants of this Land, to acknowledge, honour, respect, and obey, the said *Anthony Colve*, as Governor General; for such we judge necessary, for the Service of the Country, waiting the Approbation of our Principals. Thus done at *Fort-William-Henderick*, the 12th Day of *August*, 1673.

*Jacob Benkes.*

Signed by
*Cornelius Evertse*, jun.

The Dutch governour enjoyed his office but a very short season, for on the 9th of February, 1674, the Treaty of Peace between England and the States General was signed at Westminster; the sixth article of which, restored this country to the English. The terms of it were generally,

> That whatsoever Countries, Islands, Towns, Ports, Castles, or Forts, have or shall be taken on both Sides, since the Time that the late unhappy War broke out, either in *Europe* or elsewhere, shall be restored to the former Lord and Proprietor, in the same Condition they shall be in, when the Peace itself shall be proclaimed; after which Time, there shall be no Spoil nor Plunder of the Inhabitants, no Demolition of Fortifications, nor carrying away of Guns, Powder or other Military Stores, which belonged to any Castle or Fort, at the Time when it was taken.

The lenity which began the administration of Colonel Nicolls was continued under Lovelace. He appears to have been a man, rather of a phlegmatic than an enterprising disposition, always pursuing the common road, and scarce ever acting without the aid of his Council.[5] Instead of taking upon himself the sole determination of judicial controversies, after the example of his predecessor, he called to his assistance a few justices of the peace. This, which was called The Court of Assizes,* was

---

* This was a court both of law and equity, for the trial of causes of £20 and upwards, and ordinarily sat but once a year. Subordinate to this, were the town courts and sessions; the former took cognizance of actions under £5 and the latter, of suits between that sum and twenty pounds, seven constables and overseers were judges in the first, and in the last the justices of the peace, with a jury of seven men. The verdict of the majority was sufficient.

the principal law judicatory in those times. The legislative power under the Duke, was vested entirely in the Governour and Council. A third Estate might then be easily dispensed with, for the charge of the province was* small, and in a great measure defrayed by his Royal Highness, the proprietor of the country.

Upon conclusion of the peace in 1674, the Duke of York, to remove all controversy respecting his property, obtained a new Patent† from the King, dated the 29th of June, for the lands granted in 1664, and two days after commissioned Major, afterwards Sir Edmund Andross to be Governour of his territories in America. After the resignation of this Province, which was made to him by the Dutch possessors, on the 31st of October following, he called a court martial, to try Manning for his treacherous and cowardly Surrender.[6] The Articles of Accusation exhibited against him, were in Substance,

I. That the said Manning, on the 28th of July, 1673, having notice of the approach of the enemy's fleet, did not endeavour to put the garrison in a posture of defence; but on the contrary, slighted such as offered their assistance.

II. That while the fleet was at anchor under Staten Island, on the 30th of July, he treacherously sent on board to treat with the enemy, to the great discouragement of the garrison.

III. That he suffered the fleet to moor under the Fort, forbidding a gun to be fired on pain of death.

IV. That he permited the enemy to land, without the least opposition.

V. That shortly after he had sent persons to treat with the

* The manner of raising public money, was established by Colonel Nicolls on the first of June, 1665, and was thus. The High Sheriff issued a warrant annually, to the High Constables of every district, and they sent theirs to the petty Constables; who with the overseers of each town, made a list of all male persons above sixteen years of age, with an estimate of their rent and personal estates, and then taxed them according to certain rates, prescribed by a law. After the assessment was returned to the High Sheriff, and approved by the Governour, the Constables received warrants for levying the taxes by distress and sale.

† Some are of opinion that the second Patent was unnecessary, the Duke being revested *per post liminium.* This matter has been often disputed in the ejectments between the N. Jersey Proprietors and the Elizabeth Town Patentees. In New-York the Right of Postliminy was disregarded, and perhaps unknown; for there are many instances, especially on Long Island, of new grants from Sir Edmond Andross, for lands patented under Nicolls and Lovelace, by which the quit-rents have been artfully enlarged.

Dutch commodores, he struck his flag, even before the enemy were in sight of the garrison, the Fort being in a condition, and the men desirous, to fight.

VI. And lastly, that he treacherously caused the Fort gates to be opened, and cowardly and safely let in the enemy, yielding the garrison without Articles.

This scandalous charge, which Manning on his trial confessed to be true, is less surprising, than the lenity of the sentence pronounced against him. It was this, that though he deserved death, yet because he had since the surrender, been in England, and seen the King and the Duke, it was adjudged that his sword should be broke over his head in publick, before the City Hall, and himself rendered incapable of wearing a sword, and of serving his Majesty for the future, in any publick trust in the government.

This light censure, is however no proof, that Sir Edmond was a man of a merciful disposition; the historians of New-England, where he was afterwards Governour, justly transmit him to posterity, under the odious character of a sycophantic tool to the Duke, and an arbitrary tyrant over the people commited to his care. He knew no law, but the will of his master, and Kirk and Jefferies were not fitter instruments than he to execute the despotic projects of James II.[7]

In the year 1675, Nicholas Renslaer, a Dutch clergyman arrived here. He claimed the Manor of Renslaerwick, and was recommended by the Duke to Sir Edmond Andross for a living in one of the churches at New-York, or Albany, probably to serve the Popish cause.* Niewenhyt, minister of the church at Albany, disputed his right to administer the sacraments, because he had received an Episcopal ordination, and was not approved by the Classis of Amsterdam, to which the Dutch churches here hold themselves subordinate. In this controversy

---

* Another reason is assigned for the favour he met with from the Crown. It is said, that while Charles II was in exile, he predicted the day of his restoration. The people of Albany had a high opinion of his prophetick spirit, and many strange tales about him still prevail there. The parson made nothing of his claim, the Manor being afterwards granted, by Colonel Dongan to Killian Van Renslaer, a distant relation. This extensive tract, by the Dutch called a colony, is an oblong extending 24 miles upon Hudson's River, and as many on each side. The Patent of Confirmation was issued by special direction from the King, and is the most liberal in the privileges it grants of any one in the province.

the Governour took the part of Renslaer, and accordingly summoned Niewenhyt before him, to answer for his conduct. This minister was treated with such singular contempt, and so frequently harassed, by fruitless and expensive attendances before the Council, that the dispute became interesting, and the greater part of the people resented the usage he met with. Hence we find, that the magistrates of Albany, soon after imprisoned Renslaer, for several dubious words (as they are called in the record) delivered in a sermon. The Governour, on the other hand, ordered him to be released, and summoned the magistrates to attend him at New-York; warrants were then issued to compel them to give security in £5000 each, to make out good cause for confining the minister. Leisler, who was one of them, refused to comply with the warrant, and was thrown into Jail. Sir Edmond, fearful that a great party would rise up against him, was at last compelled to discontinue his ecclesiastical jurisdiction, and to refer the controversy to the determination of the Consistory of the Dutch Church at Albany. It is perhaps not improbable, that these popish measures, sowed the seeds of that aversion to the Duke's Government, which afterwards produced those violent convulsions in the Province under Leisler, at the time of the revolution, in favour of the Prince of Orange.

If Sir Edmond Andross's administration at New-York, appears to be less exceptionable, than while he commanded at Boston, it was through want of more opportunities to shew himself in his true light. The main course of his publick proceedings, during his continuance in the province, was spent in the ordinary acts of government, which then principally consisted in passing grants to the subject, and presiding in The Court of Assize, established by Colonel Lovelace. The publick exigencies were now in part supplied by a kind of benevolence; the badge of bad times! This appears in an entry on the records, of a letter of May the 5th, 1676, from Governour Andross, to several towns on Long Island, desiring to know, what sums they would contribute towards the war. Near the close of his administration, he thought proper to quarrel with Philip Carteret, who in 1680, exercised the government of East Jersey, under a Commission from Sir George Carteret, dated the 31st of July, 1675. Andross disputed his right, and seized and brought him prisoner to New-York; for which it is said he lost his own government, but whoever considers that Sir Edmond was immediately prefered to be Governour of Boston, will rather believe, that the Duke superseded him for some other reasons.

Before I proceed to the succeeding administration, in which our Indian Affairs began to have a powerful influence upon the publick measures, it may not be improper to present the reader with a summary view of the history and character of the Five Nations.* These, of all those innumerable tribes of savages, which inhabit the northern part of America, are of most importance to us and the French, both on account of their vicinity and warlike disposition. Before the late incorporation of the Tuscaroras, a people driven by the inhabitants of Carolina from the frontiers of Virginia, they consisted of five confederate cantons.† What in particular gave rise to this league, and when it took place, are questions which neither the natives, nor Europeans, pretend to answer. Each of these nations is divided into three Families, or Clans, of different ranks, bearing for their arms, and being distinguished by the names of, the Tortoise, the Bear, and the Wolf.‡

No people in the world perhaps have higher notions than these Indians of military glory. All the surrounding nations have felt the effects of their prowess; and many not only became their tributaries, but were so subjugated to their power, that without their consent, they durst not commence either peace or war.

Though a regular police for the preservation of harmony within, and the defence of the state against invasions from without, is not to be expected from the people of whom I am now writing, yet perhaps, they have paid more attention to it than is generally allowed. Their government is suited to their condition. A people whose riches consist not so much in abundance, as in a freedom from want;§ who are circumscribed by no

* By the Dutch called Maquaas, by the French Iroquois, and by us, Five Nations, Six Nations, and lately the Confederates. They are greatly diminished, and consist now only of about twelve hundred fighting men.

† The Tuscaroras were received upon a supposition, that they were originally of the same stock with the Five Nations, because there is some similitude between their languages.

‡ Their Instruments of Conveyances are signed by signatures, which they make with a pen, representing these animals.

§ An Indian, in answer to his question, What the white People meant by Covetousness? was told by another, that it signified, a Desire of more than a Man had need of. "That's strange!" said the querist.

boundaries, who live by hunting, and not by agriculture, must always be free, and therefore subject to no other authority, than such as consists with the liberty necessarily arising from their circumstances. All their affairs, whether respecting peace or war, are under the direction of their sachems, or chief men. Great exploits and publick virtue procure the esteem of a people, and qualify a man to advise in council, and execute the plan concerted for the advantage of his country: thus whoever appears to the Indians in this advantageous light, commences a sachem without any other ceremony.

As there is no other way of arriving at this dignity, so it ceases, unless an uniform zeal and activity for the common good, is uninterruptedly continued. Some have thought it hereditary, but that is a mistake. The son is indeed, respected for his father's services, but without personal merit, he can never share in the government; which were it otherwise, must sink into perfect disgrace. The children of such as are distinguished for their patriotism, moved by the consideration of their birth, and the perpetual incitements to virtue constantly inculcated into them, imitate their father's exploits, and thus attain to the same honours and influence; which accounts for the opinion that the title and power of sachem is hereditary.

Each of these republicks has its own particular chiefs, who hear and determine all complaints in council, and though they have no officers for the execution of justice, yet their decrees are always obeyed, from the general reproach that would follow a contempt of their advice. The condition of this people exempts them from factions, the common disease of popular governments. It is impossible to gain a party amongst them by indirect means; for no man has either honour, riches, or power to bestow.*

All affairs which concern the general interest are determined in a great assembly of the chiefs of each canton, usually held at Onondaga, the center of their country. Upon emergencies

---

* The learned and judicious author of *The Spirit of Laws*, speaking of a people who have a fixed property in lands, observes, "That if a Chief would deprive them of their Liberty, they would immediately go and seek it under another, or retire into the Woods, and live there with their Families." The Five Nations can never be enslaved, till they grow rich by agriculture and commerce. Property is the most permanent basis of power. The authority of a sachem depending only upon his reputation for wisdom and courage, must be weak and precarious, and therefore safe to the people.

they act separately, but nothing can bind the league but the voice of the general convention.

The French, upon the maxim, *divide & impera*, have tried all possible means to divide these republicks, and sometimes have even sown great jealousies amongst them. In consequence of this plan, they have seduced many families to withdraw to Canada, and there settled them in regular towns, under the command of a fort, and the tuition of missionaries.

The manners of these savages are as simple as their government. Their houses are a few crotched stakes thrust into the ground, and over-laid with bark. A fire is kindled in the middle, and an aperture left at the top for the conveyance of the smoke. Whenever a considerable number of those huts are collected, they have a castle, as it is called, consisting of a square without bastions, surrounded with pallisadoes. They have no other fortification; and this is only designed as an asylum for their old men, their wives and children, while the rest are gone out to war. They live almost entirely without care. While the women, or squaws cultivate a little spot of ground for corn, the men employ themselves in hunting. As to clothes, they use a blanket girt at the waist, and thrown loosely over their shoulders; some of their women indeed have, besides this, a sort of petticoat, and a few of their men wear shirts; but the greater part of them are generally half naked. In winter, their legs are covered with stockings of blanket, and their feet with socks of deer skin. Many of them are fond of ornaments, and their taste is very singular. I have seen rings affixed, not only to their ears, but their noses. Bracelets of silver and brass round their wrists, are very common. The women plait their hair, and tie it up behind in a bag, perhaps in imitation of the French beaus in Canada. Though the Indians are capable of sustaining great hardships, yet they cannot endure much labour, being rather fleet, than strong. Their men are taller than the Europeans, rarely corpulent, always beardless,\* streight limbed, of a tawny complection, and black uncurled hair. In their food they have no manner of delicacy, for though venison is their ordinary diet, yet some times they eat dogs, bears, and even snakes. Their cookery is of two kinds, boiled or roasted; to perform the latter, the meat is penetrated by a short sharp stick set in

---

\* Because they pluck out the hairs. The French writers, who say they have naturally no beards, are mistaken; and the reasons they assign for it are ridiculous.

the ground, inclining towards the fire, and turned as occasion requires. They are hospitable to strangers, though few Europeans would relish their highest favours of this kind, for they are very nasty both in their garments and food. Every man has his own wife, whom he takes and leaves at pleasure: a plurality, however, at the same time, is by no means admitted amongst them. They have been generally commended for their chastity, but I am informed by good authority, that they are very lascivious, and that the women, to avoid reproach, frequently destroy the foetus in the womb. They are so perfectly free, that unless their children, who generally assist the mother, may be called servants, they have none. The men frequently associate themselves for conversation, by which means they not only preserve the remembrance of their wars, and treaties, but diffuse among their youths, incitements to military glory, as well as instruction in all the subtilties of war.

Since they became acquainted with the Europeans, their warlike apparatus is a musket, hatchet,* and a long knife. Their boys still accustom themselves to bows and arrows, and are so dextrous in the use of them, that a lad of sixteen, will strike an English shilling five times in ten at twelve or fourteen yards distance. Their men are excellent marksmen, both with the gun and hatchet; their dexterity at the latter is very extraordinary, for they rarely miss the object, though at a considerable distance. The hatchet in the flight perpetually turns round, and yet always strikes the mark with the edge.

Before they go out, they have a feast upon dog's flesh, and a great war dance. At these, the warriours, who are frightfully painted with vermillion, rise up and sing their own exploits, or those of their ancestors, and thereby kindle a military enthusiasm in the whole company. The day after the dance, they march out a few miles in a row, observing a profound silence. The procession being ended, they strip the bark from a large oak, and paint the design of their expedition on the naked trunk. The figure of a canoe, with the number of men in it, determines the strength of their party; and by a deer, a fox, or some other emblem painted at the head of it, we discover against what nation they are gone out.

The Five Nations being devoted to war, every art is contrived

---

* Hence, to take up the hatchet, is with them a phrase signifying to declare war; as on the contrary to bury it, denotes the establishment of a peace.

to diffuse a military spirit through the whole body of their people. The ceremonies attending the return of a party seem calculated in particular for that purpose. The day before they enter the village, two heralds advance, and at a small distance set up a yell, which by its modulation intimates either good or bad news. If the former, the village is alarmed, and an entertainment provided for the conquerours, who in the mean time approach in sight: one of them bears the scalps stretched over a bow, and elevated upon a long pole. The boldest man in the town comes out, and receives it, and instantly flies to the hut where the rest are collected. If he is overtaken, he is beaten unmercifully; but if he out-runs the pursuer, he participates in the honour of the victors, who at their first entrance receive no compliments, nor speak a single word till the end of the feast. Their parents, wives, and children then are admited, and treat them with the profoundest respect. After these salutations, one of the conquerours is appointed to relate the whole adventure, to which the rest attentively listen, without asking a question, and the whole concludes with a savage dance.

The Indians never fight in the field, or upon equal terms, but always sculk and attack, by surprise, in small parties, meeting every night at a place of rendezvous. Scarce any enemy can escape them, for by the disposition of the grass and leaves, they follow his tract with great speed any where but over a rock. Their barbarity is shocking to human nature. Women and children they generally kill and scalp, because they would retard their progress, but the men they carry into captivity. If any woman has lost a relation, and inclines to receive the prisoner in his stead, he not only escapes a series of the most inhuman tortures, and death itself, but enjoys every immunity they can bestow, and is esteemed a member of the family, into which he is adopted. To part with him would be the most ignominious conduct, and considered as selling the blood of the deceased; and for this reason it is not without the greatest difficulty, that a captive is redeemed.

When the Indians incline to peace, a messenger is sent to the enemy with a pipe, the bowl of which is made of soft, red, marble; and a long reed beautifully painted, and adorned with the gay plumage of birds, forms the stem. This is his infallible protection from any assault on the way. The envoy makes his proposals to the enemy, who if they approve them, ratify the preliminaries to the peace, by smoking through the pipe, and from that instant, a general cessation of arms takes place. The French call it a Calumet. It is used, as far as I can learn, by all the Indian nations upon the continent. The rights of it are esteemed sacred, and have been only invaded by the Flat Heads; in just indignation for which, the Confederates maintained a war with them for near thirty years.

As to the language of the Five Nations, the best account I have had of it, is contained in a letter from the Reverend Mr. Spencer, who resided amongst them in the Year 1748, being then a missionary from the Scotch Society for propogating Christian Knowledge. He writes thus:

SIR,
Though I was very desirous of learning the *Indian* Tongue, yet through my short Residence at *Onoughquage,* and the surly Disposition of my Interpreter, I confess my Proficiency was not great.

Except the *Tuscaroras,* all the *Six Nations* speak a language radically the same. It is very masculine and sonorous, abounding with Gutturals and strong Aspirations, but without Labials. Its solemn grave Tone is owing to the generosity of its Feet, as you will observe in the following Translation of the *Lord's Prayer,* in which I have distinguished the Time of every Syllable by the common Marks used in Prosody.*

Soungwauneha, caurounkyawga, tehseetaroan, sauhsone-yousta, esa, sawaneyou, Okettauhsela, ehneauwoung, na, caurounkyawga, nughwonshauga, neattewehnesalauga, taugwaunautoronoantoughsick, toantaugweleewheyoustaung, cheneeyeut, chaquatautalehwheyoustaunna, toughsau, taugwaussareneh, tawautottenaugaloughtoungga, nasawne, sacheautaugwass, coantehsalohaunzaickaw, esa, sawauneyou, esa, sashautzta, esa, soungwasoung, chenneauhaungwa, auwen.

The extraordinary Length of *Indian* Words, and the guttural Aspirations, necessary in pronouncing them, render the Speech extremely rough and difficult. The Verbs never change in their Terminations, as in *Latin, Greek,* and *Hebrew,* but all their Variations are prefixed. Besides the singular and plural,

---

* If we had a good dictionary, marking the quantity as well as emphasis of every syllable in the English language, it would conduce to an accuracy and uniformity of pronunciation. The dignity of style, so far as the ear is concerned, consists principally in generous feet; and perhaps it may be a just remark that no sentence, unless in a dialogue, ends well without a full sound. Gordon and Fordyce rarely swerve from this rule, and Mr. Mason, an ingenious author, has lately written with great applause, on this attribute of style.

they have also the dual Number. A strange Transposition of Syllables of different Words, *Euphoniae gratiâ,* is very common in the *Indian* Tongue, of which I will give an Instance. OGILLA signifies *Fire,* and CAWAUNNA *great,* but instead of joining the Adjective and Substantive to say *great Fire,* CAWAUNNA OGILLA, both Words would be blended into this one, CO-GILLA-WAUNNA. The Dialect of the *Oneydas,* is softer than that of the other Nations; and the Reason is, because they have more Vowels, and often supply the Place of harsh Letters with Liquids Instead of R, they always use L: *Rebecca* would be pronounced *Lequecca.*

The art of publick Speaking is in high esteem among the Indians, and much studied. They are extremely fond of method, and displeased with an irregular harangue, because it is difficult to be remembered. When they answer, they repeat the whole, reducing it into strict order. Their speeches are short, and the sense conveyed in strong metaphors. In conversation they are sprightly, but solemn and serious in their messages relating to publick affairs. Their speakers deliver themselves with surprising force and great propriety of gesture. The fierceness of their countenances, the flowing blanket, elevated tone, naked arm and erect stature, with a half circle of auditors seated on the ground, and in the open air, cannot but impress upon the mind, a lively idea of the ancient orators of Greece and Rome.

At the close of every important part of the speech, ratifying an old covenant, or creating a new one, a belt is generally given, to perpetuate the remembrance of the transaction. These belts are about four inches wide, and thirty in length. They consist of strings of conque shell beads fastened together.*

With respect to religion, the Indians may be said to be under the thickest gloom of ignorance. If they have any, which is much to be questioned, those who affirm it, will find it difficult to tell us wherein it consists. They have neither priest nor temple, sacrifice nor altar. Some traces indeed appear, of the original law writen upon their hearts; but they have no system of doctrines, nor any rites and modes of publick worship. They are sunk, unspeakably beneath the polite pagans of antiquity. Some confused notions, indeed, of beings superiour to themselves,

* Those beads which pass for money, are called by the Indians, Wampum, and by the Dutch, Sewant; six beads were formerly valued at a Styver. There are always several poor families at Albany, who support themselves by coining this cash for the traders.

they have, but of the deity and his natural and moral perfections, no proper or tolerable conceptions; and of his general and particular providence they know nothing. They profess no obligations to him, nor acknowledge their dependence upon him. Some of them, it is said, are of opinion, that there are two distinct, powerful beings, one able to help, the other to do them harm. The latter they venerate most, and some alledge, that they address him by a kind of prayer. Though there are no publick monuments of idolatry to be seen in their country, yet the missionaries have discovered coarse imagery in wooden trinkets, in the hands of their jugglers, which the converts deliver up as detestable. The sight of them would remind a man of letters, of the *Lares* and *Penates* of the ancients, but no certain judgement can be drawn of their use. The Indians sometimes assemble in large numbers, and retire far into the wilderness, where they eat and drink in a profuse manner. These conventions are called Kenticoys. Some esteem them to be debauched revels or Bacchanalia; but those, who have privately followed them into these recesses, give such accounts of their conduct, as naturally lead one to imagine, that they pay a joint homage and supplication to some invisible being. If we suppose they have a religion, it is worse than none, and raises in the generous mind, most melancholy ideas of their depraved condition. Little has been done to illuminate these dark corners of the earth, with the light of the gospel. The French priests boast indeed of their converts, but they have made more proselytes to politicks than religion. Queen Anne sent a missionary amongst them, and gave him an appointment out of the Privy Purse. He was a man of a good life, but slow parts, and his success very inconsiderable. The Reverend Mr. Barclay afterwards resided among the Mohawks, but no suitable provision being made for an interpreter, he was obliged to break up the mission. If the English Society for propagating the Gospel, that truly venerable body, instead of maintaining missionaries in rich Christian congregations along the Continent, expended half the amount of their annual contributions on evangelists among the heathen, besides the unspeakable religious benefits that would, it is to be hoped, accrue to the natives, such a proceeding would conduce greatly to the safety of our colonies, and his Majesty's service. Much has been written upon this subject in America;* and why noth-

---

* See Mr. Hobart's Letters to the Episcopalians in New-England. The account of the Scotch Mission at Stockbridge. Douglass's Summary, &c.

ing to purpose has yet been attempted in England, towards so laudable a design, can only be attributed to the amazing falsehoods and misrepresentations, by which some of the missionaries have long imposed upon benevolent minds in Great Britain.*

As to the history of the Five Nations, before their acquaintance with the Europeans, it is wrapt up in the darkness of antiquity. It is said that their first residence was in the country about Montreal; and that the superiour strength of the Adirondacks, whom the French call Algonquins, drove them into their present possessions, lying on the South side of the Mohawks River, and the great Lake Ontario.† Towards the close of those

* This is notorious to all who give themselves the trouble of perusing the abstracts of their accounts published in England. It would be a very agreeable office to me, on this occasion, to distinguish the innocent from the guilty, but that such a task would infallibly raise up a host of enemies. Many of the missionaries are men of learning and exemplary morals. These in America are known and honoured, and cannot be prejudiced by an indiscriminate censure. Their joining in a representation for distinguishing the delinquents, who are a disgrace to the cloth, will serve as a full vindication of themselves to the society. Mr. Ogilvie is, I believe, the only person now employed by that charitable corporation among the Indians, and the greatest part even of his charge is in the city of Albany. All the Scotch missionaries are among the heathen, and their success has been sufficient to encourage any future attempts. There is a regular society of Indian converts in New Jersey; and it is worthy of remark, that not one of them has apostatized into heathenism. Some of them have made such proficiencies in practical religion, as ought to shame many of us, who boast the illuminating aids of our native Christianity. Not one of these Indians has been concerned in those barbarous irruptions, which have lately deluged the frontiers of the South-western Provinces, with blood of several hundred innocents of every age and sex. At the commencement of these ravages, they flew into the settlements, and put themselves under the protection of the government. These Indians no sooner became Christians, than they openly professed their loyalty to King George; and therefore to contribute to their conversion, was as truly politick, as nobly Christian. Those colonies which have done most for this charitable design, have escaped best from the late distressing calamities. Of all the missionaries, Mr. David Brainerd, who recovered these Indians from the darkness of paganism, was most successful. He died the 9th of October, 1747, a victim to his extreme mortification and inextinguishable zeal, for the prosperity of his mission. Those who are curious to enquire particularly into the effects of his indefatigable industry, may have recourse to his Journal, published at Philadelphia, by the American Correspondents of the Scotch Society, in whose service he was employed. Dr. Douglass, ever ready to do honour to his native country, after remarking that this self-denying clergyman rode about 4000 miles, in the year 1744, with an air of approbation, asks, "Is there any Missionary, from any of the Societies, for propagating the Gospel in Foreign Parts, that has reported the like?"

† Charlevoix, in partiality to the French, limits the country of

disputes, which continued for a long series of years, the Confederates gained advantages over the Adirondacks, and struck a general terrour into all the other Indians. The Harons on the North Side of the Lake Erie, and the Cat Indians on the South Side, were totally conquered and dispersed. The French, who settled Canada in 1603, took umbrage at their success, and began a war with them which had well nigh ruined the new colony. In Autumn 1665, Mr. Courcelles, the Governour,[8] sent out a party against the Mohawks. Through ignorance of the country, and the want of snow-shoes, they were almost perished, when they fell in with Schencetady. And even there the Indians would have sacrificed them to their barbarous rage, had not Corlear, a Dutchman, interposed to protect them.[9] For this seasonable hospitality, the French governour invited him to Canada, but he was unfortunately drowned in his passage through the Lake Champlain. It is in honour of this man, who was a favourite of the Indians, that the Governours of New-York, in all their Treaties are addressed by the name of Corlear. Twenty light companies of foot, and the whole militia of Canada, marched the next spring into the country of the Mohawks; but their success was vastly unequal to the charge and labour of such a tedious march of 700 miles, through an uncultivated desert; for the Indians, on their approach, retired into the woods, leaving behind them some old sachems, who prefered death to life, to glut the fury of their enemies. The emptiness of this parade on the one hand, and the Indian fearfulness of fire arms on the other, brought about a Peace in 1667, which continued for several years after. In this interval, both the English and French cultivated a trade with the natives very profitable to both nations. The latter, however, were most politick and vigorous, and filled the Indian country with their missionaries.

---

the Five Nations, on the North, to the 44th degree of latitude; according to which, all the country on the North side of the Lake Ontario, and the River issuing thence to Montreal, together with a considerable tract of land on the South side of that river, belongs to the French. Hennepin, a Recollect Friar, has more Regard to Truth than the Jesuit; for he tells us in Effect, that the Iroquois possessed the lands on the North, as well as the South side of the Lake, and mentions several of their villages in 1679, viz. Tejajahon, Kente, and Ganneousse. The map in his book agrees with the text. Charlevoix is at variance with his geographer; for Mr. Bellin, besides laying down these towns in the map, contained in the fifth Volume, writes on the North side of the protraction of Lake Ontario, *Les Iroquois du Nord*.

The Sieur Perot, the very year in which the peace was concluded, travelled above 1200 miles westward, making proselytes of the Indians every where to the French interest. Courcelles appears to have been a man of art and industry.[10] He took every measure in his power for the defence of Canada. To prevent the irruptions of the Five Nations, by the way of Lake Champlain, he built several forts in 1665, between that and the mouth of the River Sorel. In 1672, just before his return to France, under pretence of treating with the Indians more commodiously, but in reality, as Charlevoix expresses it, "to bridle them," he obtained their leave to erect a Fort at Cadaracqui, or Lake Ontario, which Count Frontenac, his successour, completed the following spring, and called after his own name.* The command of it was afterwards given to Mr. De la Salle, who, in 1678, rebuilt it with stone. This enterprising person, the same year, launched a bark of ten tons into the Lake Ontario, and another of sixty tons, the year after into Lake Erie; about which time he inclosed with pallisadoes, a little spot at Niagara.[11]

Though the Duke of York had preferred Colonel Thomas Dongan to the government of this Province on the 30th of September, 1682, he did not arrive here till the 27th of August, in the following year. He was a man of integrity, moderation, and genteel manners, and though a professed Papist, may be classed among the best of our Governours.[12]

The people, who had been formerly ruled at the will of the Duke's deputies, began their first participation in the legislative power under Colonel Dongan, for shortly after his arrival, he issued orders to the sheriffs, to summon the freeholders for choosing representatives, to meet him in Assembly on the 17th of October, 1683. Nothing could be more agreeable to the people, who, whether Dutch or English, were born the subjects of a free state; nor indeed, was the change, of less advantage to the Duke, than to the inhabitants. For such a general disgust had prevailed, and in particular in Long Island, against the old form which Colonel Nicolls had introduced, as threatened the total subversion of the publick tranquility. Colonel Dongan saw the disaffection of the people at the East end of the Island, for he landed there on his first arrival in the country; and to extin-

* In May 1721, it was a square with four bastions, built of stone, being a quarter of a French league in circumference; before it, are many small islands, and a good harbour, and behind it a morass. Charlevoix.

guish the fire of discontent, then impatient to burst out, gave
them his promise, that no laws or rates for the future should be
imposed, but by a general Assembly. Doubtless, this alteration
was agreeable to the Duke's orders, who had been strongly importuned for it,* as well as acceptable to the people, for they sent
him soon after an address, expressing the highest sense of gratitude, for so beneficial a change in the government.[13] It would
have been impossible for him much longer to have maintained
the old model over free subjects, who had just before formed
themselves into a colony for the enjoyment of their liberties,
and had even already sollicited the protection of the colony of
Connecticut, from whence the greatest part of them came. Disputes relating to the limits of certain townships at the East end
of Long Island, sowed the seeds of enmity against Dongan, so
deeply in the hearts of many who were concerned in them, that
their representation to Connecticut, at the Revolution, contains
the bitterest invectives against him.

Dongan surpassed all his predecessours, in a due attention to
our affairs with the Indians, by whom he was highly esteemed.
It must be remembered to his honour, that though he was ordered by the Duke, to encourage the French priests, who were
come to reside among the natives, under pretence of advancing
the Popish cause, but in reality to gain them over to a French
interest; yet he forbid the Five Nations to entertain them. The
Jesuits, however, had no small success. Their proselytes are
called Praying Indians, or Caghnuagaes, and reside now in
Canada, at the Fall of St. Lewis, opposite to Montreal. This village was begun in 1671, and consists of such of the Five Nations, as have formerly been drawn away by the intrigues of
the French priests, in the times of Lovelace and Andross, who
seem to have paid no attention to our Indians affairs.† It was
owing to the instigation also of these priests, that the Five Nations about this time, commited hostilities on the back parts of
Maryland and Virginia, which occasioned a grand convention at

* The Petition to his Royal Highness was drawn by the Council,
the Aldermen of New-York, and the Justices of the Peace at the
Court of Assize, the 29th of June, 1681. I have seen a copy in the
hands of Lewis Morris, Esq; It contains many severe reflections upon
the tyranny of Sir Edmond Andross.

† Of late some others of the Confederates have been allured to
settle at Oswegatchi, called by the French, la Gallette, near 50
miles below Frontenac. General Shirley's emissaries from Oswego
in 1755, prevailed with several of these families to return to their
old habitations.

Albany, in the year 1684. Lord Howard of Effingham, the Governour of Virginia, was present, and made a covenant with them for preventing further depredations, towards the accomplishment of which, Colonel Dongan was very instrumental,\* Doctor Colden has published this Treaty at large, but as it has no immediate connection with the affairs of this Province, I beg leave to refer the reader for a full account of it, to his History of the Five Nations.

While Lord Howard was at Albany, a messenger from De la Barre, then Governour of Canada, arrived there, complaining of the Senneca Indians, for interrupting the French in their trade with the more distant Indians, commonly included among us by the general name of the Far Nations.† Colonel Dongan, to whom the message was sent, communicated it to the Sennecas, who admited the charge, but justified their conduct, alledging, that the French supplied arms and ammunition to the Twightwies,‡ with whom they were then at war. De la Barre, at the same time, meditating nothing less than the total destruction of the Five Nations, proceeded with an army of 1700 men to the Lake Ontario. Mighty preparations were made to obtain the desired success: fresh troops were imported from France, and a letter procured from the Duke of York to Colonel Dongan, commanding him to lay no obstacles in the way. The officers posted in the out Forts, even as far as Michilimackinac, were ordered to rendezvous at Niagara, with all the Western Indians they could engage. Dongan, regardless of the Duke's orders, apprised the Indians of the French designs, and promised to assist them. After six weeks delay at Fort Frontenac, during which time a great sickness, occasioned by bad provisions, broke out in the French Army, De la Barre found it necessary to conclude the campaign with a treaty, for which purpose he crossed the lake, and came to the place which, from the distress of his army, was called la Famine. Dongan sent an interpreter among the Indians, by all means to prevent them from attending the Treaty. The Mohawks and Sennecas accordingly refused to meet De la Barre, but the Oneydoes, Onondagas, and Cayugas, influenced by the missionaries, were unwilling to hear the interpreter, ex-

---

\* This Covenant was ratified in 1685, and at several times since.

† By the Far Nations are meant, all those numerous tribes inhabiting the countries on both sides of the Lakes Huron and Erie, Westward, as far as the Missisippi, and the Southern Country along the Banks of the Ohio, and its Branches.

‡ By the French called Miamies.

cept before the priests, one La Main, and three other Frenchmen, and afterwards waited upon the French Governour. Two
days after their arrival in the camp, Monsieur De la Barre ad-
dessing himself to Garrangula, an Onondaga chief, made the
following speech, the Indians, and French officers at the same
time forming a circle round about him.

The King, my Master, being informed, that the *Five Na-*
*tions* have often infringed the Peace, has ordered me to come
hither with a Guard, and to send *Ohguesse* to the *Onondagas*,
to bring the chief *Sachems* to my Camp. The Intention of the
Great King is, that You and I may smoke the Calumet of
Peace together; but on this Condition, that you promise me,
in the Name of the *Senekas, Cayugas, Onondagas,* and *Mo-*
*hawks,* to give entire Satisfaction and Reparation to his Subjects, and for the future, never to molest them.

The *Senekas, Cayugas, Onondagas, Oneydoes,* and *Mo-*
*hawks,* have robbed and abused all the Traders that were
passing to the *Illinois* and *Miamies,* and other *Indian* Nations,
the Children of my King. They have acted, on these Occasions, contrary to the Treaty of Peace with my Predecessor. I
am ordered, therefore, to demand Satisfaction, and to tell
them, that in Case of Refusal, or their plundering us any
more, that I have express Orders to declare War. This Belt
confirms my Words. The Warriours of the *Five Nations* have
conducted the *English* into the Lakes, which belong to the
King, my Master, and brought the *English* among the Nations
that are his Children, to destroy the Trade of his Subjects, and
to withdraw these Nations from him. They have carried the
*English* thither, notwithstanding the Prohibition of the late
Governour of *New-York,* who foresaw the Risque that both
they and you would run. I am willing to forget those Things,
but if ever the like shall happen for the future, I have express
Orders to declare War against you. This Belt confirms my
Words. Your Warriours have made several barbarous Incursions on the *Illinois* and *Umameis;* they have massacred Men,
Women, and Children, and have made many of these Nations
Prisoners, who thought themselves safe in their Villages in
Time of Peace; these People, who are my King's Children,
must not be your Slaves; you must give them their Liberty,
and send them back into their own Country. If the *Five Na-*
*tions* shall refuse to do this, I have express Orders to declare
War against them. This Belt confirms my Words.

This is what I have to say to *Garrangula,* that he may carry
to the *Senekas, Onondagas, Oneydoes, Cayugas,* and *Mo-*

*hawks,* the Declaration which the King, my Master, has commanded me to make. He doth not wish them to force him to send a great Army to *Cadarackui* Fort, to begin a War, which must be fatal to them. He would be sorry that this Fort, *that was the Work of Peace,* should become the Prison of your Warriours. We must endeavour, on both Sides, to prevent such Misfortunes. The *French,* who are the Brethren and Friends of the *Five Nations,* will never trouble their Repose, provided that the Satisfaction which I demand, be given; and that the Treaties of Peace be hereafter observed. I shall be extremely grieved, if my Words do not produce the Effect, which I expect from them; for then I shall be obliged to join with the Governour of *New-York,* who is commanded by his Master, to assist me, and burn the Castles of the *Five Nations,* and destroy you. This Belt confirms my Words.

Garrangula heard these threats with contempt, because he had learnt the distressed state of the French Army, and knew that they were incapable of executing the designs with which they set out; and therefore, after walking five or six times round the circle, he answered the French Governour, who sat in an Elbow chair, in the following strain:

YONNONDIO,

I honour you, and the Warriours that are with me likewise honour you. Your Interpreter has finished your Speech; I now begin mine. My Words make haste to reach your Ears; hearken to them.

Yonnondio, you must have believed, when you left *Quebeck,* that the Sun had burnt up all the Forests, which render our Country inaccessible to the *French,* or that the Lakes had so far overflown the Banks, that they had surrounded our Castles, and that it was impossible for us to get out of them. Yes, Yonnondio, surely you must have dreamt so, and the Curiosity of seeing so great a Wonder, has brought you so far. Now you are undeceived, since that I and the Warriours here present, are come to assure you, that the *Senekas, Cayugas, Onondagas, Oneydoes,* and *Mohawks,* are yet alive. I thank you, in their Name, for bringing back into their Country the Calumet, which your Predecessor received from their Hands. It was happy for you, that you left under Ground that murdering Hatchet that has been so often died in the Blood of the *French.* Hear, Yonnondio, I do not sleep, I have my Eyes open, and the Sun, which enlightens me, discovers to me a great Captain at

the Head of a Company of Soldiers, who speaks as if he
were dreaming. He says, that he only came to the Lake to
smoke on the great Calumet with the *Onondagas.* But
*Garrangula* says, that he sees the contrary, that it was to
knock them on the Head, if Sickness had not weakened the
Arms of the *French.*

I see *Yonnondio* raving in a Camp of sick Men, whose
Lives the great Spirit has saved, by inflicting this Sickness on
them. Hear, *Yonnondio,* our Women had taken their Clubs,
our Children and old Men had carried their Bows and
Arrows into the Heart of your Camp, if our Warriors had
not disarmed them, and kept them back, when your
Messenger, *Ohguesse,* came to our Castles. It is done, and
I have said it. Hear, *Yonnondio,* we plundered none of the
*French,* but those that carried Guns, Powder, and Ball to
the *Twightwies* and *Chictaghicks,* because those Arms might
have cost us our Lives. Herein we follow the Example of
the Jesuits, who stave all the Caggs of Rum brought to our
Castles, lest the drunken *Indians* should knock them on
the Head. Our Warriors have not Beaver enough to pay for
all these Arms, that they have taken, and our old Men
are not afraid of the War. This Belt preserves my Words.

We carried the *English* into our Lakes, to trade there
with the *Utawawas* and *Quatoghies* as the *Adirondacks*
brought the *French* to our Castles, to carry on a Trade, which
the *English* say is theirs. We are born free; we neither
depend on *Yonnondio* nor *Corlear.*

We may go where we please, and carry with us whom
we please, and buy and sell what we please: if your Allies
be your Slaves, use them as such, command them to receive
no other but your People. This Belt preserves my words.

We knocked the *Twightwies* and *Chictaghicks* on the
Head, because they had cut down the Trees of Peace, which
were the Limits of our Country. They have hunted Beavers
on our Lands: they have acted contrary to the Customs
of all *Indians;* for they left none of the Bevers alive, they
killed both male and female. They brought the *Satanas**
into the Country, to take Part with them, after they had
concerted ill Designs against us. We have done less than
either the *English* or *French,* that have usurped the Lands of
so many *Indian* Nations, and chased them from their own
Country. This Belt preserves my words.

Hear, *Yonnondio,* what I say, is the Voice of all the *Five
Nations;* hear what they answer; open your Ears to what

* By the French called Sauounons.

they speak. The *Senekas, Cayugas, Onondagas, Oneydoes,*
and *Mohawks* say, that when they buried the Hatchet
at *Cadarackui* (in the Presence of your Predecessor) in the
Middle of the Fort; they planted the Tree of Peace in the
same Place, to be there carefully preserved, that, in place of
a Retreat for Soldiers, that Fort might be a Rendezvous
for Merchants: that in place of Arms and Ammunition of
War, Bevers and Merchandise should only enter there.

Hear, *Yonnondio,* take care for the future, that so great
a Number of Soldiers as appear there do not choke the
Tree of Peace planted in so small a Fort. It will be a great
Loss, if, after it had so easily taken Root, you should stop its
Growth, and prevent its covering your Country and ours
with its Branches. I assure you, in the Name of the *Five
Nations,* that our Warriors shall dance to the Calumet of
Peace under its Leaves, and shall remain quiet on their
Matts, and shall never dig up the Hatchet, till their Brother
*Yonnondio* or *Corlear* shall either jointly or separately
endeavour to attack the Country, which the great Spirit has
given to our Ancestors. This Belt preserves my Words,
and this other, the Authority which the *Five Nations* have
given me.

Then Garrangula, addressing himself to Monsieur La Main,
said

Take Courage *Ohguesse,* you have Spirit, speak, explain
my Words, forget nothing, tell all that your Brethren and
Friends say to *Yonnondio,* your Governor, by the Mouth of
*Garrangula,* who loves you, and desires you to accept of
this Present of Beaver, and take Part with me in my Feast,
to which I invite you. This Present of Beaver is sent to
*Yonnondio,* on the Part of the *Five Nations.*

Enraged at this bold reply, De la Barre as soon as the Peace
was concluded, retired to Montreal, and ingloriously finished
an expensive campaign, as Doctor Colden observes, in a scold
with an old Indian.[14]

De la Barre was succeeded by the Marquis De Nonville,
Colonel of the Dragoons, who arrived with a reinforcement of
troops in 1685. The Marquis was a man of courage and an
enterprising spirit, and not a little animated by the consideration, that he was sent over to repair the disgrace, which his
predecessour had brought upon the French Colony. The year

after his arrival at Quebec, he wrote a letter to the Minister
in France, recommending the scheme of erecting a stone-fort,
sufficient to contain four or five hundred men, at Niagara, not
only to exclude the English from the lakes, but to command
the fur trade and subdue the Five Nations. Dongan, who was
jealous of his designs, took umbrage at the extraordinary supplies sent to Fort Frontenac, and wrote to the French Governours, signifying that if he attacked the Confederates, he would
consider it, as a breach of the Peace subsisting between the
two Crowns; and to prevent his building a Fort at Niagara, he
protested against it, and claimed the country as dependent
upon the Province. De Nonville, in his answer, denied that he
intended to invade the Five Nations, tho' the necessary preparations for that purpose were then carrying on, and yet Charlevoix commends him for his piety and uprightness, *"egalement
estimable* (says the Jesuit) *pour sa Valeur, sa droiture & sa
Pieté."* Colonel Dongan, who knew the importance of our Indian alliance, placed no confidence in the declarations of the
Marquis, but exerted himself in preparing the Confederates
for a war; and the French authour, just mentioned, does him
honour, while he complains of him as a perpetual obstacle, in
the way of the execution of their schemes. Our allies were
now triumphing in their success over the Chigtaghics, and
mediating a war with the Twightwies, who had disturbed them
in their beaver-hunting. De Nonville, to prevent the interruption of the French trade with the Twightwies, determined to
divert the Five Nations and carry the war into their country.
To that end, in 1687, he collected 2000 troops and 600 Indians
at Montreal, and issued orders to all the officers in the more
westerly country, to meet him with additional succours at Niagara, on an expedition against the Senecas. An English party
under one McGregory, at the same time was gone out to trade
on the Lakes, but the French, notwithstanding the Peace then
subsisting between the two Crowns, intercepted them, seized
their effects, and imprisoned their persons. Monsieur Fonti,
Commandant among the Chictaghics, who was coming to the
General's rendezvous at Niagara, did the like to another English
Party, which he met with in Lake Erie.* The Five Nations, in
the mean time, were preparing to give the French Army a suit-

---

* Both these attacks were open infractions of the Treaty at
Whitehall executed in Nov. 1686; by which it was agreed, that the
Indian trade in America, should be free to the English and French.

able reception. Monsieur Companie, with two or three hundred Canadians in an advanced party, surprised two villages of the Confederates, who at the invitation and on the faith of the French, seated themselves down about eight leagues from Lake Cadarackui or Ontario. To prevent their escape with intelligence to their country men, they were carried to the Fort, and all but thirteen died in torments at the stake, singing with an heroick spirit, in their expiring moments, the perfidy of the French. The rest according to the express orders of the French King, were sent to the galleys in Europe. The Marquis having embarked his whole Army in canoes, set out from the Fort at Cadurackui on the 23rd of June, one half of them passing along the North, and the other on the South side of the Lake; and both arrived the same day at Tirondequait, and shortly after set out on their march towards the chief village of the Sennecas at about seven leagues distance. The main body was composed of the regulars and militia, the front and rear of the Indians and traders. The scouts advanced the second day of their march, as far as the corn of the village, and within pistol-shot of 500 Sennecas, who lay upon their bellies undiscovered. The French, who imagined the enemy were all fled, quickened their march to overtake the women and old men. But no sooner had they reached the foot of a hill, about a mile from the village, than the Sennecas raised the war shout, and in the same instant charged upon the whole army both in the front and rear. Universal confusion ensued. The battalions divided, fired upon each other, and flew into the wood. The Sennecas improved the disorder of the enemy, till they were repulsed by the French Indians. According to Charlevoix's account, which may be justly suspected, the enemy lost but six men, and had twenty wounded in the conflict. Of the Sennecas, he says, sixty were wounded and forty five slain. The Marquis was so much dispirited, that he could not be persuaded to pursue the enemy that day; which gave the Sennecas an opportunity to burn their village and get off. Two old men remained in the castle to receive the general, and regale the barbarity of his Indian allies. After destroying the corn in this and several other villages, the Army retired to the banks of the Lake, and erected a Fort with four bastions on the South-east side of the streights at Niagara, in which they left 100 men, under the command of Le Chevalier de la Troye, with eight months provisions; but these being closely blocked up, all, except seven or eight of them, who were accidentally relieved, perished thro' Famine.* Soon after this expedition, Colonel Dongan met the Five Nations at Albany. To what intent, appears from the speech he made to them on the 5th of August, which I choose to lay before the reader, to shew his vigilance and zeal for the interest of his master, and the common weal of the Province commited to his care.

BRETHREN,

I am very glad to see you here in this House, and am heartily glad that you have sustained no greater Loss by the *French,* tho' I believe it was their Intention to destroy you all, if they could have surprised you in your Castles.

As soon as I heard their Design to war with you, I gave you Notice, and came up hither myself, that I might be ready to give all the Assistance and Advice, that so short a Time would allow me.

I am now about sending a Gentleman to *England,* to the King, my Master, to let him know, *That the* French *have invaded his Territories on this Side of the great Lake,* and warred upon the Brethren *his Subjects.* I therefore would willingly know, whether the Brethren have given the Governor of *Canada* any Provocation or not; and if they have, how, and in what Manner; because I am obliged to give a true Account of this Matter. This Business may cause a War between the King of *England,* and the *French* King, both in *Europe* and here, and therefore I must know the Truth.

I know the Governor of *Canada* dare not enter into the King of *England's* Territories, in a hostile Manner, without Provocation, if he thought the Brethren were the King of *England's* Subjects; but you have, two or three Years ago, made a Covenant-chain with the *French,* contrary to my Command (which I knew could not hold long) being void of itself among the Christians; for as much as Subjects (*as you are*) ought not to treat with any foreign Nation, it not lying in your Power. You have brought this Trouble on

* Nothing can be more perfidious and unjust, than this attack upon our Confederates. The two Crowns had but just concluded a Treaty for the preservation of the Peace: La Hontan, one of the French historians censures De Nonville's conduct, and admits the British title to the command of the Lakes, but Charlevoix blames him, as he does Hennepin, De L'Isle and every other authour, who confesses the truth, to the prejudice of the ambitious claims of the court of France.

yourselves, and, as I believe, this is the only Reason of their falling on you at this Time.

Brethren, I took it very ill, that *after you had put yourselves into the Number of the great King of* England's *Subjects,* you should ever offer to make Peace or War, without my Consent. You know that we can live without you, but you cannot live without us; you never found that I told you a Lie, and I offered you the Assistance you wanted, provided that you would be advised by me; for I know the *French* better than any of you do.

Now since there is a War begun upon you by the Governor of *Canada;* I hope without any Provocation by you given, I desire and command you, that you hearken to no Treaty but by my Advice; which if you follow, you shall have the Benefit of the great Chain of Friendship between the great King of *England,* and the King of *France,* which came out of *England* the other Day, and which I have sent to *Canada* by *Anthony le Junard;* in the mean Time, I will give you such Advice as will be for your Good; and will supply you with such Necessaries as you will have need of.

*1st,* My Advice is, as to what Prisoners of the *French* you shall take, that you draw not their Blood, but bring them home, and keep them to exchange for your People, which they have Prisoners already, or may take hereafter.

*2dly,* That if it be possible, that you can order it so, I would have you take one or two of your wisest Sachems, and one or two of your chief captains of each Nation, to be a Council to manage all Affairs of the War. They, to give Orders to the rest of the Officers what they are to do, that your Designs may be kept private; for after it comes among so many People, it is blazed abroad, and your Designs are often frustrated; and those chief Men should keep a Correspondence with me by a trusty Messenger.

*3dly,* The great Matter under Consideration with the Brethren is, how to strengthen themselves, and weaken their Enemy. My Opinion is, that the Brethren should send Messengers to the *Utawawas, Twichtwies,* and the farther *Indians,* and to send back likewise some of the Prisoners of these Nations, if you have any left, to bury the Hatchet, and to make a Covenant-Chain, that they may put away all the *French* that are among them, and that you will open a Path for them this Way (they being the King of England's Subjects likewise, though the *French* have been admitted to trade with them; for all that the *French* have in *Canada,* they had it of the great King of *England*) that, by that Means, they may come hither freely, where they may have

every thing cheaper than among the *French:* that you
and they may join together against the *French*, and make so
firm a League, that whoeever is an Enemy to one, must
be to both.

*4thly*, Another Thing of Concern is, that you ought to
do what you can to open a Path for all the north *Indians* and
*Mahikanders* that are among the *Utawawas* and further
Nations. I will endeavour to do the same to bring them home.
For, they not daring to return home your Way, the *French*
keep them there on purpose to join with the other Nations
against you, for your Destruction, for you know, that one
of them is worse than six of the others; therefore all Means
must be used to bring them home, and use them kindly
as they pass through your country.

*5thly*, My Advice further is, that Messengers go, in behalf
of all the *Five Nations*, to the Christian *Indians* at *Canada*,
to persuade them to come home to their native country.
This will be another great Means to weaken your Enemy;
but if they will not be advised, you know what to do
with them.

*6thly*, I think it very necessary, for the Brethrens Security
and Assistance, and to the endamaging the *French*, to build
a Fort upon the Lake, where I may keep Stores and
Provisions in Case of Necessity; and therefore I would have
the Brethren let me know what Place will be most
convenient for it.

*7thly*, I would not have the Brethren keep their Corn in
their Castles, as I hear the *Onondagas* do, but bury it a great
way in the Woods, where few People may know where it
is, for fear of such an Accident as has happened to
the *Sennekas*.

*8thly*, I have given my Advice in your general Assembly,
by Mr. *Dirk Wessels* and *Akus*, the Interpreter, how you
are to manage your Parties, and how necessary it is to get
Prisoners, to exchange for your own Men that are Prisoners
with the *French*, and I am glad to hear that the Brethren
are so united as Mr. *Dirk Wessels* tells me you are, and
that there was no rotten Members nor *French* Spies
among you.

*9thly*, The Brethren may remember my Advice, which
I sent you this Spring, not to go to *Cadarackui;* if you had,
they would have served you, as they did your People that
came from hunting thither, for I told you that I knew the
*French* better than you did.

*10thly*, There was no Advice or Proposition that I made
to the Brethren all the time that the Priest lived at

*Onondaga,* but what he wrote to *Canada,* as I found by one
of his Letters, which he gave to an *Indian* to carry to
*Canada,* but which was brought hither; therefore, I desire
the Brethren not to receive him, or any *French* Priest
any more, having sent for *English* Priests, with whom you
may be supplied to your Content.

*11thly,* I would have the Brethren look out sharp, for
fear of being surprised. I believe all the Strength of
the *French* will be at their Frontier Places, *viz.* at *Cadarackui*
and *Oniagara,* where they have built a Fort now, and at
*Trois Rivieres, Montreal* and *Chambly.*

*12thly,* Let me put you in mind again, not to make
any Treaties without my Means, which will be more
advantageous for you, than your doing it by yourselves, for
then you will be looked upon *as the King of* England's
*Subjects,* and let me know, from Time to Time, every thing
that is done.

Thus far I have spoken to you relating to the War.

Not long after this interview, a considerable party of Mohawks and Mahikanders, or River Indians, beset Fort Chambly,
burnt several houses, and returned with many captives to Albany. Forty Onondagas, about the same time, surprised a few
soldiers near Fort Frontenac, whom they confined instead of
the Indians sent home to the galleys, notwithstanding the utmost address was used to regain them, by Lamberville, a
French priest, who delivered them two belts, to engage their
kindness to the prisoners, and prevent their joining the quarrel
with the Sennecas. The belts being sent to Colonel Dongan, he
wrote to De Nonville, to demand the reason of their being
delivered. Pere le Vaillant was sent here about the beginning
of the Year 1688, under colour of bringing an answer, but in
reality as a spy. Colonel Dongan told him, that no Peace could
be made with the Five Nations, unless the Indians sent to the
galleys, and the Caghnuaga proselytes were returned to their
respective cantons, the Forts at Niagara and Frontenac raised,
and the Sennecas had satisfaction made them, for the damage
they had sustained. The Jesuit, in his return, was ordered not
to visit the Mohawks.

Dongan, who was fully sensible of the importance of the
Indian interest to the English colonies, was for compelling the
French to apply to him in all their affairs with the Five Nations; while they, on the other hand, were for treating with
them independent of the English. For this reason, among oth-

ers, he refused them the assistance they frequently required, till they acknowledged the dependence of the Confederates on the English Crown. King James, a poor bigotted, popish, priest-ridden Prince, ordered his Governour to give up this Point, and to persuade the Five Nations to send messengers to Canada, to receive proposals of peace from the French. For this purpose, a cessation of arms and mutual redelivery of prisoners was agreed upon. Near 1200 of the Confederates attended this negotiation at Montreal, and in their speech to De Nonville, insisted with great resolution, upon the terms proposed by Colonel Dongan to Father Le Vaillant. The French Governour declared his willingness to put an end to the war, if all his allies might be included in the Treaty of Peace, if the Mohawks and Sennecas would send deputies to signify their concurrence, and the French might supply Fort Frontenac with provisions. The Confederates, according to the French accounts, acceded to these conditions, and the Treaty was ratified in the field. But a new rupture not long after ensued, from a cause entirely unsuspected. The Dinondadies had lately inclined to the English trade at Missilimakinac, and their alliance was therefore become suspected by the French. Adario, their chief, thought to regain the ancient confidence, which had been reposed in his country men, by a notable action against the Five Nations; and for that purpose put himself at the head of 100 men: nothing was more disagreeable to him, than the prospect of peace between the French and the Confederates; for that event would not only render the amity of the Dinondadies useless, but give the French an Opportunity of resenting their late favourable conduct towards the English. Impressed with these sentiments, out of affection to his country, he intercepted the ambassadours of the Five Nations, at one of the falls in Cadarackui River, killed some, and took others prisoners, telling them that the French Governour had informed him, that fifty warriours of the Five Nations were coming that way. As the Dinondadies and Confederates were then at war, the ambassadours were astonished at the perfidy of the French Governour, and could not help communicating the design of their journey. Adario, in prosecution of his crafty scheme, counterfeited the utmost distress, anger, and shame, on being made the ignominious tool of De Nonville's treachery, and addressing himself to Dekanesora, the principal ambassadour, said to him, "Go, my Brethren, I untie your Bonds, and send you Home again, though our Nations be at War. The French Governor has made me commit so black an Action, that I shall never be easy after it, till the Five Nations shall have taken full Revenge." This outrage and indignity upon the rights of ambassadours, the truth of which they did not in the least doubt, animated the Confederates, to the keenest thirst after revenge; and accordingly 1200 of their men, on the 26th of July 1688, landed on the South side of the island of Montreal, while the French were in perfect security; burnt their houses, sacked their plantations, and put to the sword all the men, women, and children, without the skirts of the town. A thousand French were slain in this invasion, and twenty six carried in captivity and burnt alive. Many more were made prisoners in another attack in October, and the lower part of the island wholly destroyed. Only three of the Confederates were lost, in all this scene of misery and desolation.*

Never before did Canada sustain such a heavy blow. The news of this attack on Montreal no sooner reached the garrison at the Lake Ontario, than they set fire to the two barks, which they had built there, and abandoned the Fort, leaving a match to 28 barrels of powder, designed to blow up the works. The soldiers went down the river in such precipitation, that one of the battoes[15] and her crew were all lost in shooting a fall. The Confederates in the mean time seized the fort, the powder, and the stores; and of all the French allies, who were vastly numerous only the Nepicirinians and Kikapous adhered to them in their calamities. The Utawawas and seven other nations instantly made peace with the English; and but for the uncommon sagacity and address of the Sieur Perot, the Western Indians would have murdered every Frenchman amongst them. Nor did the distresses of the Canadians end here. Numerous scouts from the Five Nations, continually infested their borders. The frequent depredations that were made, prevented them from the cultivation of their fields, and a distressing famine raged through the whole country. Nothing but the ignorance of the Indians, in the art of attacking fortified places, saved Canada from being now utterly cut off. It was therefore unspeakably fortunate to the French, that the Indians had no

* I have followed Dr. Colden in the account of this attack, who differs from Charlevoix. That Jesuit tells us, that the invasion was late in August, and the Indians 1500 strong; and as to the loss of the French, he diminishes it only to 200 souls.

assistance from the English, and as unfortunate to us, that our colonies were then incapable of affording succours to the Confederates, through the malignant influence of those execrable measures, which were pursued under the infamous reign of King James the Second. Colonel Dongan, whatever his conduct might have been in civil affairs, did all that he could in those relating to the Indians, and fell at last into the King's displeasure, through his zeal for the true interest of the Province.

While these things were transacting in Canada, a scene of the greatest importance was opening at New-York. A general disaffection to the government prevailed among the people. Papists began to settle in the colony under the smiles of the Governour. The Collector of the Revenues, and several principal officers, threw off the mask, and openly avowed their attachment to the doctrines of Rome. A Latin school was set up, and the teacher strongly suspected for a Jesuit. The people of Long-Island, who were disappointed in their expectation of mighty boons, promised by the Governour on his arrival, were become his personal enemies; and in a word, the whole body of the people trembled for the Protestant cause. Here the leaven of opposition first began to work. Their intelligence from England, of the designs there in favour of the Prince of Orange, blew up the coals of discontent, and elevated the hopes of the disaffected. But no man dared to spring in action, till after the rupture in Boston, Sir Edmond Andross, who was perfectly devoted to the arbitrary measures of King James, by his tyranny in New-England, had drawn upon himself the universal odium of a people, animated with the love of liberty and in the defence of it resolute and courageous; and therefore, when they could no longer endure his despotic rule, they seized and imprisoned him, and afterwards sent him to England. The government, in the mean time, was vested in the hands of a Committee for the Safety of the People, of which Mr. Bradstreet, was chosen president. Upon the news of this event, several Captains of our militia convened themselves to concert measures, in favour of the Prince of Orange. Amongst these, Jacob Leisler was the most active. He was a man in tolerable esteem among the People, and of a moderate fortune, but destitute of every qualification necessary for the enterprise.

Milborne, his son-in-law, an Englishman, directed all his councils, while Leisler as absolutely influenced the other officers.[16]

The first thing they contrived, was to seize the garrison in New-York; and the custom, at that time, of guarding it every night by the militia, gave Leisler a fine opportunity of executing the design. He entered it with forty nine men, and determined to hold it till the whole militia should join him. Colonel Dongan, who was about to leave the Province, then lay embarked in the Bay, having a little before resigned the government to Francis Nicholson, the Lieutenant Governour. The Council, civil officers, and magistrates of the city, were against Leisler, and therefore many of his friends were at first fearful of openly espousing a cause disapproved by the gentlemen of figure. For this reason, Leisler's first Declaration in favour of the Prince of Orange, was subscribed only by a few, among several companies of the trained bands. While the people, for four days successively, were in the utmost perplexity to determine what part to choose, being sollicited by Leisler on the one hand, and threatened by the Lieutenant Governour on the other, the town was alarmed with a report, that three ships were coming up, with orders from the Prince of Orange. This falsehood was very seasonably propagated to serve the interest of Leisler; for on that day, the 3d of June 1689, his party was augmented by the addition of six captains and 400 men in New-York, and a company of 70 men from East-Chester, who all subscribed a second Declaration,* mutually covenanting to hold the Fort for the Prince. Colonel Dongan continued till this time in the harbour, waiting the issue of these commotions; and Nicholson's party being now unable to contend with their opponents were totally dispersed, the Lieutenant Gover-

---

* I have taken an exact copy of it for the satisfaction of the reader. "Whereas our Intention, tended only but to the Preservation of the Protestant Religion, and the Fort of this Citty, to the end that we may avoid and prevent, the rash Judgment of the World, in so a just Design; wee have thought fitt, to let every Body know by these publick Proclamation, that till the safe Arryvell of the Ships, that wee expect every Day, from his Royal Highness the Prince of Orange, with Orders for the Government of this Country in the Behalf of such Person, as the said Royal Highness had chosen, and honored with the Charge of a Governour, that as soon as the Bearer of the said Orders, shall have let us see his Power, then, and without any Delay, we shall execute the said Orders punctually; declaring that we do intend to submit and obey, not only the said Orders, but also the Bearer thereof, committed for the Execution of the same. In Witness hereof, we have signed these Presents, the third of June 1689."

nour himself absconding, the very night after the last Declaration was signed.

Leisler being now in compleat possession of the Fort, sent home an address to King William and Queen Mary, as soon as he received the news of their accession to the Throne. It is a tedious, incorrect, ill-drawn narrative of the grievances which the people had endured, and the methods lately taken to secure themselves, ending with a recognition of the sovereignty of the King and Queen over the whole English Dominions.

This address was soon followed, by a private letter from Leisler to King William, which, in very broken English, informs His Majesty of the State of the garrison, the repairs he had made to it, and the temper of the people, and concludes with strong protestations of his sincerity, loyalty, and zeal. Jost Stoll, an ensign, on the delivery of this letter to the King, had the honour to kiss his Majesty's hand, but Nicholson the Lieutenant-Governour, and one Ennis, an Episcopal clergyman, arrived in England before him; and by falsely representing the late measures in New-York, as proceeding rather from their aversion to the Church of England, than zeal for the Prince of Orange, Leisler and his party missed the rewards and notice, which their activity for the Revolution justly deserved. For tho' the King made Stoll the bearer of his thanks to the people for their fidelity, he so little regarded Leisler's complaints against Nicholson, that he was soon after preferred to the government of Virginia. Dongan returned to Ireland, and it is said succeeded to the Earldom of Limerick.

Leisler's sudden investiture with supreme power over the Province, and the probable prospects of King William's approbation of his conduct, could not but excite the envy and jealousy of the late Council and magistrates, who had refused to join in the glorious Work of the Revolution; and hence the spring of all their aversion, both to the man and his measures. Colonel Bayard, and Courtland the Mayor of the city, were at the head of his opponents, and finding it impossible to raise a party against him in the City, they very early retired to Albany, and there endeavoured to foment the opposition. Leisler, on the other hand, fearful of their influence, and to extinguish the jealousy of the people, thought it prudent, to admit several trusty persons to a participation of that power, which the militia on the 1st of July had commited solely to himself. In conjunction with these (who, after the Boston example,

were called The Committee of Safety) he exercised the government, assuming to himself only, the honour of being President
in their Councils. This model continued till the month of December, when a packet arrived with a letter from the Lords
Carmarthen, Hallifax, and others, directed "To Francis Nicholson, Esq; or in his Absence, to such as for the Time being,
take Care for preserving the Peace and administring the Laws,
in their Majesties Province of New-York, in America." This
letter was dated the 29th of July, and was accompanied with
another from Lord Nottingham, dated the next day, which
after empowering Nicholson to take upon him the chief command, and to appoint for his assistance as many of the principal freeholders and inhabitants as he should think fit, requiring
also "to do every Thing, appertaining to the Office of Lieutenant-Governor, according to the Laws and Customs of New-York
untill further Orders."

Nicholson being absconded when this packet came to hand,
Leisler considered the letter as directed to himself, and from
this time issued all kinds of commissions in his own name,
assuming the title, as well as authority, of Lieutenant-Governour. On the 11th of December, he summoned the Committee
of Safety, and agreeable to their advice, swore the following
persons for his Council. Peter de Lanoy, Samuel Staats, Hen-
drick Jansen, and Johannes Vermilie, for New-York. Gerardus
Beekman, for King's County. For Queen's County, Samuel Ed-
sel; Thomas Williams for West-Chester, and William Lawrence
for Orange County.

Except the Eastern inhabitants of Long Island, all the Southern part of the colony, chearfully submited to Leisler's command. The principal freeholders, however, by respectful letters,
gave him hopes of their submission, and thereby prevented his
betaking himself to arms, while they were privately solliciting
the colony of Connecticut, to take them under its jurisdiction.
They had indeed no aversion to Leisler's authority, in favour
of any other party in the Province, but were willing to be
incorporated with a people, from whence they had originally
colonized; and therefore, as soon as Connecticut declined their
request, they openly appeared to be advocates for Leisler. At
this juncture the Long-Island representation was drawn up,
which I have more than once had occasion to mention.

The people of Albany, in the mean time, were determined
to hold the garrison and city for King William, independent of

Leisler, and on the 26th of October, which was before the packet arrived from Lord Nottingham, formed themselves into a Convention for that purpose. As Leisler's attempt, to reduce this country to his command, was the original cause of the future divisions in the Province, and in the end brought about his own ruin, it may not be improper to see the resolution of the Convention, a copy of which was sent down to him at large.

| | | |
|---|---|---|
| Peter Schuyler, Mayor, | Claes Ripse, | |
| Dirk Wessels, Recorder, | David Schuyler, | Aldermen. |
| Jan Wendal, | Albert Ryckman, | |
| Jan Jansen Bleeker, | | |

| | |
|---|---|
| Killian V. Renslaer, Justice, | John Cuyler, |
| Capt. Marte Gerritse, Justice, | Gerrit Ryerse, |
| Capt. Gerrit Teunisse, | Evert Banker, |
| Dirk Teunise, Justice, | Rynier Barentse. |
| Lieut. Robert Saunders, | |

Resolved, since we are informed by Persons coming from *New-York*, that Capt. *Jacob Leisler* is designed to send up a Company of armed Men, upon Pretence to assist us in this Country, who intend to make themselves Master of their Majesties Fort and this City, and carry divers Persons and chief Officers of this City Prisoners to *New-York*, and so disquiet and disturb their Majesties liege People, that a Letter be writ to Alderman *Levinus Van Shaic*, now at *New-York*, and *Lieutenant Jochim Staets*, to make narrow Enquiry of the Business, and to signify to the said *Leisler*, that we have received such Information; and withal acquaint him, that notwithstanding we have the Assistance of ninety five Men from our Neighbours of *New-England*, who are now gone for, and one hundred Men upon Occasion, to command, from the County of *Ulster*, which we think will be sufficient this Winter, yet we will willingly accept any such Assistance as they shall be pleased to send for the Defence of their Majesties County of *Albany*: Provided, they be obedient to, and obey such Orders and Commands, as they shall, from Time to Time, receive from the Convention; and that by no means they will be admitted, to have the Command of their Majesties Fort or this City; which we intend by God's Assistance, to keep and preserve for the Behoof of their Majesties *William* and *Mary*, King and Queen of *England*, as we hitherto have done since their Proclamation; and if you hear, that they persevere with such Intentions, so to disturb the Inhabitants of this County, that you then, in the Name and Behalf of the Convention and Inhabitants of the City and County of *Albany,* protest against the said *Leisler,* and all such Persons that shall make Attempt, for all Losses, Damages, Blood-shed, or whatsoever Mischiefs may ensue thereon; which you are to communicate with all Speed, as you perceive their Design.

Taking it for granted that Leisler at New-York, and the Convention at Albany, were equally affected to the Revolution, nothing could be more egregiously foolish, than the conduct of both parties, who by their intestine divisions, threw the province into Convulsions, and sowed the seeds of mutual hatred and animosity, which for a long time after, greatly embarrassed the publick affairs of the colony. When Albany declared for the Prince of Orange, there was nothing else that Leisler could properly require: and rather than sacrifice the publick peace of the Province, to the trifling honour of resisting a man who had no evil designs, Albany ought in prudence to have delivered the garrison into his hands, till the King's definitive orders should arrive. But while Leisler, on the one hand, was inebriated with his new-gotten power, so on the other, Bayard, Courtland, Schuyler, and others, could not brook a submission to the authority of a man, mean in his abilities, and inferior in his degree. Animated by these principles, both parties prepared, the one to reduce, if I may use the expression, the other to retain, the garrison of Albany. Mr. Livingston, a principal agent for the Convention, retired into Connecticut, to sollicit the aid of that colony, for the protection of the frontiers against the French.[17] Leisler suspecting that they were to be used against him, endeavoured not only to prevent these supplies, but wrote letters, to have Livingston apprehended, as an enemy to the reigning powers, and to procure succours from Boston, falsely represented the Convention, as in the interest of the French and King James.

Jacob Milborne was commissioned for the reduction of Albany. Upon his arrival there, a great number of the inhabitants armed themselves and repaired to the Fort, then commanded by Mr. Schuyler, while many others followed the other members of the Convention, to a conference with him at the City-Hall. Milborne, to proselyte the crowd, declaimed much against

King James, Popery, and arbitrary power; but his Oratory was lost upon the hearers, who after several meetings, still adhered to the Convention. Milborne then advanced with a few men up to the Fort, and Mr. Schuyler had the utmost difficulty to prevent both his own men, and the Mohawks who were then in Albany, and perfectly devoted to his service, from firing upon Milborne's party, which consisted of an inconsiderable number. In these circumstances, he thought proper to retreat, and soon after departed from Albany. In the spring, he commanded another party upon the same errand, and the distress of the Country on an Indian irruption, gave him all the desired success. No sooner was he possessed of the garrison, than most of the principal members of the Convention absconded. Upon which, their effects were arbitrarily seized and confiscated, which so highly exasperated the sufferers, that their posterity, to this day, cannot speak of these Troubles, without the bitterest invectives against Leisler and all his adherents.

In the Midst of those intestine confusions at New-York, the people of New-England, were engaged in a war with the Owenagungas, Ourages, and Penocoks. Between these and the Schakook Indians, there was then a friendly communication, and the same was suspected of the Mohawks, among whom, some of the Owenagungaes had taken sanctuary. This gave rise to a conference, between several commissioners from Boston, Plymouth, and Connecticut, and the Five Nations, at Albany, in September 1689, the former endeavouring to engage the latter, against those Eastern Indians, who were then at war with the New-England colonies. Tahajadoris, a Mohawk sachem, in a long oration, answered the English message, and however improbable it may seem to Europeans, repeated all that had been said the preceding day. The art they have in assisting their memories is this. The sachem who presides, has a bundle of sticks prepared for the purpose, and at the close of every principal article of the message delivered to them, gives a stick to another sachem charging him with the remembrance of it. By this means the orator, after a previous conference with the Indians, is prepared to repeat every part of the message, and give it its proper reply. This custom is invariably pursued in all their publick treaties.

The conference did not answer the expectation of the people of New-England, the Five Nations discovering a great disinclination to join in the hostilities against the Eastern Indians.

To atone for which, they gave the highest protestations of their willingness to distress the French, against whom the English had declared war, on the 7th of May preceding. That part of the speech ratifying their friendship, with the English Colonies, is singularly expressed.

> We promise to preserve the chain inviolably, and wish
> that the Sun may always shine in Peace, over all our Heads
> that are comprehended in this Chain.* We give two Belts.
> One for the Sun, and the other for its Beams. We make fast
> the Roots of the Tree of Peace and Tranquility which is
> planted in this Place. Its Roots extend as far as the utmost
> of your Colonies, if the *French* should come to shake this
> Tree, we would feel it by the Motion of its Roots, which ex-
> tend into our Country. But we trust it will not be in the
> Governor of *Canada's* Power to shake this Tree, which has
> been so firmly, and long planted with us.

Nothing could have been more advantageous to these colonies, and especially to New-York, than the late success of the Five Nations against Canada. The miseries to which the French were reduced, rendered us secure against their inroads, till the work of the Revolution was in a great measure accomplished; and to their distressed condition, we must principally ascribe the defeat of the French design, about this time, to make a conquest of the Province. De Calliers, who went to France in 1688, first projected the scheme;† and the troubles in England encouraged the French Court to make the attempt. Cassiniere commanded the ships, which sailed for that purpose from Rochefort; subject, nevertheless, to the Count De Frontenac, who was General of the land forces, destined to march from Canada by the rout of Sorel-River and the Lake Champlain. The fleet and troops arrived at Chebucta, the place of rendezvous, in September; from whence the Count proceeded to Que-

---

* The Indians conception of the League between them and us, is couched under the idea of a chain extended from a ship to a tree, and every renewal of this league they call brightening the chain.

† Charlevoix has published an extract of the Memorial presented to the French King. The force demanded for this enterprise, was to consist of 1300 regulars and 300 Canadians. Albany was said to be fortified only by an inclosure of stockadoes and a little fort with four bastions; and that it contained but 150 soldiers and 300 inhabitants. That New York the capital of the Province was open, had a stone fort with four bastions, and about four hundred inhabitants, divided into eight companies.

beck, leaving orders with Cassiniere to sail for New-York, and continue in the Bay, in sight of the city, but beyond the fire of our cannon, till the 1st of December: when, if he received no intelligence from him, he was ordered to return to France, after unlading the ammunition, stores, and provisions at Port-Royal.* The Count was in high spirits, and fully determined upon the enterprise, till he arrived at Quebeck; where the news of the success of the Five Nations against Montreal, the loss of his favourite fort at Lake Ontario, and the advanced season of the year, defeated his aims, and broke up the expedition. De Nonville who was recalled, carried the news of this disappointment to the Court of France, leaving the chief command of the country in the hands of Count Frontenac. This gentleman was a man of courage, and well acquainted with the affairs of that country. He was then in the 68th year of his age, and yet so far from consulting his ease, that in a few days after he landed at Quebeck, he re-embarked in a canoe for Montreal, where his presence was absolutely necessary, to animate the inhabitants and regain their Indian alliances. A war, between the English and French Crowns, being broke out; the Count betook himself to every art, for concluding a peace between Canada and the Five Nations; and for this purpose, the utmost civilities were shewn to Taweraket and the other Indians, who had been sent to France by De Nonville, and were now returned. Three of those Indians, who doubtless were struck with the grandeur and glory of the French monarch, were properly sent on the important message of conciliating the friendship of the Five Nations. These, agreeable to our alliance, sent two sachems to Albany, in December, with notice, that a Council for that purpose was to be held at Onondaga. It is a just reflection upon the people of Albany, that they regarded the treaty so slightly, as only to send four Indians and the interpreter with instructions, in their name, to dissuade the Confederates from a cessation of arms; while the French, on the other hand, had then a Jesuit among the Oneydoes. The Council began on the 22d of January 1690, and consisted of eighty sachems. Sadekanaghtie, an Onondaga chief, opened the Conference. The whole was managed with great art and formality, and concluded in shewing a disposition to make peace with the French, without perfecting it; guarding, at the same time, against giving the least umbrage to the English.[18]

* Now Annapolis.

Among other measures to detach the Five Nations from the British interest, and raise the depressed spirit of the Canadians, the Count De Frontenac thought proper to send out several parties against the English colonies. D'Aillebout, De Mantel, and Le Moyne, commanded that against New-York, consisting of about two hundred French and some Caghnuaga Indians, who being proselytes from the Mohawks, were perfectly acquainted with that country. Their orders were, in general, to attack New-York; but pursuing the advice of the Indians, they resolved, instead of Albany, to surprise Schenectady, a village seventeen miles North-west from it, and about the same distance from the Mohawks. The people of Schenectady, tho' they had been informed of the designs of the enemy, were in the greatest security; judging it impracticable, for any men to march several hundred miles, in the depth of winter, thro' the snow, bearing their provisions on their backs. Besides, the village was in as much confusion as the rest of the Province; the officers, who were posted there, being unable to preserve a regular watch, or any kind of military order. Such was the state of Schenectady, as represented by Colonel Schuyler, who was at that time Mayor of the city of Albany, and at the head of the Convention. A copy of his letter to the neighbouring colonies, concerning this descent upon Schenectady, dated the 15th of February 1689–90, I have now lying before me, under his own hand.

After two and twenty days march, the enemy fell in with Schenectady, on the 8th of February; and were reduced to such streights, that they had thoughts of surrendering themselves prisoners of war. But their scouts, who were a day or two in the village entirely unsuspected, returned with such encouraging accounts of the absolute security of the people, that the enemy determined on the attack. They entered, on Saturday night about eleven o'clock, at the gates, which were found unshut; and, that every house might be invested at the same time, divided into small parties of six, or seven men. The inhabitants were in a profound sleep, and unalarmed, till their doors were broke open. Never were people in a more wretched consternation. Before they were risen from their beds, the enemy entered their houses; and began the perpetration of the most inhuman Barbarities. No tongue, says Colonel Schuyler, can express the cruelties that were commited. The whole village was instantly in a Blaze. Women with child ripped open, and their infants cast into the flames, or dashed against the posts of the doors. Sixty persons perished in the massacre, and twenty seven were carried into captivity. The rest fled naked towards Albany, thro' a deep snow which fell that very night in a terrible storm; and twenty five of these fugitives, lost their limbs in the flight, thro' the severity of the frost. The news of this dreadful tragedy reached Albany, about break of day; and universal dread seized the inhabitants of that city, the enemy being reported to be one thousand four hundred strong. A party of horse was immediately dispatched to Schenectady, and a few Mohawks then in town, fearful of being intercepted, were with difficulty sent to apprise their own castles.

The Mohawks were unacquainted with this bloody scene, till two days after it happened; our messengers being scarce able to travel thro' the great depth of the snow. The enemy, in the mean time, pillaged the town of Schenectady till noon the next day; and then went off with their plunder, and about forty of their best horses. The rest, with all the cattle they could find, lay slaughtered in the streets.

The design of the French, in this attack, was to alarm the fears of our Indian allies, by shewing that we were incapable of defending them. Every art also was used to conciliate their friendship, for they not only spared those Mohawks who were found in Schenectady, but several other particular persons, in compliment to the Indians, who requested that favour. Several women and children were also released at the desire of Captain Glen, to whom the French offered no violence; the officer declaring he had strict orders against it, on the score of his wife's civilities to certain French captives in the time of Colonel Dongan.

The Mohawks, considering the cajoling arts of the French, and that the Caghnuagas who were with them, were once a part of their own body, behaved as well as could be reasonably expected. They joined a party of young men from Albany, fell upon the rear of the enemy, and either killed or captivated five and twenty. Several sachems, in the mean time, came to Albany, and very affectingly addressed the inhabitants, who were just ready to abandon the country; urging their stay, and exciting an union of all the English colonies against Canada. Their sentiments concerning the French, appear from the following speech of Condolence. "Brethren, we do not think, that what the French have done can be called a Victory: it is only a further Proof of their cruel Deceit: the Governor of Canada, sent to Onondaga, and talks to us of Peace with our whole house; but War was in his Heart, as you now see by woeful Experience. He did the same, formerly, at Cadaracqui, and in the Seneca's Country. This is the third Time he has acted so deceitfully. He has broken open our House, at both Ends; formerly in the Sennecas Country, and now here. We hope however to be revenged of them."

Agreeable to this declaration, the Indians soon after treated the Chevalier D'Eau and the rest of the French messengers, who came to conclude the peace proposed by Taweraket, with the utmost indignity; and afterwards delivered them up to the English. Besides this, their scouts harassed the borders of the enemy, and fell upon a party of French and Indians, in the river, about one hundred and twenty miles above Montreal, under the command of Louvigni, a Captain who was going to Missilimakinac, to prevent the conclusion of the Peace, between the Utawawas and Quatoghies, with the Five Nations. The loss in this skirmish was nearly equal on both sides. One of our prisoners was delivered to the Utawawas, who ate him. In revenge for this barbarity, the Indians attacked the island of Montreal at Trembling Point, and killed an officer and twelve men; while another party carried off about fifteen prisoners taken at Riviere Puante, whom they afterwards slew through fear of their pursuers, and others burnt the French plantations at St. Ours. But what rendered this year most remarkable, was the expedition of Sir William Phips against Quebeck. He sailed up the river with a fleet of thirty two sail and came before the city in October.[19] Had he improved his time and strength, the conquest would have been easy; but by spending three days in idle consultations, the French Governour brought in his forces, and entertained such a mean opinion of the English Knight, that he not only despised his summons to surrender, but sent a verbal answer, in which he called King William an usurper, and poured the utmost contempt upon his subjects. The messenger who carried the summons insisted upon a written answer, and that within an hour; but the Count De Frontenac absolutely refused it, adding "I'll answer your Master by the Mouth of my Cannon, that he may learn that a Man of my Condition is not to be summoned in this Manner." Upon this, Sir William made two attempts to land below the town, but was repulsed by the enemy, with considerable loss of men, cannon, and baggage. Several of the ships also cannonaded the city, but without any success. The forts at the same returned the fire, and obliged them to retire in disorder. The French writers, in their accounts of this expedition, universally censure the conduct of Sir William, though they confess the valour of his troops. La Hontan, who was then at Quebeck, says, he could not have acted in a manner more agreeable to the French, if he had been in their interest.*

---

* Dr. Colden supposes this attack was made upon Quebeck in 1691, but he is certainly mistaken: see *Life of Sir Williams Phips* published at London in 1697. *Oldmixon's Brit. Empire,* and *Charlevoix.*

Among the causes of the ill success of the fleet, the authour of the Life of Sir William Phips, mentions the neglect of the conjoined troops of New-York, Connecticut, and the Indians, to attack Montreal, according to the original plan of operations. He tells us that they marched to the lake, but there found themselves unprovided with battoes, and that the Indians were dissuaded from the attempt. By what authority these assertions may be supported, I know not. Charlevoix says our army was disappointed in the intended diversion, by the small-pox, which seized the camp, killed three hundred men, and terrified our Indian allies.

# Part III

## From the Revolution to the Second Expedition Against Canada

While our Allies were faithfully exerting themselves against the common enemy, Colonel Henry Sloughter, who had a Commission to be Governour of this Province, dated the 4th of January 1689, arrived here, and published it on the 19th of March 1691. Never was a governour more necessary to the Province, than at this critical conjuncture; as well for reconciling a divided people, as for defending them against the wiles of a cunning adversary. But either through the hurry of the King's affairs, or the powerful interest of a favorite, a man was sent over, utterly destitute of every qualification for government, licentious in his morals, avaricious, and poor. The Council present at his arrival were

| | |
|---|---|
| Joseph Dudley, | Gabriel Mienvielle, |
| Frederick Philipse, | Chudley Brook, |
| Stephen Van Courtland, | Thomas Willet, |
| | William Pinhorne. |

If Leisler had delivered the garrison to Colonel Sloughter, as he ought to have done, upon his first landing, besides extinguishing, in a great degree, the animosities then subsisting, he would, doubtless, have attracted the favourable notice, both of the Governour and the Crown. But being a weak man, he was so intoxicated with the love of power, that though he had been well informed of Sloughter's appointment to the government, he not only shut himself up in the Fort with Bayard and Nichols, whom he had, before that time, imprisoned, but refused to deliver them up, or to surrender the garrison. From this moment, he lost all credit with the Governour, who joined the other party against him. On the second demand of the Fort, Milborne and Delanoy came out, under pretence of confering with his excellency, but in reality to discover his designs. Sloughter, who considered them as rebels, threw them both into gaol. Leisler, upon this event, thought proper to abandon the Fort, which Colonel Sloughter immediately entered. Bayard and Nichols were now released from their confinement, and sworn of the Privy Council. Leisler having thus ruined his cause, was apprehended with many of his adherents, and a Commission of Oyer and Terminer issued to Sir Thomas Robinson, Colonel Smith, and others, for their trials.

In vain did they plead the merit of their zeal for King William, since they had so lately opposed his governour. Leisler, in particular, endeavoured to justify his conduct, insisting that Lord Nottingham's letter entitled him to act in the quality of Lieutenant Governour. Whether it was through ignorance or sycophancy, I know not: but the judges instead of pronouncing their own sentiments upon this part of the prisoners defence, referred it to the Governour and Council, praying their opinion, whether that letter "or any other Letters, or Papers, in the Packet from White-Hall, can be understood, or interpreted, to be and contain, any Power, or Direction to Captain Leisler, to take the Government of this province upon himself, or that the Administration thereupon be holden good in Law." The answer was, as might have been expected, in the negative; and Leisler and his son were condemned to death for high-treason. These violent measures drove many of the inhabitants, who were fearful of being apprehended, into the neighbouring colonies, which shortly after occasioned the passing an Act of General Indemnity.

From the surrender of the Province to the year 1683, the inhabitants were ruled by the Duke's governours and their councils, who, from time to time, make rules and orders, which were esteemed to be binding as laws. These, about the year 1674, were regularly collected under alphabetical titles; and a fair copy of them remains, amongst our records, to this day. They are commonly known by the name of *The Duke's Laws.* The title page of the book, writen in the old court hand is in these bald words.

JUS
NOVAE EBORACENSIS;
VEL,
LEGES ILLUSTRISSIMO PRINCIPE JACOBI DUCE
EBORACI ET ALBANAE, etc.
INSTITUTAE ET ORDINATAE,
AD OBSERVANDUM IN TERRITORIIS AMERICAE;
TRANSCRIPTAE
ANNO DOMINI
MDCLXXIV.[1]

Those Acts, which were made in 1683, and after the Duke's accession to the Throne, when the people were admited to a participation of the legislative power, are for the most part rotten, defaced, or lost. Few minutes relating to them remain on the Council books, and none in the Journals of the House.

As this Assembly, in 1691, was the first after the revolution, it may not be improper to take some particular notice of its transactions.*

It began the 9th of April, according to the writs of summons issued on the 20th of March preceding. The Journal of the House opens with a list of the members returned by the sheriffs.

*City and County of New-York.*
James Graham,
William Merrett,
Jacobus Van Courtlandt,
Johannes Kipp.

*County of Richmond.*
Elias Dukesbury,
John Dally.

*County of West-Chester.*
John Pell.

*City and County of Albany.*
Derrick Wessels,
Levinus Van Scayck.

*County of Suffolk.*
Henry Pierson,
Matthew Howell.

*Ulster and Dutchess County.*
Henry Beekman,
Thomas Garton.

*Queen's County.*
John Bound,
Nathaniel Percall.

*King's County.*
Nicholas Stillwell.
John Poland.

The members for Queen's County, being Quakers, were afterwards dismissed, for refusing the oaths directed by the Gov-

---

* All laws made here, antecedent to this period, are disregarded both by the Legislature and the Courts of Law. In the collection of our Acts published in 1752, the compilers were directed to begin at this Assembly. The validity of the old grants of the powers of government, in several American colonies, is very much doubted in this province.

ernour's Commission, but all the rest were qualified before two Commissioners appointed for that purpose.

James Graham was elected their Speaker, and approved by the Governour.

The majority of the members of this Assembly were against the measures, which Leisler pursued in the latter part of his time, and hence we find the House, after considering a petition signed by sundry persons against Leisler, unanimously resolved, that his dissolving the late Convention, and imprisoning several persons, was tumultuous, illegal, and against their Majesties right, and that the late depredations on Schenectady, were to be attributed to his usurpation of all power.

They resolved, against the late forcible seizures made of effects of the people, and against the levying of money on their Majesties subjects. And as to Leisler's holding the Fort against the Governour, it was voted to be an Act of Rebellion.

The House having, by these agreeable resolves, prepared the way of their access to the Governour, addressed him in these words.

May it please your Excellency,
    We their Majesties most dutiful and loyal Subjects, convened, by their Majesties most gracious Favour, in General Assembly, in this Province, do, in all most humble Manner, heartily congratulate, your Excellency, that as, in our Hearts, we do abhor and detest all the rebellious, arbitrary and illegal Proceedings of the late Usurpers of their Majesties Authority, over this Province, so we do, from the Bottom of our Hearts, with all Integrity, acknowledge and declare, that there are none, that can or ought to have, Right to rule and govern their Majesties Subjects here, but by their Majesties Authority, which is now placed in your Excellency; and therefore we do solemnly declare, that we will, with our Lives and Fortunes, support and maintain, the Administration of your Excellency's Government, under their Majesties, against all their Majesties Enemies whatsoever: and this we humbly pray your Excellency to accept, as the sincere Acknowledgement of all their Majesties good Subjects, within this their Province; praying for their Majesties long and happy Reign over us, and that your Excellency may long live and rule, as according to their Majesties most excellent Constitution of Governing their Subjects by a general Assembly.
Before this House proceeded to pass any Acts, they unanimously resolved. That all the Laws consented to by the gen-

eral Assembly, under *James* Duke of *York,* and the Liberties and Privileges therein contained, granted to the People, and declared to be their Rights, not being observed, nor ratified and approved by his Royal Highness, nor the late King, are null and void, and of none Effect; and also, the several Ordinances, made by the late Governors and Councils, being contrary to the Constitution of *England,* and the Practice of the Government of their Majesties other Plantations in *America,* are likewise null and void, and of no Effect, nor Force, within this Province."[2]

Among the principal laws enacted at this session, we may mention that for establishing the revenue, which was drawn into precedent. The sums raised by it, were made payable into the hands of the Receiver-General, and issued by the Governour's warrant. By this means the Governour became, for a season, independent of the people, and hence we find frequent instances of the Assemblies' contending with him for the discharge of debts to private persons, contracted on the faith of the Government.

Antecedent to the Revolution, innumerable were the controversies relating to publick townships and private rights; and hence, an Act was now passed, for the confirmation of ancient patents and grants, intended to put an end to those debates. A law was also passed for the Establishment of Courts of Justice, tho' a perpetual Act had been made to that purpose in 1683, and the old Court of Assize entirely dissolved in 1684. As this enacted in 1691, was a temporary law, it may hereafter be disputed, as it has been already, whether the present establishment of our courts, for general jurisdiction, by an ordinance, can consist even with the preceding Act, or the general Rules of Law. Upon the erection of the Supreme Court, a Chief Justice, and four Assistant Judges, with an Attorney General, were appointed. The Chief Justice, Joseph Dudley, had a salary of £130 per annum: Johnson the second Judge £100 and both were payable out of the Revenue; but William Smith, Stephen Van Courtlandt, and William Pinhorne, the other Judges, and Newton the Attorney-General, had nothing allowed for their services.

It has, more than once, been a subject of animated debate, whether the People, in this colony, have a right to be represented in Assembly, or whether it be a privilege enjoyed, thro' the grace of the Crown. A memorable Act passed this session, virtually declared in favour of the former opinion, upon that, and several other of the principal and distinguishing liberties of Englishmen. It must, nevertheless, be confessed, that King William was afterwards pleased to repeal that law, in the year 1697.*

Colonel Sloughter proposed, immediately after the session, to set out to Albany, but as Leisler's party were enraged at his imprisonment, and the late sentence against him, his enemies were afraid new troubles would spring up in the absence of the Governour; for this reason, both the Assembly and Council advised that the prisoners should be immediately executed.[3] Sloughter, who had no inclination to favour them in this request, chose rather to delay such a violent step, being fearful of cutting off two men, who had vigorously appeared for the King, and so signally, contributed to the Revolution. Nothing could be more disagreeable to their enemies, whose interest was deeply concerned in their destruction. And therefore, when no other measures could prevail with the Governour, tradition informs us, that a sumptuous feast was prepared, to which Colonel Sloughter was invited. When his Excellency's reason was drowned in his cups, the entreaties of the company prevailed with him to sign the death warrant, and before he recovered his senses, the prisoners were executed. Leisler's son afterwards carried home a complaint to King William, against the Governour. His petition was referred, according to the common course of plantation affairs, to the Lords Commissioners of Trade, who, after hearing the whole matter, reported on the 11th of March 1692, "That they were humbly of Opinion, that Jacob Leisler and Jacob Milborne deceased, were condemned and had suffered according to Law." Their Lordships, however, interceded for their families, as fit objects of mercy, and this induced Queen Mary, who approved the report, on the 17th of March, to declare, "That upon the humble Application of the Relations of the said Jacob Leisler and Jacob Milborne deceased, her Majesty will order the Estates of Jacob Leisler and John Milborne, to be restored to their Families, as Objects of her Majesty's Mercy." The bodies of these unhappy sufferers were afterwards taken up and interred, with great pomp, in the old Dutch church, in the city of New-York. Their estates were

* It was entitled, "An Act declaring what are the Rights and Privileges of their Majesties Subjects inhabiting within their province of New-York."

restored to their families, and Leisler's children, in the publick estimation, are rather dignified, than disgraced, by the fall of their ancestor.

These distractions, in the Province, so entirely engrossed the publick attention, that our Indian allies, who had been left solely to contend with the common enemy, grew extremely disaffected. The Mohawks, in particular, highly resented this conduct, and, at the instance of the Caghnuagaes, sent a messenger to Canada, to confer with Count Frontenac about a peace. To prevent this, Colonel Sloughter had an interview at Albany, in June, with the other four nations, who expressed their joy at seeing a governour again in that place. They told him, that their ancestors, as they had been informed, were greatly surprised at the arrival of the first ship in that country, and were curious to know what was in its huge belly. That they found Christians in it, and one Jacques, with whom they made a chain of friendship, which they had preserved to this day. All the Indians, except the Mohawks, assured the Governour at this meeting, of their resolution to prosecute the war. The Mohawks confessed their negotiations with the French, that they had received a belt from Canada, and prayed the advice of the Governour, and afterwards renewed their League with all our colonies.

Sloughter soon after returned to New-York, and ended a short, weak, and turbulent administration, for he died suddenly on the 23d of July 1691. Some were not without suspicions, that he came unfairly to his end, but the certificate of the physician and surgeons who opened his body, by an Order of Council, confuted these conjectures, and his remains were intered in Stuyvesant's vault, next to those of the old Dutch Governour.

At the time of Sloughter's decease, the Government devolved, according to the late Act for declaring the rights of the people of this Province, on the Council, in which Joseph Dudley had a right to preside; but they commited the chief command to Richard Ingolsby,[4] a captain of an independent company, who was sworn into the office of President on the 26th of July 1691. Dudley, soon afterwards, returned to this Province, from Boston, but did not think proper to dispute Ingolsby's authority, though the latter had no title, nor the greatest abilities for government, and was besides obnoxious to the party who had joined Leisler, having been an agent in the measures which accomplished his ruin. To the late troubles, which were then recent, and the agreement subsisting between the Council and Assembly we must ascribe it, that the former tacitly acknowledged Ingolsby's right to the President's Chair; for they concurred with him, in passing several laws, in Autumn and the spring following, the validity of which have never yet been disputed.[5]

This summer Major Schuyler,* with a party of Mohawks, passed through the Lake Champlain, and made a bold irruption upon the French settlements, at the north end of it.† De Callieres, the Governour of Montreal, to oppose him, collected a small army, of eight hundred men, and encamped at La Prairie. Schuyler had several conflicts with the enemy, and slew about three hundred of them, which exceeded in number his whole party. The French, ashamed of their ill success, attribute it to the want of order, too many desiring to have the command. But the true cause was the ignorance of their officers in the Indian manner of fighting. They kept their men in a body, while ours posted themselves behind trees, hidden from the enemy. Major Schuyler's design, in this descent, was to animate the Indians, and preserve their enmity against the French. They, accordingly, continued their hostilities, and, by frequent incursions, kept the country in constant alarm.

In the midst of these distresses, the French Governour preserved his sprightliness and vigour, animating every body about him. After he had served himself of the Utawawas, who came to trade at Montreal, he sent them home under the care of a captain and one hundred and ten men; and to secure their attachment to the French interest, gave them two Indian prisoners, and, besides, sent very considerable presents to the Western Indians, in their alliance. The captives were afterwards burnt. The Five Nations, in the mean time, grew more and more incensed, and continually harassed the French borders. Mr. Beaucour, a young gentleman, in the following winter, marched a body of about three hundred men to attack them at the

* The French, from his great influence at Albany, and activity among the Indians, concluded that he was Governour of that city; and hence, their historians honour him with that title, though he was then only Mayor of the Corporation. "Pitre Schuyler (says Charlevoix) etoit un fort honnête Homme."

† Dr. Colden relates it as a transaction of the year 1691, which is true: but he supposes it was before Sir William Phips's Attack upon Quebeck, and thus falls into an anachronism, of a whole year, as I have already observed.

isthmus, at Niagara. Incredible were the fatigues they underwent in this long march over the snow, bearing their provisions on their backs. Eighty men, of the Five Nations, opposed the French party and bravely maintained their ground, till most of them were cut off. In return for which, the Confederates, in small parties, obstructed the passage of the French through Lake Ontario, and the river issuing out of it, and cut off their communication with the Western Indians. An Indian called Black Kettle, commanded in these incursions of the Five Nations, and his successes, which continued the whole summer, so exasperated the Count, that he ordered an Indian prisoner to be burnt alive. The bravery of this savage was as extraordinary, as the torments inflicted on him were cruel. He sung his military achievements without interruption, even while his bloody executioners practiced all possible barbarities. They broiled his feet, thrust his fingers into red hot pipes, cut his joints, and twisted the sinews with Bars of Iron. After this his scalp was ripped off, and hot sand poured on the wound.

In June 1692, Captain Ingolsby met the Five Nations at Albany, and encouraged them to persevere in the war. The Indians declared their enmity to the French, in the strongest terms, and as heartily professed their friendship to us. "Brother Corlear," said the Sachem, "We are all Subjects of one great King and Queen, we have one Head, one Heart, one Interest, and are all engaged in the same War." The Indians, at the same time, did not forget, at this interview, to condemn the inactivity of the English, telling them, that the destruction of Canada would not make one summer's work, against their united strength, if vigorously exerted.

Colonel Benjamin Fletcher arrived, with a Commission to be Governour, on the 29th of August, 1692, which was published the next day, before the following members, in Council:

| Frederick Philipse, | Nicholas Bayard, | William Nicoll, |
| Stephen Van Courtlandt, | Gabriel Mienville, | Thomas Johnston. |
| Thomas Willet, | Chudley Brooke, | |

William Pinhorne, one of that board, being a non-resident was refused the oaths; and Joseph Dudley, for the same reason, removed, both from his seat in Council, and his office of Chief Justice, Caleb Heathcote and John Young succeeded them in Council; and William Smith[6] was seated, in Dudley's place, on the bench.

Colonel Fletcher brought over with him a present to the

colony of arms, ammunition, and warlike stores; in gratitude for which, he exhorted the Council and Assembly, who were sitting at his arrival, to send home an address of thanks to the King. It consists, principally, of a representation of the great expence the Province was continually at to defend the frontiers, and praying his Majesty's direction, that the neighbouring colonies might be compelled to join their Aid, for the support of Albany. The following passage in it shews the sense of the legislature, upon a Matter which has since been very much debated.

> When these Counties were possessed by the *Dutch West-India* Company, they always had Pretences (and had the most Part of it within their actual Jurisdiction) to all that Tract of Land (with the Islands adjacent) extending, from the West Side of *Connecticut* River, to the Lands lying on the West Side of *Delaware* Bay, as a suitable Portion of Land for one Colony or Government; all which, including the Lands on the West of *Delaware* Bay or River, were in the Duke of *York's* Grant, from his Majesty King *Charles* the Second, whose Governours also possessed those Lands on the West Side of *Delaware* Bay or River. By several Grants, as well from the Crown, as from the Duke, the said Province has been so diminished, that it is now decreased to a very few Towns and Villages; the Number of Men fit to bear Arms, in the whole Government, not amounting to 3000, who are all reduced to great Poverty.

Fletcher was by profession a soldier, a man of strong passions, and inconsiderable talents, very active, and equally avaricious. Nothing could be more fortunate to him, than his early acquaintance with Major Schuyler, at Albany, at the Treaty, for confirmation of the Indian alliance, the fall after his arrival. No man, then in this province, understood the state of our affairs with the Five Nations better than Major Schuyler. He had so great an influence over them, that whatever Quider,* as they called him, recommended or disapproved, had the force of a law. This power over them was supported, as it had been obtained, by repeated offices of kindness; and his singular bravery and activity in the defence of his country. These qualifications rendered him singularly serviceable and necessary, both to the Province and the Governour. For this reason,

* Instead of Peter which they could not pronounce.

Fletcher took him into his confidence, and, on the 25th of October, raised him to the Council Board. Under the tutelage of Major Schuyler, the Governour became daily more and more acquainted with our Indian affairs; his constant application to which, procured and preserved him a reputation and influence in the colony. Without this knowledge, and which was all that he had to distinguish himself, his incessant sollicitations for money, his passionate temper and bigoted principles, must necessarily have rendered him obnoxious to the people, and kindled a hot fire of contention in the Province.[7]

The old French Governour, who found that all his measures for accomplishing a peace with the Five Nations, proved abortive, was now meditating a blow on the Mohawks. He accordingly collected an army of six or seven hundred French and Indians, and supplied them with every thing necessary for a winter campaign. They set out from Montreal, on the 15th of January, 1693; and after a march, attended with incredible hardships, they passed by Schenectady on the 6th of February, and, that night, captivated five men, and some women and children, at the first castle of the Mohawks. The second castle was taken with equal ease, the Indian inhabitants being in perfect security, and, for the most part, at Schenectady. At the third, the enemy found about forty Indians in a war dance, designing to go out, upon some enterprise, the next day. Upon their entering the castle a conflict ensued, in which the French lost about thirty men. Three hundred of our Indians were made captives, in this descent; and, but for the intercession of the savages in the French interest, would all have been put to the sword.*

The Indians were enraged, and with good reason, at the people of Schenectady, who gave them no assistance against the enemy, though they had notice of their marching by that village. But this was atoned for by the succours from Albany. Colonel Schuyler, voluntarily, headed a party of two hundred men, and went out against the enemy. On the 15th of February, he was joined by near three hundred Indians, ill armed, and many of them boys. A pretended deserter, who came to dissuade the Indians from the pursuit, informed him, the next

* Dr. Colden and the Jesuit Charlevoix are not perfectly agreed in the history of this irruption. I have followed, sometimes the former, and at other times the latter; according as the facts, more immediately, related to the conduct of their respective countrymen.

day, that the French had built a fort, and waited to fight him; upon which he sent to Ingolsby the Commandant at Albany, as well for a reinforcement, as for a supply of provisions; for the greatest part of his men came out, with only a few biscuits in their pockets, and at the time they fell in with the enemy, on the 17th of the month, had been several days without any kind of food. Upon approaching the French Army, sundry skirmishes ensued; the enemy endeavouring to prevent our Indians from felling trees for their protection. Captain Syms, with eighty Regulars of the independent companies, and a supply of provisions, arrived on the 19th, but the enemy had marched off the day before, in a great snow storm. Our party however pursued them, and would have attacked their rear, if the Mohawks had not been averse to it. When the French reached the North branch of Hudson's River, luckily a cake of ice, served them to cross over it, the river being open both above and below. The frost was now extremely severe, and the Mohawks fearful of an engagement; upon which Schuyler who had retaken about fifty Indian captives, desisted from the pursuit on the 20th of February; four of his men and as many Indians being killed, and twelve wounded. Our Indians, at this time, were so distressed for provisions, that they fed upon the dead bodies of the French; and the enemy in their turn, were reduced before they got home, to eat up their shoes. The French in this enterprise lost eighty men, and had above thirty wounded.

Fletcher's extraordinary dispatch up to Albany, upon the first news of this descent, gained him the esteem both of the publick and our Indian allies.

The express reached New-York on the 12th of February, at ten o'clock in the night, and in less than two days, the Governour embarked with three hundred volunteers. The river, which was heretofore very uncommon at that season, was open.* Fletcher landed at Albany, and arrived at Schenectady, the 17th of the month, which is about one hundred and sixty miles from New-York; but he was still too late to be of any other use than to strengthen the ancient alliance. The Indians, in commendation of his activity on the occasion, gave him the name of Cayenguirago, or, The great Swift Arrow.

---

* The climate of late years is much altered, and this day (February 14, 1756.) three hundred recruits sailed from New-York for the Army under the command of General Shirley, now quartered at Albany, and last year, a sloop went up the river a month earlier.

Fletcher returned to New-York, and, in March, met the Assembly, who were so well pleased with his late vigilance, that, besides giving him the thanks of the House, they raised £6000 for a year's pay of three hundred volunteers, and their officers, for the defence of the frontiers.

As the greatest part of this Province consisted of Dutch inhabitants, all our Governours, as well in the Duke's time, as after the Revolution, thought it good policy to encourage English preachers and schoolmasters in the colony. No man could be more bent upon such a project than Fletcher, a bigot to the Episcopal form of church government. He, accordingly, recommended this matter to the Assembly, on his first arrival, as well as at their present meeting. The House, from their attachment to the Dutch language, and the model of the Church of Holland, secured by one of the articles of surrender, were entirely disinclined to the scheme, which occasioned a warm rebuke from the Governour, in his speech at the close of the session, in these words, "Gentlemen, the first thing that I did recommend to you, at our last Meeting, was to provide for a Ministry, and nothing is done in it. There are none of you, but what are big with the Privileges of Englishmen and Magna Charta, which is your Right; and the same Law doth provide for the Religion of the Church of England, against Sabbath breaking and all other Profanity. But as you have made it last, and postponed it this session, I hope you will begin with it the next meeting, and do somewhat toward it effectually."

The news of the arrival of the recruits and ammunition at Canada, the late loss of the Mohawks, and the unfulfilled promises of assistance, made from time to time, by the English, together with the incessant sollicitations of Milet, the Jesuit,[8] all conspired to induce the Oneydoes to sue for a peace with the French. To prevent so important an event, Fletcher met the Five Nations at Albany, in July 1693, with a considerable present of knives, hatchets, clothing, and ammunition, which had been sent over, by the Crown, for that purpose. The Indians consented to a renewal of the ancient League, and expressed their gratitude, for the King's Donation, with singular force. "Brother Cayenguirago, we roll and wallow in Joy, by reason of the great Favour the great King and Queen have done us, in sending us Arms and Ammunition at a Time when we are in the greatest need of them; and because there is such Unity among the Brethren." Colonel Fletcher pressed their delivering up to him Milet, the old priest, which they promised, but never performed. On the contrary, he had influence enough to persuade all, but the Mohawks, to treat about the Peace at Onondaga, tho' the Governour exerted himself to prevent it.

Soon after this interview, Fletcher returned to New-York; and, in September, met a new Assembly, of which James Graham was chosen speaker. The Governour laboured, at this session, to procure the establishment of a Ministry throughout the colony, a revenue to his Majesty for life, the repairing the Fort in New-York, and the erection of a chapel. That part of his speech, relating to the ministry, was in these words: "I recommended to the former Assembly, the setling of an able Ministry, that the Worship of God may be observed among us, for I find that great and first Duty very much neglected. Let us not forget that there is a God that made us, who will protect us if we serve him. This has been always the first Thing I have recommended, yet the last in your Consideration. I hope you are all satisfied of the great Necessity and Duty, that lies upon you to do this, as you expect his Blessing upon your Labours." The zeal with which this affair was recommended, induced the House, on the 12th of September, to appoint a Committee of eight members, to agree upon a scheme for settling a ministry, in each respective precinct, throughout the Province. This committee made a report the next day, but it was recommited till the afternoon, and then deferred to the next morning. Several debates arising about the report, in the House, it was again "recommited for farther Consideration." On the 15th of September it was approved, the establishment being then limited to several parishes in four counties, and a bill ordered to be brought in accordingly; which the Speaker (who on the 18th of September, was appointed to draw all their bills) produced on the 19th. It was read twice on the same day, and then refered to a Committee of the whole House. The third reading was on the 21st of September, when the bill passed, and was sent up to the Governour and Council, who immediately returned it with an amendment, to vest his Excellency with an Episcopal power of inducting every incumbent, adding to that part of the bill near the end, which gave the right of presentation to the people, these words "and presented to the Governour to be approved and collated." The House declined their consent to the addition, and immediately returned the bill, praying, "that it may pass without the Amendment, having, in the drawing of the Bill, had a due Regard to that pious Intent of settling a Ministry, for the Benefit of the People." Fletcher was so exasperated with their refusal, that he no sooner received the answer of the House, than he convened them before him, and in an angry speech broke up the session. I shall lay that part of it, relating to this bill, before the reader, because it is characteristick of the man.

GENTLEMEN,

There is also a Bill for settling a Ministry in this City, and some other Countries of the Government. In that very Thing you have shewn a great deal of Stiffness. You take upon you, as if you were Dictators. I sent down to you an Amendment of three or four Words in that Bill, which, tho' very immaterial, yet was positively denied. I must tell you, it seems very unmannerly. There never was an Amendment yet desired by the Council Board, but what was rejected. It is the Sign of a stubborn ill Temper, and this have also passed.

But, Gentlemen, I must take leave to tell you, if you seem to understand by these Words, that none can serve without your Collation or Establishment, you are far mistaken. For I have the Power of collating or suspending any Minister, in my Government, by their Majesties Letters Patent; and whilst I stay in the Government, I will take Care, that neither Heresy, Sedition, Schism, or Rebellion, be preached among you, nor Vice and Profanity encouraged. It is my Endeavour, to lead a virtuous and pious Life amongst you, and to give a good Example: I wish you all to do the same. You ought to consider, that you have but a third Share in the legislative Power of the Government; and ought not to take all upon you, nor be so peremptory. You ought to let the Council have a Share. They are in the Nature of the House of Lords, or upper House; but you seem to take the whole Power in your Hands, and set up for every Thing. You have set a long Time, to little Purpose, and have been a great Charge to the Country. Ten Shillings a Day is a large Allowance, and you punctually exact it. You have been always forward enough to pull down the Fees of other Ministers in the Government. Why did you not think it expedient to correct your own, to a more moderate Allowance?

Gentlemen, I shall say no more, at present, but that you do withdraw to your private Affairs in the Country. I do prorogue you to the tenth of *January* next, and you are hereby prorogued to the tenth Day of *January* next ensuing.

The violence of this man's temper, is very evident in all his speeches and messages to the Assembly; and it can only be attributed to the ignorance of the times, that the members of that House, instead of asserting their equality, peaceably put up with his rudeness. Certainly they deserved better usage at his hands. For the revenue, established the last year, was, at this session, continued five years longer than was originally intended. This was rendering the Governour for a time independent of the people. For, at that day, the Assembly had no treasure, but the amount of all taxes went of course into the hands of the Receiver-General, who was appointed by the Crown. Out of this fund, monies were only issuable by the Governour's warrant; so that every officer in the government, from Mr. Blaithwait,[9] who drew annually five per cent out of the revenue, as Auditor-General, down to the meanest servant of the publick, became dependent, solely, of the Governour. And hence we find the House, at the close of every session, humbly addressing his Excellency, for the trifling wages of their own clerk. Fletcher was, notwithstanding, so much displeased with them, that, soon after the prorogation, he dissolved the Assembly.

The members of the new Assembly met according to the writ of summons, in March 1694, and chose Colonel Peirson, for their Speaker, Mr. Graham being left out at the election for the city. The shortness of this session, which continued only to the latter end of the month, was owing to the disagreeable business the House began upon, of examining the state of the publick accounts, and in particular the muster rolls of the volunteers, in the pay of the Province. They, however, resumed it again in September, and formally entered their dissatisfaction, with the Receiver-General's accounts. The Governour, at the same time, blew up the coals of contention, by a demand of additional pay, for the King's soldiers, then just arrived, and new supplies for detachments in defence of the frontiers. He at last prorogued them, after obtaining an Act for supporting one hundred men upon the borders. The same disputes revived again in the spring 1695; and proceeded to such lengths, that the Assembly asked the Governour's leave to print their minutes, that they might appeal to the publick. It was at this session, on the 12th of April 1695, that upon a petition of five church wardens and vestrymen of the city of New-York, the House declared it to be their opinion, "That the Vestrymen and Church Wardens have Power to call a dissenting Protestant

Minister, and that he is to be paid and maintained as the Act directs." The intent of this petition was to refute an opinion, which prevailed, that the late Ministry Act was made for the sole benefit of Episcopal clergymen.

The quiet, undisturbed, state of the frontiers, while the French were endeavouring to make a peace with the Five Nations, and the complaints of many of the volunteers, who had not received their pay, very much conduced to the backwardness of the Assembly, in answering Fletcher's perpetual demands of money. But when the Indians refused to comply with the terms of peace demanded by the French Governour, which were to suffer him to rebuild the fort at Cadaraqui, and to include the Indian allies, the war broke out afresh, and the Assembly were obliged to augment both their detachments and supplies. The Count Frontenac, now leveled his wrath, principally, against the Mohawks, who were more attached, than any other of the Five Nations to our interest: but as his intentions had taken air, he prudently changed his measures, and sent a party of three hundred men, to the isthmus at Niagara, to surprise those of the Five Nations, that might be hunting there. Among a few that were met with, some were killed, and others taken prisoners, and afterwards burnt at Montreal. Our Indians imitated the Count's example, and burnt ten Dewagunga captives.

Colonel Fletcher and his Assembly having come to an open rupture, in the spring, he called another in June, of which James Graham was chosen Speaker. The Count Frontenac was then repairing the old fort at Cadaraqui, and the intelligence of this, and the King's assignment of the quotas of the several colonies, for an united force* against the French, were the principal matters which the Governour laid before the Assembly. The list of the quotas was this.

* As such an union appeared to be necessary so long ago, it is very surprising that no effectual scheme for that purpose has hitherto been carried into full execution. A plan was concerted, in the great Congress consisting of Commissioners from several colonies, met at Albany, in 1754; but what approbation it received at home, has not hitherto been made publick. The danger to Great Britain, apprehended fom our united force, is founded in a total ignorance of the true state and character of the colonies. None of His Majesty's subjects are more loyal, or more strongly attached to Protestant principles; and the remarkable attestation, in the elegant address of the Lords of the 13th of November 1755, in our favour, "That we are a great Body of brave and faithful Subjects," is as justly due to us, as it was nobly said by them.

| Pennsylvania, | £ 80. | Rhode Island and Providence, | |
|---|---|---|---|
| Massachusetts Bay, | 350. | Plantation, | £ 48. |
| Maryland, | 160. | Connecticut, | 120. |
| Virginia, | 240. | New-York, | 200. |

As a number of forces were now arrived, the Assembly were in hopes, the Province would be relieved from raising any more men for the defence of the frontiers; and, to obtain this favour of the Governour, ordered £1000 to be levied, one half to be presented to him, and the rest he had leave to distribute among the English officers and soldiers. A bill for this purpose was drawn, but though his Excellency thanked them for their favourable intention, he thought it not for his honour to consent to it. After passing several laws, the session broke up in perfect harmony, the Governour in his great grace, recommending it to the House, to appoint a Committee to examine the publick accounts against the next sessions.

In September, Fletcher went up to Albany, with very considerable presents to the Indians; whom he blamed for suffering the French to rebuild the fort at Cadaraqui, or Frontenac, which commands the entrance from Canada, into the great Lake Ontario.

While these works were carrying on, the Dionandadies, who were then poorly supplied by the French, made overtures of a peace with the Five Nations, which the latter readily embraced, because it was owing to their fears of these Indians, who lived near the Lake Misilimachinac, that they never dared to march with their whole strength against Canada. The French Commandant was fully sensible of the importance of preventing this alliance. The civilities of the Dionandadies to the prisoners, by whom the Treaty to Prevent a Discovery, was negotiated, gave the officer the first suspicion of it. One of these wretches had the unhappiness to fall into the hands of the French, who put him to the most exquisite torments, that all future intercourse with the Dionandadies might be cut off. Dr. Colden, in just resentment for this inhuman barbarity, has published the whole process from La Potherie's History of North America, and it is this:

> The Prisoner being first made fast to a Stake, so as to have room to move round it; a *Frenchman* began the horrid Tragedy, by broiling the Flesh of the Prisoner's Legs, from his

Toes to his Knees, with the red-hot Barrel of a Gun. His Example was followed by an *Utawawa,* who being desirous to outdo the *French* in their refined Cruelty, split a Furrow from the Prisoner's Shoulder to his Garter, and filling it with Gun Powder, set fire to it. This gave him exquisite Pain, and raised excessive Laughter in his Tormentors. When they found his Throat so much parched, that he was no longer able to gratify their Ears with his Howling, they gave him Water, to enable him to continue their Pleasure longer. But at last his Strength failing, an *Utawawa* fleaed off his Scalp, and threw burning hot Coals on his Scull. Then they untied him, and bid him run for his Life. He began to run, tumbling like a drunken Man. They shut up the Way to the East, and made him run Westward, the Country, as they think, of departed miserable Souls. He had still Force left to throw Stones, till they put an End to his Misery by knocking him on the Head. After this every one cut a Slice from his Body, to conclude the Tragedy with a Feast.

From the time Colonel Fletcher received his instruction, respecting the quotas of these colonies, for the defence of the frontiers, he repeatedly, but in vain, urged their compliance with the King's Direction; he then carried his complaints against them home to His Majesty, but all his applications were defeated by the agents of those colonies, who resided in England. As soon therefore, as he had laid this matter before the assembly, in autumn 1695, the House appointed William Nicol, to go home in the quality of an agent for this Province, for which they allowed him £1000.[10] But his sollicitations proved unsuccessful, and the instruction, relating to these quotas, which is still continued, remains unnoticed to this day. Fletcher maintained a good correspondence with the Assembly, through the rest of his administration; and nothing appears, upon their Journals, worth the reader's attention.

The French never had a governour, in Canada, so vigilant and active as the Count De Frontenac. He had no sooner repaired the old Fort, called by his name, than he formed a design of invading the country of the Five Nations with a great army. For this purpose, in 1696, he convened at Montreal, all the regulars, as well as militia, under his command; the Owenagungas, Quatoghies of Loretto, Adirondacks, Sokakies, Nipiciriniens, the proselyted praying Indians of the Five Nations, and a few Utawawas. Instead of waggons and horses, which are useless in such a country as he had to march through, the army was conveyed through rivers and lakes, in light barks, which are portable, whenever the rapidity of the stream and the crossing an isthmus rendered it necessary. The Count left La Chine, at the South end of the island of Montreal, on the 7th of July. Two battalions of regulars, under the command of Le Chevalier de Callieres, headed by a number of Indians, led the van, with two small pieces of cannon, the mortars, grenadoes, and ammunition. After them followed the provisions: then the main body, with the Count's houshold, a considerable number of voluntiers, and the engineer; and four battalions of the militia commanded by Monsieur De Ramezai, Governour of Trois Rivieres.

Two battalions of regulars and a few Indians, under the Chevalier De Vaudrueil, brought up the rear. Before the army went a parcel of Scouts, to descry the tracts and ambuscades of the enemy. After twelve days march, they arrived at Cadaracqui, about one hundred and eighty miles from Montreal, and then crossed the lake to Oswego. Fifty men marched on each side of the Onondaga River, which is narrow and rapid. When they entered the little lake,* the army divided into two parts, coasting along the edges, that the enemy might be uncertain as to the place of their landing, and where they did land, they erected a fort. The Onondagas had sent away their wives and children, and were determined to defend their castle, till they were informed by a deserter of the superior strength of the French, and the nature of bombs, which were intended to be used against them, and then, after setting fire to their village, they retired into the woods. As soon as the Count heard of this, he marched to their huts in order of battle; being himself carried in an elbow chair, behind the artillery. With this mighty apparatus he entered it, and the destruction of a little Indian corn was the great acquisition. A brave sachem, then about a hundred years old, was the only person, who tarried in the castle to salute the old General. The French Indians put him to torment, which he endured with astonishing presence of mind. To one who stabbed him with a knife, "you had better," says he, "make me die by Fire, that these French Dogs may learn how to suffer like Men:

---

*The Onondaga or Oneida Lake, noted for a good salt pit at the South east end; which, as it may be very advantageous to the garrison at Oswego, it is hoped the Government will never grant to any private company.

you Indians, their Allies, you Dogs of Dogs, think of me when you are in the like Condition."* This sachem was the only man, of all the Onondagas, that was killed; and had not thirty five Oneydoes, who waited to receive Vaudrueil at their castles, been afterwards basely carried into captivity, the Count would have returned without the least mark of triumph. As soon as he began his retreat, the Onondagas followed, and annoyed his army by cuting off several batteaus.

This expensive enterprise, and the continued incursions of the Five Nations, on the country near Montreal, again spread a famine through all Canada. The Count, however, kept up his spirits to the last; and sent out scalping parties, who infested Albany, as our Indians did Montreal, till the Treaty of Peace signed at Ryswick, in 1697.

Richard, Earl of Bellomont, was appointed to succeed Colonel Fletcher, in the year 1695, but did not receive his Commission till the 18th of June, 1697; and as he delayed his voyage till after the Peace of Ryswick, which was signed the 10th of September following, he was blown off our coast to Barbadoes, and did not arrive here before the 2d of April, 1698.

During the late war, the seas were extremely infested with English pirates, some of whom sailed out of New-York; and it was strongly suspected that they had received too much countenance here, even from the government, during Fletcher's administration. His Lordship's promotion to the chief command of the Massachussets Bay and New Hampshire, as well as this Province, was owing partly to his rank, but principally to the affair of the pirates; and the multiplicity of business, to which the charge of three colonies would necessarily expose him, induced the Earl to bring over with him John Nanfan, his kinsman, in the quality of our Lieutenant Governour.† When Lord Bellomont was appointed to the government of these provinces, the King did him the honour to say "that he thought him a Man of Resolution and Integrity, and with these Qualities more likely than any other he could think of, to put a stop to the Growth of Piracy."

Before the Earl set out for America, he became acquainted

---

* "Never perhaps (says Charlevoix) was a Man treated with more Cruelty, nor did any ever bear it with superior Magnanimity and Resolution."
† His Commission was dated the 1st of July, 1697.

with* Robert Livingston, Esq; who was then in England, soliciting his own affairs before the Council and the Treasury. The Earl took occasion, in one of his conferences with Mr. Livingston, to mention the scandal the Province was under on account of the pirates. The latter, who confessed it was not without reason, brought the Earl acquainted with one Kid, whom he recommended as a man of integrity and courage, that knew the pirates and their rendezvous, and would undertake to apprehend them, if the King would employ him in a good sailing frigate of 30 guns and 150 men. The Earl laid the proposal before the King, who consulted the Admiralty upon that subject; but this project dropped, thro' the uncertainty of the adventure, and the French war, which gave full employment to all the ships in the Navy. Mr. Livingston then proposed a private adventure against the pirates, offering to be concerned with Kid, a fifth part in the ship and charges, and to be bound for Kid's faithful execution of the Commission. The King then approved of the design, and reserved a tenth share, to shew that he was concerned in the enterprise. Lord Chancellor Somers, the Duke of Shrewsbury, the Earls of Romney and Oxford, Sir Edmond Harrison and others, joined in the scheme, agreeing to the expence of £6000. But the management of the whole affair was left to Lord Bellomont, who gave orders to Kid to pursue his Commission, which was in common form. Kid sailed, from Plymouth, for New-York, in April, 1696; and afterwards turned pirate, burnt his ship, and came to Boston, where the Earl apprehended him. His Lordship wrote to the Secretary of State, desiring that Kid might be sent for. The Rochester Man-of-War was dispatched upon this service, but being driven back, a general suspicion prevailed in England, that all was collusion between the ministry and the adventurers, who, it was thought, were unwilling Kid should be brought home, lest he might discover that the Chancellor, the Duke, and others, were confederates in the piracy. The matter even proceeded to such lengths, that a motion

* This gentleman was a son of Mr. John Livingston, one of the Commissioners from Scotland to King Charles II while he was an exile at Breda. He was a clergyman distinguished by his zeal and industry; and for his opposition to Episcopacy, became so obnoxious after the Restoration to the English Court, that he left Scotland, and took the pastoral charge of an English Presbyterian church in Rotterdam. His descendants are very numerous in this Province, and the family in the first rank for their wealth, morals, and education. The original diary, in the hand-writing of their common ancestor, is still amongst them, and contains a history of his life.

was made, in the House of Commons, that all who were concerned in the adventure might be turned out of their employments, but it was rejected by a great majority.[11]

The Tory Party, who excited these clamours, though they lost their motion in the House, afterwards impeached several Whig Lords; and, among other articles, charged them with being concerned in Kid's piracy. But these prosecutions served only to brighten the innocency of those, against whom they were brought; for the impeached Lords were honourably acquited by their peers.

Lord Bellomont's Commission was published in Council, on the day of his arrival; Colonel Fletcher, who still remained Governour under the proprietors of Pennsylvania, and Lieutenant-Governour Nanfan, being present. The members of the Council were,

|  |  |
|---|---|
| Frederick Philipse, | William Smith, |
| Stephen Van Cortlandt, | William Nicoll, |
| Nicholas Bayard, | Thomas Willet, |
| Gabriel Mienvielle, | William Pinhorne, |
|  | John Lawrence. |

After the Earl had dispatched Captain John Schuyler, and Dellius, the Dutch Minister of Albany, to Canada, with the account of the peace, and to solicit a mutual exchange of prisoners; he laid before the Council the letters from Secretary Vernon and the East-India Company, relating to the pirates; informing that board, that he had an affidavit, that Fletcher had permited them to land their spoils in this province, and that Mr. Nicoll bargained for their protections, and received for his services 800 Spanish dollars. Nicoll confessed the receipt of the money for protections, but said it was in virtue of a late Act of Assembly, allowing privateers on their giving security; but he denied the receipt of any money from known pirates. One Weaver was admitted, at this time, into the council-chamber, and acted in the quality of King's Council, and in answer to Mr. Nicoll, dened that there was any such Act of Assembly as he mentioned. After considering the whole matter, the Council advised his Excellency to send Fletcher home, but to try Nicoll here, because his estate would not bear the expence of a trial in England. Their advice was never carried into execution, which was probably owing to a want of evidence against the parties accused. It is nevertheless certain, that the pirates were frequently in the

sound, and supplied with provisions by the inhabitants of Long
Island, who, for many years afterwards, were so infatuated with
a notion, that the pirates buried great quantities of money along
the coast, that there is scarce a point of land, or an island,
without the marks of their Auri sacra Fames.[12] Some credulous
people have ruined themselves by these researches, and propagated a thousand idle fables, current to this day, among our
country farmers.

As Fletcher, thro' the whole of his administration, had been
entirely influenced by the enemies of Leisler; nothing could be
more agreeable to the numerous adherents of that unhappy
man, than the Earl's disaffection to the late Governour. It was
for this reason, they immediately devoted themselves to his
Lordship, as the head of their party.

The majority of the members of the Council were Fletcher's
friends, and there needed nothing more to render them obnoxious to his Lordship. Leisler's advocates, at the same time, mor-
tally hated them; not only because they had imbrued their
hands in the blood of the principal men of their party, but
also because they had engrossed the sole confidence of the
late Governour, and brought down his resentment upon them.
Hence, at the commencement of the Earl's administration, the
members of the Council had every thing to fear; while the
party they had depressed, began once again to erect its head
under the smiles of a governour, who was fond of their aid,
as they were solicitous to conciliate his favour. Had the Earl
countenanced the enemies, as well as the friends of Leisler,
which he might have done, his administration would doubtless
have been easier to himself and advantageous to the Province.
But his inflexible aversion to Fletcher prevented his acting with
that moderation, which was necessary to enable him to govern
both parties. The fire of his temper appeared very early, on
his suspending Mr. Nicoll from the Board of Council, and
obliging him to enter into a recognizance in £2000 to answer
for his conduct relating to the protections. But his speech to
the new Assembly, convened on the 18th of May, gave the
fullest evidence of his abhorrence of the late administration.
Philip French was chosen Speaker, and waited upon his Excellency with the House, when his Lordship spoke to them in the
following manner:

"I cannot but observe to you, what a Legacy my Predecessor has left me, and what Difficulties to struggle with;

a divided People, an empty Purse, a few miserable, naked, half-starved Soldiers, not half the Number the King allowed Pay for: the Fortifications and even the Governour's House very much out of Repair, and in a Word the whole Government out of Frame. It hath been represented to the Government in *England*, that this Province has been a noted Receptacle of Pirates, and the Trade of it under no Restriction but the Acts of Trade violated by the Neglect and Connivance of those, whose Duty it was to have prevented it."

After this introduction, he puts them in mind that the revenue was near expiring. "It would be hard, says he, if I that come among you with an honest Mind, and a Resolution to be just to your Interest, should meet with greater Difficulties, in the Discharge of his Majesty's Service, than those that have gone before me. I will take Care there shall be no Misapplication of the public Money. I will pocket none of it myself, nor shall there be any Embezzlement by others; but exact Accounts shall be given you, when, and as often, as you shall require."

It was customary with Fletcher, to be present in the field, to influence elections; and as the Assembly consisted, at this time, of but nineteen members, they were too easily influenced to serve the private ends of a faction. For that reason, his Lordship was warm in a scheme of increasing their number, at present, to thirty, and so, in proportion, as the colony became more populous; and hence we find the following clause in his speech. "You cannot but know, what Abuses have been formerly in Elections of Members, to serve in the general Assembly, which tends to the Subversion of your Liberties. I do therefore recommend the making of a Law to provide against it."

The House, tho' unanimous in a hearty address of thanks to the Governour for his speech, could scarce agree upon any thing else. It was not till the beginning of June, before they had finished the controversies relating to the late turbulent elections; and even then six members seceded from the House, which obliged his Excellency to dissolve the Assembly on the 14th of June, 1698. About the same time, the Governour dismissed two of the Council; Pinhorne, for disrespectful words of the King, and Brook, the Receiver-General, who was also turned out of that office, as well as removed from his place on the Bench.

In July, the disputes with the French, concerning the exchanging of prisoners, obliged his Excellency to go up to Albany. When the Earl sent the account of the conclusion of the peace to the Governour of Canada, all the French prisoners, in our custody, were restored, and as to those among the Indians, he promised to order them to be safely escorted to Montreal. His Lordship then added, "I doubt not, Sir, that you, on your Part, will also issue an Order to relieve the Subjects of the King, captivated during the War, whether Christians or Indians."

The Count, fearful of being drawn into an implicit acknowledgement, that the Five Nations were subject to the English Crown, demanded the French prisoners, among the Indians, to be brought to Montreal; threatening, at the same time, to continue the war against the Confederates, if they did not comply with his request. After the Earl's interview with them, he wrote a second letter* to the Count, informing him that they had importunately begged to continue *under the Protection of the* English *Crown, professing an inviolable Subjection and Fidelity to his Majesty;* and that the Five Nations were always considered as subjects, which, says his Lordship, "can be manifested to all the World by authentick and solid Proofs." His Lordship added, that he would not suffer them to be insulted, and threatens to execute the laws of England upon the missionaries, if they continued any longer in the Five Cantons. A resolute spirit runs through the whole letter, which concludes in these words: "if it is necessary, I will arm every Man in the Provinces, under my Government, to oppose you; and redress the Injury that you may perpetrate against our *Indians."* The Count, in his answer, proposed to refer the dispute to the Commissaries, to be appointed according to the Treaty of Ryswick;† but the Earl continued the claim, insisting that the French prisoners should be delivered up at Albany.

The French Count dying while this matter was controverted, Monsieur De Callieres, his successor, sent ambassadours, the next year, to Onondaga, there to regulate the exchange of pris-

* Charlevoix has published both these letters, at large, together with Count Frontenac's answer. I have had no opportunity of enquiring into the Jesuit's integrity, in these transcripts, being unable to find his Lordship's letters in the Secretary's office.
† The Count misunderstood the treaty. No provision was made by it for commissaries to settle the limits between the English and French Possessions, but only to examine and determine the controverted rights and pretensions to Hudson's Bay.

oners, which was accomplished without the Earl's consent; and thus the important point, in dispute, remained unsettled. The Jesuit Bruyas, who was upon this embassage, offered to live at Onondaga; but the Indians refused his belt, saying that Corlear, or the Governour of New-York, had already offered them ministers for their instruction.

Great alterations were made in Council, at his Excellency's return from Albany. Bayard,[13] Meinvielle, Willet, Townley, and Lawrence, were all suspended on the 28th of September; and Colonel Abraham Depeyster, Robert Livingston, and Samuel Staats, called to that board. The next day, Frederick Philipse resigned his seat, and Robert Walters was sworn in his stead.

The new Assembly, of which James Graham was chosen Speaker, met in the spring. His Excellency spoke to them on the 21st of March, 1699.

As the late Assembly was principally composed of Anti-Leislerians, so this consisted, almost entirely, of the opposite party. The elections were attended with great outrage and tumult, and many applications made, relating to the returns; but as Abraham Governeur, who had been Secretary to Leisler, got returned for Orange County, and was very active in the House,* all the petitions were rejected without ceremony.

Among the principal acts, passed at this session, there was one for indemnifying those who were excepted out of the general pardon in 1691; another against pirates; one for the settlement of Milborne's estate; and another to raise fifteen hundred pounds, as a present to his Lordship, and five hundred pounds for the Lieutenant-Governour, his kinsman. Besides which, the revenue was continued for six years longer. A necessary law was also made for the regulation of elections, containing the substance of the English statutes of 8 *Hen.* VI. Chap. VII. and the 7 and 8 *Will.* III.

This Assembly took, also, into consideration sundry extravagant grants of land, which Colonel Fletcher had made to several of his favourites. Among these, two grants to Dellius, the Dutch Minister, and one to Nicholas Bayard, were the most considerable. Dellius was one of the commissioners for Indian affairs, and had fraudulently obtained the Indian deeds, according to which the patents had been granted. One of the grants included all the lands within twelve miles on the East side of Hudson's River, and extended twenty miles in length,

---

* Mr. Governeur married Milborne's Widow.

from the North bounds of Saraghtoga. The second patent, which was granted to him in company with Pinhorne, Bancker, and others, contained all the lands, within two miles on each side of the Mohawks River, and along its banks to the extent of fifty miles. Bayard's grant was also for lands in that country, and very extravagant. Lord Bellomont, who justly thought these great patents, with the trifling annual reservation of a few skins, would impede the settlement of the country, as well as alienate the affections of our Indian allies, wisely procured recommendatory instructions from the Lords Justices, for vacating those patents, which was now regularly accomplished by a law, and Dellius thereby suspended from his ministerial function.

The Earl having thus carried all his points at New-York, set out for Boston in June, whence, after he had settled his salary, and apprehended the Pirate Kidd, he returned here again in the fall.

The revenue being settled for six years, his Lordship had no occasion to meet the Assembly till the summer of the year 1700, and then indeed little else was done, than to pass a few laws. One for hanging every Popish priest, that came voluntarily into the Province, which was occasioned by the great number of French Jesuits, who were continually practising upon our Indians. By another, provision was made for erecting a fort in the country of the Onondagas, but as this was repealed a few months after the King's providing for that purpose, so the former continues, as it for ever ought, in full force to this day.

The Earl was a man of art and polite manners, and being a mortal enemy to the French, as well as a lover of liberty, he would doubtless have been of considerable service to the colony; but he died here on the 5th of March in 1701, when he was but just become acquainted with the colony.[14]

The Earl of Bellomont's death was the source of new troubles, for Nanfan, the Lieutenant-Governour, being then absent in Barbadoes, high disputes arose among the counsellors, concerning the exercise of the powers of government. Abraham de Peyster, Samuel Staats, Robert Walters, and Thomas Weaver, who sided with the party that adhered to Leisler, insisted that the government was devolved upon the Council, who had a right to act by a majority of voices; but Colonel Smith[15] contended that all the powers of the late Governour were devolved upon him, as President, he being the eldest member of that board. Colonel Schuyler and Robert Livingston, who did not arrive in town till the 21st of March, joined Mr. Smith, and refused to appear at the Council-Board, till near the Middle of April. The Assembly, which was convened on the 2d of that month, were in equal perplexity, for they adjourned from day to day, waiting the issue of this rupture. Both parties continuing inflexible, those members, who opposed Colonel Smith, sent down to the House a representation of the controversy, assigning a number of reasons for the siting of the Assembly, which the House took into their consideration, and on the 16th of April resolved, that the execution of the Earl's Commission and instructions, in the absence of the Lieutenant-Governour, was the right of the Council by majority of voices, and not of any single member of that board; and this was afterwards the opinion of the Lords of Trade.[16] The disputes, nevertheless, continuing in the Council strenuously supported by Mr. Livingston, the House, on the 19th of April, thought proper to adjourn themselves to the first Tuesday in June.

In this interval, on the 19th of May, John Nanfan, the Lieutenant-Governour, arrived, and settled the controversy, by taking upon himself the supreme command.

Upon Mr. Nanfan's arrival, we had the agreeable news that the King had given two thousand pounds sterling, for the defence of Albany and Schenectady, as well as five hundred pounds more for erecting a fort in the country of the Onondagas. And not long after, an ordinance was issued, agreeable to the special direction of the Lords of Trade, for erecting a court of chancery, to sit the first Thursday in every month. By this ordinance the powers of the Chancellor were vested in the Governour and Council, or any two of that board: commissions were also granted, appointing masters, clerks, and a register: so that this court was compleatly organized on the 2d of September 1701.

Atwood, who was then Chief Justice of the Supreme Court, was now sworn of the Council. Abraham de Peyster and Robert Walters were his assistants on the Bench; and the former was also made Deputy Auditor-General, under Mr. Blaithwait. Sampson Shelton Broughton was the Attorney-General, and came into that office when Atwood took his seat on the Bench, before the decease of Lord Bellomont. Both these had their commissions from England. The Lieutenant-Governour, and the major part of the Board of Council, together with the several officers above named, being strongly in the interest of the Leislerian party, it was not a little surprising, that Mr. Nanfan dissolved the late Assembly on the 1st of June last.

Great were the struggles at the ensuing elections, which however generally prevailed in favour of those, who joined Leisler at the Revolution; and hence, when the new Assembly met on the 19th of August 1701, Abraham Governeur was elected for their Speaker. Dutchess was thought heretofore incapable of bearing the charge of a representation; but the people of that county, now animated by the heat of the times, sent Jacob Rutsen and Adrian Garretsen to represent them in Assembly.[17]

Mr. Nanfan, in his speech to the House, informs them of the memorable grant made to the crown, on the 19th of July, by the Five Nations, of a vast tract of land, to prevent the necessity of their submitting to the French in case of a war; that his Majesty had given out of his Exchequer two thousand five hundred pounds sterling for forts, and eight hundred pounds to be laid out in presents to the Indians; and that he had also settled a salary of three hundred pounds on a Chief Justice, and one hundred and fifty pounds on the Attorney-General, who were both now arrived here.

The fire of contention, which had lately appeared in the tumultuous elections, blazed out afresh in the House. Nicoll, the late Counsellor, got himself elected for Suffolk, and was in hopes of being seated in the chair: but Abraham Governeur was chosen Speaker. Several members contended, that he, being an alien, was unqualified for that station. To this it was answered, that he was in the Province in the year 1683, at the time of passing an Act to naturalize all the free inhabitants, professing the Christian religion; and that for this reason, the same objection against him had been over-ruled at the last Assembly. In return for this attack, Governeur disputed Nicoll's right of sitting as a member of that House. And succeeded in a resolve, that he and Mr. Wessels, who had been returned for Albany, were both unqualified according to the late Act, they being neither of them residents in the respective counties for which they were chosen. This occasioned an imprudent secession of seven members, who had joined the interest of Mr. Nicoll; which gave their adversaries an opportunity to expell them, and introduce others in their stead.

Among the first opposers of Captain Leisler, none was more considerable than Mr. Livingston. The measures of the Convention at Albany were very much directed by his advice; and he was peculiarly obnoxious to his adversaries, because he was a man of sense and resolution, two qualifications rarely to be found united in one person at that day. Mr. Livingston's intimacy with the late Earl, had, till this time, been his defence, against the rage of the party which he had formerly opposed; but as that Lord was now dead, and Mr. Livingston's conduct in Council, in favour of Colonel Smith, had given fresh provocation to his enemies, they were fully bent upon his destruction. It was in execution of this scheme, that as soon as the disputed elections were over, the House proceeded to examine the state of the publick accounts, which they partly began at the late Assembly.

The pretence was, that he refused to account for the publick monies he had formerly received out of the excise; upon which, a committee of both Houses advised the passing a bill to confiscate his estate, unless he agreed to account by a certain day. But instead of this, an Act was afterwards passed to oblige him to account for a sum amounting to near eighteen thousand pounds. While this matter was transacting, a new complaint was forged, and he was summoned before another committee of both Houses, relating to his procuring the Five Nations to signify their desire that he should be sent home to sollicit their affairs. The criminality of this charge can be seen only through the partial opticks, with which his enemies then scanned his behaviour. Besides, there was no evidence to support it, and therefore the Committee required him to purge himself by his own oath. Mr. Livingston, who was better acquainted with English law and liberty, than to countenance a practice so odious, rejected the insolent demand with disdain; upon which, the House, by advice of the Committee, addressed the Lieutenant-Governour, to pray his Majesty to remove him from his office of Secretary of Indian Affairs, and that the Governour, in the mean time, would suspend him from the exercise of his Commission.*

It was at this favourable conjuncture, that Jacob Leisler's petition to the King, and his Majesty's letter to the late Earl of

---

* Mr. Livingston's reason for not accounting was truly unanswerable; his books and vouchers were taken into the hands of the Government, and detained from him.

Bellomont, were laid before the Assembly. Leisler, displeased with the report of the Lords of Trade, that his father and his brother Milborne had suffered according to law, laid his case before the Parliament, and obtained an act to reverse the attainder.[18] After which, he applied to the King, complaining that his father had disbursed about four thousand pounds, in purchasing arms and forwarding the Revolution; in consequence of which he procured the following letter to Lord Bellomont, dated at Whitehall the 6th of February 1699/1700.

My Lord,

The King being moved upon the Petition of Mr. *Jacob Leisler,* and having a gracious Sense of his Father's Services and Sufferings, and the ill Circumstances the Petitioner is thereby reduced to, his Majesty is pleased to direct, that the same be transmitted to your Lordship, and that you recommend his Case to the general Assembly of *New-York,* being the only Place, where he can be relieved, and the Prayer of his Petition complyed with. I am,

My Lord, your Lordship's

*Most obedient and humble Servant,*

Jersey.

As soon as this letter and the petition was brought into the House, a thousand pounds were ordered to be levied for the benefit of Mr. Leisler, as well as several sums for other persons, by a bill for paying the debts of the government; which nevertheless did not pass into a law, till the next sessions. Every thing that was done at this meeting of the Assembly, which continued till the 18th of October, was under the influence of a party spirit; and nothing can be a fuller evidence of it, than an incorrect, impertinent, address to his Majesty, which was drawn up by the House, at the close of the session, and signed by fourteen of the members. It contains a tedious narrative of their proceedings, relating to the disputed elections, and concludes with a little incense, to regale some of the then principal agents in the publick affairs, in these words:

This necessary Account of ourselves and our unhappy divisions, which we hope the Moderation of our Lieutenant-Governor, the Wisdom and Prudence of *William Atwood,* Esq; our Chief Justice, and *Thomas Weaver,* Esq; your Majesty's Collector and Receiver-General, might have healed, we lay before your Majesty with all Humility, and deep Sense of your Majesty's Goodness to us, lately expressed in sending over so excellent a Person to be our Chief Justice.

The news of the King's having appointed Lord Cornbury to succeed the Earl of Bellomont, so strongly animated the hopes of the Anti-Leislerian Party, that about the commencement of the Year 1702, Nicholas Bayard promoted several addresses to the King, the Parliament, and Lord Cornbury, which were subscribed at a tavern kept by one Hutchins, an alderman of the city of New-York. In that to his Majesty, they assure him, "That the late Differences were not grounded on a Regard to his Interest, but the corrupt Designs of those, who laid hold on an Opportunity to enrich themselves by the Spoils of their Neighbours." The petition to the Parliament says, that Leisler and his adherents gained the fort at the Revolution without any opposition; that he oppressed and imprisoned the people without cause, plundered them of their goods, and compelled them to flee their country, tho' they were well affected to the Prince of Orange. That the Earl of Bellomont appointed indigent sheriffs, who returned such members to the Assembly as were unduly elected, and in his Lordship's esteem. That he suspended many from the Board of Council, who were faithful servants of the Crown, introducing his own tools in their stead. Nay they denied the authority of the late assembly, and added, that the House had bribed both the Lieutenant-Governour and the Chief Justice; the one to pass their bills, and the other to defend the legality of their proceedings. A third address was prepared, to be presented to Lord Cornbury, to congratulate his arrival, as well to prepossess him in their favour, as to prejudice him against the opposite party.

Nothing could have a more natural tendency to excite the wrath of the Lieutenant-Governour, and the revenge of the Council and Assembly, than the reflections contained in those several Addresses. Nanfan had no sooner received intelligence of them than he summoned Hutchins to deliver them up to him, and upon his refusal committed him to jail, on the 19th of January; the next day Nicholas Bayard, Rip Van Dam, Philip French, and Thomas Wenham, hot with party zeal, sent an imprudent address to the Lieutenant-Governor, boldly justifying the legality of the address, and demanding his discharge out of custody. I have before taken notice, that upon Sloughter's arrival in 1691, an Act was passed, to recognize the right of King William and Queen Mary to the sovereignty of this Province. At the end of that law, a clause was added in these words, "That whatsoever Person or Persons, shall by any Manner of Ways, or upon any Pretence whatsoever, endeavour by Force of Arms or otherwise, to disturb the Peace, Good, and Quiet of their Majesties Government, as it is now established, shall be deemed and esteemed as Rebels and Traytors unto their Majesties, and incur the Pains, Penalties, and Forfeitures, as the Laws of *England* have for such Offenses made and provided." Under pretext of this Law, which Bayard himself had been personally concerned in enacting, Mr. Nanfan issued a warrant for commiting him to jail as a traitor, on the 21st of January; and lest the mob should interpose, a company of soldiers, for a week after, constantly guarded the prison.[19]

Through the uncertainty of the time of Lord Cornbury's arrival, Mr. Nanfan chose to bring the prisoner to his trial, as soon as possible; and for that purpose issued a Commission of Oyer and Terminer, on the 12th of February, to William Atwood, the Chief Justice, and Abraham De Peyster and Robert Walters, who were the puisne Judges of the Supreme Court; and not long after Bayard was arraigned, indicted, tried, and convicted of high treason. Several reasons were afterwards offered in arrest of judgment; but as the prisoner was unfortunately in the hands of an enraged party, Atwood overruled what was offered, and condemned him to death on the 16th of March. As the process of his trial has been long since printed in the State Trials at large, I leave the reader to his own remarks upon the conduct of the judges, who are generally accused of partiality.

Bayard applied to Mr. Nanfan for a reprieve, till his Majesty's pleasure might be known; and obtained it, not without great difficulty, nor till after a seeming confession of guilt was extorted. Hutchins, who was also convicted, was bailed upon the payment of forty pieces of eight to the Sheriff, but Bayard, who refused to procure him the gift of a farm, of about fifteen hundred pounds value, was not released from his confinement, till after the arrival of Lord Cornbury, who not only gave his consent to an Act for reversing the late attainders, but procured the Queen's confirmation of it, upon their giving security according to the advice of Sir Edward Northey, not to bring any suits against those who were concerned in their prosecution;

which the Attorney-General thought proper, as the Act ordained all the proceedings to be obliterated.[20]

After these trials, Nanfan erected a Court of Exchequer, and again convened the Assembly, who thanked him for his late measures, and passed an Act to out-law Philip French, and Thomas Wenham, who absconded upon Bayard's commitment; another to augment the number of representatives, and several others, which were, all but one, afterwards repealed by Queen Anne. During this session, Lord Cornbury being daily expected, the Lieutenant-Governor suspended Mr. Livingston from his seat in Council, and thus continued to abet Leisler's Party, to the end of his administration.

Lord Cornbury's arrival quite opened a new scene. His father, the Earl of Clarendon, adhered to the cause of the late abdicated King, and always refused the oaths both to King William and Queen Anne. But the son recommended himself at the Revolution, by appearing very early for the Prince of Orange, being one of the first officers that deserted King James's army. King William, in gratitude for his services, gave him a Commission for this government, which, upon the death of the King, was renewed by Queen Anne, who at the same time, appointed him to the chief command of New-Jersey, the government of which the Proprietors had lately surrendered into her hands. As Lord Cornbury came to this Province, in very indigent circumstances, hunted out of England by a host of hungry creditors, he was bent upon getting as much money, as he could squeeze out of the purses of an impoverished people. His talents were, perhaps, not superior to the most inconsiderable of his predecessors; but in his zeal for the Church [of England] he was surpassed by none. With these bright qualifications he began his administration on the 3d of May, 1702, assisted by a Council consisting of the following members,

| | |
|---|---|
| William Atwood, | Thomas Weaver, |
| William Smith, | Sampson Shelton Broughton, |
| Peter Schuyler, | Wolfgang William Romar, |
| Abraham De Peyster, | William Lawrence, |
| Samuel Staats, | Gerardus Beekman, |
| Robert Walters, | Rip Van Dam. |

His Lordship, without the least disguise, espousing the Anti-Leislerian faction, Atwood, the Chief Justice,[21] and Weaver, who acted in quality of Sollicitor-General, thought proper to retire from his frowns to Virginia, whence they sailed to England: the former concealing himself under the name of Jones, while the latter called himself Jackson. Colonel Heathcote and Doctor Bridges succeeded in their places at the Council Board.

The following summer was remarkable for an uncommon mortality, which prevailed in the City of New-York, and makes a grand epoch among our inhabitants, distinguished by the "Time of the great Sickness."* On this occasion Lord Cornbury had his residence and court at Jamaica, a pleasant village on Long-Island, distant about twelve miles from the city.

The inhabitants of Jamaica consisted, at that time, partly of original Dutch planters, but mostly of New-England emigrants, encouraged to settle there, after the surrender, by the Duke of York's CONDITIONS FOR PLANTATIONS, one of which was in these words: "That every Township should be obliged to pay their own Ministers, according to such Agreements as they should make with him; the Minister being elected by the major Part of the Housholders and Inhabitants of the Town." These people had erected an edifice for the worship of God, and enjoyed a handsome donation of a parsonage-house and glebe, for the use of their minister. After the Ministry Act was passed, by Colonel Fletcher, in 1693, a few Episcopalians crept into the town, and viewed the Presbyterian Church with a jealous Eye. The town vote, in virtue of which the building had been erected, contained no clause to prevent its being hereafter engrossed by any other sect. The Episcopal Party, who knew this, formed a design of seizing the edifice for themselves, which they shortly after carried into execution, by entering the church between the morning and evening service, while the Presbyterian minister and his congregation were in perfect security, unsuspicious of the zeal of their adversaries, and a fraudulent ejectment, on a day consecrated to sacred rest.

Great outrage ensued among the people, for the contention being *pro Aris & Focis*,²² was animating and important. The original Proprietors of the House tore up their seats, and afterwards got the key and the possession of the church, which were shortly after again taken from them by force and violence. In

---

* The fever killed almost every patient seized with it, and was brought here in a vessel from St. Thomas in the West Indies, an island remarkable for contagious diseases.

these controversies the Governour abetted the Episcopal zealots, and harassed the others by numberless prosecutions, heavy fines, and long imprisonments; through fear of which, many, who had been active in the dispute, fled out of the Province. Lord Cornbury's noble descent and education should have prevented him from taking part in so ignominious a quarrel; but his Lordship's sense of honour and justice was as weak and indelicate, as his bigotry was rampant and uncontroulable: and hence we find him guilty of an act complicated of a number of vices, which no man could have perpetrated without violence to the very slightest remains of generosity and justice. When his Excellency retired to Jamaica, one Hubbard, the Presbyterian minister, lived in the best house in the town. His Lordship beged the loan of it for the use of his own family, and the Clergyman put himself to no small inconveniencies to favour the Governour's request; but in return for the generous benefaction, his Lordship perfidiously delivered the parsonage-house into the hands of the Episcopal Party, and encouraged one Cardwel, the Sheriff, a mean fellow, who afterwards put an end to his own life, to seize upon the glebe, which he surveyed into lots, and farmed for the benefit of the Episcopal Church. These tyrannical measures justly inflamed the indignation of the injured sufferers, and that again the more embittered his Lordship against them. *They* resented, and *he* prosecuted: nor did he confine his pious rage to the people of Jamaica. He detested all who were of the same denomination; nay, averse to every sect except his own, he insisted that neither the ministers nor schoolmasters of the Dutch, the most numerous persuasion in the Province, had a right to preach or instruct without his gubernatorial licence; and some of them tamely submited to his unauthoritative rule.[23] A general account of his Lordship's singular zeal, is preserved under the title of the WATCH TOWER, in a number of papers published in the *New-York Weekly Mercury* for the year 1755.

While his Excellency was exerting his bigotry, during the summer season, at Jamaica; the elections were carrying on, with great heat, for an Assembly, which met him, at that village, in the fall. It consisted principally of the party, which had been borne down by the Earl of Bellomont and his kinsman; and hence we find Philip French, who had lately been out-lawed, was returned a Representative for New-York, and William Nicoll elected into the Speaker's Chair. Several extracts from my Lord's speech are proper to be laid before the reader, as a specimen of his temper and designs.

> It was an extream Surprise to me, (says his Lordship), to find this Province, at my Landing at *New-York,* in such a Convulsion as must have unavoidably occasioned its Ruin, if it had been suffered to go on a little longer. The many Complaints that were brought to me, against the Persons I found here in Power, sufficiently proved against them; and the miserable Accounts I had of the Condition of our Frontiers, made me think it convenient to delay my Meeting you in general Assembly, till I could inform myself, in some measure, of the Condition of this Province, that I might be able to offer to your Consideration, some few of those Things, which will be necessary to be done forthwith, for the Defence of the Country.

He then recommends their fortifying the port of New-York, and the frontiers; adding, that he found the soldiers naked and unarmed: after which, he proposes a militia bill, the erection of publick schools, and an examination of the provincial debts and accounts; and not only promises to make a faithful application of the monies to be raised, but that he would render them an account. The whole speech is sweetened with this gracious conclusion:

> Now, Gentlemen, I have no more to trouble you with, but to assure you, in the Name of the great Queen of *England,* my Mistress, that you may safely depend upon all the Protection that good and faithful Subjects can desire or expect, from a sovereign whose greatest Delight is the Welfare of her People, under whose auspicious Reign we are sure to enjoy what no Nation in the World dares claim but the Subjects of *England;* I mean, the free Injoyment of the best Religion in the World, the full Possession of all lawful Liberty, and the undisturbed Injoyment of our Freeholds and Properties. These are some, of the many, Benefits which I take the Inhabitants of this Province to be well intitled to by the Laws of *England;* and I am glad of this Opportunity to assure you, that as long as I have the Honour to serve the Queen in the Government of this Province, those Laws shall be put in Execution, according to the Intent with which they were made; that is, for the Preservation and Protection of the People, and not for their Oppression. I heartily rejoice to see, that the free Choice of the People has fallen upon Gentlemen, whose constant Fidelity to the Crown, and un-

wearied Application to the Good of their Country, is so universally known.

The House echoed back an address of high compliment to his Lordship, declaring, "That being deeply sensible of the Misery and Calamity the Country lay under at his Arrival, they were not sufficiently able to express the Satisfaction they had, both in their Relief and their Deliverer."

Well pleased with a governour who headed their party, the Assembly granted him all his requests; eighteen hundred pounds were raised for the support of one hundred and eighty men, to defend the frontiers, besides two thousand pounds more, as a present towards defraying the expences of his voyage. The Queen, by her letter of the 20th of April, in the next year, forbad any such donations for the future. It is observable, that tho' the county of Dutchess had no representatives at this Assembly, yet such was then the known indigence of that now populous and flourishing county, that but eighteen pounds were apportioned for their quota of these levies.

Besides the acts above-mentioned, the House brought up a militia bill, and continued the revenue to the 1st of May, 1709; and a law passed to establish a grammar-school, according to his Lordship's recommendation. Besides the great harmony that subsisted between the Governour and his Assembly, there was nothing remarkable except two resolves against the Court of Chancery erected by Mr. Nanfan, occasioned by a petition of several disappointed suitors, who were displeased with a decree. The resolutions were in these words: "That the setting up a Court of Equity in this Colony, without Consent of general Assembly, is an Innovation without any former Precedent, inconvenient and contrary to the *English* Law." And again: "That the Court of Chancery, as lately erected, and managed here, was and is unwarrantable, a great Oppression to the Subject, of pernicious Example and Consequence; that all Proceedings, Orders, and Decrees in the same, are, and of Right ought to be, declared null and void; and that a Bill be brought in, according to these two Resolutions," which was done: but tho' his Lordship was by no means disinclined to fix contempt on Nanfan's Administration, yet as this bill would diminish his own power, himself being the Chancellor, the matter was never moved farther, than to the order for the ingrossment of the bill upon the second reading.

Tho' a war was proclaimed by England on the 4th of May,

1702, against France and Spain, yet as the Five Nations had entered into a Treaty of Neutrality with the French in Canada, this Province, instead of being harassed on its borders by the enemy, carried on a trade very advantageous to all those who were concerned in it. The Governour, however, continued his sollicitations for money, with unremited importunity, and by alarming the Assembly, which met in April, 1703, with his expectation of an attack by sea, fifteen hundred pounds were raised, under pretence of erecting two batteries at the Narrows; which, instead of being employed for that use, his Lordship, notwithstanding the Province had expended twenty-two thousand pounds during the late peace, was pleased to appropriate to his private advantage.[24] But let us do him the justice to confess, that while he was robbing the publick, he at the same time consented to several other laws for the emolument of the clergy.

Whether it was owing to the extraordinary sagacity of the House, or their presumption that his Lordship was as little to be trusted as any of his predecessors, that, after voting the above sum for the batteries, they added, that it should be "for no other Use whatsoever," I leave the reader to determine. It is certain they now began to see the danger of throwing the publick money into the hands of a Receiver-General appointed by the Crown, from whence the Governour, by his warrants, might draw it at his pleasure. To this cause we must assign it, that in an address to his Lordship, on the 19th of June, 1703, they "desire and insist, that some proper and sufficient Person might be commissioned Treasurer, for the receiving and paying such Monies now intended to be raised for the publick Use, as a Means to obstruct Misapplications for the future." Another address was sent home to the Queen, complaining of the ill state of the revenue, thro' the frauds which had formerly been commited, the better to facilitate the important design of having a treasurer dependent on the Assembly. The success of these measures will appear in the sequel.

Tho' our frontiers enjoyed the profoundest tranquillity all the next winter, and we had expended thirteen hundred pounds, in supporting one hundred fuzileers about Albany, besides the four independent companies in the pay of the Crown, yet his Excellency demanded provisions for one hundred and fifty men, at the next meeting of the Assembly, in April, 1704. The House having reason to suspect, that the several sums of eighteen and thirteen hundred pounds, lately raised for the publick service, had been prodigally expended or embezzled, prudently declined any farther aids, till they were satisfied that no misapplication had been made. For this purpose they appointed a committee, who reported that there was a balance of near a thousand pounds due to the colony. His Lordship, who had hitherto been treated with great complaisance, took offence at this parsimonious scrutiny, and ordered the Assembly to attend him; when, after the example of Fletcher, whom, abating that man's superior activity, his Lordship mostly resembled, he made an angry speech, in which he charges them with innovations never attempted by their predecessors, and hopes they would not force him to exert "CERTAIN POWERS" vested in him by the Queen. But what he more particularly took notice of, was their insisting in several late bills, upon the title of *"General Assembly,"* and a saving of the *"Rights of the House,"* in a resolve agreeing to an amendment for preventing delay; with respect to which, his Lordship has these words: "I know of no Right that you have as an Assembly, but such as the Queen is pleased to allow you." As to the vote, by which they found a balance due to the colony, of nine hundred and thirteen pounds, fifteen shillings, "it is true," says his Lordship, "the Queen is pleased to command me, in her Instructions, to permit the Assembly, from Time to Time, to view and examine the Accounts of Money, or Value of Money, disposed by Virtue of the Laws made by them; but you can in no wise meddle with that Money; but if you find any Misapplication of any of that Money, you ought to acquaint me with it, that I may take Care to see those Mistakes rectified, which I shall certainly do."

The House bore these rebukes with the utmost passiveness, contenting themselves with little else than a general complaint of the deficiency of the revenue, which became the subject of their particular consideration in the fall.[25] The Governour, on the one hand, then proposed an additional duty of ten per cent. on certain goods, not immediately imported from Europe, to which the Assembly, on the other, were utterly averse, and as soon as they resolved against it, the very printer, clerk, and door-keeper, were denied the payment of their salaries. Several other demands being made for the publick debts, the House resolved to address his Lordship for an exact account of the revenue, which, together with their refusal, to admit the Council's amendment to a money bill, gave him such high provocation, that he was induced to dissolve an Assembly, whose prodigal liberality had justly exposed them to the resentment of the people.[26] The new Assembly, which met on the 14th of June, 1705, neglected the affair of the revenue and the additional duty, though his Lordship strongly recommended them both. Among the principal acts passed at this meeting, is that for the benefit of the clergy, who were entitled to the salaries formerly established by Colonel Fletcher; which, tho' less than his Lordship recommended, was doubtless a grateful offering to his unceasing zeal for the Church, manifested in a part of his speech at the opening of the session, in these words:

The Difficulties which some very worthy Ministers of the Church of *England* have met with, in getting the Maintainance settled upon them, by an Act of the general Assembly of this Province, passed in the Year 1693, moves me to propose to you the passing an Act, explanatory of the forementioned Act, that those worthy good Men, who have ventured to come so far, for the Service of God in his Church, and the Good and Edification of the People, to the Salvation of their Souls, may not for the future be vexed, as some of them have been; but may injoy in Quiet, that Maintainance, which was by a Law provided for them.* I farther recommend to you, the passing an Act to provide for the Maintainance of some Ministers, in some of the Towns at the East End of *Long-Island,* where I don't find any Provision has been yet made for propagating Religion.

Our harbour being wholly unfortified, a French privateer actually entered it in 1705, and put the inhabitants into great consternation. The Assembly, at their session in June, the next year, were not disinclined, thro' the importunity of the people, to put the city in a better posture of defence for the future; but being fully convinced, by his Lordship's embezzlement of £1500 formerly raised for two batteries at the Narrows, and near £1000 levied for the protection of the frontiers, that he was no more to be trusted with publick monies, offered a bill for raising £3000 for fortifications, appointing that sum to be deposited in the hands of a private person of their own nomination; but his Excellency did not pass it till their next meeting

* The majority of our people are of a contrary opinion, if my Lord thought the establishment was designed only for the Episcopal clergy.

in the fall, when he informed them that he had received the queen's commands, "to permit the general Assembly to name their own Treasurer, when they raised extraordinary Supplies for particular Uses, and which are no Part of the standing and constant Revenue; the Treasurer being accountable to the three Branches of the Legislature, and the Governor always acquainted with the Occasion of issuing such warrants."[27]

His Lordship's renewing the proposal of raising fortifications at the Narrows, which he had himself hitherto scandalously prevented, is a proof of his excessive effrontery and contempt of the people; and the neglect of the House, to take the least notice, either of that matter or the revenue, occasioned another dissolution.

Before I proceed to the transactions of the new Assembly, which did not meet till the year 1708, it will not be improper to lay before the reader, the account of a memorable proof of that persecuting spirit, which influenced Lord Cornbury's whole administration.

The inhabitants of the city of New-York consisted, at this time, of Dutch Calvinists, upon the plan of the Church of Holland; French refugees, on the Geneva model; a few English Episcopalians; and a still smaller number of English and Irish Presbyterians; who having neither a minister nor a church, used to assemble themselves, every Sunday, at a private house, for the worship of God. Such were their circumstances, when Francis McKemie and John Hampton, two Presbyterian ministers, arrived here in January, 1707. As soon as Lord Cornbury, who hated the whole persuasion, heard that the Dutch had consented to McKemie's preaching in their church, he arbitrarily forbid it; so that the publick worship, on the next Sabbath, was performed, with open doors, at a private house. Mr. Hampton preached, the same day, at the Presbyterian Church in New-Town, distant a few miles from the city. At that village both these ministers were two or three days after apprehended, by Cardwel the Sheriff, pursuant to his Lordship's warrant, for preaching without his licence. From hence they were led in triumph a circuit of several miles through Jamaica to New-York. They appeared before his Lordship with an undaunted courage, and had a conference with him, in which it is difficult to determine, whether my Lord excelled in the character of a savage bigot, or an ill-mannerly tyrant. The ministers were no lawyers, or they would not have founded their justification on the supposed extent of the English Act of Toleration. They know not that the Ecclesiastical Statutes had no relation to this colony; and that its religious state consisted in a perfect parity between Protestants of all denominations. They erroneously supposed that all the penal laws extended to this Province, and relied, for their defence, on the Toleration, offering testimonials of their having complied with the Act of Parliament in Virginia and Maryland, and promised to certify the House, in which McKemie had preached, to the next sessions. His Lordship's discourse with them was the more ridiculous, because he had Bickly, the Attorney-General, to assist him. Against the extension of the statute, they insisted that the penal laws were limited to England, and so also the Toleration Act, because the sole intent of it was to take away the penalties formerly established. But grant the position, and the consequence they drew from it, argues that my Lord and Mr. Attorney were either very weak, or influenced by evil designs. If the penal laws did not extend to the plantations, then the prisoners were innocent, for where there is no law there can be no transgression; but according to these incomparable sages, if the penal laws and the Toleration were restricted to the realm of England, as they contended, then the poor clergymen, for preaching without his licence, were guilty of a heinous crime, against his private, unpublished instructions; and for this cause he issued an informal precept to the Sheriff of New-York, for their commitment to jail, till further orders. They continued in confinement, through the absence of Mompesson, the Chief Justice, who was in New-Jersey, six weeks and four days; but were then brought before him by writ of *Habeas Corpus.* Mompesson being a man of learning in his profession, and his Lordship now apprised of the illegality of his first warrant, issued another, on the very day of the test of the writ, in which he virtually contradicts what he had before insisted on, at his conference with the prisoners. For according to this, they were imprisoned for preaching without being qualified as the Toleration Act required, tho' they had offered themselves to the sessions during their imprisonment. They were then bailed to the next Supreme Court, which began a few days after. Great pains were taken to secure a grand jury for the purpose, and among those who found the indictment, to their shame be it remembered, were several Dutch and French Protestants.

Mr. McKemie returned to New-York, from Virginia, in June; and was now come to his trial on the indictment found at the last court. As to Mr. Hampton, he was discharged, no evidence being offered to the grand jury against him.

Bickley, the Attorney-General, managed the prosecution in the name of the Queen; Reignere, Nicoll, and Jamison appeared for the defendant. The trial was held on the 6th of June, and being a cause of great expectation, a numerous audience attended. Roger Mompesson sat on the Bench as Chief Justice,[28] with Robert Milward and Thomas Wenham for his assistants. The indictment was, in substance, that Francis McKemie, pretending himself to be a Protestant dissenting minister, contemning and endeavouring to subvert the Queen's ecclesiastical supremacy, unlawfully preached without the Governour's license first obtained, in derogation of the royal authority and prerogative: that he used other rites and ceremonies, than those contained in the Common-prayer Book. And lastly, that being unqualified by law to preach, he nevertheless did preach at an illegal conventicle: and both these last charges were laid to be contrary to the form of the English statutes. For it seems that Mr. Attorney was now of opinion, that the penal laws did extend to the American plantations, tho' his sentiments were the very reverse at the first debate before his Excellency: but Bickley was rather remarkable for a voluble tongue, than a penetrating head or much learning. To support this prosecution, he endeavoured to prove the Queen's ecclesiastical supremacy in the colonies, and that it was delegated to her noble cousin the Governour; and hence he was of opinion, that his Lordship's Instructions relating to church matters, had the force of a law. He, in the next place, contended for the extention of the Statutes of Uniformity, and, upon the whole, was pleased to say, that he did not doubt the jury would find a verdict for the Queen. Reignere, for the defendant, insisted, that preaching was no crime by the Common Law, that the Statutes of Uniformity, and the Act of Toleration did not extend here, and that the Governour's Instructions were not laws. Nicoll spoke to the same purpose, and so did David Jamison; but McKemie concluded the whole defence in a speech, which sets his capacity in a very advantageous light. The reader may see it in the narrative of this trial, which was first published at the time, and since reprinted at New-York in the year 1755. The Chief Justice, in his charge, advised a special verdict, but the jury found no difficulty to acquit the defendant, who thro' the shame-

ful partiality of the court, was not discharged from his recognizance, till they had illegally extorted all the fees of his prosecution, which, together with his expences, amounted to eighty-
three pounds, seven shillings, and six pence.[29]

Lord Cornbury was now daily losing the favour of the people.
The friends of Leisler had him in the utmost abhorrence from
the beginning; and being all spies upon his conduct, it was impossible for his Lordship to commit the smallest crime unnoticed. His persecution of the Presbyterians very early increased the number of his enemies. The Dutch too were fearful
of his religious rage against them, as he disputed their right to
call and settle ministers, or even schoolmasters, without his
special licence. His excessive avarice, his embezzlement of the
publick money, and his sordid refusal to pay his private debts,
bore so heavily upon his reputation, that it was impossible for
his adherents, either to support him, or themselves, against the
general opposition. Such being the temper of the people, his
Lordship did not succeed according to his wishes in the new
Assembly, which met on the 19th of August, 1708. The members were all against him, and William Nicoll was again chosen
speaker.

Among the several things recommended to their consideration, the affair of the revenue, which was to expire in May following, and the propriety of making presents to the Indians,
were the chief. The House were not insensible of the importance of the Indian interest, and of the infinite arts of the
French to seduce them from our alliance: but suspicious that
his Lordship, who heretofore had given himself little concern
about that Matter, was seeking a fresh opportunity to defraud
the publick, they desired him to give them a list of the articles
of which the presents were to consist, together with an estimate
of the charge, before they would provide for that donation.

With respect to the revenue, his Lordship was not so successful, for the Assembly resolutely refused to continue it; tho' they
consented to an Act to discharge him from a contract of £250
and upwards, which he had made with one Hanson for the
publick service. Thomas Byerly was, at that time, Collector and
Receiver-General; and by pretending that the Treasury was exhausted, the debts of the government were unpaid. This gave
rise to many petitions to the Assembly to make provision for

their discharge. Colonel Schuyler, who had expended large sums on the publick credit, was among the principal sufferers, and joined with several others in an aplication to the House, that Byerly might be compelled to account. The disputes, relating to this matter, took up a considerable part of the session, and were litigated with great heat. Upon the whole, an Act was passed for refunding £700 which had been misapplied.

The resolutions of the Committee of Grievances, approved by the House, shew the general objections of the people to his Lordship's administration. These were made at the beginning of the session, and yet we find this haughty Lord subdued by the opposition against him, and so dispirited thro' indigence, and the incessant sollicitations of his creditors, that he not only omitted to justify himself, but to shew even an impotent resentment. For after all the censures of the House, he tamely thanked them, for passing the bill to discharge him from a small debt, which they could not, in justice, have refused. The resolutions were in these words:

> *Resolved,* That it is the Opinion of this Committee, that the appointing Coroners in this Colony, without their being chosen by the People, is a Grievance, and contrary to Law.\*
>
> *Resolved,* That it is, and always has been, the unquestionable Right of every Free-man in this Colony, that he hath a perfect and entire Property in his Goods and Estate.
>
> *Resolved,* That the imposing and levying of any Monies upon her Majesty's Subjects of this Colony, under any Pretence or Colour whatsoever, without Consent in general Assembly, is a Grievance, and a Violation of the People's Property.
>
> *Resolved,* That for any Officer whatsoever, to extort from the People, extravagant and unlimited Fees, or any Money whatsoever, not positively established and regulated by Consent in general Assembly, is unreasonable and unlawful, a great Grievance, and tending to the utter Destruction of all Property in this Plantation.
>
> *Resolved,* That the erecting a Court of Equity without Consent in general Assembly, is contrary to Law, without Precedent, and of dangerous Consequence to the Liberty and Property of the Subjects.
>
> *Resolved,* That the raising of Money for the Government,

\* See Lord Bacon's *Works,* fol. edit. 2 vol. 152. and yet the coroners in every county are still appointed by the Governour.

or other necessary Charge, by any Tax, Impost, or Burthen
on Goods imported, or exported; or any Clog, or Hindrance,
on Traffick or Commerce, is found by Experience to be the
Expulsion of many, and the Impoverishing of the Rest of
the Planters, Freeholders, and Inhabitants of this Colony; of
most pernicious Consequence, which, if contained, will unavoidably prove the Ruin of the Colony.

*Resolved,* That the excessive Sums of Money *screwed* from
Masters of Vessels trading here, under the Notion of Port-
Charges, visiting the said Vessels by supernumerary Officers,
and taking extraordinary Fees, is the great Discouragement
of Trade, and Strangers coming amongst us, beyond the
Precedent of any other Port, and without Colour of Law.

*Resolved,* That the compelling any Man upon Trial by a
Jury, or otherwise, to pay any Fees for his Prosecution, or
any Thing whatsoever, unless the Fees of the Officers whom
he employs for his necessary Defence, is a great Grievance,
and contrary to Justice.*

Lord Cornbury was no less obnoxious to the people of New-
Jersey, than to those of New-York. The Assembly of that Province, impatient of his tyranny, drew up a complaint against
him, which they sent home to the Queen.

Her Majesty graciously listened to the cries of her injured
subjects, devested him of his power, and appointed Lord Lovelace in his stead; declaring that she would not countenance
her nearest relations in oppressing her people.

As soon as my Lord was superseded, his creditors threw him
into the custody of the Sheriff of New-York; and he remained
here till the death of his father, when succeeding to the Earldom of Clarendon, he returned to England.

We never had a Governour so universally detested, nor any
who so richly deserved the publick abhorrence. In spite of his
noble descent, his behaviour was trifling, mean, and extravagant.

It was not uncommon for him to dress himself in a woman's
habit, and then to patrole the fort in which he resided.[30] Such
freaks of low humour exposed him to the universal contempt of
the people; but their indignation was kindled by his despotick
rule, savage bigotry, insatiable avarice, and injustice, not only
to the publick, but even his private creditors. For he left some

---

* This had a special relation to the late prosecution of Mr.
McKemie.

of the lowest tradesmen in his employment unsatisfied in their just demands.[31]

John Lord Lovelace, Baron of Hurley, was appointed to this government, in the spring, 1708, but did not arrive here till the 18th of December following. Lord Cornbury's oppressive, mean, administration had long made the people very desirous of a change; and therefore his successor was received with universal joy. Having dissolved the General Assembly, soon after his accession to the government, he convened a new one on the 5th of April, 1709, which consisting of Members of the same interest with the last, re-elected William Nicoll, the former Speaker, into the chair. His Lordship told them, at the beginning of the session, "That he had brought with him large Supplies of Soldiers and Stores of War, as well as Presents for the *Indians*," than which nothing could be more agreeable to the people. He lamented the greatness of the provincial debts, and the decay of publick credit; but still recommended their raising a revenue, for the same term with that established by the Act in the 11th year of the last reign. He also pressed the discharge of the debts of the government, and their examination of the publick accounts, "that it may be known," says he, "what this Debt is, and that it may appear hereafter to all the World, that it was not contracted in my Time." This oblique reflection upon his predecessor, who was now ignominiously imprisoned by his creditors, was displeasing to no body.

Tho' the Assembly, in their answer, heartily congratulated his Lordship's arrival, and thanked the Queen for her care of the Province, yet they sufficiently intimated their disinclination to raise the revenue, which the Governour had requested. "Our earnest Wishes," to use the Words of the Address, "are, that suitable Measures may be taken, to incourage the few Inhabitants left to stay in it, and others to come. The just Freedom injoyed by our Neighbours, by the tender Indulgence of the Government, has extremely drained and exhausted us both of People and Stock; whilst a different Treatment, the wrong Methods too long taken, *and Severities practised here,* have averted and deterred the usual Part of Mankind from settling and coming hitherto." Towards the close, they assure him, "That as the Beginning of his Government gave them a delightful Prospect of Tranquility, so they were come with Minds prepared to consult the Good of the Country and his Satisfaction."

The principal matter which engaged the attention of the Assembly, was the affair of the revenue. Lord Cornbury's conduct had rendered them utterly averse to a permanent support for the future, and yet they were unwilling to quarrel with the new Governour. They, however, at last agreed on the 5th of May, to raise £2500 to defray the charges of the government to the 1st of May ensuing, £1600 of which was voted to his Excellency, and the remaining sums towards a supply of firewood and candles to the several forts in New-York, Albany, and Schenectady; and for payment of small salaries to the printer, clerk of the Council, and Indian interpreter.

This new project of providing, annually, for the support of government, was contrived to prevent the mischiefs, to which the long revenues had formerly exposed us. But as it rendered the Governour, and all the other servants of the Crown dependent upon the Assembly, a rupture, between the several branches of the Legislature, would doubtless have ensued; but the very day, in which the vote passed the House, his Lordship died of a disorder contracted in crossing the ferry at his first arrival in the city of New-York. His Lady continued here, long after his death, soliciting for the sum voted to her husband; but tho' the Queen interposed, by a letter, in her behalf, nothing was allowed till several years afterwards.

## Part IV

*From the* Canada *Expedition in 1709*
*to the Arrival of Governour* Burnet

Lord Lovelace being dead, the chief command devolved upon Richard Ingoldsby, the Lieutenant-Governour, the same who had exercised the government several years before, upon the decease of Colonel Sloughter. His short administration is remarkable, not for his extraordinary talents, for he was a heavy man, but for a second fruitless attempt against Canada. Colonel Vetch, who had been, several years before, at Quebeck, and sounded the river of St. Lawrence, was the first projector of this enterprise.[1] The Ministry approved of it, and Vetch arrived in Boston, and prevailed upon the New-England Colonies to join in the scheme. After that, he came to New-York, and concerted the plan of operations with Francis Nicholson, formerly our Lieutenant-Governour, who, at the request of Ingoldsby, the Council, the Assembly, Gurdon Saltonstal the Governour of Connecticut, and Charles Gookin Lieutenant-Governour of Pennsylvania, accepted the chief command of the provincial forces, intended to penetrate into Canada, by the way of Lake Champlain. Impoverished as we were, the Assembly joined heartily in the enterprise. It was at this juncture, our first act for issuing bills of credit was passed; an expedient without which we could not have contributed to the expedition, the Treasury being then totally exhausted. Universal joy now brightened every man's countenance, because all expected the compleat reduction of Canada, before the ensuing fall. Big with the pleasing prospect of an event, which would put a period to all the ravages of an encroaching, merciless, enemy, extend the British Empire, and augment our trade, we exerted ourselves to the utmost, for the success of the expedition. As soon as the design was made known to the House, twenty ship and house carpenters were impressed into the service for building batteaus. Commissioners also were appointed to purchase provisions and other necessaries, and empowered to break open houses for that purpose; and to impress men, vessels, horses, and waggons, for transporting the stores. Four hundred and eighty-seven men, besides the Independent Companies, were raised and dispatched to Albany, by the 27th of June; from whence they advanced, with the main body, to the Wood Creek. Three forts were built there, besides many block-houses and stores for the provisions, which were transported with great dispatch. The Province of New-York (all things considered) has the merit of having contributed more than any of her neighbours towards this expedition. Pennsylvania gave no kind of aid, and New-Jersey was only at the expence of £3000. One hundred batteaus, as many birch canoes, and two of the forts, were built entirely, and the other fort, for the most part, at the charge of this government. All the provisions and stores for the army, were transported at our expence; and besides our quota of volunteers and the independent companies, we procured and maintained six hundred Indians, and victualed a thousand of their wives and children at Albany, during the campaign.[2]

Having thus put ourselves to the expence of above twenty thousand pounds towards this enterprise, the delay of the arrival of the fleet spread a general discontent through the country; and early in the fall, the Assembly addressed the Lieutenant-Governour to recall our forces from the camp. Vetch and Nicholson soon after broke up the campaign, and retired to New-Port in Rhode-Island, where there was a Congress of Governours. Ingoldsby, who was invited to it, did not appear, in compliance with the inclination of the Assembly, who incensed at the publick disappointment, harboured great jealousies of all the first promoters of the design. As soon, therefore, as Lord Sunderland's letters, which arrived here on the 21st of October, were laid before the House, they resolved to send an address to the Queen, to lay before her a true account of the manner, in which this province exerted itself in the late undertaking.

Had this expedition been vigorously carried on, doubtless it would have succeeded. The publick Affairs at home were conducted by a wise Ministry. The allied army triumphed in repeated successes in Flanders; and the Court of France was in no condition to give assistance to so distant a colony as Canada. The Indians of the Five Nations were engaged, thro' the indefatigable solicitations of Colonel Schuyler, to join heartily in the attempt; and the Eastern colonies had nothing to fear from the Ouwenagungas, because those Indians had, a little before, concluded a peace with the Confederates. In America every thing was ripe for the attack. At home, Lord Sunderland, the Secretary of State, had proceeded so far, as to dispatch orders to the Queen's ships at Boston, to hold themselves in readiness, and the British troops were upon the point of their embarkation. At this juncture, the news arrived of the defeat of the Portuguese, which reducing our allies to great streights, the forces intended for the American adventure were then ordered to their assistance, and the thoughts of the Ministry entirely diverted from the Canada expedition.

As we had not a man in this Province, who had more extended views of the importance of driving the French out of Canada, than Colonel Schuyler, so neither did any person more heartily engage in the late expedition. To preserve the friendship of the Five Nations, without which it would be impossible to prevent our frontiers from becoming a field of blood, he studied all the arts of insinuating himself into their favour. He gave them all possible encouragement and assistance, and very much impaired his own fortune, by his liberality to their chiefs. They never came to Albany but they resorted to his house, and even dined at his table; and by this means he obtained an ascendency over them, which was attended with very good consequences to the Province, for he could always, in a great degree, obviate or eradicate the prejudices and jealousies, by which the French Jesuits were incessantly labouring to debauch their fidelity.

Impressed with a strong sense of the necessity of some vigorous measures against the French, Colonel Schuyler was extremely discontented at the late disappointment; and resolved to make a voyage to England, at his private expence, the better to inculcate on the Ministry, the absolute necessity of reducing Canada to the Crown of Great-Britain. For that purpose he proposed to carry home with him five Indian chiefs. The House no sooner heard of his design, than they came to a resolution, which, in justice to his distinguished merit, I ought not to suppress. It was this:

Resolved, *Nemine contradicente,* That the humble Address of the Lieutenant-Governor, Council, and general Assembly of this Colony to the Queen, representing the present State of this Plantation, be committed to his Charge and Care, to be presented by himself to her sacred Majesty; he being a Person, who not only in the last War, when he commanded the Forces of this Colony in chief at *Canada,* but also in the present, has performed faithful Services, to this and the neighbouring Colonies; and behaved himself in the Offices, with which he has been intrusted, with good Reputation, and the general Satisfaction of the People in these Parts.[3]

The arrival of the five sachems in England, made a great bruit thro' the whole kingdom.[4] The mob followed wherever they went, and small cuts of them were sold among the people. The Court was at that time in mourning for the death of the Prince of Denmark: these American Kings* were therefore dressed in black under cloths, after the English manner; but, instead of a blanket, they had each a scarlet-in-grain cloth mantle, edged with gold, thrown over all their other garments. This dress was directed by the dressers of the playhouse, and given by the Queen, who was advised to make a shew of them. A more than ordinary solemnity attended the audience they had of her Majesty. Sir Charles Cotterel conducted them, in two coaches, to St. James's; and the Lord Chamberlain introduced them into the royal presence. Their speech, on the 19th of April, 1710, is preserved by Oldmixon, and was in these words:

*Great Queen,*
  We have undertaken a long Voyage, which none of our Predecessors could be prevailed upon to undertake, to see our great Queen, and relate to her those Things, which we thought absolutely necessary for the Good of her, and us her Allies, on the other Side of the Water.
  We doubt not but our great Queen has been acquainted with our long and tedious War, in Conjunction with her Children, against her Enemies the *French;* and that we have been as a strong Wall for their Security, even to the Loss of our best Men. We were mightily rejoiced, when we heard our great Queen had resolved to send an Army to reduce *Canada,* and immediately, in Token of Friendship, we hung up the Kettle, and took up the Hatchet, and, with one Consent,

* This title is commonly bestowed on the sachems, tho' the Indians have no such dignity or office amongst them.

assisted Colonel *Nicholson* in making Preparations on this Side of the Lake; but, at length, we were told our great Queen, by some important Affairs, was prevented in her Design, at present, which made us sorrowful, lest the *French,* who had hitherto dreaded us, should now think us unable to make War against them. The Reduction of *Canada* is of great Weight to our free Hunting; so that if our great Queen should not be mindful of us, we must, with our Families, forsake our Country, and seek other Habitations, or stand neuter, either of which will be much against our Inclinations.

In Token of the Sincerity of these Nations, we do, in their Names, present our great Queen with these Belts of *Wampum,* and in Hopes of our great Queen's Favour, leave it to her most gracious Consideration.

While Colonel Schuyler was at the British Court, Captain Ingoldsby was dispatched, and Gerardus Beekman exercised the powers of government, from the 10th of April, 1710, till the arrival of Brigadier Hunter, on the 14th of June following. The Council then present were,

| | |
|---|---|
| Mr. Beekman, | Mr. Mompesson, |
| Mr. Van Dam, | Mr. Barbarie, |
| Colonel Renslaer, | Mr. Philipse. |

Hunter was a native of Scotland, and, when a boy, put apprentice to an apothecary. He left his master, and went into the army; and being a man of wit and personal beauty, recommended himself to Lady Hay, whom he afterwards married. In the year 1707, he was appointed Lieutenant-Governour of Virginia, but being taken by the French in his voyage to that colony, he was carried into France, and upon his return to England, appointed to succeed Lord Lovelace in the government of this and the Province of New-Jersey. Dean Swift's letter to him, during his captivity, shews that he had the honour of an intimacy with Mr. Addison and others, who were distinguished for their good sense and learning; and perhaps it was by their interest, he was advanced to this profitable place.[5]

Governour Hunter brought over with him near three thousand palatines, who the year before fled to England from the rage of persecution in Germany. Many of these people seated themselves in the city of New-York, where they built a Lutheran Church, which is now in a declining condition. Others settled on a tract of several thousand acres, in the manor of Living-

ston.[6] Their village there, called the Camp, is one of the pleasantest situations on Hudson's River: right opposite, on the
West bank, are many other families of them. Some went into
Pennsylvania, and by the favourable accounts of the country,
which they transmited to Germany, were instrumental to the
transmigration of many thousands of their countrymen into
that Province. Queen Anne's liberality to these people, was not
more beneficial to them, than serviceable to this colony. They
have behaved themselves peaceably, and lived with great industry. Many are rich, all are Protestants, and well affected to the
government.[7] The same must be said of those who have lately
settled amongst us, and planted the lands Westward of Albany.
We have not the least ground for jealousy with respect to them.
Amongst us they are few in number, compared to those in Pennsylvania. There they are too numerous, to be soon assimilated
to a new constitution. They retain all the manners and principles which prevail in their native country, and as many of them
are Papists, some are not without their fears, that sooner or
later, they will become dangerous to our colonies.*

The late attempt to attack Canada proving abortive, exposed
us to consequences equally calamitous, dreaded, and foreseen.
While the preparations were making to invade it, the French
exerted themselves in cajoling their Indian allies to assist in the
repulse; and as soon as the scheme droped, numerous parties
were sent out to harass the English frontiers. These irruptions
were, principally, made on the Northern parts of New-England,
where the most savage cruelties were daily commited. New-York
had, indeed, hitherto escaped, being covered by the Indians of
the Five Nations; but the danger we were in induced Governour
Hunter, soon after his arrival, to make a voyage to Albany,
where he met the Confederate chiefs, and renewed the old
covenant. While there, he was strongly solicited, by the New-
England governments, to engage our Indians in a war with
those who were daily ravaging their borders; but he prudently
declined a measure, which might have exposed his own Prov-

---

* The surprising importation of Germans into that colony, gave
rise to the scheme, of dispersing English clergymen and schoolmasters amongst them. The project is founded on principles of
sound polity. If a political mission among the Indians had been
seasonably encouraged, the Province of Pennsylvania might have
escaped all that shocking devastation, which ensued the fatal
defeat of General Braddock's Army on the 9th of July, 1755; and
would, perhaps, have prevented even the erection of Fort Quesne,
which has already cost the nation so much blood and treasure.

ince to a general devastation. A Treaty of Neutrality subsisted, at that time, between the Confederates and the Canada French and their Indians; which, depending upon the faith of lawless savages, was, at best, but precarious, and yet the only security we had for the peace of our borders. A rupture between them would have involved us in a scene of misery, at a time, of all others, most unseasonable. However the people of New-England might censure the Governour, it was a proof of his wisdom to refuse their request. For besides a want of men and arms to defend us, our forts were fallen down, and the Treasury exhausted.[8]

The new Assembly met, at New-York, on the 1st of September. Mr. Nicoll, the Speaker, Mr. Livingston, Mr. De Lancey, and Colonel Morris, were the members most distinguished for their activity in the House. Mr. De Lancey was a Protestant refugee, a native of Caen in Normandy; and by marrying a daughter of Mr. Courtlandt, connected with a family, then, perhaps, the most opulent and extensive of any in the Province. He was an eminent merchant, and, by a successful trade, had amassed a very considerable fortune. But of all these, Colonel Morris had the greatest influence on our publick affairs. He was a man of letters, and, tho' a little whimsical in his temper, was grave in his manners and of penetrating parts. Being excessively fond of the society of men of sense and reading, he was never wearied at a Sitting, till the spirits of the whole company were dissipated. From his infancy, he had lived in a manner best adapted to teach him the nature of man, and to fortify his mind for the vicissitudes of life. He very early lost both his father and mother, and fell under the patronage of his uncle, formerly an officer, of very considerable rank, in Cromwell's Army; who, after the Restoration, disguised himself under the profession of Quakerism, and settled on a fine farm, within a few miles of the city, called, after his own name, Morrisania. Being a boy of strong passions, the general indications of a fruitful genius, he gave frequent offence to his uncle, and, on one of these occasions, thro' fear of his resentment, strolled away into Virginia, and thence to Jamaica in the West-Indies,* where, to support

* Hugh Coppathwait, a Quaker zealot, was his preceptor: the pupil taking advantage of his enthusiasm, hid himself in a tree, and calling to him, ordered him to preach the Gospel among the Mohawks. The credulous Quaker took it for a miraculous call, and was upon the point of seting out when the cheat was discoverd.

himself, he set up for a scrivener. After several years spent in
this vagabond life, he returned again to his uncle, who received
the young prodigal with joy; and, to reduce him to regularity,
brought about his marriage with a daughter of Mr. Graham, a
fine lady, with whom he lived above fifty years, in the possession of every enjoyment, which good sense and polite manners
in a woman could afford. The greatest part of his life, before
the arrival of Mr. Hunter, was spent in New-Jersey,* where he
signalized himself in the the service both of the proprietors and
the Assembly. The latter employed him to draw up their complaint against my Lord Cornbury, and he was made the bearer
of it to the Queen. Tho' he was indolent in the management of
his private affairs, yet, thro' the love of power, he was always
busy in matters of a political nature, and no man in the colony
equaled him in the knowledge of the law and the arts of in-
trigue. From this character, the reader will easily perceive that
Governour Hunter shewed his prudence, in taking Mr. Morris
into his confidence, his talents and advantages rendering him
either a useful friend or formidable foe. Such were the acting
members of this Assembly. When Brigadier Hunter spoke to
them, he recommended the settling a revenue, the defence of
the frontiers, and the restoration of the publick credit, which
Lord Cornbury had almost entirely destroyed. To stifle the remaining sparks of our ancient feuds, he concluded with these
words: "If any go about to disturb your Peace, by reviving buried Parties or Piques, or creating new ones, they shall meet with
no Countenance or Incouragement from me; and I am sure they
deserve as little from you." The address of the House was perfectly agreeable to the Governour. They promised to provide for
the support of government, and to restore the publick credit, as
well as to protect the frontiers. In answer to the close of his
speech, they declare their hope, "That such as excited party
Contentions might meet with as *little Credit,* and as *much
Disgrace,* as they deserve." This unanimity, however, was soon
interrupted. Colonel Morris, for some warm words dropped in
a debate, was expelled the House; and soon after a dispute
arose, between the Council and Assembly, concerning some

* He was one of the Council in that Province, and a judge of the
Supreme Court there, in 1692. Upon the surrender of the government to Queen Anne, in 1702, he was named to be Governour of
the colony; but the appointment was changed in favour of Lord
Cornbury, the Queen's cousin.

amendments, made by the former, to a bill *"For the Treasurer's paying sundry Sums of Money."* The design of it, in mentioning the particular sums, and rendering them issuable by their own officer, was to restrain the Governour from repeating the mis-applications which had been so frequent in a late administration. The Council, for that reason, opposed it, and adhered to their amendments; which occasioned a prorogation, on the 25th of November, after the passing of several other necessary laws.

Mr. Hunter cautiously avoided entering, publickly, into the dispute between the two Houses, till he knew the sentiments of the Ministry, and then he opened the spring sessions with a speech too singular not to be inserted.

Gentlemen: I hope you are now come with a Disposition to answer the Ends of your Meeting, that is, to provide a suit-able Support for her Majesty's Government here, in the Man-ner she has been pleased to direct; to find out Means to restore the publick Credit, and to provide better for your own Security.

They abuse you, who tell you, that you are hardly dealt by in the Augmentation of Salaries. Her Majesty's Instructions, which I communicated to you at our last Meeting, might have convinced you that it was her Tenderness towards her Sub-jects in the Plantations, who suffered under an established Custom of making considerable Presents to their Governours, by Acts of Assembly, that induced her to allot to each of them such a Salary as she judged sufficient for their Support, in their respective Stations, with a strict Prohibition of all such Presents for the future; which instruction has met with a chearful and grateful Compliance in all the other Colonies.

If you have been in any Thing distinguished, it is by an extraordinary Measure of her royal Bounty and Care. I hope you will make suitable Returns, lest some Insinuations, much repeated of late Years, should gain Credit at last, that how-ever your Resentment has fallen upon the *Governor*, it's the *Government* you dislike.

It is necessary, at this Time, that you be told also, that giv-ing Money for the Support of Government, and disposing of it at your Pleasure, is the same with giving none at all. Her Majesty is the sole Judge of the Merits of her Servants. This Right has never yet been disputed at Home, and should I con-sent to give it up abroad, I should render myself unworthy, not only of the Trust reposed in me, but of the Society of my Fellow-Subjects, by incurring her higest Displeasure. If I have tired you by a long Speech, I shall make Amends by putting you to the Trouble of a very short Answer.

Will you support her Majesty's Government, in the Manner she has been pleased to direct, or are you resolved that Burden shall lie still upon the Governor, who cannot accuse himself of any Thing that may have deserved this Treatment at your Hands?

Will you take Care of the Debts of the Government; or, to increase my Sufferings, must I continue under the Torture of the daily Cries of such as have just Demands upon you, and are in Misery, without the Power of giving them any Hopes of Relief?

Will you take more effectual Care of your own Safety, in that of your Frontiers; or are you resolved for the future to rely upon the Security of an open Winter, and the Caprice of your savage Neighbours? I shall be very sorry if this Plainness offends you. I judge it necessary towards the establishing and cultivating a good Understanding betwixt us. I hope it will be so construed, and wish heartily it may have that Effect.

Perplexed with this remarkable speech, the Assembly, after a few days, concluded, that as his Excellency had prorogued them in February, while he was at Burlington, in the Province of New-Jersey, they could not sit and act as a House; upon which, they were the same day dissolved.

The five Indian Kings, carried to England by Colonel Schuyler, having seen all the curiosities in London, and been much entertained by many persons of distinction, returned to Boston, with Commodore Martin and Colonel Nicholson; the latter of whom commanded the forces designed against Port-Royal and the coast of Nova-Scotia. In this enterprise the New-England colonies, agreeable to their wonted courage and loyalty, lent their assistance; and the reduction of the garrison, which was then called Annapolis-Royal, was happily completed on the 2d of October, 1710. Animated by this, and some other successes in Newfoundland, Nicholson again urged the prosecution of the scheme for the reduction of Canada; which having been strongly recommended by the Indian chiefs, as the only effectual means to secure the northern colonies, was now again resumed.

Towards the execution of this project, five thousand troops from England and Flanders, were sent over under the command of Brigadier Hill, the brother of Mrs. Masham, the Queen's new confident [following] on the disgrace of the Dutchess of Marl-borough. The fleet of transports, under the convoy of Sir Hove-den Walker, arrived, after a month's passage, at Boston, on the 4th of June, 1711. The provisions, with which they expected to be supplied there, being not collected, the troops landed. Nichol-son, who was to command the land-forces, came immediately to New-York, where Mr. Hunter convened the Assembly, on the 2d of July. The re-election of the same members, who had served in the last, was a sufficient proof of the general aversion to the establishment of a revenue. Robert Livingston, junior, who mar-ried the only daughter of Colonel Schuyler, came in for Albany; and together with Mr. Morris, who was again chosen for the borough of West-Chester, joined the Governour's interest. Briga-dier Hunter informed the Assembly of the intended expedition, and the arrival of the fleet and forces; that the quota of this Province, settled by the Council of War, at New-London, was 600 private sentinels and their officers: besides which, he rec-ommended their making provision for building batteaus, trans-porting the troops and provisions, subsisting the Indians, and for the contingent charges: nor did he forget to mention the support of government and the publick debts.

The House was so well pleased with the design upon Canada, that they voted an address of thanks to the Queen, and sent a committee to Nicholson, to congratulate his arrival, and make an honourable acknowledgement of his *"sedulous Application to her Majesty for reducing Canada."* In a few days time, an act was passed for raising forces; and the Assembly, by a resolu-tion, according to the Governour's advice, restricted the price of provisions to certain particular sums. Bills of credit, for for-warding the expedition, were now also struck, to the amount of £10,000 to be sunk in five years, by a tax on estates real and personal. After these supplies were granted, the Governour pro-rogued the Assembly; tho' nothing was done relating to the ordinary support of government.

While these preparations were making at New-York, the fleet, consisting of twelve men of war, forty transports, and six store-ships, with forty horses, a fine train of artillery and all manner of warlike stores, sailed for Canada, from Boston, on the 30th of July; and, about a month afterwards, Nicholson appeared at Albany, at the head of an army of four thousand men, raised in this and the colonies of New-Jersey and Connecticut: the sev-eral regiments being commanded by Colonel Ingoldsby, Colonel

Whiting, and Colonel Schuyler, the latter of whom procured 600 of the Five Nations to join our army.

The French, in Canada, were not unapprised of these designs. Vaudreuil, the Governour General, sent his orders, from Montreal, to the Sieur De Beaucourt, to hasten the works he was about at Quebeck, and commanded that all the regulars and militia should be held in readiness to march on the first warning. Four or five hundred Indians, of the more distant nations, arrived at the same time at Montreal, with Messieurs St. Pierre and Tonti, who, together with the Caughnuaga proselytes, took up the hatchet in favour of the French. Vaudreuil, after dispatching several Indians and two missionaries among the Five Nations, to detach them from our interest, went to Quebeck, which Beaucourt the engineer had sufficiently fortified to sustain a long siege. All the principal posts below the city, on both sides of the river, were prepared to receive the British troops in case of their landing. On the 14th of August, Sir Hoveden Walker arrived with the fleet in the mouth of St. Lawrence River; and fearing to lose the company of the transports, the wind blowing fresh at North-West, he put into Gaspe Bay, and continued there till the 20th of the same month. Two days after he sailed from thence, the fleet was in the utmost danger, for they had no soundings, were without sight of land, the wind high at East-South-East, and the sky darkened by a thick fog. In these circumstances the fleet brought to, by the advice of the pilots, who were of opinion, that if the ships lay with their heads to the Southward, they might be driven by the stream into the midst of the channel: but instead of that, in two hours after, they found themselves on the North shore, among rocks and islands, and upon the point of being lost. The men of war escaped, but eight transports, containing eight hundred souls, officers, soldiers, and seamen, were cast away. Two or three days being spent, in recovering what they could from the shore, it was determined, at a consultation of sea officers, to return to some bay or harbour, till a further resolution could be taken. On the 14th of September they arrived at Spanish-River Bay, where a council of war, consisting of land and sea officers, considering that they had but ten weeks provision, and judging that they could not depend upon a supply from New-England, unanimously concluded to return home, without making any farther attempts; and they accordingly arrived at Portsmouth on the 9th of October, when, in addition to our misfortunes, the Edgar, a 70 gun ship, was blown up, having on board above four hundred men, besides many persons who came to visit their friends.

As soon as the Marquis de Vaudreuil, by the accounts of the fishermen and two other ships, had reason to suspect that our fleet was returned, he went to Chambly, and formed a camp of three thousand men to oppose Nicholson's Army, intended to penetrate Canada, at that end. But he was soon informed that our troops were returned, upon the news of the disaster which had befallen the fleet, and that the people of Albany were in the utmost consternation.

The new Ministry are generally censured for their conduct in this expedition by the Whigs, who condemn both the project and the measures taken towards its execution. The scheme was never laid before the Parliament, tho' it was then sitting; but this, it is said, was for the greater secrecy, and for the same reason, the fleet was not fully victualed at home. They relied upon New-England for supplies, and this destroyed the design. For the ships tarried at Boston, till the season for the attack was over.

According to Lord Harley's account of this expedition, the whole was a contrivance of Bolingbroke, Moore, and the Lord Chancellor Harcourt, to cheat the publick of twenty thousand pounds. The latter of these was pleased to say "No Government was worth serving, that would not admit of such advantageous Jobs."

Apprehensive that the enemy would fall upon our borders, as they afterwards really did, in small parties, upon the miscarriage of that enterprise; Governour Hunter pressed the Assembly, in autumn, to continue a number of men in pay the ensuing winter, and to repair the out forts. After the House had passed several votes to this purpose, his Excellency, during the session, went up to Albany, to withdraw the forces of the colony, and give orders for the necessary repairs.

The publick debts, by this unfortunate expedition, were become greatly enhanced, and the Assembly, at last, entered upon measures for the support of the government, and sent up to the Council several bills for that purpose. The latter attempted to make amendments, which the other would not admit, and a warm controversy arose between those two branches of the legislature. The Council assigned instances, that amendments had formerly been allowed; and, besides this argument, drawn from precedent, insisted that they were a part of the legislature, constituted as the Assembly were "by the meer Grace of the Crown;" adding that the Lords of Trade had determined the matter in their favour. The House, nevertheless, adhered to their resolutions, and answered in these words:

> 'Tis true, the Share the Council have (if any) in the Legislation, does not flow from any Title they have from the Nature of that Board, which is only to advise; or from their being another distinct State, or Rank of People in the Constitution, which they are not, being all Commons; but only from the meer Pleasure of the Prince signified in the Commission. On the contrary, the inherent Right the Assembly have to dispose of the Money of the Freemen of this Colony, does not proceed from any Commission, Letters Patent, or other Grant from the Crown; but from the free Choice and Election of the People, who ought not to be divested of their Property (nor justly can) without their Consent. Any former Condescensions, of other Assemblies, will not prescribe to the Council, a Privilege to make any of those Amendments, and therefore they have it not. If the Lords Commissioners for Trade and Plantations, did conceive no Reason why the Council should not have Right to amend Money Bills, this is far from concluding there are none. The Assembly understand them very well, and are sufficiently convinced of the Necessity they are in, not to admit of any Encroachment so much to their prejudice.

Both Houses adhered obstinately to their respective opinions: in consequence of which, the publick debts remained unpaid, though his Excellency could not omit passing a bill for paying to himself 3750 ounces of plate.

Upon the return of the fleet, Dudley, Saltonstal, and Cranston, the Governours of the eastern colonies, formed a design of engaging the Five Nations in a rupture with the French, and wrote on that head to Mr. Hunter; who, suspicious that his Assembly would not approve of any project that might increase the publick debts, laid their letter before the House, and, according to his expectations, they declared against the scheme.

About this time Colonel Hunter, by the advice of his Council, began to exercise the Office of Chancellor, having, on the 4th of October, appointed Messieurs Van Dam and Philipse Masters, Mr. Whileman Register, Mr. Harrison Examiner, and Messieurs Sharpas and Broughton Clerks. A proclamation was then issued, to signify the sitting of the court on Thursday in every week.

This gave rise to these two resolutions of the House. "*Resolved,* That the erecting a Court of Chancery, without Consent in general Assembly, is contrary to Law, without Precedent, and of dangerous Consequence to the Liberty and Property of the Subjects. That the establishing Fees, without Consent in general Assembly, is contrary to Law." The Council made these votes the subject of part of a long representation, which they shortly after transmited to the Lords of Trade, who, in a letter to the Governour, in answer to it, approved of his erecting a court of equity, and blamed the Assembly; adding, "That her Majesty has an undoubted Right of appointing such, and so many Courts of Judicature, in the Plantations, as she shall think necessary for the Distribution of Justice."

At the next meeting, in May 1712, Colonel Hunter strongly recommended the publick debts to the consideration of the Assembly, informing them, that the Lords of Trade had signified their opinion, with respect to the amending money bills, in favour of the Council. The House neglected the matters laid before them, and the Governour broke up the sessions by a short prorogation of three days. After which they soon passed an Act for paying his Excellency 8025 ounces of plate. Our publick affairs never wore a more melancholy aspect than at this juncture.[9]

Among the Five Nations many emissaries from the French were daily seducing them from the British interest, and our late ill success gave such a powerful influence to their solicitations, that the Indians even at Catt's Kill sent a belt of wampum to those in Dutchess County to prepare for a war. The Senecas and Shawanas were also greatly disaffected, and it was generally apprehended that they would fall upon the inhabitants along Hudson's River. An invasion was strongly suspected, by sea, on the city of New-York, where they had been alarmed, in April, by an insurrection of the Negroes; who, in execution of a plot to set fire to the town, had burnt down a house in the night, and killed several people who came to extinguish the fire, for which nineteen of them were afterwards executed.[10] But distressed as the colony then was, the Assembly were inflexibly averse to the establishment of a revenue, which had formerly been wickedly misapplied and exhausted. At the ensuing session, in the fall, Colonel Hunter proposed a scheme to the Assembly, which was, in substance, that the Receiver-General should give security, residing in the colony, for the due execution of his office; and, every quarter, account, to the Governour and Council, for the sums he might receive. That the creditors of the government should, every three months, deliver in their demands to the Governour and Council; when, if that quarter's revenue equaled the amount of such debts, the Governour, by the advice of council, should draw for it: but if the revenue, for that quarter, should fall short of the Governour's demands; then the warrants were to be drawn for so much only as remained, and the creditors should afterwards receive new drafts for their balances in the next quarter. That no warrant should be issued, until the quarterly account of the revenue was given in; but that then they should be paid in course, and an action of debt be given against the Receiver-General in case of refusal. That he should account also to the Assembly when required, and permit all persons to have recourse to his books. The House turned a deaf ear to this plausible project, and displeased with a letter from the Lords of Trade, favouring the Council's claim to amend money bills, they agreed upon an address to the Queen, protesting their willingness to support her government, complaining of misapplications in the treasury, intimating their suspicions that they were misrepresented, and praying an instruction to the Governour to give his consent to a law, for supporting an agent to represent them at the Court of Great-Britain. Provoked by this conduct, and to put an end to the disputes subsisting between the two Houses, his Excellency dissolved the Assembly.

Before the meeting of the next Assembly, the Peace of Utrecht was concluded, on the 31st of March, 1713. A peace, in the judgment of many, dishonourable to Great-Britain, and injurious to her allies. I shall only consider it with relation to our Indian affairs. The reader doubtless observed, that Lord Bellomont, after the Peace at Ryswick, contended with the Governour of Canada, that the Five Nations ought to be considered as subjects of the British Crown, and that the point was disputed even after the death of Count Frontenac. It does not appear that any decision of that matter was made between the two crowns, till the Treaty of Utrecht, the XVth Article of which is in these words:

> The Subjects of *France* inhabiting *Canada*, and others, shall hereafter give no Hindrance or Molestation to the *Five Nations*, or Cantons of *Indians*, subject to the Dominion of

*Great Britain,* nor to the other Nations of *America* who are Friends to the same. In like Manner, the Subjects of *Great-Britain* shall behave themselves peaceably towards the *Americans,* who are Subjects or Friends to *France;* and on both Sides they shall enjoy full Liberty of going and coming on account of Trade. Also the Natives of these Countries shall, with the same Liberty, resort, as they please, to the *British* and *French* Colonies, for promoting Trade on one Side and the other, without any Molestation or Hindrance, either on the Part of the *British* Subjects, or of the *French.* But it is to be exactly and distinctly settled by Commissaries, who are, and who ought to be, accounted the Subjects of *Britain* or of *France.*

In consequence of this treaty, the British Crown became entitled, at least for any claim that could justly be interposed by the French, to the sovereignty over the country of the Five Nations, concerning the extent of which, as it never was adjusted by Commissaries, it may not be improper to say a few words.

When the Dutch began the settlement of this country, all the Indians on Long-Island, and the northern shore of the Sound, on the banks of Connecticut, Hudson's, Delaware, and Susquehana Rivers, were in subjection to the Five Nations; and, within the memory of persons now living, acknowledged it by the payment of an annual tribute.* The French historians of Canada, both ancient and modern, agree, that the more northern Indians were driven before the superior martial powers of the Confederates. The author of the book entitled, *Relation de ce qui s'est passé de plus remarquable aux Mission de Peres de la Compagnie de Jesus, en la nouvelle France,* published with the privilege of the French King, at Paris, in 1661, writes with such singular simplicity, as obviates the least suspicion of those sinister views, so remarkable in the late French histories. He informs us, that all the Northern Indians, as far as Hudson's Bay, were harassed by the Five Nations "Partout," (says he, speaking in the name of the missionaries), "nous trouvons Iroquois, qui comme un Phantome importun, nous obsede en tous lieux."[11] In the account he gives of the travels of a Father, in 1658, we are told, that the banks of the upper lake were lined with the Algonkins, "Ou la Crainte des Irequois leur a fait chercher un

---

* A little tribe settled at the Sugar-Loaf Mountain in Orange County, to this day make a yearly payment of about £20 to the Mohawks.

Asyle." Writing of the Hurons, "La Nation la plus sedentaire & la plus propre pour les Semences de la Foy,"[12] he represents them as totally destroyed by the Confederates. Charlevoix, whose history of New France is calculated to countenance the encroachments of the French, gives the following description of the territory of the Confederates.

"The Country of the *Irequois*," (says he), "extends itself between the 41st and 44th Degrees of North Latitude, about 70 or 80 Leagues from East to West, from the Head of the River, bearing for its Name that of *Richlieu* and *Sorel;*\* that is, from Lake *St. Sacrament* to *Niagara*, and a little above forty Leagues from North to South, or rather North-East and South-West from the Head of the *Mohawks* River to the River *Ohio*. Thus the last mentioned River and *Pennsylvania* bound it on the South. On the West it has Lake *Ontario;* and Lake *Erie* on the North-West. *St. Sacrament* and the River *St. Lawrence* on the North; on the South and South-East, the Province of *New-York*. It is watered with many Rivers. The Land is in some Places broken, but, generally speaking, very fertile.

In this partial description, the Jesuit is neither consistent with his geographer, nor several other French authours, and yet both his history and Mr. Bellin's maps, in 1744,† which are bound up with it, furnish many strong evidences in favour of the British claims. I will point out a few instances. The ancient

---

\* The river issuing from Lake Champlain, is called, Rivieres des Irequois de Richelieu & Sorel, but the last is now most commonly used.

† Mr. Bellin published a new set of maps in 1745, the first plate being thought too favourable to our claims, especially in the protraction of the North side of the Bay of Fundy, for Nova Scotia, which, in the second plate, was called "the South Part of *New France*." General Shirley, one of the *British* Commissaries for settling the disputed limits, took occasion to speak of this alteration to Mr. Bellin at Paris, and informed him that 100 copies of his first maps were dispersed to London, upon which he discovered some surprise; but instead of urging any thing in support of the variation in this new draft, said, smiling, *"We in* France *must follow the Command of the Monarch."* I mention this to shew, that since the French Government interposes in the construction of their maps, they are proper evidence against them. Among the English, Dr. Mitchel's is the only authentick one extant. None of the rest, concerning America, have passed under the examination, or received the sanction of any publick board; and, for this reason, they ought not to be construed to our prejudice. Add, that they generally copy from the French.[13]

country of the Hurons is laid down on the North side of Lake Erie, by which we are ascertained of the extent of territory, to which the Five Nations are entitled by their conquest of that people. The right of the Confederates to the South side of that lake, is also established by their dispersion of the Cat Indians, to whom it originally belonged. The land, on both sides of the Lake Ontario, is admitted to be theirs by this geographer, who writes on the North, "Les Iroquois du Nord," and on the South side, "Pays des Iroquois." Hennepin, La Hontan and Delisle, all concur with Bellin, in extending the right of the Five Nations, to the lands on the North side of Lake Ontario. The first of these, besides what appears from his map, speaking of that lake, has these words, *"There are likewise on the North Side these* Iroquois *Villages,* Tejajahon, Kente, *and* Ganneousse"; every one of which is laid down even in Bellin's, and almost all the maps I have seen of that country, whether French or English. What renders Hennepin's account the more remarkable is, that these villages were there in 1679, seven years after the erection of Fort Frontenac. From whence it may fairly be argued, that their not opposing those works, was by no means a cession of the country to the French; and indeed Charlevoix himself represents that matter as carried on by a fraud, for, says he, *"Under Pretext of seeking their Advantage, the Governor had nothing in View, que de les tenir en Bride."*[14]

To these attestations, which are the more to be depended upon, because they are given by the French writers, whose partiality leads them to confine the Five Nations to contracted limits,* we may add, that our Indians universally concur in the claim of all the lands, not sold to the English, from the mouth of Sorel River, on the South side of the Lakes Erie and Ontario, on both sides of the Ohio, till it falls into the Mississippi; and on the North side of those lakes, that whole territory between the Outawais River and the Lake Huron, and even beyond the streights between that and Lake Erie. This last tract, and the land on the North side of the Lakes Erie and Ontario, were

---

* Mr. Bellin was engineer of the Marine, and tells us, that Charlevoix performed his travels in this country, by order of the French Court; that he was a man of attention and curiosity, and had a determined resolution to collect all possible intelligence, which he designed to make publick. To give the greater credit to the Jesuit's history and his own map, he adds, that Charlevoix was never without the instruments proper for a voyager, *"partout la Boussole à la main."*[15]

contained in their surrender to King William in 1701; of which
I took notice in its proper place: and doubtless to that, and Lord
Bellomont's contest with Count Frontenac, we must ascribe it,
that the Five Nations were afterwards so particularly taken
notice of in the Treaty of Utrecht.

The British title to Fort Frontenac, and the lands on the
North-west side of Cadaracqui River, has of late been drawn
into question by some, who, from jealousy, or other motives
equally shameful, were bent upon finding fault with every measure planned by General Shirley. The advocates for the French
claim, relied much on a late map of the middle British colonies,
and two pamphlets published by Lewis Evans.

"The *French*," says he, "being in Possession of Fort *Frontenac*,
at the Peace of *Ryswick*, which they attained during their War
with the Confederates, gives them an undoubted Title to the Acquisition of the North-West Side of *St. Lawrence* River, from
thence to their settlement at *Montreal*." The Writer adds, "It was
upon the Faith and Honour of King *William's* Promise (by the
fourth Article of the Treaty of *Ryswick*) of not disturbing the
*French* King in the free Possession of the Kingdoms, Counties,
Lands, or Dominions he then injoyed, that I said the *French* had
an *undoubted Title* to their Acquisition of the North-West Side
of *St. Lawrence* River, from *Frontenac* to *Montreal*."

Whether the treaty ought to be considered, as having any relation to this matter, is a question which I shall not take upon
me to determine. The map-maker supposes it to be applicable,
and, for the present, I grant it. The XIIth Article of this treaty
is in these words: "The most Christian King shall restore to the
King of *Great-Britain* all Countries, Islands, Forts, and Colonies,
wheresoever situated, which the *English* did possess before the
Declaration of the present War. And in like Manner, the King
of *Great-Britain* shall restore to the most Christian King, all
Countries, Islands, Forts, and Colonies, wheresoever situated,
which the *French* did possess before the said Declaration of
War." If therefore the British subjects were in possession of
Fort Frontenac at the commencement of the war, the French,
who attained it during its continuance, according to this treaty,
ought to have surrendered it to the British Crown.

Whatever the French title to Fort Frontenac might have been,
antecedent to the year 1688, in which the island of Montreal
was invaded by the Five Nations, it is certain, that it was then
abandoned, and that the Indians entered it, and demolished a

great part of the works.* But the authour of the map affirms, "that the *English* did *not* possess Fort *Frontenac* before the Declaration of War terminated by the Peace of *Ryswick.*" To which I reply, that the Indians acquired a title in 1688, either by conquest or dereliction, or both; and that the Crown of Great-Britain had a right to take advantage of their acquisition, in virtue of its sovereignty over the Five Cantons. That they were our dependents, was strongly and often insisted upon by Governour Dongan and Lord Bellomont, and the point remained *sub Judice* till the Treaty of Utrecht. Then a decision was solemnly made in our favour, which looks back, as the determination of all disputes do, at least as far as the first rise of the controversy; posterior to which, and prior to King William's War, his Indian subjects obtained the possession of the Fort in question.†
Whence I think it may be fairly deduced, if we take the Treaty of Ryswick for our rule, that Fort Frontenac, which was regained by the French during their war with us, ought to have been surrendered to the British Crown. Every publick transaction between the French and the Five Nations, without the participation of the government of Great-Britain, since the Indians were claimed as our dependents, is perhaps absolutely void, and particularly the Treaty of Peace made between the Indians and the Chevalier De Callieres, after the death of Count Frontenac.‡

* LeFort de Catarocouy étoit évacué & ruiné. Charlevoix.
† The Five Nations entered the fort in 1688, and the war against France was not proclaimed till May 1689.
‡ Evans's map and first pamphlet, or analysis, were published in the summer 1755, and that part in favour of the French claim to Frontenac, was attacked by two papers in the *New-York Mercury*, in January 1756. This occasioned his publication of the second pamphlet the next spring, in which he endeavours to support his map. He was a man in low circumstances, in his temper precipitate, of violent passions, great vanity, and rude manners. He pretended to the knowledge of everything, and yet had very little learning. By his inquisitive turn, he filled his head with a considerable collection of materials, and a person of more judgment than he had, might, for a few days, receive advantages from his conversation. He piqued himself much upon his two maps, which are however justly chargeable with many errours. His ignorance of language is evident, both in them and the two pamphlets of his analysis, the last of which is stuffed with groundless aspertions on General Shirley, who deserves so well from these colonies, that on that account, and to weaken the authority of a map prejudicial to his Majesty's rights, I beg the reader's excuse for this infraction of the old rule, *de mortuis nil nisi bonum.*[16] He died at New-York, June 12, 1756, under an arrest for a gross slander, uttered against Mr. Morris, the Governour of Pennsylvania.

The possession of any part of the country of the Five Nations by the French, either before or since the close of Queen Anne's War, cannot prejudice the British title, because the Treaty of Aix la Chapelle, renews and confirms that executed at Utrecht in 1713, and expressly stipulates, that the dominions of the contracting parties shall be in the same condition, "which they ought of Right to have been in before the late War." Commissaries were soon after appointed to adjust the controverted limits, who accordingly met at Paris, and continued the negotiation, till the French King perfidiously seized upon several parts of Nova-Scotia, or Acadia, the settlement of the bounds of which, was part of the very business of the Commissaries. This gave rise to the present operations, and the longest sword will determine the controversy.

Brigadier Hunter was disappointed in his expectations upon the late dissolution, for though the elections vere very hot, and several new members came in, yet the majority were in the interest of the late Assembly, and on the 27th of May, 1713, chose Mr. Nicoll into the Chair. The Governour spoke to them with great plainness, informing them, that it would be in vain to endeavour to lodge the money alloted for the support of government, in any other than the hands of the Queen's officers. "Nevertheless," says he, "if you are so resolved, you may put the Country to the Expence of a Treasurer, for the Custody of Money raised for extraordinary Uses." He added, that he was resolved to pass no law, till provision was made for the government. The members were therefore reduced to the dilemma of passing a bill for that purpose, or breaking up immediately. They chose the former, and the Governour gave his assent to that, and an Excise Bill on strong liquors, which continues to this day, producing into the Treasury about one thousand pounds *per annum.* After a short recess, several other laws were enacted in the fall. But the debts of the government still remained unnoticed, till the summer of the year 1714. A long session was then almost entirely devoted to that single affair. Incredible were the numbers of the publick creditors. New demands were every day made. Petitions came in from all quarters, and even for debts contracted before the Revolution. Their amount was near twenty eight thousand pounds. To pay this prodigious sum, recourse was had to the circulation of bills of credit to that value. These were lodged in the hands of the Province Treasurer, and issued by him only, according to the directions of the Act.[17]

The news of the Queen's death arriving in the ensuing fall, a dissolution ensued of course; and a new House met in May, 1715, which continued only to the 21st of July. For the Governour being now determined to subdue those, whom he could not allure, again dissolved the Assembly. He succeeded in his Design, for though Mr. Nicoll was re-elected into the Chair on the 9th of June, 1716, yet we plainly perceive, by the harmony introduced between the several Branches of the legislature, that the majority of the House were now in the interest of the Governour.

An incontestible evidence of their good understanding, appeared at the session in autumn, 1717, when the Governour informed them of a memorial, which had been sent home, reflecting upon his administration. The House immediately voted an address to him, which was conceived in terms of the utmost respect, testifying their abhorrence of the memorial, as a false and malicious libel. It was supposed to be writen by Mulford, a Representative for Suffolk County, who always opposed the measures that were taken to preserve the friendship of the Five Nations, and foolishly projected a scheme to cut them off. It was printed in England, and delivered to the Members at the door of the House of Commons, but never had the authour's intended effect.

It was at this meeting, the Council, on the 31st of October, sent a message by Mr. Alexander,[18] then Deputy Secretary, to the House, desiring them, "to appoint proper Persons, for running the Division Line between this Colony and the Province of *New-Jersey,* his Excellency being assured the Legislature of the Province of *New-Jersey* will bear half the Expence thereof." The Assembly had a bill before them, at that time, which afterwards passed into a law, for the payment of the remaining debts of the government, amounting to many thousand pounds;[19] in which, after a recital of the general reasons, for ascertaining the limits between New-York and New-Jersey on the one side, and Connecticut on the other, a clause was added, to defray the expence of those services. Seven hundred and fifty ounces of plate were enacted "to be issued by Warrant, under the Hand and Seal of the Governour of this Province for the Time being, by and with the Advice and Consent of his Majesty's Council, in such Parts and Portions as shall be requisite for that Service, when the Survey, ascertaining, and running the said Line, Limit, and Boundary, shall be begun, and carried on, by the mutual Consent and Agreement of his Excellency and Council of this

Province, and the Proprietors of the Soil of the said Province of
*New-Jersey.*" According to this law, the line "agreed on by the
Surveyors and Commissioners of each Colony was to be conclusive." Another sum was also provided by the same clause, for
running the line between New-York and Connecticut; and in the
year, 1719, an Act was passed for the settlement of that limit,
of which I shall have occasion to take notice in a succeeding
administration.

Whether it was because Mr. Nicoll was disgusted with the
Governour's prevailing interest in the House, or to his infirm
state of health, that he desired, by a letter to the general Assembly, on the 18th of May, 1718, to be discharged from the
Speaker's place, is uncertain. His request was readily granted,
and Robert Livingston, Esq; chosen in his stead. The concord
between the Governour and this Assembly, was now wound up
to its highest pitch. Instead of other evidences of it, I shall lay
before the reader his last speech to the House on the 24th of
June, 1719, and their address in answer to it.

> Gentlemen, I have now sent for you, that you may be
> Witnesses to my Assent to the Acts passed by the general
> Assembly in this Session. I hope that what remains unfin-
> ished, may be perfected by To-morrow, when I intend to put a
> Close to this Session.
>
> I take this Opportunity also to acquaint you, that my late
> uncertain State of Health, the Care of my little Family, and
> my private Affairs, on the other Side, have at last determined
> me, to make Use of that License of Absence, which has been
> some Time ago so graciously granted me; but with a firm
> Resolution to return to you again, if it is his Majesty's Pleas-
> ure that I should do so: but if that proves otherwise, I assure
> you that whilst I live, I shall be watchful and industrious to
> promote the Interest and Welfare of this Country, of which I
> think I am under the strongest Obligations, for the future, to
> account myself a Countryman.
>
> I look with Pleasure on the present Quiet and flourishing
> State of the People here, whilst I reflect on that in which I
> found them at my Arrival. As the very Name of Party or
> Faction seems to be forgotten, may it for ever lye buried in
> Oblivion, and no Strife ever happen amongst you, but that
> laudable Emulation, who shall approve himself the most zeal-
> ous Servant and most dutiful Subject of the best of Princes,
> and most useful Member of a well established and flourishing
> Community, of which you Gentlemen have given a happy

Example, which I hope will be followed by future Assemblies. I mention it to your Honour, and without Ingratitude and Breach of Duty I could do no less.

Colonel Morris and the new Speaker, were the authours of the answer to this speech, tho' it was signed by all the members. Whether Mr. Hunter deserved the elogium they bestowed upon him, I leave the reader to determine. It is certain that few plantation governours have the honour to carry home with them such a testimonial as this:

> Sir, when we reflect upon your past Conduct, your just, mild, and tender Administration, it heightens the Concern we have for your Departure, and makes our Grief such as Words cannot truly express. You have governed well and wisely, like a prudent Magistrate, like an affectionate Parent; and wherever you go, and whatever Station the Divine Providence shall please to assign you, our sincere Desires and Prayers for the Happiness of you and yours, shall always attend you.
>
> We have seen many Governours, and may see more; and as none of those, who had the Honour to serve in your Station, were ever so justly fixed in the Affections of the Governed, so those to come will acquire no mean Reputation, when it can be said of them, their Conduct has been like yours.
>
> We thankfully accept the Honour you do us, in calling yourself our Countryman; give us Leave then to desire, that you will not forget this as your Country, and, if you can, make haste to return to it.
>
> But if the Service of our Sovereign will not admit of what we so earnestly desire, and his Commands deny us that Happiness; permit us to address you as our Friend, and give us your Assistance, when we are oppressed with an Administration the Reverse of yours.

Colonel Hunter departing the Province, the chief command devolved, the 31st of July, 1719, on Peter Schuyler, Esq; then the eldest member of the Board of Council. As he had no interview with the Assembly during his short administration, in which he behaved with great moderation and integrity; there is very little observable in his time, except a treaty, at Albany, with the Indians, for confirming the ancient League; and the transactions respecting the Partition Line between this and the colony of New-Jersey: concerning the latter of which, I shall now lay before the reader a very summary account.

The two provinces were originally included in the grant of King Charles to the Duke of York. New-Jersey was afterwards conveyed by the Duke to Lord Berkley and Sir George Carteret. This again, by a deed of partition, was divided into East and West Jersey, the former being released to Sir George Carteret, and the latter to the assigns of Lord Berkley. The line of division extended from Little Egg Harbour to the North partition point on Delaware River, and thus both those tracts became concerned in the limits of the Province of New-York. The original rights of Lord Berkley and Sir George Carteret, are vested in two different sets, consisting each of a great number of persons, known by the general name of the Proprietors of East and West Jersey, who, tho' they surrendered the powers of government to Queen Anne, in the year 1702, still retained their property in the soil. These were the persons interested against the claim of New-York. It is agreed on all sides, that the deed to New-Jersey is to be first satisfied, out of that great tract granted to the Duke, and that the remainder is the right of New-York. The Proprietors insist upon extending their Northern limits to a line drawn from the latitude of 41° 40′ on Delaware, to the latitude of 41°, on Hudson's River; and alledge, that before the year 1671, the latitude of 41°, was reputed to be fourteen miles to the Northward of Tappan Creek, part of those lands being settled under New-Jersey till 1684. They farther contend, that in 1684 or 1685, Dongan and Lawrie, (the former, Governour of New-York, and the latter, of New-Jersey,) with their respective councils agreed, that the latitude on Hudson's River was at the mouth of Tappan Creek, and that a line from thence to the latitude of 41° 40′ on Delaware should be the boundary line. In 1686, Robinson, Wells, and *Keith, surveyors of the three several provinces, took two observations, and found the latitude of 41° to be 1′ and 25″ to the Northward of the Yonker's Mills, which is four miles and forty five chains to the Southward of the mouth of Tappan Creek. But against these observations the Proprietors offer sundry objections, which it is not my business to enumerate. It is not pretended by any of the litigants, that a line

* The same who left the Quakers, and took orders in the Church of England. Burnet's *History of his Own Times.*

according to the stations settled by Dongan and Lawrie was actually run; so that the limits of these contending provinces, must long have existed in the uncertain conjectures of the inhabitants of both; and yet the inconveniencies of this unsettled state, through the infancy of the country, were very inconsiderable. In the year 1701, an Act passed in New-York, relating to elections, which annexed Wagachemeck; and great and little Minisink, certain settlements near Delaware, to Ulster County. The intent of this law was to quiet disputes before subsisting between the inhabitants of those places, whose votes were required both in Orange and Ulster. The natural conclusion from hence is, that the legislature of New York then deemed those plantations not included within the New-Jersey grant.

Such was the state of this affair till the year 1717, when provision was made by this Province for running the line. The same being done in New-Jersey the succeeding year, commissions for that purpose under the great seals of the respective colonies, were issued in May, 1719. The commissioners, by indenture dated the 25th of July, fixed the North Station point on the Northermost branch of Delaware, called the Fish-Kill; and from thence a random line was run to Hudson's River, terminating about five miles to the Northward of the mouth of Tappan Creek. In August, the surveyors of East-Jersey met for fixing the Station on Hudson's River. All the commissioners not attending thro' sickness, nothing further was done. What had already been transacted, however, gave a general alarm to many persons interested in several patents under New-York, who before imagined their rights extended to the Southward of the random line. The New-York surveyor afterwards declined proceeding in the work, complaining of faults in the instrument, which had been used in fixing the North Station on Delaware. The Proprietors, on the other hand, think they have answered his objections, and the matter rested, without much contention, till the year 1740. Frequent quarrels multiplying after that period, relating to the rights of soil and jurisdiction Southward of the line in 1719, a probationary Act was passed, in New-Jersey, in February, 1748, for running the line ex parte, if the Province of New-York refused to join in the work. Our Assembly, soon after, directed their agent, to oppose the King's confirmation of that Act; and it was accordingly dropped, agreeably to the advice of the Lords of Trade, whose report of the

18th of July, 1753, on a matter of so much importance, will doubtless be acceptable to the reader.[20]

To the King's Most Excellent Majesty:

*May it please your Majesty,*
    We have lately had under our Consideration, an Act passed in your Majesty's Province of *New-Jersey* in 1747–8, entitled, *An Act for running and ascertaining the Line of Partition and Division betwixt this Province of* New-Jersey, *and the Province* of New-York.
    And having been attended by Mr. *Paris,* Solicitor in Behalf of the Proprietors of the Eastern Division of *New-Jersey;* with Mr. *Hume Campbell* and Mr. *Henley* his Counsel in Support of the said Act; and by Mr. *Charles,* Agent for the Province of *New-York,* with Mr. *Forrester* and Mr. *Pratt* his Counsel against the said Act; and heard what each Party had to offer thereupon; we beg Leave humbly to represent to your Majesty, that the Considerations which arise upon this Act, are of two Sorts, *viz.* such as relate to the Principles upon which it is founded, and such as relate to the Transactions and Circumstances which accompany it.
    As to the first, it is an Act of the Province of *New-Jersey* interested in the Determination of the Limits, and in the consequential Advantages to arise from it.
    The Province of *New-Jersey,* in its distinct and separate Capacity, can neither make nor establish Boundaries: it can as little prescribe Regulations for deciding Differences between itself and other Parties concerned in Interest.
    The established Limits of its Jurisdiction and Territory, are such as the Grants under which it claims have assigned. If those Grants are doubtful, and Differences arise upon the Constructions, or upon the Matters of them, we humbly apprehend that there are but two Methods of deciding them: either by the Concurrence of all Parties concerned in Interest, or by the regular and legal Forms of judicial Proceedings: and it appears to us, that the Method of Proceeding must be derived from the immediate Authority of the Crown itself, signified by a Commission from your Majesty under the great Seal: the Commission of subordinate Officers and of derivative Powers being neither competent nor adequate to such Purposes: to judge otherwise would be, as we humbly conceive, to set up *ex parte* Determinations and incompetent Jurisdictions in the Place of Justice and legal Authority.
    If the Act of *New-Jersey* cannot conclude other Parties,

it cannot be effectual to the Ends proposed; and that
it would not be effectual to form an absolute Decision in
this Case, the Legislature of that Province seems sensible,
whilst it endeavors to leave to your Majesty's Determination,
the Decision of one Point relative to this Matter, and of
considerable Importance to it; which Power your Majesty
cannot derive from them, without their having the Power to
establish the Thing itself, without the Assistance of your
Majesty.

As we are of Opinion, that the present Act without
the Concurrence of other Parties concerned in Interest, is
unwarrantable and ineffectual; we shall in the next Place
consider what Transactions and Proceedings have passed,
towards obtaining such Concurrence.

The Parties interested are your Majesty and the two
Provinces of *New-York* and *New-Jersey.* Your Majesty is
interested with Respect to your Sovereignty, Seigneurie,
and Property; and the said Provinces with Respect to their
Government and Jurisdiction.

With regard to the Transactions on the Part of *New-York,*
we beg Leave to observe, that whatever Agreements have
been made formerly between the two Provinces for settling
their Boundaries; whatever Acts of Assembly have
passed, and whatever Commissions have been issued by the
respective Governours and Governments; the Proceedings under them have never been perfected, the Work
remains unfinished, and the Disputes between the two
Provinces subsist with as much Contradiction as ever; but
there is a Circumstance that appears to us to have still
more Weight, namely, that those Transactions were never
properly warranted on the Part of the Crown: the Crown
never participated in them, and therefore cannot be bound
with Respect to its Interests by Proceedings so authorised.

The Interest which your Majesty has in the Determination
of this Boundary, may be considered in three Lights:
either as Interests of Sovereignty, respecting mere Government; of Seigneurie, which respect Escheats, and Quitrents;
or of Property, as relative to the Soil itself; which last
Interest, takes Place in such Cases, where either your
Majesty has never made any Grants of the Soil, or where
such Grants have by Escheats reverted to your Majesty.

With Regard to the first of these Interests, *viz.* that of
Sovereignty, it has been alledged to us in Support of the
Act, that it is not materially affected by the Question,
as both Provinces are under your Majesty's immediate
Direction and Government: but they stand in a very

different Light with Respect to your Majesty's Interest in the
Quitrents and Escheats; in both which Articles the Situation
of the two Provinces appears to us to make a very material
Alteration: for altho' the Province of *New-Jersey* is not
under Regulations of Propriety or Charter with Respect to its
Government, yet it is a proprietary Province with Respect
to the Grant and Tenure of its Territory, and consequently
as *New-York* is not in that Predicament, the Determination
of the Boundary in Prejudice to that Province, will affect
your Majesty's Interest with Respect to the Tenure of
such Lands as are concerned in this Question: it being
evident, that whatever Districts are supposed to be included
in the Limits of *New-Jersey*, will immediately pass to
the Proprietors of that Province, and be held of them, by
which Means your Majesty would be deprived of your
Escheats, and the Quitrents would pass into other Hands.

To obviate this Objection, it has been alledged, that
the Crown has already made absolute Grants of the whole
Territory that can possibly come in Question under the
Denomination of this Boundary, and reserved only trifling
and inconsiderable Quitrents on those Grants. But this
Argument does not seem to us to be conclusive, since it
admits an Interest in your Majesty, the Greatness or Small-
ness of which is merely accidental; and therefore does
not affect the essence of the Question: and we beg Leave
to observe, that in the Case of exorbitant Grants with
inconsiderable Quitrents; and where consequently it may
reasonably be supposed, that the Crown has been deceived in
such Grants by its Officers; your Majesty's contingent
Right of Property in Virtue of your Seigneurie, seems rather
to be enlarged than diminshed.

This being the Case, it appears to us, that Governor
*Hunter*, ought not to have issued his Commission for running the Line above mentioned, without having previously
received the royal Direction and Instruction for that
Purpose; and that a Commission issued without such Authority, can be considered, with Respect to the Interests of the
Crown, in no other Light than as a mere Nullity: and even
with Respect to *New-York*, we observe, that the said
Commission is questionable, as it does not follow the Directions of the above-mentioned Act, passed in 1717, which
declares, that the Commission to be issued, shall be granted
under the joint Authority of the Governor and Council
of that Province.

But it has been further urged, that the Crown has
since confirmed these Transactions, either by previous

Declarations or by subsequent Acquiescence, and consequently participated in them, so far as to conclude itself: we
shall therefore, in the next Place, beg Leave to consider
the Circumstances urged for this Purpose.

It has been alledged, that the Crown, by giving Consent
to the aforesaid Act, passed in *New-York* in 1717, for paying
and discharging several Debts due from that Colony,
&c. concluded and bound itself, with Respect to the subsequent Proceedings had under the Commission issued by
Governor *Hunter;* but the View and Purport of that
Act appears to us so entire, and so distinctly formed for the
Purpose of raising Money and establishing Funds; so
various and so distinct from any Consideration of the Disputes subsisting in the two Provinces, with Respect to the
Boundaries; that we cannot conceive a single Clause in
so long and so intricate an Act, can be a sufficient Foundation to warrant the Proceedings of Governor *Hunter*
subsequent to it, without a special Authority from the Crown
for that Purpose; and there is the more Reason to be of
this Opinion, as the Crown, by giving its Assent to that Act,
can be construed to have assented only to the levying Money
for a future Purpose; which Purpose could not be effected
by any Commission, but from itself; and therefore can never
be supposed to have, thereby, approved a Commission
from another Authority, which was at that Time already
issued, and carrying in Execution, previous to such Assent.

We further beg leave humbly to represent to your
Majesty, that the Line of Partition and Division between
your Majesty's Province of *New-York* and Colony of
*Connecticut,* having been run and ascertained, pursuant to
the Directions of an Act passed, at *New-York,* for that
Purpose, in the Year 1719, and confirmed by his late Majesty
in 1723; the Transactions between the said Province and
Colony, upon that Occasion, have been alledged to be
similar to, and urged as, a Precedent, and even as an Approbation, of the Matter now in Question: but we are humbly
of Opinion, that the two Cases are materially, and essentially, different. The Act passed in *New-York,* in 1719, for
running and ascertaining the Lines of Partition and Division
between that Colony and the Colony of *Connecticut* recites,
that in the Year 1683, the Governor and Council of
*New-York,* and the Governor and Commissioners of *Connecticut,* did, in Council, conclude an Agreement concerning
the Boundaries of the two Provinces; that, in Consequence of
this Agreement, Commissioners and Surveyors were appointed on the Part of each Government, who did actually

agree, determine, and ascertain, the Lines of Partition; marked out a certain Part of them, and fixed the Point from whence the remaining Part should be run: that the several Things agreed on and done by the said Commissioners, were ratified by the respective Governors; entered on Record in each Colony, in *March* 1700; approved and confirmed by Order of King *William,* the third, in his Privy Council; and by his said Majesty's Letter to his Governor of *New-York.* From this Recital it appears to us, that those Transactions were not only carried on with the Participation, but confirmed by the express Act and Authority of the Crown; and that Confirmation made the Foundation of the Act passed, by *New-York,* for settling the Boundaries between the two Provinces; of all which Authority and Foundation the Act, we now lay before your Majesty, appears to us to be entirely destitute.

Upon the whole, as it appears to us, that the Act in Question, cannot be effectual to the Ends proposed; that your Majesty's Interest may be materially affected by it, and that the Proceedings, on which it is founded, were not warranted in the first Instance, by the proper Authority, but carried on without the Participation of the Crown; we cannot think it advisable, to lay this Act before your Majesty, as fit to receive your royal Approbation.

Which is most humbly submitted,

*Dunk  Halifax,*
*F.  Grenville,*
*James  Oswald,*
*Andrew  Stone.*

*Whitehall,*
*July* 18, 1753.

# Part V

*From the Year 1720, to the Commencement of the Administration of Colonel* Cosby

William Burnet, Esq; took upon him the government of this Province, on the 17th of September, 1720. The Council named in his instructions, were

| | |
|---|---|
| Colonel Schuyler, | Mr. Barbarie, |
| Colonel Depeyster, | Mr. Philipse, |
| Captain Walter, | Mr. Byerly, |
| Colonel Beekman, | Mr. Clarke, |
| Mr. Van Dam, | Dr. Johnston, |
| Colonel Heathcote, | Mr. Harison. |

Mr. Burnet was a son of the celebrated bishop of that name, whose piety and erudition, but especially his zeal and activity, for the Glorious Revolution and Protestant Succession, will embalm his memory to the most distant ages.[1] The Governour was a man of sense and polite breeding, a well read scholar, sprightly, and of a social disposition. Being devoted to his books, he abstained from all those excesses, into which his pleasurable relish would otherwise have plunged him. He studied the arts of recommending himself to the people, had nothing of the moroseness of a scholar, was gay and condescending, affected no pomp, but visited every family of reputation, and often diverted himself in free converse with the ladies, by whom he was very much admired. No Governour, before him, did so much business in Chancery. The Office of Chancellor was his delight. He made a tolerable figure in the exercise of it, tho' he was no lawyer, and had a foible very unsuitable for a judge, I mean his resolving too speedily, for he used to say of himself, "I act first, and think afterwards." He spoke however always sensibly, and by his great reading was able to make a literary parade.—As to his fortune it was very inconsiderable, for he suffered much in the South Sea scheme.[2] While in England, he had the office of comptroller of the customs at London, which he resigned to Brigadier Hunter, as the latter, in his favour, did the government of this and the colony of New-Jersey. Mr. Burnet's acquaintance with that gentleman gave him a fine opportunity, before his arrival, to obtain good intelligence both of persons and things. The Brigadier recommended all his old friends to the favour of his successor, and hence we find that he made few changes amongst them.* Mr. Morris, the Chief Justice, was his principal confident. Dr. Colden and Mr. Alexander, two Scotch gentlemen, had the next place in his esteem. He shewed his wisdom in that choice, for they were both men of learning, good morals, and solid parts. The former was well acquainted with the affairs of the Province, and particularly those which concerned the French in Canada and our Indian allies. The latter was bred to the law, and tho' no speaker, at the head of his profession for sagacity and penetration; and in application to business no man could surpass him. Nor was he unacquainted with the affairs of the publick, having served in the Secretary's office, the best school in the Province, for instruction in matters of government; because the Secretary enjoys a plurality of offices, conversant with the first springs of our provincial oeconomy. Both those gentlemen Mr. Burnet soon raised to the Council Board, as he also did Mr. Morris, jun., Mr. Van Horn, whose daughter he married, and Mr. Kennedy, who succeeded Byerly, both at the Council Board, and in the office of Receiver-general.

Of all our governours none had such extensive and just views of our Indian affairs, and the dangerous neighbourhood of the French, as Governour Burnet, in which Mr. Livingston was his principal assistant. His attention to these matters appeared at the very commencement of his administration, for in his first speech to the Assembly, the very fall after his arrival, he laboured to implant the same sentiments in the breasts of the

---

* Colonel Schuyler and Mr. Philipse were, indeed, removed from the Council Board, by his representations; and their opposing, in Council, the continuance of the Assembly, after his arrival, was the cause of it.

members; endeavouring to alarm their fears, by the daily advances of the French, their possessing the main passes, seducing our Indian allies, and increasing their new settlements in Louisania.

Chief Justice Morris, whose influence was very great in the House, drew the address in answer to the Governour's speech, which contained a passage manifesting the confidence they reposed in him. "We believe that the Son of that worthy Prelate, so eminently instrumental under our glorious Monarch, William the Third, in delivering us from arbitrary Power, and its Concomitants, Popery, Superstition, and Slavery; has been educated in, and possesses, those Principles, that so justly recommended his Father to the Council and Confidence of protestant Princes; and succeeds our former Governor, not only in Power, but Inclination, to do us good."

From an Assembly, impressed with such favourable sentiments, his Excellency had the highest reason, to expect a submissive compliance, with every thing recommended to their notice. The publick business proceeded without suspicion or jealousy, and nothing intervened to disturb the tranquillity of the political state. Among the most remarkable acts, passed at this session, we may reckon that, for a five years support; another for laying a duty of two per cent. prime cost, on the importation of European goods, which was soon after repealed by the King; and a third, for prohibiting the sale of Indian goods to the French. The last of these was a favourite act of the Governour's, and tho' a law very advantageous to the Province, became the source of an unreasonable opposition against him, which continued thro' his whole administration. From the conclusion of the Peace of Utrecht, a great trade was carried on between Albany and Canada, for goods saleable among the Indians. The chiefs of the Confederates, wisely foresaw its ill consequences, and complained of it to the Commissioners of Indian Affairs,* who wrote to Mr. Hunter, acquainting him

* The Governours residing at New-York, rendered it necessary, that some persons should be commissioned, at Albany, to receive intelligence from the Indians, and treat with them upon emergencies. This gave rise to the office of Commissioners of Indian Affairs, who in general transact all such matters as might be done by the Governour. They receive no salaries, but considerable sums are deposited in their hands for occasional presents. There are regular minutes of their transactions from the year 1675. These were in separate quires, till Mr. Alexander, who borrowed them for his Perusal in 1751, had them bound up in four large volumes in folio.

of their dissatisfaction. The letter was laid before the House, but no effectual step taken to prevent the mischief, till the passing of this act, which subjected the traders to a forfeiture of the effects sold, and the penalty of £100. Mr. Burnet's scheme was to draw the Indian trade into our own hands; to obstruct the communication of the French with our allies, which gave them frequent opportunities of seducing them from their fidelity; and to regain the Caghnuagas, who became interested in their disaffection, by being the carriers between Albany and Montreal. Among those who were more immediately prejudiced by this new regulation, the importers of those goods, from Europe, were the chief; and hence the spring of their opposition to the Governour.[3]

All possible arts were used, both here and at home, to preserve the good temper of the Assembly. Brigadier Hunter gave the Ministry such favourable accounts of the members, that Colonel Schuyler, during his presidentship, had orders from Mr. Secretary Craggs, neither to dissolve them himself, nor permit them to be dissolved,[4] and at the spring session, in the year 1721, Mr. Burnet informed them, that his continuance of them, was highly approved at home. Horatio Walpole, the Auditor-General, who had appointed Mr. Clarke for his deputy, thought this a favourable conjuncture, for procuring 5 per cent out of the Treasury. But the House were averse to his application, and on the 2d of June, Abraham Depeyster, jun. was appointed Treasurer by the Speaker's warrant, with the consent of the Governour, in the room of his father, who was infirm; upon which he entered into a recognizance of £5000 to the King, before a judge of the Supreme Court, for the faithful execution of his trust, which was lodged in the Secretary's office.[5] The House, at the same time, in an address, declared their willingness that the treasurer should account; but utterly refused to admit of any draughts upon the Treasury,

---

Here all our Indian treaties are entered. The books are kept by a secretary, commissioned in England, whose appointment is an annual salary of £100 proclamation out of the quit-rents. The commandant at Oswego is generally a commissioner. The office would probably have been more advantageous than it has been, if the Commissioners were not traders themselves, than which nothing is more ignoble in the judgment of the Indians. Sir William Johnson is at present the sole Commissioner, and within nine months after the arrival of General Braddock, received £10,000 sterling, to secure the Indian interest.

for the Auditor-General, who was constrained to depend entirely upon the revenue, out of which he received about £200 per annum.

Mr. Burnet being well acquainted with the geography of the country, wisely concluded, that it was to the last degree necessary, to get the command of the great Lake Ontario, as well for the benefit of the trade, and the security of the friendship of the Five Nations, as to frustrate the French designs, of confining the English colonies to narrow limits, along the sea coast, by a chain of forts on the great passes from Canada to Louisania. Towards the subversion of this scheme, he began the erection of a trading house at Oswego, in the county of the Senecas, in 1722; and recommended a provision for the residence of trusty persons among them, and the Onondagas, which last possess the center of the Five Cantons.[6] This year was remarkable for a congress of several Governours and Commissioners, on the renewal of the ancient friendship with the Indians at Albany. Mr. Burnet prevailed upon them to send a message, to threaten the Eastern Indians with a war, unless they concluded a peace with the English, who were very much harassed by their frequent irruptions. On the 20th of May, in the year following, the Confederates were augmented by their reception of above 80 Nicariagas, besides women and children, as they had been formerly, by the addition of the Tuscaroras. The country of the Nicariagas was on the North side of Missilimakinack, but the Tuscaroras possessed a tract of land, near the sources of James's River, in Virginia, from whence the encroachments of the English, induced them to remove, and settle near the South-East end of the Oneyda Lake.

The strict union subsisting between the several branches of the legislature, gave a handle to Mr. Burnet's enemies to excite a clamour against him. Jealousies were industriously sown in the breasts of the people. The continuance of an Assembly, after the accession of a new Governour, was represented as an anti-constitutional project; and tho' the affairs of the publick were conducted with wisdom and spirit, many were so much imposed upon, that a rupture between the Governour and the Assembly was thought to be absolutely necessary for the weal and safety of the community. But this was not the only stratagem of those who were disaffected by the prohibition of the French trade. The London merchants were induced to petition the King for an order to his Governour, prohibiting the revival of the Act made against it, or the passing any new law of that tendency. The petition was referred to the Board of Trade, and backed before their Lordships, with suggestions of the most notorious falsehoods. The Lords of Trade prudently advised, that no such directions should be sent to Mr. Burnet, till he had an opportunity of answering the objections against the Act. They were accordingly sent over to him, and he laid them before his Council. Dr. Colden and Mr. Alexander exerted themselves in a memorable report in answer to them, which drew upon them the resentment of several merchants here, who had first excited the London petition, and laid the foundation for a variance between their families, which has manifested itself on many occasions. In justice to Mr. Burnet's memory, and to shew the propriety of his measures for obstructing the French trade, I cannot refrain the republication of the Council's report at full length.

*May it please your Excellency,*
   In Obedience to your Excellency's Commands, in Council, the 29th of October, referring to us a Petition of several Merchants in London, presented to the King's most excellent Majesty, against renewing an Act passed in this Province, entitled, *"An Act for Encouragement of the* Indian *Trade, and rendering it more effectual to the Inhabitants of this Province, and for prohibiting the Selling of* Indian *Goods to the* French." As likewise the several Allegations of the said Merchants before the right honourable the Lords of Trade and Plantations, we beg Leave to make the following Remarks.
   In order to make our Observations the more distinct and clear, we shall gather together the several Assertions of the said Merchants, both in their Petition, and delivered verbally before the Lords of Trade, as to the Situation of this Province, with Respect to the French and Indian Nations; and observe on them, in the first Place, they being the Foundation on which all their other Allegations are grounded. Afterwards we shall lay before your Excellency, what we think necessary to observe, on the other Parts of the said Petition, in the Order they are in the Petition, or in the Report of the Lords of Trade.
   In their geographical Accounts they say, *"Besides the Nations of* Indians *that are in the* English *Interest, there are very many Nations of* Indians, *who are at present in the Interest of the* French, *and who lie between* New-York *and*

*the Nations of* Indians *in the* English *Interest.—The*
French *and their* Indians *would not permit the* English
Indians *to pass over by their Forts." The said Act "restrains
them (the* Five Nations) *from a free Commerce with
the Inhabitants of* New-York.

*The five* Indian *Nations are settled upon the Banks
of the River* St. Lawrence, *directly opposite to* Quebeck, *two
or three hundred Leagues distant from the nearest*
British *Settlements in* New-York.

*They (the five Nations of* Indians) *were two or three
hundred Leagues distant from* Albany; *and that they could
not come to trade with the* English, *but by going down
the River* St. Lawrence, *and from thence through a Lake,
which brought them within eighteen Leagues of* Albany."

These Things the Merchants have thought it safe for
them, and consistent with their Duty to his sacred Majesty,
to say in his Majesty's Presence, and to repeat them
afterwards before the right honourable the Lords of Trade,
though nothing can be more directly contrary to the
Truth. For there are no Nations of *Indians* between *New-
York* and the Nations of *Indians* in the *English* Interest, who
are now six in Number, by the Addition of the *Tuscaroras.*
The *Mohawks* (called *Annies** by the *French*) one of
the *Five Nations*, live on the South Side of a Branch of
*Hudson's* River, (not on the North Side as they are placed in
the *French* Maps) and but forty Miles directly West from
*Albany*, and within the *English* Settlements; some of
the *English* Farms, upon the same River, being thirty Miles
further West. The *Oneydas* (the next of the *Five Nations*)
lie likewise West from *Albany*, near the Head of the
*Mohawks* River, about one hundred Miles from *Albany*. The
*Onondagas* lie about one hundred and thirty Miles West
from *Albany;* and the *Tuscaroras* live partly with the
*Oneydas* and partly with the *Onondagas*. The *Cayugas* are
about one hundred and sixty Miles from *Albany;* and
the *Senecas* (the furthest of all these Nations, are not above
two hundred and forty Miles from *Albany*, as may appear
from Mr. *De L'Isle's*† Map of *Louisania*, who lays down the
*Five Nations* under the Name of *Iroquois:* and Goods are
daily carried, from this Province, to the *Senecas*, as well as
to those Nations that lie nearer, by Water, all the Way, except three Miles (or in the dry Seasons five Miles) where
the Traders carry over Land between the *Mohawks* River and

* *Agniès.*
† *De L'Isle.*

the *Wood Creek*, which runs into the *Oneydas* Lake, without going near either *St. Lawrence* River, or any of the Lakes upon which the *French* pass, which are intirely out of their Way.

The nearest *French* Forts or Settlements to *Albany*, are *Chambly* and *Montreal*, both of them lying about North and by East from *Albany*, and are near two hundred Miles distant from it. *Quebeck* lies about three hundred and eighty Miles North-East from *Albany*. So far is it from being true, that the *Five Nations* are situated upon the Banks of the River *St. Lawrence*, opposite to *Quebeck*, that *Albany* lies almost directly between *Quebeck* and the *Five Nations*. And to say that these *Indians* cannot come to trade at *Albany*, but by going down the River *St. Lawrence*, and then into a Lake eighteen Leagues from *Albany* (we suppose they mean Lake *Champlain*) passing by the *French* Forts, is to the same Purpose as if they should say, that one cannot go from *London* to *Bristol*, but by Way of *Edinburgh*.

Before we go on to observe other Particulars, we beg Leave further to remark, that it is so far from being true, that the *Indians* in the *French* Interest, lie between *New-York* and our *Five Nations* of *Indians;* that some of our Nations of *Indians* lie between the *French* and the *Indians*, from whence the *French* bring the far greatest Quantity of their Furs: for the *Sennekas* (whom the *French* call *Sonontouons\**) are situated between Lake *Erie* and *Cadaracqui* Lake, (called by the *French*, *Ontario*) near the great Fall of *Iagara†*, by which all the *Indians* that live round Lake *Erie*, round the Lake of the *Hurons*, round the Lake of the *Illenois*, or *Michegan*, and round the great upper Lake, generally pass in their Way to *Canada*. All the *Indians* situated upon the Branches of the *Misissippi*, must likewise pass by the same Place, if they go to *Canada*. And all of them likewise, in their Way to *Canada*, pass by our Trading-place upon the *Cadaracqui* Lake, at the Mouth of the *Onondaga* River. The nearest and safest Way of carrying Goods upon the *Cadaracqui* Lake, towards *Canada*, being along the South Side of that Lake, (near where our *Indians* are settled, and our Trade of late is fixed) and not by the north side and *Cadaracqui*, or *Frontinac* Fort, where the *French* are settled.

Now that we have represented to your Excellency, that not one Word of the Geography of these Merchants is true, upon which all their Reasoning is founded; it might seem needless to trouble your Excellency with any further Remarks, were

\* *Isonnontouans.*
† Sometimes *Oniagara, Ochniagara,* but commonly *Niagara.*

it not to show with what Earnestness they are promoting the *French* Interest, to the Prejudice of all his Majesty's Colonies in *North America,* and that they are not ashamed of asserting any Thing for that End, even in the royal Presence.

First they say, "That by the Act passed in this Province, entitled, An Act for the Encouragement of the *Indian* Trade, *&c.* All Trade whatsoever is prohibited in the strictest Manner, and under the severest Penalties, between the Inhabitants of *New-York* Government, and the *French* of *Canada.*"

This is not true; for only carrying Goods to the *French,* which are proper for the *Indian* Trade, is prohibited. The Trade, as to other Things, is left in the same State it was before that Act was made, as it will appear to any Person that shall read it: and there are, yearly, large Quantities of other Goods, openly, carried to *Canada,* without any Hindrance from the Government of *New-York.* Whatever may be said of the Severity and Penalties in that Act, they are found insufficient to deter some from carrying Goods clandestinely to the *French;* and the Legislature of this Province are convinced, that no Penalties can be too severe, to prevent a Trade, which puts the Safety of all his Majesty's Subjects of *North America* in the greatest Danger.

Their next Assertion is, *"All the* Indian *Goods have by this Act been raised* 25 *l.* to 30 *l. per Cent."* This is the only Allegation in the whole Petition that there is any Ground for. Nevertheless, tho' the common Channel of Trade cannot be altered without some Detriment to it in the Beginning; we are assured from the Custom-house Books, that there has been every Year, since the passing of this Act, more Furs exported from *New-York,* than in the Year immediately before the passing of this Act. It is not probable that the greatest Difference between the Exportation, any Year before this Act, and any Year since, could so much alter the Price of Beaver, as it is found to be this last Year. Beaver is carried to *Britain* from other Parts besides *New-York,* and it is certain that the Price of Beaver is not so much altered here by the Quantity in our Market, as by the Demand for it in *Britain.* But as we cannot be so well informed here, what occasions Beaver to be in greater Demand in *Britain,* we must leave that to be enquired after in *England.* However, we are fully satisfied that it will be found to be for very different Reasons from what the Merchants alledge.

The Merchants go on and say, "Whereas, on the other Hand, this Branch of the *New-York* Trade, by the Discouragements brought upon it by this Act, is almost wholly engrossed by the *French,* who have already by this Act, been encouraged

to send proper *European* Goods to *Canada,* to carry on this
Trade, so that should this Act be continued, the *New-York*
Trade, which is very considerable, must be wholly lost to us,
and center in the *French.*—Though *New-York* should not
furnish them, the *French* would find another Way to be supplied therewith, either from some other of his Majesty's
Plantations, or it might be directly from *Europe.*—Many of
the Goods, which the *Indians* want, being as easy to be had
directly from *France* or *Holland,* as from *Great-Britain."*

This is easily answered, by informing your Excellency,
that the principal of the Goods proper for the *Indian* Market,
are only of the Manufactures of *Great-Britain,* or of the
*British* Plantations, *viz.* Strouds,[7] or Stroud-waters, and other
Woollens, and Rum.—The *French* must be obliged to buy
all their Woollens (the Strouds especially) in *England,* and
thence carry them to *France,* in Order to their Transportation to *Canada.*

The Voyage to *Quebeck,* through the Bay of *St. Lawrence,*
is well known to be the most dangerous of any in the World,
and only practicable in the Summer Months. The *French*
have no Commodities in *Canada,* by Reason of the Cold and
Barrenness of the Soil, proper for the *West-India* Markets;
and therefore have no Rum but by Vessels from *France,*
that touch at their Islands in the *West-Indies. New-York*
has, by Reason of its Situation, both as to the Sea and the
*Indians,* every Way the Advantage of *Canada.* The *New-York*
Vessels make always two Voyages in a Year from *England,*
one in Summer, and another in Winter, and several Voyages
in a Year to the *West-Indies.* It is manifest, therefore, that
it is not in the Power of the *French* to import any Goods near
so cheap, to *Canada,* as they are imported to *New-York.*

But to put this out of all Controversy, we need only observe
to your Excellency, that Strouds (without which no considerable Trade can be carried on with the *Indians*) are sold at
*Albany* for £10 a Piece: they were sold at *Montreal,* before
this Act took Place, at £13 2s. 6 d. and now they are sold
there for £25 and upwards; which is an evident Proof, that
the *French* have not in these four Years Time (during the
Continuance of this Act) found out any other Way to supply
themselves with Strouds; and likewise that they cannot trade
without them, seeing they buy them at so extravagant a
Price.

It likewise appears, that none of the neighbouring Colonies have been able to supply the *French* with these Goods,
and those that know the Geography of the Country, know it
is impracticable to do it at any tolerable Rate, because they

must carry their Goods ten Times further by Land than we need to do.

We are likewise assured, that the Merchants of *Montreal* lately told Mr. *Vaudreuil* their Governor, that if the Trade from *Albany* be not by some Mean or other encouraged, they must abandon that Settlement. We have Reason therefore to suspect, that these Merchants (at least some of them) have been practised upon by the *French* Agents in *London;* for no doubt, the *French* will leave no Method untried to defeat the present Designs of this Government, seeing they are more afraid of the Consequences of this Trade between *New-York* and the *Indians* than of all the warlike Expeditions that ever were attempted against *Canada.*

But to return to the Petitioners. "They conceive nothing can tend more to the withdrawing the Affections of the *Five Nations* of *Indians* from the *English* Interest, than the Continuance of the said Act, which in its Effects restrains them from a free Commerce with the Inhabitants of *New-York*, and may too probably estrange them from the *English* Interest; whereas by a Freedom of Commerce, and an encouraged Intercourse of Trade with the *French* and their *Indians*, the *English* Interest might, in Time be greatly improved and strengthened."

It seems to us a strange Argument to say, that an Act, the whole Purport of which is to encourage our own People to go among the *Indians*, and to draw the far *Indians* through our *Indian* Country to *Albany* (and which has truly produced these Effects) would, on the contrary, restrain them from a free Commerce with the Inhabitants of *New-York*, and may too probably estrange them from the *English* Interest; and therefore that it would be much wiser in us to make Use of the *French*, to promote the *English* Interest; and for which End, we ought to encourage a free Intercourse between them and our *Indians*. The Reverse of this is exactly true, in the Opinion of our *Five Nations;* who in all their publick Treaties with this Government, have represented against this Trade, as *the building the* French *Forts with* English *Strouds:* that the encouraging a Freedom of Commerce with our *Indians*, and the *Indians* round them, who must pass through their Country to *Albany*, would certainly increase both the *English* Interest and theirs, among all the Nations to the Westward of them; and that the carrying the *Indian* Market to *Montreal* in *Canada*, draws all the far *Indians* thither.

The last Thing we have to take Notice, is what the Merchants asserted before the Lords of Trade, *viz.* "That there has not been half the Quantity of *European* Goods exported

since the passing of this Act, that used to be."—'We are well
assured, that this is no better grounded than the above Facts
they assert with the same Positiveness. For it is well known,
almost to every Person in *New-York,* that there has not been
a less, but rather a greater, Quantity of *European* Goods imported into this Place, since the passing of this Act than was
at any Time before it, in the same Space of Time. As this
appears by the Manifests in the Custom-house here, the same
may likewise be easily proved by the Custom-house Books in
*London.*

As all the Arguments of the merchants run upon the ill
Effects this Act has had upon the Trade and the Minds of
the *Indians,* every one of which we have shown to be asserted,
without the least Foundation to support them; there nothing
now remains, but to shew the good Effects this Act has produced, which are so notorious in this Province, that we know
not one Person that now opens his Mouth against the Act.

Before this Act passed, none of the People of this Province
travelled into the *Indian* Countries to trade. We have now
above forty young Men, who have been several Times as far
as the Lakes a trading, and thereby become well acquainted,
not only with the Trade of the *Indians,* but likewise with their
Manners and Languages; and those have returned with such
large Quantities of Furs, that greater Numbers are resolved
to follow their Example; so that we have good Reason to
hope, that in a little Time, the *English* will draw the whole
*Indian* Trade of the inland Countries to *Albany,* and into the
Country of the *Five Nations.* This Government has built a
publick Trading-house upon *Cataracqui* Lake, at *Irondequat*
in the *Sennekas* Land, and another is to be built, next Spring,
at the Mouth of the *Onondagas* River. All the far *Indians* pass
by these Places, in their Way to *Canada,* and they are not
above half so far from the *English* Settlements, as they are
from the *French.*

So far is it from being true what the Merchants say, "That
the *French* Forts interrupt all Communication between the
*Indians* and the *English";* that if these Places be well supported, as they easily can be from our Settlements, in case
of a Rupture with the *French,* it will be in the Power of this
Province, to intercept the greatest Part of the Trade between
*Canada* and the *Indians* round the Lakes and the Branches
of the *Misissippi.*—Since this Act passed, many Nations have
come to *Albany* to trade; and Peace and Friendship, whose
Names had not so much as been heard of among us.—In the
Beginning of *May,* 1723, a Nation of *Indians* came to *Albany*
singing and dancing, with their Calumets before them, as
they always do when they come to any Place, where they have

not been before. We do not find that the Commissioners of
*Indian* Affairs, were able to inform themselves what Nation
this was.

Towards the End of the same Month, eighty Men, besides
the Women and Children, came to *Albany* in the same
Manner. These had one of our *Five Nations* with them for an
Interpreter, by whom they informed the Commissioners, that
they were of a great Nation, called *Nehkereages*, consisting of
six Castles and Tribes; and that they lived near a Place called
by the *French, Missillimakinah,* between the upper Lake and
the Lake of the *Hurons.* These *Indians* not only desired a free
Commerce, but likewise to enter into a strict League of
Friendship with us and our *Six Nations,* that they might be
accounted the seventh Nation in the League, and being received accordingly, they left their Calumet as a Pledge of
their Fidelity.—In *June* another Nation arrived, but from
what Part of the Continent we have not learned.

In *July,* the *Twightwies* arrived, and brought an *Indian*
Interpreter of our Nations with them, who told, that they
were called by the *French, Miamies,* and that they live upon
one of the Branches of the River *Misissippi.*—At the same
Time some of the *Tahsagrondie Indians,* who live between
Lake *Erie* and the Lake *Hurons,* near a *French* Settlement,
did come and renew their League with the *English,* nor
durst the *French* hinder them.—In *July* this Year, another
Nation came, whose Situation and Name we know not; and
in *August* and *September,* several Parties of the same *Indians*
that had been here last Year: but the greatest Numbers of
these far *Indians* have been met this Year in the *Indian*
Country by our Traders, every one of them endeavouring to
get before another, in order to reap the Profits of so advantageous a Trade, which has all this Summer long, kept about
forty Traders constantly employed, in going between our
Trading-places, in our *Indian* Country, and *Albany.*

All these Nations of *Indians,* who came to *Albany,* said,
that the *French* had told them many strange Stories of the
English, and did what they could to hinder their coming to
*Albany,* but that they had resolved to break through by Force.
The Difference on this Score between the *Taksagrondie In-*
*dians* and the *French* (who have a Fort and Settlement there,
called by them *Le Detroit*) rose to that Height, this Summer,
that Mr. *Tonti,* who commanded there, thought it proper to
retire, and return to *Canada* with many of his Men.

We are, for these Reasons, well assured, that this Year
there will be more Beaver exported for *Great-Britain,* than
ever was from this Province in one Year; and that if the
Custom-house Books at *London* be looked into, it will be

found, that there will be a far greater Quantity of Goods for the *Indians* (Strouds especially) sent over next Spring, than ever was at any one Time to this Province. For the Merchants here tell us, that they have at this Time ordered more of these Goods, than ever was done at any one Time before.

These Matters of Fact prove, beyond Contradiction, that this Act has been of the greatest Service to *New-York*, in making us acquainted with many Nations of *Indians*, formerly entirely unknown, and Strangers, to us; withdrawing them from their Dependence upon the *French*, and in uniting them to us and our *Indians*, by Means of Trade and mutual Offices of Friendship.—Of what great Consequence this may be to the *British* Interest in general, as to Trade, is apparent to any Body. It is no less apparent likewise, that it is of the greatest Consequence to the Safety of all the *British* Colonies in *North America*. We feel, too sensibly, the ill Effects of the *French* Interest in the present War betwixt *New-England*, and only one Nation of *Indians* supported by the *French*. Of what dismal Consequences then might it be, if the *French* should be able to influence, in the same Manner, so many and such numerous Nations, as lie to the Westward of this Province, *Pensylvania* and *Maryland?*—On the other Hand, if all these Nations (who assert their own Freedom, and declare themselves Friends to those that supply them best with what they want) be brought to have a Dependance upon the *English* (as we have good Reason to hope in a short Time they will) the *French* of *Canada*, in Case of a War, must be at the Mercy of the *English*.

To these Advantages must be added, that many of our young Men having been induced by this Act to travel among the *Indians*, they learn their Manners, their Languages, and the Situation of all their Countries, and become inured to all Manner of Fatigues and Hardships; and a great many more being resolved to follow their Example, these young Men, in Case of War with the *Indians*, will be of ten Times the Service, that the same Number of the common Militia can be of.—The Effects of this Act have likewise so much quieted the Minds of the People, with Respect to the Security of the Frontiers, that our Settlements are now extended above thirty Miles further West towards the *Indian* Countries, than they were before it passed.

The only Thing that now remains to answer, is an Objection which we suppose may be made, What can induce the Merchants of *London* to petition against an Act, which will be really so much for their Interest in the End? The Reason is, in all Probability, because they only consider their present

Gain; and that they are not at all concerned for the Safety of this Country, in encouraging the most necessary Undertaking, if they apprehend their Profit for two or three Years may be lessened by it. This Inclination of the Merchants has been so notorious, that few Nations, at War with their Neighbours, have been able to restrain them from supplying their Enemies with Ammunition and Arms. The Count *D'Estrade*, in his Letters in 1638, says, that when the *Dutch* were besieging *Antwerp*, one *Beiland*, who had loaded four Fly-boats with Arms and Powder for *Antwerp*, being taken up by the Prince of *Orange*'s Order, and examined at *Amsterdam*, said boldly, that the Burghers of *Amsterdam* had a Right to trade every where: that he could name a hundred that were Factors for the Merchants at *Antwerp*, and that he was one. "That Trade cannot be interrupted, and that for his Part he was very free to own, that if to get any Thing by Trade it were necessary to pass through Hell, he would venture to burn his Sails." 'When this Principle, so common to Merchants, is considered, and that some in this Place have got Estates by trading many Years to *Canada*, it is not to be wondered, that they have acted as Factors for *Canada* in this Affair, and that they have transmitted such Accounts to their Correspondents in *London*, as are consistent with the Trust reposed in them by the Merchants of *Canada*.

In the last Place, we are humbly of Opinion, that it may be proper to print the Petition of the Merchants of *London*, and their Allegations before the Lords of Trade, together with the Answers your Committee has made thereto, in Vindication of the Legislature of this Province, of which we have the Honour to be a Part, if your Excellency shall approve of our Answers; that what we have said may be exposed to the Examination of every one in this Place, where the Truth of the Matters of Fact is best known, and that the Correspondents of these Merchants may have the most publick Notice to reply, if they shall think it proper, or to disown, in a publick Manner, that they are the Authors of such groundless Informations. All which is unanimously and humbly submitted by

*Your Excellency's*

*Most obedient humble Servants,*

| | |
|---|---|
| *R. Walter,* | *Cadwallader Colden,* |
| *Rip Van Dam,* | *James Alexander,* |
| *John Barbarie,* | *Abraham Van Horne.* |
| *Fr. Harrison,* | |

Governour Burnet transmited this report to the Board of Trade, and it had the intended effect.[8]


About the latter end of the year 1724, an unfortunate dispute commenced in the French Church, of which, because it had no small influence on the publick affairs of the government, I shall lay before the reader a short account.

The Persecutions in France, which ensued upon the revocation of the Edict of Nantz, drove the Protestant subjects of Louis XIV into the territories of other princes. Many of them fled even into this Province: the most opulent settled in the city of New-York, others went into the country and planted New Rochelle, and a few seated themselves at the New Paltz in Ulster County. Those who resided in New-York soon erected a church, upon the principles and model of that in Geneva; and by their growth and foreign accessions, formed a congregation, for numbers and riches, superior to all but the Dutch. They had two ministers; Rou, the first called, was a man of learning, but proud, pleasurable, and passionate. Moulinaars, his colleague, was most distinguished for his pacifick spirit, dull parts, and unblameable life and conversation. Rou despised his fellow labourer, and for a long time commanded the whole congregation, by the superiority of his talents for the pulpit. The other impatient of repeated affronts and open contempt, raised a party in his favour, and this year succeeded in the election of a set of elders, disposed to humble the delinquent. Rou being suspicious of the design, refused to acknowledge them duly elected. Incensed at this conduct, they entered an Act in their minutes, dismissing him from the pastoral charge of the church, and procured a ratification of the Act under the hands of the majority of the people. Governour Burnet had, long before this time, admitted Rou into his familiarity, on the score of his learning; and that consideration encouraged a petition to him, from Rou's adherents, complaining against the elders. The matter was then referred to a committee of the Council, who advised that the congregation should be admonished, to bring their differences to an amicable conclusion. Some overtures, to that end, were attempted; and the elders offered to submit the controversy to the Dutch ministers. But Rou, who knew that the French Church, in this country, without a Synod was unorganized, and could not restrain him, chose rather to bring his bill in Chancery before the Governour.

Mr. Alexander was his counsel, and Mr. Smith,* a young lawyer, of the first reputation as a speaker,[9] appeared for the elders. He pleaded to the jurisdiction of the court, insisting that the matter was entirely ecclesiastical, and, in the prosecution of his argument, entered largely into an examination of the government of the Protestant churches in France. According to which, he shewed that the Consistory were the proper judges of the point in dispute, in the first instance; and that from thence an appeal lay to a collogue, next to a provincial, and last of all to a national synod. Mr. Burnet nevertheless over-ruled the plea, and the defendants, being fearful of a decree, that might expose their own estates to the payment of Rou's salary, thought it advisable to drop their debates, reinstate the minister, and leave the church.

All those who opposed Rou were disobliged with the Governour: among these Mr. De Lancey was the most considerable for his wealth and popular influence. He was very rigid in his religious profession, one of the first builders, and by far the most generous benefactor, of the French Church, and therefore left it with the utmost reluctance. Mr. Burnet, before this time, had considered him as his enemy, because he had opposed the prohibition of the French trade; and this led him into a step, which, as it was a personal indignity, Mr. De Lancey could never recollect without resentment. This gentleman was returned for the city of New-York, in the room of a deceased member, at the meeting of the Assembly in September 1725. When he offered himself for the oaths, Mr. Burnet asked him how he became a subject of the Crown? He answered, that he was denized in England, and his Excellency dismissed him, taking time to consider the matter. Mr. De Lancey then laid before the House an Act of a notary publick, certifying that he was named in a Patent of Denization, granted in the reign of James the Second—A patent of the same kind, under the Great Seal of this Province, in 1686—And two certificates, one of his having taken the Oath of Allegiance, according to an Act passed here in 1683, and another of his serving in several former Assemblies. The Governour, in the mean time, consulted the Chief Justice, and transmitted his opinion† to the House,

* These gentlemen came into the colony in the same ship in 1715. The latter was born at Newport Pagnel in Buckinghamshire. They were among the principal agents in the political struggles during the administration of Col. Cosby.[10]

† What Colonel Morris's opinion was, I have not been able to discover. Governour Burnet's conduct was thought to be unconstitu-

who resolved in favour of Mr. De Lancey. Several other new representatives came in, at this session, upon the decease of the old members; and Adolph Philipse, who was sometime before dismissed from the Council Board, was elected into the Speaker's Chair, in the absence of Mr. Livingston.[11] The majority, however, continued in the interest of the Governour; and consented to the revival of the several acts, which had been passed for prohibiting the French trade; which in spite of all the restraints laid upon it, was clandestinely carried on by the people of Albany. Oswego, nevertheless, grew considerable for its commerce: fifty-seven canoes went there this summer, and returned with seven hundred and thirty-eight packs of beaver and deer skins.

Nothing could more naturally excite the jealousy of the French, than the erection of the new trading house at the mouth of the Onandaga River. Fearful of losing a profitable trade, which they had almost entirely engrossed, and the command of the Lake Ontario, they launched two vessels in it in 1726, and transported materials, for building a large store-house, and repairing the fort at Niagara. The scheme was not only to secure to themselves the entrance into the West end of the Lake, as they already had the East, by the fraudulent erection of Fort Frontenac, many years before; but also to carry their trade more westerly, and thus render Oswego useless, by shortening the travels of the Western Indians, near two hundred miles. Baron De Longueil, who had the chief command in Canada, on the death of the Marquis de Vaudreuil in October 1725, was so intent upon this project, that he went, in person, to the Onondago canton, for leave to raise the store-house at Niagara: and as those Indians were most of all exposed to the intrigues of the Jesuits, who constantly resided amongst them; he prevailed upon them by fraud and false representations to consent to it, for their protection against the English. But as soon as this matter was made known to the other nations, they declared the permission granted by the Onondagas to be absolutely void; and sent deputies to Niagara, with a message, signifying that the country in which they were at work, belonged solely to the Sennecas; and required them immediately to desist. The French, notwithstanding, were regard-

---

tional, and an invasion of the rights of the Assembly, who claim the exclusive privilege of determining the qualifications of their own members.

less of the embassage, and pushed on their enterprise with all
possible dispatch, while Joncaire[12] exerted all his address among
the Indians, to prevent the demolition of the works. Canada
was very much indebted to the incessant intrigues of this man.
He had been adopted by the Sennecas, and was well esteemed
by the Onondagas. He spoke the Indian language as Charlevoix
informs us, "avec la plus sublime eloquence Iroquoise," and had
lived amongst them, after their manner, from the beginning of
Queen Anne's reign. All these advantages he improved for the
interest of his country; he facilitated the missionaries in their
progress through the cantons, and more than any man contributed to render their dependence upon the English, weak and
precarious. Convinced of this, Colonel Schuyler urged the Indians, at his treaty with them, in 1719, to drive Joncaire out
of their country, but his endeavours were fruitless.*

The Jesuit Charlevoix does honour to Mr. Burnet, in declaring that he left no stone unturned, to defeat the French designs
at Niagara. Nor is it much to be wondered at. For besides sup-
planting his favourite trade at Oswego, it tended to the defection of the Five Nations; and in case of a rupture, exposed the
frontiers of our Southern colonies to the ravages of the French
and their allies. Mr. Burnet, upon whom these considerations
made the deepest impression, laid the matter before the house,
remonstrated against the proceedings to Longuiel in Canada,
wrote to the Ministry in England, who complained of them to
the French Court, and met the Confederates at Albany, endeavouring to convince them of the danger they themselves
would be in, from an aspiring, ambitious, neighbour. He spoke
first about the affair privately to the sachems, and afterwards,
in the publick conference, informed them of all the encroachments which the French had made upon their fathers, and the
ill usage they had met with, according to La Potherie's account,
published with the privilege of the French King, at Paris, in
1722. He then reminded them of the kind treatment they had
received from the English, who constantly fed and cloathed
them, and never attempted any act of hostilities to their prejudice. This speech was extremely well drawn, the thoughts being
conceived in strong figures, particularly expressive and agree-

---

* The same thing has since been frequently laboured, but to no
purpose. His son continued the course of intrigues begun by the
father, till General Shirley, while he was at Oswego in 1755,
prevailed upon the Sennecas to order him to Canada.

able to the Indians. The Governour required an explicit declaration of their sentiments, concerning the French transactions at Niagara, and their answer was truly categorical. "We speak now in the Name of all the *Six Nations,* and come to you howling. This is the Reason why we howl, that the Governour of *Canada* incroaches on our Land and builds thereon." After which they entreated him to write to the King for succour. Mr. Burnet embraced this favourable opportunity to procure from them a deed, surrendering their country to his Majesty, to be protected for their use, and confirming their grant in 1701, concerning which there was only an entry in the books of the Secretary for Indian Affairs.* It happened very unfortunately, that his Excellency's hands were then more weakened than ever, by the growing disaffection in the House. The intrigues of his adversaries, and the frequent deaths of the members, had introduced such a change in the Assembly, that it was with difficulty he procured a three years support. The clamours of the people ran so high without doors for a new election, that he was obliged to dissolve the House, and soon after another dissolution ensued on the death of the King. The French, in the mean time, completed their works at Niagara, and Mr. Burnet, who was unable to do any thing else, erected a fort, in 1727, for the protection of the post and trade at Oswego. This necessary undertaking was pregnant with the most important consequences, not only to this, but all our colonies; and though the Governour's seasonable activity, deserved the highest testimonials of our gratitude, I am ashamed to confess, what I am bound to relate, that he built the fort at his private expence, and that a balance of above £56 principal, though frequently demanded, remains due to his estate to this very day.

Beauharnois, the Governour of Canada, who superseded Longuiel, was so incensed at the building of the fort, that he sent a written summons, in July, to the officer posted there, to abandon it; and though his predecessor had done the same, a

---

* Besides the territories at the West end of Lake Erie, and on the North side of that, and the Lake Ontario, which were ceded in 1701; the Indians now granted, for the same purpose, all their habitations from Oswego to Cayahoga River, which disembogues into Lake Erie, and the country extending sixty miles from the Southermost banks of those lakes. Though the first surrender, through negligence was not made by the execution of a formal deed under seal; yet as it was transacted with all the solemnity of a treaty, and as the second surrender confirms the first, no intermediate possession by the French can prejudice the British title derived by the cession in 1701.

little before, at Niagara, in the country of the Sennecas, the acknowledged subjects of the British Crown,* yet, with a singular effrontery, he dispatched De la Chassaigne, a Man of Parts and Governour of Trois Rivieres, to New-York, with the strongest complaints to Mr. Burnet upon that head. His Excellency sent him a polite, but resolute, answer on the 8th of August; in which he refuted the arguments urged by the French Governour General; and remonstrated against the proceedings, of the last year, at Niagara.[13]

The new Assembly met in September 1727, and consisted of members all ill affected to the Governour. The long continuance of the last, the clamours which were excited by several late important decrees in chancery, the affair of the French Church, and especially the prohibiting the Canada trade, were the causes, to which the loss of his interest is to be ascribed.[14] Mr. Philipse, the Speaker, was piqued at a Decree in Chancery against himself, which very much affected his estate; no wonder then that the members, who were very much influenced by him, came, on the 25th of November, into the following resolutions. Colonel Hicks, from the Committee of Grievances, reported,

That as well by the Complaints of several People, as by the general Cry of his Majesty's Subjects inhabiting this Colony, they find that the Court of Chancery, as lately assumed to be set up here, renders the Liberties and Properties of the said Subjects extreamly precarious; and that by the violent Measures taken in, and allowed by it, some have been ruined, others obliged to abandon the Colony, and many restrained in it, either by Imprisonment or by excessive Bail exacted from them not to depart, even when no Manner

* Though the sovereignty over the Five Nations was ceded to Great-Britain, and Charlevoix himself had acknowledged that Niagara was part of their country, yet the pious Jesuit applauds the French settlement there, which was so manifest an infraction of the Treaty of Utrecht. The Marquis De Nonville, in his letter to the Court of France in 1686, proposed the erection of a fort there, to secure the communication with the lakes, and deprive us of a trade which he computed to be worth 400,000 francs per annum. Charlevoix, perhaps, considered these advantages sufficient to justify the violation of publick faith; reasoning upon the principles of Le Chevalier de Callieres, who thought the legality of making a conquest of New-York, during the strict peace in James IId's reign, might be infered from the benefit, that would, thereby, accrue to the French colony, "que il n'y avoit point d'autre voye pour conserver la Colonie, que de nous rendre maitres de la Nouvelle York; & que cette conquête etoit legitime par la necessité."[15]

of Suits are depending against them: and therefore are of
Opinion, that the extraordinary Proceedings of that Court,
and the exorbitant Fees and Charges, countenanced to be
exacted by the Officers and Practitioners thereof, are the
greatest Grievance and Oppression this Colony hath ever felt:
and that for removing the fatal Consequences thereof, they
had come to several Resolutions, which being read, were
approved by the House, and are as follow:

*Resolved,* That the Erecting or Exercising, in this Colony, a
Court of Equity or Chancery (however it may be termed)
without Consent in General Assembly, is unwarrantable, and
contrary to the Laws of *England,* and a manifest Oppression
and Grievance to the Subjects, and of pernicious Consequences to their Liberties and Properties.

*Resolved,* That this House will at their next Meeting prepare, and pass, *An Act* to declare and adjudge all Orders,
Ordinances, Devices, and Proceedings, of the Court, so assumed to be erected and exercised as above-mentioned, to be
illegal, nill, and void, as by Law and Right they ought to be.

*Resolved,* That this House, at the same Time, will take into
Consideration, whether it be necessary, to establish a Court
of Equity or Chancery in this Colony; in whom the Jurisdiction thereof ought to be vested, and how far the Powers of it
shall be prescribed and limited.

Mr. Burnet no sooner heard of these votes, than he called
the members before him, and dissolved the Assembly. They
occasioned, however, an ordinance in the spring following, as
well to remedy sundry abuses in the practice in Chancery, as
to reduce the fees of that court, which, on account of the popular clamours, were so much diminished, that the wheels of the
Chancery, have ever since rusted upon their axes, the practice
being contemned by all gentlemen of eminence in the profession.

We are now come to the close of Mr. Burnet's administration,
when he was appointed to the chief command of the Massachuset's Bay. Though we never had a Governour, to whom the
colony is so much indebted as to him; yet the influence of a
faction, in the judgment of some, rendered his removal necessary for the publick tranquility. Insensible of his merit, the un-
distinguishing multitude were taught to consider it as a most
fortunate event; and till the ambitious designs of the French
King, with respect to America, awakened our attention to the
general welfare, Mr. Burnet's administration was as little esteemed, as that of the meanest of his predecessors.

He was very fond of New-York, and left it with reluctance. His marriage here connected him with a numerous family, and, besides an universal acquaintance, there were some gentlemen, with whom he contracted a strict intimacy and friendship.

The excessive love of money, a disease common to all his predecessors, and to some who succeeded him, was a vice, from which he was entirely free. He sold no offices, nor attempted to raise a fortune by indirect means; for he lived generously, and carried scarce any thing away with him, but his books. These and the conversation of men of letters, were to him inexhaustible sources of delight. His astronomical observations have been useful; but by his comment on the Apocalypse, he exposed himself, as other learned men have before him, to the criticisms of those who have not abilities to write half so well.

John Montgomerie, Esq; received the Great Seal of this Province from Mr. Burnet, on the 15th of April 1728, having a Commission to supersede him here and in New-Jersey. The Council Board consisted of

| | |
|---|---|
| Mr. Walters, | Mr. Alexander, |
| Mr. Van Dam, | Mr. Morris, jun. |
| Mr. Barbarie, | Mr. Van Horne, |
| Mr. Clarke, | Mr. Provoost, |
| Mr. Harrison, | Mr. Livingston, |
| Dr. Colden, | Mr. Kennedy. |

The Governour was a Scotch gentleman, and bred a soldier; but, in the latter part of his life, he had little concern with arms, having served as Groom of the Bedchamber to his present Majesty, before his accession to the Throne. This station, and a seat he had in Parliament, paved the way to his preferment in America. In his talents for government he was much inferior to his predecessor, for he had neither strength nor acuteness of parts, and was but little acquainted with any kind of literature.

As in the natural, so in the political world, a violent storm is often immediately succeeded by a peaceful calm;[16] tired by the mutual struggles of party rage, every man now ceased to act under its influence. The Governour's good humour too extinguished the flames of contention, for being unable to plan, he had no particular scheme to pursue; and thus by confining himself to the exercise of the common acts of government, our publick affairs flowed on in a peaceful, uninterrupted, stream.

The reader will, for this reason, find none of those events in

Colonel Montgomerie's short administration, which only take rise under the superintendency of a man of extensive views. Indeed he devoted himself so much to his ease, that he has scarce left us any thing to perpetuate the remembrance of his time.

The two rocks, upon which the publick Tranquility was shipwrecked in the late administration, he carefully avoided; for he dissolved the Assembly, called by his predecessor, before they had ever been convened: and as to the Chancery he himself countenanced the clamours against it, by declining to sit; till enjoined to exercise the office of Chancellor by special orders from England. He then obeyed the command, but not without discovering his reluctance; and modestly confessing to the practisers, that he thought himself unqualified for the station. Indeed the Court of Chancery was evidently his aversion, and he never gave a single decree in it, nor more than three orders; and these, both as to matter and form, were first settled by the Council concerned.

Mr. Philipse was chosen Speaker of the Assembly which met, on the 23d of July, and continued siting in perfect harmony till autumn. After his Excellency had procured a five years support,[17] and several other laws to his mind, of less considerable moment; he went up to Albany, and, on the 1st of October, held a treaty with the Six Nations for a renewal of the ancient covenant. He gave them great presents, and engaged them in the defence of Oswego. Nothing could be more seasonable than this interview, for the French who eyed that important garrison and our increasing trade there, with the most restless jealousy, prepared, early in the spring following, to demolish the works. Governour Burnet gave the first intelligence of this design, in a letter to Colonel Montgomerie, dated at Boston the 31st of March, 1729. The garrison was thereupon immediately reinforced by a detachment from the independent companies;[18] which together with the declared revolution of the Indians to protect the fort, induced the French to desist from the intended invasion.*

* From that time, to the year 1754, this garrison was guarded only by a lieutenant and five and twenty men. General Shirley's parting from the forces destined against Fort Du Quesne, and proceeding with half the army to Oswego in 1755, was extremely fortunate to our colonies; the French being then determined and prepared to possess themselves of that post. Besides the vessels launched there to secure the command of the lake, the General, before he returned to winter quarters, erected two strong square forts, with bastions, commanding as well the entrance into the Onondaga River, as the

Thus far our Indian affairs appeared to be under a tolerable direction; but these fair prospects were soon obscured by the King's repealing, on the 11th of December, 1729, all the Acts which Mr. Burnet, with so much labour and opposition, procured for the prohibition of an execrable trade between Albany and Montreal. To whose intrigues this event is to be ascribed, cannot be certainly determined. But that it was pregnant with the worst consequences, time has sufficiently evinced. Nothing could more naturally tend to undermine the trade at Oswego, to advance the French commerce at Niagara, to alienate the Indians from their fidelity to Great-Britain, and particularly to rivet the defection of the Caghnuagas. For these residing on the South side of St. Lawrence, nearly opposite to Montreal, were employed by the French as their carriers; and thus became interested against us, by motives of the most prevailing nature. One would imagine, that after all the attention bestowed on this affair in the late administration, the objections against this trading intercourse with Canada, must have been obvious to the meanest capacity; and yet so astonishing has been our conduct, that from the time Mr. Burnet removed to Boston, it has rather been encouraged than restrained. This trade, indeed, was subject to duties, but that at Oswego always was, and still is, exposed to the same incumbrance; while the French trade, in the interval between the years 1744 and 1750, was perfectly free: and as the duty, by the law then made, is laid only on goods sold in the City and County of Albany, the trader to elude the Act, is only exposed to the trouble of transporting his merchandize, beyond the scant district of the city ascertained in the charter. But how much soever our inattention to this matter may deserve censure, I cannot in justice to my Countrymen help observing, that from the severest scrutiny I could make, our people are free from the charge of selling ammunition to the French, which has so unjustly exposed the inhabitants of Albany, to the odium of all the colonies in New-England.*

The Year 1731 was distinguished, only by the complete settlement of the disputed boundary between this Province and the

---

old fort; in the situation of which, little regard was had to any thing besides the pleasantness of the prospect.

* Ever since the year 1729, the sale of arms and ammunition to the French, has been exempt both from duties and a prohibition; which I attribute to the confidence of the government, that the calumny is entirely groundless.

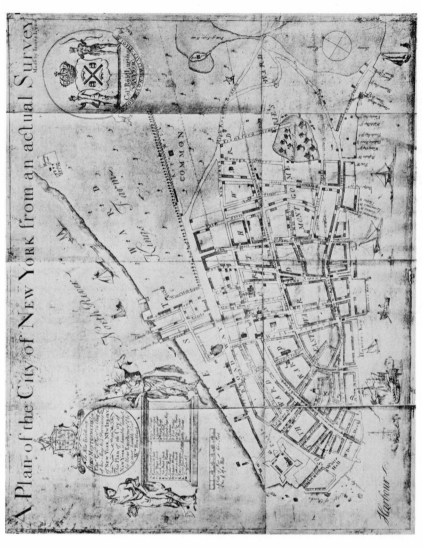

*The Bradford Map or Lyne Survey of New York, about 1730*

colony of Connecticut. An event, considering the late colonizing spirit and extensive claims of the people of New-England, of no small importance, and concerning which it may be proper to give a succinct account.

The partition line agreed upon, in 1664, being considered as fraudulent, or erroneous; a second agreement, suspended only for the King's and the Duke's approbation, was concluded, on the 23d of November 1683, between Colonel Dongan and his Council, and Robert Trent, Esq; then Governour of Connecticut, and several other Commissioners appointed by that colony. The line of partition, then agreed to be established, was to begin at the Mouth of Byram Brook,

> Where it falleth into the *Sound*, at a Point called *Lyon's Point*, to go as the said River runneth, to the Place where the common Road, or wading Place, over the said River is; and from the said Road or wading Place, to go North North-west into the Country, as far as will be eight *English* Miles from the foresaid *Lyon's Point*; and that a Line of twelve Miles, being measured from the said *Lyon's Point*, according to the Line or general Course of the *Sound* Eastward: where the said twelve Miles endeth, another Line shall be run from the *Sound*, eight Miles into the Country North North-west, and also, that a fourth Line be run (that is to say) from the Northermost End of the eight Miles Line, being the third mentioned Line, which fourth Line with the first mentioned Line, shall be the Bounds where they shall fall to run; and that from the Eastermost End of the fourth mentioned Line (which is to be twelve Miles in Length) a Line parrallel to *Hudson's* River, in every Place twenty Miles distant from *Hudson's* River, shall be the Bounds there, between the said Territories or Province of *New-York*, and the said Colony of *Connecticut* so far as *Connecticut* Colony doth extend North-wards; that is to the South Line of the *Massachusets* Colony: only it is provided, that in Case the Line from *Byram* Brook's Mouth, North North-west eight Miles, and the Line, that is then to run twelve Miles to the End of the third fore mentioned Line of eight Miles, do diminish or take away Land, within twenty Miles of *Hudson's* River, that then so much as is in Land diminished of twenty Miles of *Hudson's* River thereby, shall be added out of *Connecticut* Bounds unto the Line aforementioned, parallel to *Hudson's* River and twenty Miles distant from it; the Addition to be made the whole Length of the said parrallel Line, and in such Breadth, as

will make up, Quantity for Quantity, what shall be diminished as aforesaid.

Pursuant to this agreement some of the lines were actually run out, and a report made of the survey, which, on the 24th of February 1684, was confirmed by the Governour of each colony at Milford in Connecticut. Here the matter rested, till a dispute arose concerning the right of jurisdiction over the towns of Rye and Bedford, which occasioned a solicitation at home; and on the 28th of March 1700, King William was pleased to confirm the agreement in 1683.

Nineteen years afterwards, a Probationary Act was passed, empowering the Governour to appoint Commissioners, as well to run the line parallel to Hudson's River, as to re-survey the other lines and distinguish the boundary. The Connecticut agent opposed the King's confirmation of this Act *totis viribus,*[19] but it was approved on the 23d of January 1723. Two years after, the commissioners and surveyors of both colonies met at Greenwich, and entered first into an agreement, relating to the method of performing the work.[20]

The survey was immediately after executed in part, the report being dated on the 12th of May 1725; but the complete settlement, was not made till the 14th of May 1731, when indentures, certifying the execution of the agreement in 1725, were mutually signed by the commissioners and surveyors of both colonies. Upon the establishment of this partition, a tract of land lying on the Connecticut side, consisting of above 60,000 acres, from its figure called the Oblong, was ceded to New-York, as an equivalent for lands near the Sound surrendered to Connecticut.*

The very day after the surrender, made by that colony, a patent passed in London to Sir Joseph Eyles and others, intended to convey the whole Oblong. A grant posterior to the other was also regularly made here, to Hauley and Company,[21] of the greatest part of the same tract, which the British patentees brought a bill in Chancery to repeal. But the defendants filed an answer, containing so many objections against the English Patent, that the suit remains still unprosecuted, and the American Proprietors have ever since held the possession. Mr. Harison, of the Council, solicited this controversy for Sir Joseph

* See Douglas's late Plan of the British Dominions of New-England.

Eyles and his partners, which contributed, in a great degree, to the troubles, so remarkable, in a succeeding administration.

Governour Montgomerie died on the 1st of July 1731; and being a man of a kind and humane disposition, his death was not a little lamented. The chief command then devolved upon Rip Van Dam, Esq; he being the oldest counsellor, and an eminent merchant of a fair estate, though distinguished more for the integrity of his heart, than his capacity to hold the reins of government. He took the oaths before

| Mr. Alexander, | Mr. De Lancey,* and |
| Mr. Van Horne, | Mr. Courtlandt. |
| Mr. Kennedy, | |

This administration is unfortunately signalized by the memorable encroachment at Crown Point. An enemy despised at first for his weakness, generally grows formidable for his activity and craft. This observation is true, applied to private persons, religious sects, or publick states. The French, in Canada, have always been jealous of the increasing strength of our colonies; and a motive of fear led them, naturally, to concert a regular system of conduct for their defence.[22] Confining us to scant limits along the sea coast, is the grand object they have long had in view; and seizing the important passes from Canada to Louisania, seducing our Indian allies, engrossing the trade, and fortifying the routes into their country, were all proper expedients towards the execution of their plan. By erecting Fort St. Frederick, they secured the absolute command of Lake Champlain, through which we must pass, if ever a descent be made upon Canada, either to conquer the country, or harass its out-settlements. The garrison was, at first, situated on the East side of the Lake, near the South end; but was afterwards built upon a commodious point on the opposite Side. Of all their infractions of the Treaty of Utrecht, none was more palpable than this. The country belonged to the Six Nations, and the very spot, upon which the fort stands, is included within a Patent, to Dellius the Dutch Minister of Albany, granted under the Great Seal of this Province in 1696. Besides, nothing could

---

* This gentleman being a youth of fine parts, was called up to the Council Board on the 26th of *January* 1729, just after his return from the university. Mr. *Morris*, jun. was suspended on the same day, for words dropped in a dispute relating to the governour's draughts upon the revenue.

be more evident than the danger to which it exposed us. Through this lake the French parties made their ancient bloody incursions upon Schenectady, the Mohawks castles, and Deerfield; and the erection of this fort was apparently adapted, to facilitate the inroads of the enemy, upon the frontiers of the colonies of New-York, Massachusets Bay, and New-Hampshire.[23] For it served not only as an asylum to fly to, after the perpetration of their inhumanities, but for a magazine of provisions and ammunition; and though it was much above 120 miles from the very city of Albany, yet by the conveyance through Sorel River and the lake, it may be reinforced from Montreal in three or four days.*

The Massachusets government foresaw the dangerous consequences of the French fort at Crown Point, and Governour Belcher gave us the first information of it, in a letter from Boston to Mr. Van Dam. He informed him of the vote of the General Court, to bear their proportion of the charge of an embassage to Canada, to forbid the works, and pressed him to engage the opposition of the Six Nations. Van Dam laid the letter before his Council, on the 4th of February 1732; who, with singular calmness, advised him to write to the Commissioners of Indian Affairs, at Albany, ordering them to enquire, whether the land belonged to the Confederates or the River Indians. That Mr. Van Dam ever wrote to the Commissioners, I have not been able to discover; nor whether any complaint of the encroachment was sent home, according to the second advice of Council on the 11th of February; who, besides the first step, were now pleased to recommend his transmiting Governour Belcher's letter and the Boston vote to the several Southwestern colonies.

The Passiveness we discovered, on this impudent and dangerous invasion of his Majesty's rights, is truly astonishing; and the more so, as the Crown had, at that time, four independent companies, which had long been posted here for our protection, at the annual expence of about £7500 sterling. A very

* The present fort at Crown Point is said to be a square with four bastions, and a high castle within the walls. It has no ditch, but is strengthened by a redoubt, and mounts six and thirty small cannon. While the colony forces, consisting of about 4000 militia, lay at Lake George, employed in erecting Fort William Henry in 1755, the French threw up an advanced work at Ticononderoge, near the North-east end of Lake George: an important pass about 16 miles to the Southward of Fort St. Frederick.

good scheme, in some measure, to repair this shameful misconduct, was afterwards projected, by settling the lands near Lake George, with loyal Protestant Highlanders from Scotland. Captain Laughlin Campbel, encouraged by a proclamation to that purpose, came over in 1737, and ample promises were made to him. He went upon the land, viewed and approved it; and was entreated to settle there, even by the Indians, who were taken with his Highland dress. Mr. Clarke, the Lieutenant Governour, promised him, in a printed advertisement, the grant of 30,000 acres of land, free from all but the charges of the survey and the King's quit rent. Confiding on the faith of the government, Captain Campbel went home to Isla, sold his estate, and, shortly after, transported, at his own expence, 83 Protestant families, consisting of 423 adults, besides a great number of children. Private faith and publick honour loudly demanded the fair execution of a project, so expensive to the undertaker and beneficial to the colony. But it unfortunately droped, through the sordid views of some persons in power, who aimed at a share in the intended grant; to which Campbel, who was a man of spirit, would not consent.[24]

Captain Campbel, afterwards, made an attempt to redress himself, by an application to the Assembly here, and then to the Board of Trade in England. The first proved abortive, and such were the difficulties attending the last, that he left his colonists to themselves; and with the poor remains of his broken fortune purchased a small farm in this Province. No man was better qualified than he, for the business he had engaged in. He had a high sense of honour and a good understanding: was active, loyal, and of a military disposition. For upon the news of the late rebellion in Scotland, he went home: fought under the Duke, returned to his family and soon after died; leaving a widow and several children, who still feel the consequences of his disappointments.

Mr. Van Dam finished his administration, on the 1st of August 1732; when William Cosby, Esq; arrived, with a Commission, to govern this and the Province of New-Jersey. The history of our publick transactions, from this period, to the present time, is full of important and entertaining events, which I leave others to relate. A very near relation to the authour[25] had so great a concern in the publick controversies with Colonel Cosby, that the history of those times will be better received from a more disinterested pen. To suppress truth on the one hand, or exaggerate it, on the other, are both inexcusable faults, and perhaps it would be difficult for me to avoid those extremes. Besides, a writer, who exposes the conduct of the living, will inevitably meet with their fury and resentment. The prudent historian of his own times will always be a coward, and never give fire, till death protects him from the malice and stroke of his enemy.

# Six Appendixes, called "Chapters" to the History of New York

## Chapter I  A Geographical Description of the Country

The Province of New-York, at present, contains Long Island, Staten Island, and the lands, on the East side of Hudson's River, to the bounds of Connecticut. From the division line between that colony and the Massachusets Bay, Northward, to the line between us and the French, we claim an extent to Connecticut River.* On the West side of Hudson's River from the

---

* The grounds of this claim are contained in the following report of a committee, of council, to Governour Clinton, on the 2d of March 1753, which was drawn up by Mr. Alexander.

*May it please your Excellency,*
In Obedience to your Excellency's Order, in Council, of the 3d Day of *July* last, referring to a Committee thereof, the Petitions of *Robert Livingston,* jun. Esq; and of the Owners of a certain Tract of Land called *Westenhook,* complaining of new Claims and Encroachments made upon their Lands by the Inhabitants of the *Massachusets Bay,* and also the Surveyor General's and the Attorney General's Reports on the said two Petitions: the Committee having maturely weighed and considered of the same, humbly beg Leave to report to your Excellency;
*1st,* That they apprehend the Claims of *Massachusets Bay* to the Manor of Livingston, or the said Tract of Land called *Westenhook,* cannot be well founded; because they find that the *Dutch* claimed the Colony of *New Netherland,* as extending from Cape *Cod* to Cape *Cornelius,* now called Cape *Henlopen,* Westward of *Delaware* Bay, along the Sea Coast, and as far back into the Country, as any of the Rivers within those Limits extend; and that they were actually possessed of *Connecticut* River, long before any other *European* People knew any Thing of the Existence of such a River, and were not only possessed of the Mouth of it, where they had a Fort and Garrison, but discovered the River above a hundred Miles up, had their People trading there,

sea to the latitude of 41° lies New-Jersey. The line of partition between that Province and this, from that latitude to the
other station on Delaware, is unsettled. From thence, wheresoever it may be fixed, we claim all the lands, on the East side

and purchased of the Natives almost all the Lands on both Sides
of the said River.

*2dly,* That Governor *Stuyvesant,* the *Dutch* Governor of the
said Province, by his Letter dated the 2d of *September* 1664,
New Stile, in Answer to a Letter from Governor *Richard Nicolls*
of the 20/30 *August* preceding, demanding the Surrender of all
the Forts and Places of Strength possessed by the *Dutch* under
his (Governor *Stuyvesant's*) Command, writes as follows:—"Moreover it's without Dispute, and acknowledged by all the World, that
our Predecessors by virtue of the Commission and Patent of the
said Lords the States Generals, have without Controul, and peaceably (the contrary never coming to our Knowledge) enjoyed
Fort *Orange* about 48 or 50 Years; and *Manhatans* about 41 or
42 Years; the *South River* 40 Years, and the *Fresh River* about
36 Years." Which last mentioned River, the Committee find to
be the same, that is now called *Connecticut* River.

*3dly,* That the said Dutch Governor Stuyvesant did, in the Year
1664, surrender all the Country, which the *Dutch* did then
possess, to King *Charles* the Second, and that the States General
made a Cession thereof, by the Treaty of *Breda,* in the Year 1667:
that the *Dutch* reconquered Part of this Province in 1673, and
surrendered and absolutely yielded it to King *Charles* the Second,
in 1673–4, by the Treaty of *London;* and that in the Year 1674,
King *Charles* granted to the Duke of *York,* all the Land between
*Connecticut* River and *Delaware* Bay; the whole of these Lands
being Part of the former Colony of *New Netherland.*

*4th,* That the Duke of *York* in his several Commissions to
Major *Edmund Andross,* on the 1st of *July* 1674, and to Governor
*Dongan* on the 30th of *September* 1682, among other Descriptions
of the Boundaries of this Province, mentions all the Land from
the West Side of *Connecticut* River to the East Side of *Delaware*
Bay: that their Majesties King *William* and Queen *Mary,* by their
Commission, bearing Date the fourth Day of *January,* in the first
Year of their Majesties Reign, appointed *Henry Sloughter* to be
Governour of the Province of *New-York,* and Territories depending
thereon; the Boundaries whereof to *Connecticut* River, on the
East, were notorious, by the Grant and other Commissions
aforesaid, and many other Grants and Commissions relating to
the same.

*5th,* That the Committee apprehend *Connecticut* River continued
the East Bounds of this Province, until the 28th of *March* 1700,
when, by King *William's* Confirmation of an Agreement between
this Province and *Connecticut,* the Western Bounds of that Colony
were settled at twenty Miles from *Hudson's* River: and they
cannot find any other Alteration in the Eastern Bounds of this
Province, and have no Reason to believe any other was made
before, or since, that Time.

*6th,* That King *James* the First, by Letters Patents bearing Date
the 3d of *November,* in the 18th Year of his Reign, granted unto
the Council of *Plymouth,* from forty to forty-eight Degrees of

of Delaware, to the North Line of Pennsylvania; and all the
territory, on both sides of the Mohawks River, and Westward
to the Isthmus at Niagara: in a word, all the country belonging
to the Crown of Great-Britain, not already granted; for we are

North Latitude inclusive, in which there is a Recital to this
Purpose.————Now for as much as the King has been certainly
given to understand, by divers good Subjects that have, for these
many Years frequented those Coasts and Territories, between
the Degrees of 40° and 48°, that there are no other Subjects of
any Christian King or State, or by any Authority from their
Sovereigns, Lords, or Princes, actually in Possession of any the
said Lands or Precincts, whereby any Right, Claim, Interest, or
Title, may, or ought, by that Means, to accrue or belong to them,"
&c. And also a Provisoe in these Words, "Provided always, that
the said Lands, Islands, or any of the Premisses, by the said
Letters Patent intended or meant to be granted, were not then
actually possessed or inhabited by any other Christian Power or
State." Which Patent, the Committee conceive, could not vest
any Thing in the Grantees, by Reason of the said Recital and
Condition upon which it was granted; Part of the Premisses being
then actually possessed by the *Dutch,* and most of the said Colony
of *New Netherland* being within the Bounds thereof.

7th, That the Council of Plymouth, by their Deed dated the
19th of *March,* in the third Year of King *Charles* the First, granted
to Sir *Henry Rosswell* and others, Part of what was supposed to
be granted by the said Letters Patent, which Grant, from the said
Council of *Plymouth,* the Committee take to be void, as founded
upon the said void Patent.

8th, That he the said Sir *Henry Rosswell,* and others, obtained
a Grant and Confirmation thereof, from the Crown, under the
Great Seal of *England,* dated the 4th of *March,* in the fourth
Year of King *Charles* the First, within which Grant and Confirmation, the Province of *Massachusets Bay* is included; which Grant
and Confirmation was adjudged void in the high Court of
*Chancery* of *England* in the Year 1684. And the Committee are
of Opinion, that nothing, to the Westward of *Connecticut* River,
could pass by that Grant and Confirmation; for that his Majesty
could not have had an Intention to grant the same, it being then
posessed by the *Dutch,* as before mentioned.

9th, That the Committee conceive the Inhabitants of *Massachusets Bay* can claim nothing at present, but what is granted
them by their last Charter in 1691; all their other Grants and
Charters being either void of themselves, or declared so in the
Chancery of *England.*

10th, That the Bounds granted, by this Charter, are Westward
as far as the Colonies of *Rhode Island, Connecticut,* and the
*Narraganset* Country: which Words being in the Case of a Grant
from the Crown, the Committee conceive, cannot extend their
Bounds farther than to *Connecticut* Colony, and therefore not to
*Connecticut* River, and much less to the Westward of it; because
*Connecticut* itself, at the Time of that Charter, did not, in the
Knowledge of the Crown, extend Westward of that River; nor did
till nine Years after, when, by the royal Approbation, the Agree-
ment between this Province and that Colony taking Place, (which

to consider New-York among her sister colonies, to borrow a law phrase, as a residuary legatee.

Hence we have, from the beginning, been exposed to controversies about limits. The New-Jersey claim includes several

---

was not to be in Force till such Approbation) the Bounds of that Colony were settled as is before mentioned: and the Committee conceive it to be against Reason, to suppose that the Crown intended, by the said Charter, to grant any Part of the Province of *New-York,* under the then immediate Government of the Crown, without express Mention thereof in the Charter; and without Notification thereof to *Henry Sloughter,* then Governor of this Province, that the Crown had granted such a Part of what was before within his Jurisdiction by their Majesties Commission aforesaid to him.

*11th,* That both the Patents, under which the Petitioners claim, the Committee find were granted under the Great Seal of this Province; that of the Manor of *Livingston* in 1686, and that of *Westenhook* in 1735. And that the Lands contained in the said Grants are, the Committee apprehend, within the Jurisdiction of this Province, they being both West of *Connecticut* River.

*12th,* That the Committee are of Opinion, the Attempts of the Inhabitants of the *Massachuset's Bay,* to make Encroachments upon any Lands, granted by Letters Patent under the Great Seal of *New-York,* or upon any Lands within the Jurisdiction of this Province, are disrespectful to his Majesty's Authority, tend to the Disturbance of the Subjects of this Province, and may be the Cause of great Mischiefs and Disorders.

*13th,* That the Steps taken by the said Inhabitants, even were the Bounds of this Province doubtful and unsettled, are Intrusions, and disrespectful to his Majesty's Authority.

And *lastly,* The Committee are of Opinion, that a Copy of so much of this Report, as shall be approved of by your Excellency and the Council, be transmitted to the Lieutenant Governor of the Province of *Massachuset's Bay,* requesting that he would take effectual Measures, that all Encroachments and Disturbances, by the People of that Colony, on his Majesty's Subjects of this Province, be stayed; and that he would lay this Matter before the next *General Court,* that they may inform your Excellency, by what Warrant they claim or exercise any Right to Soil or Jurisdiction, Westward of *Connecticut* River; that the same may be considered, and such Steps taken towards removing all Causes of Encroachments, or Disturbances, for the future, as may be agreeable to Equity and Justice: to the End, that good Understanding may be preserved, which ought to subsist between Fellow Subjects and neighbouring Provinces.

All which is nevertheless humbly submitted,
by Order of the Committee,
JAMES DE LANCEY, Chairman.

---

The government of the Massachuset's Bay never exhibited the reasons of their claim, in answer to this report, but continued their encroachments: and, in the Spring, 1755, surveyed and sold lands, lying several miles West of the Eastern extent of the Manor of Livingston and the Patent of Claverack.

hundred thousand acres, and has not a little impeded the settlement of the colony. The dispute with the Massachuset's Bay is still more important, and, for several years past, occasioned very considerable commotions. The New-Hampshire pretensions have, as yet, exposed us to no great trouble. But when all those claims are settled, a new controversy will probably commence with the Proprietaries of Pennsylvania.

This Province was, in 1691, divided, by an Act of Assembly, into twelve counties, which I shall describe in their order.

## The City and County of NEW-YORK

The city of New-York, at first, included only the island, called by the Indians, Manhatans; Manning's Island, the two Barn Islands and the three Oyster Islands were in the County. But the limits of the city have since been augmented by charter. The island is very narrow, not a mile wide at a medium, and about 14 miles in length. The South-west point projects into a fine spacious bay, nine miles long and about four in breadth; at the confluence of the waters of Hudson's River, and the streight between Long Island and the Northern shore. The Narrows, at the south end of the bay, is scarce two miles wide, and opens the ocean to full view. The passage up to New-York from Sandy Hook, a point that extends farthest into the sea, is safe, and not above five and twenty miles in length. The common navigation is between the East and West banks, in two or three and twenty feet water. But it is said that an eighty gun ship may be brought up, through a narrow, winding, unfrequented, channel, between the North end of the East bank and Coney Island.

The city has, in reality, no natural bason or harbour. The ships lie off in the road, on the East side of the town, which is docked out, and better built than the West side, because the freshets in Hudson's River, fill it in some winters with ice.

The city of New-York, as I have elsewhere had occasion to mention, "consists of about two thousand five hundred Buildings. It is a Mile in Length, and not above half that in Breadth. Such is its Figure, its Center of Business, and the Situation of the Houses, that the mean Cartage from one Part to another, does not exceed above one Quarter of a Mile, than which nothing can be more advantageous to a trading City."

It is thought to be as healthy a spot as any in the world. The

East and South parts, in general, are low, but the rest is situated on a dry, elevated, soil. The streets are irregular, but being paved with round pebbles are clean, and lined with well built brick houses, many of which are covered with tiled roofs.

No part of America is supplied with markets abounding with greater plenty and variety. We have beef, pork, mutton, poultry, butter, wild fowl, venison, fish, roots, and herbs, of all kinds, in their seasons. Our oysters are a considerable article in the support of the poor. Their beds are within view of the town; a fleet of two hundred small craft, are often seen there, at a time, when the weather is mild in winter; and this single article is computed to be worth annually 10 or £12,000.

This city is the metropolis and grand mart of the Province, and, by its commodious situation, commands also all the trade of the Western part of Connecticut and that of East Jersey. "No Season prevents our Ships from launching out into the Ocean. During the greatest Severity of Winter, an equal, unrestrained, Activity runs through all Ranks, Orders, and Employments."

Upon the South-west point of the city stands the fort, which is a square with four bastions. Within the walls is the house in which our governours usually reside; and opposite to it brick barracks, built formerly, for the independent companies. The Governour's house is in heighth three stories, and fronts to the West; having, from the second story, a fine prospect of the bay and the Jersey Shore. At the South end there was formerly a chapel, but this was burnt down in the Negroe conspiracy of the spring 1741.[1] According to Governour Burnet's observations, this fort stands in the latitude of 40° 42 N.

Below the walls of the garrison, near the water, we have lately raised a line of fortifications, which commands the entrance into the Eastern road and the mouth of Hudson's River. This battery is built of stone, and the merlons[2] consist of cedar joists, filled in with earth. It mounts 92 cannon, and these are all the works we have to defend us. About six furlongs, Southeast of the fort, lies Notten Island, containing about 100 or 120 acres, reserved by an Act of Assembly as a sort of demesne for the Governours, upon which it is proposed to erect a strong castle, because an enemy might from thence easily bombard the city, without being annoyed either by our battery, or the fort. During the late war a line of palisadoes was run from Hudson's to the East River, at the other end of the city, with blockhouses at small distances. The greater part of these still remain as a monument of our folly, which cost the Province about £8000.

The inhabitants of New-York are a mixed people, but mostly descended from the original Dutch planters. There are still two churches, in which religious worship is performed in that language. The old building is of stone and ill built, ornamented within by a small organ loft and brass branches. The new church is a high, heavy, edifice, has a very extensive area, and was completed in 1729. It has no galleries, and yet will perhaps contain a thousand or twelve hundred auditors. The steeple of this church affords a most beautiful prospect, both of the city beneath and the surrounding country. The Dutch congregation is more numerous than any other, but as the language becomes disused, it is much diminished; and unless they change their worship into the English tongue, must soon suffer a total dissipation. They have at present two ministers: the Reverend Messieurs Ritzma and De Ronde, who are both strict Calvinists. Their church was incorporated on the 11th of May, 1696, by the name of *The Minister, Elders, and Deacons, of the Reformed Protestant Dutch Church of the City of New-York*, and its estate, after the expiration of sundry long leases, will be worth a very great income.*

All the Low Dutch congregations, in this and the Province of New-Jersey, worship after the manner of the reformed churches in the United Provinces. With respect to government, they are in principle Presbyterians; but yet hold themselves in subordination to the Classis of Amsterdam, who sometimes permit, and at other times refuse, them the powers of ordination. Some of their ministers consider such a subjection as anti-constitutional, and hence in several of their late annual conventions, at New-York, called the Caetus, some debates have arisen amongst them; the majority being inclined to erect a classis, or ecclesiastical judicatory, here, for the government of their churches. Those of their ministers, who are natives of Europe, are, in general, averse to the project. The expence attending the ordination of their candidates, in Holland, and the reference of their disputes to the classis of Amsterdam, is very considerable; and with what consequences, the interruption of their correspondence with the European Dutch, would be attended, in case of a war, well deserves their consideration.[3]

There are, besides the Dutch, two Episcopal churches in this city, upon the plan of the Established Church in South Britain.

---

* Their charter was confirmed by a late Act of Assembly ratified by his Majesty, which recites the VIIIth Article of the surrender in 1664.

Trinity Church was built in 1696, and afterwards enlarged in 1737. It stands very pleasantly upon the banks of Hudson's River, and has a large cemetery, on each side, inclosed in the front by a painted paled fence. Before it a long walk is railed off from the broad-way, the pleasantest street of any in the whole town. This building is about 148 feet long, including the tower and chancel, and 72 feet in breadth. The steeple is 175 feet in height, and over the door facing the river is the following inscription.

### PER ANGUSTAM.

Hoc Trinitatis Templum fundatum est Anno Regni illus-trissimi, supremi, Domini Gulielmi tertii, Dei Gratiâ, Angliae, Scotiae, Franciae et Hiberniae Regis, Fidei Defensoris, &c. Octavo, Annoq; Domini 1696.

Ac voluntariâ quorundam Contributione ac Donis Aedifi-catum, maximè autem, dilecti Regis Chiliarchae BENJAMINI FLETCHER, hujus Provinciae strataeci & Imperatoris, Munifi-centiâ animatum et auctum, cujus tempore moderaminis, hujus Civitatis incolae, Religionem protestantem Ecclesiae Anglicanae, ut fecundum Legem nunc stabilitae profitentes, quodam Diplomate, sub Sigillo Provinciae incorporati sunt, atque alias Plurimas, ex Re suâ familiari, Donationes notabiles eidem dedit.[4]

The church is, within, ornamented beyond any other place of publick worship amongst us. The head of the chancel is adorned with an altarpiece, and opposite to it, at the other end of the building, is the organ. The tops of the pillars, which support the galleries, are decked with the gilt busts of angels winged. From the cieling are suspended two glass branches, and on the walls hang the arms of some of its principal benefactors. The allies are paved with flat stones.

The present rector of this church is the Rev. Mr. Henry Barclay, formerly a missionary among the Mohawks, who receives a £100 a year, levied upon all the other clergy and laity in the city, by virtue of an Act of Assembly procured by Governour Fletcher. He is assisted by Dr. Johnson and Mr. Auchmuty.

This congregation, partly by the arrival of strangers from Europe, but principally by proselytes from the Dutch churches, is become so numerous, that though the old building will contain 2000 hearers, yet a new one was erected in 1752. This, called

St. George's Chapel,\* is a very neat edifice, faced with hewn stone and tiled. The steeple is lofty,† but irregular; and its situation in a new, crowded, and ill-built, part of the town.

The rector, churchwardens, and vestrymen of Trinity Church, are incorporated by an Act of Assembly, which grants the two last the Advowson or Right of Presentation; but enacts, that the rector shall be instituted and inducted in a manner most agreeable to the King's Instructions to the Governour, and the canonical right of the Bishop of London. Their worship is conducted after the mode of the Church of England; and with respect to government, they are empowered to make rules and orders for themselves, being, if I may use the expression, an independent, ecclesiastical, corporation.

The revenue of this church is restricted, by an Act of Assembly, to £500 per annum; but it is possessed of a real estate, at the North end of the town, which having been lately divided into lots and let to farm, will, in a few years, produce a much greater income.

The Presbyterians increasing after Lord Cornbury's return to England, called Mr. Anderson, a Scotch minister, to the pastoral charge of their congregation; and Dr. John Nicol, Patrick Mac-Night, Gilbert Livingston and Thomas Smith, purchased a piece of ground and founded a church, in 1719. Two years afterwards they petitioned Colonel Schuyler, who had then the chief command, for a Charter of Incorporation, to secure their estate for religious worship, upon the plan of the church in North-Britain; but were disappointed in their expectations, through the opposition of the Episcopal party. They, shortly after, renewed their request to Governour Burnet, who refered the petition to his Council. The Episcopalians again violently opposed the grant, and the Governour, in 1724, wrote upon the subject to the Lords of Trade for their direction. Counsellor West, who was then consulted, gave his opinion in these words: "Upon Consideration of the several Acts of Uniformity that have passed in *Great-Britain,* I am of Opinion that they do not extend to *New-York,* and consequently an Act of Toleration is of no Use in that Province; and, therefore, as there is no Provincial Act for Uniformity, according to the Church of *England,* I am of Opinion, that by Law

---

\* The length, exclusive of the chancel, 92 feet, and its breadth 20 feet less.

† One hundred and seventy-five feet.

such Patent of Incorporation may be granted, as by the Petition is desired. *Richard West, 20 August, 1724.*"

After several years solicitation for a charter in vain, and fearful that those who obstructed such a reasonable request, would watch an opportunity to give them a more effectual wound; those, among the Presbyterians, who were invested with the fee simple of the church and ground, "conveyed it, on the 16th of *March,* 1730, to the Moderator of the General Assembly of the Church of *Scotland* and the Commission thereof, the Moderator of the Presbytery of *Edinburgh,* the Principal of the College of *Edinburgh,* the Professor of Divinity therein, and the Procurator and Agent of the Church of *Scotland,* for the Time being, and their Successors in Office, as a Committee of the General Assembly. On the 15th of *August,* 1732, the Church of *Scotland,* by an Instrument under the Seal of the General Assembly," and signed by Mr. Niel Campbell, Principal of the University of Glasgow, and Moderator of the General Assembly and Commission thereof; Mr. James Nesbit, one of the ministers of the Gospel at Edinburgh, moderator of the Presbytery of Edinburgh; Mr. William Hamilton, Principal of the University of Edinburgh; Mr. James Smith, Professor of Divinity therein; and Mr. William Grant, Advocate Procurator for the Church of Scotland, for the time being; pursuant to an Act of the General Assembly, dated the 8th of May, 1731, did declare,

> That notwithstanding the aforesaid Right made to them and their Successors in Office, they were desirous, that the aforesaid Building and Edifice and Appurtenances thereof, be preserved for the pious and religious Purposes for which the same were designed; and that it should be free and lawful to the Presbyterians then residing, or that should at any Time, thereafter, be resident, in, or near, the aforesaid City of *New-York,* in *America,* or others joining with them, to convene, in the foresaid Church, for the Worship of God in all the Parts thereof, and for the Dispensation of all Gospel Ordinances; and generally to use and occupy the said Church and its Appurtenances, fully and freely in all Times coming, they supporting and maintaining the Edifice and Appurtenances at their own Charge.

Mr. Anderson was succeeded, in April 1727, by the Rev. Mr. Ebenezer Pemberton, a man of polite breeding, pure morals, and warm devotion; under whose incessant labours the congregation greatly increased, and was enabled to erect the present edifice in 1748. It is built of stone, railed off from the street, is 80 feet long and in breadth 60. The steeple, raised on the South-west end, is in height 145 feet. In the front to the street, between two long windows, is the following inscription gilt and cut in a black slate six feet in length.[5]

AUSPICANTO DEO

HANC AEDEM

CULTUI DIVINO SACRAM

IN PERPETUUM

CELEBRANDO,

AD. MDCCXIX.

PRIMO SUNDATAM;

DENUO PENITUS REPARATAM

ET

AMPLIOREM ET ORNATIOREM

AD. MDCCXLVIII

CONSTRUCTAM,

NEO-EBORANCENSES PRESBYTERIANI

IN SUUM ET SUORUM USUM

CONDENTES,

IN HAC VOTIVA TABULA

D D D Q.

\* \* \*

CONCORDIA, AMORE

NECNON FIDEI CULTUS ET MORUM

PURITATE

SUFFULTA, CLARIUSQ; EXORNATA,

ANNUENTE CHRISTO,

LONGUM PERDURET IN AEVUM.[6]

Mr. Alexander Cumming, a young gentleman of learning and singular penetration, was chosen colleague to Mr. Pemberton, in 1750; but both were dismissed, at their request, about three years afterwards; the former, through indisposition, and the latter, on account of trifling contentions kindled by the bigotry and ignorance of the lower sort of people. These debates continued till they were closed, in April 1756, by a decision of the Synod, to which, almost all our Presbyterian churches, in this and the Southern provinces are subject. The congregation consists, at present, of 12 or 1400 souls, under the pastoral charge of the Rev. Mr. David Bostwick, who was lately translated from Jamaica to New-York, by a synodical decree. He is a gentleman of a mild, catholick, disposition; and being a man of piety, prudence, and zeal, confines himself entirely to the proper business of his function. In the art of preaching, he is one of the most distinguished clergymen in these parts. His discourses are methodical, sound and pathetick; in sentiment, and in point of diction, singularly ornamented. He delivers himself without notes, and yet with great ease and fluency of expression; and performs every part of divine worship with a striking solemnity.

The French church, by the contentions in 1724, and the disuse of the language, is now reduced to an inconsiderable handful. The building which is of stone nearly a square,* plain both within and without. It is fenced from the street, has a steeple and a bell, the latter of which was the gift of Sir Henry Asshurst of London. On the front of the church is the following inscription,

AEDES SACRA

GALLOR. PROT.

REFORM.

FVNDA. 1704.

PENITVS

REPAR. 1741.[7]

The present minister, Mr. Carle, is a native of France, and succeeded Mr. Rou in 1754. He bears an irreproachable character, is very intent upon his studies, preaches moderate Calvinism, and speaks with propriety, both of pronunciation and gesture.

The German Lutheran churches are two. Both their places of worship are small: one of them has a cupola and bell.

The Quakers have a meeting-house, and the Moravians, a new sect amongst us, a church, consisting principally of female proselytes from other societies. Their service is in the English tongue.

The Anabaptists assemble at a small meeting-house, but have as yet no regular settled congregation. The Jews, who are not inconsiderable for their numbers, worship in a synagogue erected in a very private part of the town, plain without, but very neat within.

The City Hall is a strong brick building, two stories in

* The area is seventy feet long and in breadth fifty.

heighth, in the shape of an oblong, winged with one at each end, at right angles with the first. The floor below is an open walk, except two jails and the jailor's apartments. The cellar underneath is a dungeon, and the garret above a common prison. This edifice is erected in a place where four streets meet, and fronts, to the South-west, one of the most spacious streets in town. The Eastern wing, in the second story, consists of the Assembly Chamber, a lobby, and a small room for the Speaker of the House. The West wing, on the same floor, forms the Council Room and a library; and in the space between the ends, the Supreme Court is ordinarily held.

The library consists of 1000 volumes, which were bequeathed to The Society for the Propagation of the Gospel in Foreign Parts, by Dr. Millington, rector of Newington. Mr. Humphrys, the Society's secretary, in a letter of the 23d of September 1728, informed Governour Montgomerie, that the Society intended to place these books in New-York, intending to establish a Library, for the use of the clergy and gentlemen of this and the neighbouring governments of Connecticut, New-Jersey, and Pennsylvania, upon giving security to return them; and desired the Governour to recommend it to the Assembly, to provide a place to reposit the books, and to concur in an Act for the preservation of them and others that might be added. Governour Montgomerie sent the letter to the Assembly, who ordered it to be laid before the city corporation, and the latter in June 1729, agreed to provide a proper repository for the books, which were accordingly soon after sent over. The greatest part of them are upon theological subjects, and through the carelessness of the keepers many are missing.[8]

In 1754, a set of gentlemen undertook to carry about a subscription towards raising a publick library, and in a few days collected near £600 which were laid out in purchasing, about 700 volumes of new, well chosen, books. Every subscriber, upon payment of £5 principal, and the annual sum of 10 s. is entitled to the use of these books. His right by the articles is assignable, and for non-compliance with them may be forfeited. The care of this library, is commited to twelve trustees, annually elected by the subscribers, on the last Tuesday of April, who are restricted from making any rules repugnant to the fundamental subscription. This is the beginning of a library, which in process of time will probably become vastly rich and voluminous; and it would be very proper for the company to have a charter for its security and encouragement. The books are deposited in the same room with those given by the Society.[9]

Besides the City Hall, there belong to the corporation, a large alms-house or place of correction, and the exchange, in the latter of which there is a large room raised upon brick arches, generally used for publick entertainments, concerts of musick, balls, and assemblies.

Though the city was put under the government of a mayor, &c. in 1665, it was not regularly incorporated till 1686. Since that time several charters have been passed: the last was granted by Governour Montgomerie on the 15th of January 1730.

It is divided into seven wards, and is under the government of a mayor, recorder, seven aldermen, and as many assistants or common councilmen. The mayor, a sheriff, and coroner, are annually appointed by the Governour. The recorder has a patent during pleasure. The aldermen, assistants, assessors and collectors, are annually elected by the freemen and freeholders of the respective wards. The mayor has the sole appointment of a deputy, and, together with four aldermen, may appoint a chamberlain. The mayor or recorder, four aldermen, and as many assistants, form *"The Common Council of the City of New-York;"* and this body, by a majority of voices, hath power to make bye-laws for the government of the city, which are binding only for a year, unless confirmed by the Governour and Council. They have many other privileges relating to ferriages, markets, fairs, the assize of bread, wine, &c. and the licensing and regulation of tavern keepers, cartage, and the like. The mayor, his deputy, the recorder and aldermen, are constituted justices of the peace; and may hold not only a court of record once a week, to take cognizance of all civil causes, but also a court of general quarter sessions of the peace. They have a common clerk, commissioned by the Governour, who enjoys an appointment worth about four or five hundred pounds per annum. The annual revenue of the corporation is near two thousand pounds. The standing militia of the island consists of about 2300 men,* and the city has in reserve, a thousand stand of arms for seamen, the poor and others, in case of an invasion.[10]

---

* The whole number of the inhabitants, exclusive of females above sixty, according to a list returned to the Governour, in the spring 1756, amounted to 10,468 whites, and 2275 Negroes; but that account is erroneous. It is most probable that there are in the city 15,000 souls.

The North-Eastern part of New-York island, is inhabited, principally, by Dutch farmers, who have a small village there called Harlem, pleasantly situated on a flat cultivated for the city markets.

## West-Chester

This county is large, and includes all the land beyond the island of Manhatans along the Sound, to the Connecticut line which is its Eastern boundary. It extends Northward to the middle of the highlands, and Westward to Hudson's River, A great part of this county is contained in the manors of Philipsburgh, Pelham, Fordham, and Courtlandt, the last of which has the privilege of sending a representative to the General Assembly.[11] The county is tolerably settled. The lands are in general rough but fertile, and therefore the farmers run principally on grazing. It has several towns, East-Chester, West-Chester, New-Rochelle, Rye, Bedford, and North-Castle. The inhabitants are either English or Dutch Presbyterians, Episcopalians, Quakers and French Protestants. The former are the most numerous. The two Episcopal missionaries are settled at Rye and East-Chester, and receive each £60 annually taxed upon the county. The town of West-Chester is an incorporated borough, enjoying a mayor's court, and the right of being represented by a member in Assembly.

## Dutchess

This county adjoins to West-Chester, which bounds it on the South, the Connecticut line on the East,* Hudson's River on the West, and the county of Albany on the North. The South part of this county is mountainous and fit only for iron works, but the rest contains a great quantity of good upland well watered. The only villages in it are Poghkeepsing and the Fish-Kill, though they scarce deserve the name. The inhabitants on the banks of the river are Dutch, but those more Easterly Englishmen, and, for the most part, emigrants from Connecticut and Long Island. There is no Episcopal church in it. The growth of this county has been very sudden, and commenced but a few years ago. Within the memory of persons now living, it did not contain

* In describing the limits of the several counties, I regard their bounds according to the jurisdiction as now exercised in each, rather than the laws relating to them, which are very imperfect, especially the general Act in 1691. The greatest part of Hudson's River is not included in any of our counties.

above twelve families; and according to the late returns of the militia, it will furnish at present above 2500 fighting men.

## Albany

This county extends from the South bounds of the manor of Livingston on the East side, and Ulster on the West side of Hudson's River; on the North its limits are not yet ascertained. It contains, a vast quantity of fine low land. Its principal commodities are wheat, pease, and pine boards.

The city of Albany, which is near 150 miles from New-York, is situated on the West side of the river. There our governours usually treat with the Indian dependents upon the British Crown. The houses are built of brick in the Dutch taste, and are in number about 350. There are two churches in it. That of the Episcopalians, the only one in this large county, is a stone building. The congregation is but small, almost all the inhabitants resorting to the Dutch Church, which is a plain, square, stone, edifice. Besides these they have no other publick buildings, except the City Hall and the fort; the latter of which is a stone square, with four bastions, situated on an eminence which overlooks the town, but is itself commanded by higher ground. The greatest part of the city is fortified only by palisadoes, and in some places there are small cannon planted in block-houses. Albany was incorporated by Colonel Dongan in 1686, and is under the government of a mayor, recorder, six aldermen, and as many assistants. It has also a sheriff, town clerk, chamberlain, clerk of the markets, one high constable, three sub-constables, and a marshal. The corporation is empowered besides to hold a mayor's court for the trial of civil causes, and a court of general quarter sessions.

Sixteen or eighteen miles North-west from Albany lies Schenectady, on the banks of the Mohawks Branch, which falls into Hudson's River 12 miles to the North of Albany. This village is compact and regular, built principally of brick, on a rich flat of low land, surrounded with hills. It has a large Dutch church, with a steeple and town clock near the center. The windings of the river through the town, and the fields (which are often overflowed in the spring) form, about harvest, a most beautiful prospect. The lands in the vale of Schenectady are so fertile, that they are commonly sold at £45 per acre. Though the farmers use no kind of manure they till the fields every year, and they always produce full crops of wheat or pease. Their church was incorporated by Governour Cosby, and the town has the privilege of sending a member to the Assembly.

From this village our Indian traders set out in battoes for Oswego. The Mohawk's River, from hence to Fort Hunter, abounds with rifts and shoals, which in the spring give but little obstruction to the navigation. From thence to its head, or rather to the portage into the Wood Creek, the conveyance is easy and the current less rapid. The banks of this river are, in general, low, and the soil exceeding good. Our settlements, on the North side, extend to Burnet's Field, a flat inhabited by Germans, which produces wheat and pease in surprising plenty. On the South side, except a few Scotch Irish in Cherry Valley at the head of Susquehanna, we have but few farms West of the three German towns on Schohare, a small creek which empties itself into the Mohawk's River, about 20 miles west of Schenectady. The fur trade at Oswego, is one of the principal advantages of this county. The Indians resort thither in May, and the trade continues till the latter end of July. A good road might be made from Schenectady to Oswego. In the summer 1755, fat cattle were easily driven there for the army under the command of General Shirley.

The principal settlements to the Northward of Albany are Connestigiune, Eastward of Schenectady on the Mohawk's River, which a little lower tumbles down a precipice of about 70 feet high, called the Cahoes. The surprise, which as one might imagine, would naturally be excited by the view of so great a cataract, is much diminished by the heighth of the banks of the river; besides, the fall is as uniform as a mill-dam, being uninterrupted by the projection of rocks.

At Scaghtahook, on the East side of the North branch of Hudson's River, there are a few farms, but many more several miles to the Eastward, and about 25 miles from Albany, in the Patent of Hosick. These were all broke up by an irruption of French and Indians, who on the 28th of August 1754, killed and scalped two persons, and set fire to the houses and barns.

About 40 miles to the Northward of Albany, on the West side of the river, lies Saragtoga, a fine tract of low land, from which several families were driven by the French Indians, in the late war. A project of purchasing these lands from the Proprietors, settling them with Indians, raising a fort there and cultivating the soil for them, has been often talked of since Captain Camp-

*The South View of Oswego on Lake Ontario*

bell's disappointment, as a proper expedient to curb the scalping parties sent out from Crown Point.

In the Southern part of the county of Albany, on both sides of Hudson's River, the settlements are very scattered, except within twelve miles of the city, when the banks become low and accessible. The islands here, which are many, contain perhaps the finest soil in the world.

There are two manors in the county, Renslaerwick and Livingston, which have each the privilege of sending a member to the Assembly. The tenants of these manors, and of the Patents of Claverack, have free farms at the annual rent of a tenth of the produce, which has as yet been neither exacted nor paid. At Ancram in the Manor of Livingston is an iron furnace, about 14 miles from the river. Its best and most improved lands lie at Tachanic in the Eastern parts, which have of late been much disturbed by the inroads of the Massachuset's Bay, on this and the Patents of Westernhook and Claverack.

The winters in this county are commonly severe, and Hudson's River freezes so hard a hundred miles to the Southward of Albany, as to bear sleds loaded with great burdens. Much snow is very serviceable to the farmers here, not only in protecting their grain from the frost, but in facilitating the transportation of their boards and other produce, to the banks of the river against the ensuing spring.

## Ulster

This county joins to that of Albany, on the West side of Hudson's River. Its Northern extent is fixed at Sawyer's Rill: the Rivers Delaware and Hudson bound it East and West, and a West line from the mouth of Murderer's Creek is its Southern limit.

The inhabitants are Dutch, French, English, Scotch, and Irish, but the first and the last are most numerous. The Episcopalians in this county are so inconsiderable, that their church is only a mean log-house. The most considerable town is Kingston, situated about two miles from Hudson's River. It contains about 150 houses mostly of stone, is regularly laid out on a dry level spot, and has a large stone church and court-house near the center. It is thought to resemble Schenectady, but far exceeds it in its elevation: On the North side of the town, the Esopus Kill winds through rich and beautiful lawns. The people of Ulster having long enjoyed an undisturbed tranquility, are some of the most opulent farmers in the whole colony.

This county is most noted for fine flour, beer, and a good breed of draught horses. At the commencement of the range of the Apalachian Hills, about 10 miles from Hudson's River, is an inexhaustible quarry of millstones, which far exceed those from Colen in Europe, formerly imported here, and sold at £80 a pair. The Marbletown millstones cost not a fourth part of that sum. This and the counties of Dutchess and Orange abound with lime-stone, and on the banks of Hudson's River are found great bodies of blue slate.

The principal villages, besides Kingston, are Marbletown, Hurley, Rochester, New Paltz, and the Wall-kill, each of which is surrounded with fine tracts of low land. The militia of Ulster is about 15 or 1600 men and a company of horse.

## Orange

County is divided by a range of mountains, stretching Westward from Hudson's River, called The Highlands. On the North side the lands are very broken but fertile, and inhabited by Scotch, Irish, and English Presbyterians. The Society's missionary in Ulster preaches here sometimes to a small congregation of the Episcopal persuasion, which is the only one in the county. Their villages are Goshen, Bethlehem, and Little Britain, all remarkable for producing, in general, the best butter made in the colony. The people on the South side of the mountains are all Dutch; and Orange Town, more commonly called by the Indian name Tappan, is a small but very pleasant inland village, with a stone court-house and church. The militia consists of about 1300 fighting men.

This county joins to the Province of New-Jersey on the South; and the non-settlement of the partition line has been the greatest obstruction to its growth.

There is a very valuable tract called the Drowned Lands on the North side of the mountains, containing about 40 or 50,000 acres. The waters, which descend from the surrounding hills, being but slowly discharged by the river issuing out of it, cover these vast meadows every winter, and hence they become extremely fertile. The fires kindled up in the woods by the deer hunters in autumn, are communicated by the leaves to these meadows, before the waters rise above the channel of the river, and a dreadful, devouring conflagration over-runs it, consuming the herbage for several days. The Walkill River, which runs through this extensive, amphibious tract, if I may use the expression, is in the spring stored with eels of uncommon size and plenty, very useful to the farmers residing on its banks. The river is about two chains in breadth where it leaves the drowned lands, and has a considerable fall. The bottom of it is a broken rock, and I am informed by Mr. Clinton, a gentleman of ingenuity and a mathematical turn, that the channel might, for less than £2000 be sufficiently deepened to draw off all the water from the meadows. Some parts near the banks of the upland, have been already redeemed from the floods. These spots are very fertile, and produce English grass, hemp, and Indian corn.

The mountains, in the county of Orange, are clothed thick with timber, and abound with iron ore, ponds, and fine streams for iron works. Goshen is well supplied with white cedar, and in some parts of the woods is found great plenty of black walnut.

Before I proceed to the description of the southern counties, I beg leave to say a few words concerning Hudson's River.

Its source has not, as yet, been discovered. We know, in general, that it is in the mountainous, uninhabited, country, between the Lakes Ontario and Champlain. In its course Southward it approaches the Mohawks River within a few miles at Saucondauga. From thence it runs North and Northeasterly towards Lake St. Sacrement, now called Lake George, and is not above 8 or 10 miles distant from it. The course then to New-York is very uniform, being in the main South 12 or 15° West.

The distance from Albany to Lake George is computed at 65 miles. The river in that interval is navigable only to batteaus, and interrupted by rifts, which occasion two portages of half a mile each.* There are three routes from Crown Point to Hudson's River in the way to Albany; one through Lake George, another through a branch of Lake Champlain, bearing a southern course, and terminating in a bason, several miles East of Lake George, called the South Bay. The third is by ascending the Wood Creek, a shallow stream about one hundred feet broad, which, coming from the South-east, empties itself into the South branch of the Lake Champlain.

* In the passage from Albany to Fort Edward, the whole land carriage is about 12 or 13 miles.

The place, where these routes meet on the banks of Hudson's River, is called the Carrying Place. Here Fort Lyman, since called Fort Edward, is built; but Fort William Henry, a much stronger garrison, was erected at the South end of Lake George, after the repulse of the French forces under the command of Baron Dieskau on the 8th of September 1755. General Shirley thought it more advisable, to strengthen Fort Edward in the concurrence of three routes, than to erect the other at Lake George 17 miles to the Northward of it; and wrote a very pressing letter upon that head to Sir William Johnson, who then commanded the provincial troops.

The banks of Hudson's River are, for the most part, rocky cliffs, especially on the Western shore. The passage through the highlands, affords a wild romantick scene, for sixteen miles, through steep and lofty mountains. The tide flows a few miles above Albany. The navigation is safe, and performed in sloops of about 40 or 50 tons burden, extremely well accommodated to the river. About sixty miles above the city of New-York the water is fresh, and in wet seasons much lower. The river is stored with variety of fish, which renders a summer's passage to Albany, exceedingly diverting to such as are fond of angling.

The advantages of this river for penetrating into Canada, and protecting the Southern colonies from the irruptions of the French, by securing the command of the lakes, and cuting off the communication between the French settlements on St. Lawrence and the Mississippi, though but lately attended to, must be very apparent to every judicious observer of the maps of the inland part of North America.

The French, as appears from the intended invasion in 1689, have long eyed the English possession of this Province with jealousy; and it becomes us to fall upon every method for its protection and defence.

The singular conveniency of Hudson's River to this Province in particular, was so fully shewn in one of the late papers, published in 1753, under the title of the *Independent Reflector*, that I cannot help reprinting the passage relating to it.

> High Roads, which, in most trading Countries, are extremely expensive, and awake a continual Attention for their Reparation, demand from us, comparatively speaking, scarce any *public* Notice at all. The whole Province is contained in two narrow Oblongs, extending from the City

East and North, having Water Carriage from the Extremity
of one, and from the Distance of one hundred and sixty
Miles of the other; and by the most accurate Calculation, has
not, at a Medium, above twelve Miles of Land Carriage,
throughout its whole Extent. This is one of the strongest
Motives to the Settlement of a new Country, as it affords the
easiest and most speedy Conveyance from the remotest
Distances, and at the lowest Expence. The Effects of
this Advantage are greater than we usually observe, and are
therefore not sufficiently admired.

The Province of *Pensylvania*, has a fine Soil, and,
through the Importation of *Germans*, abounds with Inhabitants; but being a vast inland Country, its Produce must,
of Consequence, be brought to a Market over a great
Extent of Ground, and all by Land Carriage. Hence it is,
that *Philadelphia* is crowded with Waggons, Carts, Horses,
and their Drivers: a Stranger, at his first Entrance,
would imagine it to be a Place of Traffick, beyond any one
Town in the Colonies; while at *New-York*, in particular, to
which the Produce of the Country is all brought by Water,
there is more Business, at least, Business of Profit,
though with less Shew and Appearance. Not a Boat in our
River is navigated with more than two or three Men at
most; and these are perpetually coming in from, and returning to, all Parts of the adjacent Country, in the same
Employments, that fill the City of *Philadelphia* with some
Hundreds of Men, who, in Respect to the public Advantage
may justly be said, to be laboriously idle: for, let any
one nicely compute the Expence of a Waggon, with its
Tackling; the Time of two Men in attending it; their
Maintenance; four Horses and the Charge of their Provender,
on a Journey of one, though they often come, two
hundred Miles; and he will find, these several Particulars
amount to a Sum far from being inconsiderable. All this
Time the *New-York* Farmer is in the Course of his proper
Business, and the unincumbered Acquisitions of his Calling;
for, at a Medium, there is scarce a Farmer in the
Province, that cannot transport the Fruits of a Year's Labour,
from the best Farm, in three Days, at a proper Season,
to some convenient Landing, where the Market will be
to his Satisfaction, and all the Wants from the Merchant,
cheaply supplied: besides which, one Boat shall steal into the
Harbour of *New-York*, with a Lading of more Burden and
Value, than *forty* Waggons, *one hundred and sixty*
Horses, and *eighty* Men, into *Philadelphia;* and perhaps with
less Noise, Bluster, or Shew than one.

Prodigious is the Advantage we have in this Article alone, I shall not enter into an abstruse Calculation, to evince the exact Value of it, in all the Lights in which it may be considered; thus much is certain, that barely on Account of our easy Carriage, the Profits of Farming with us, exceed those in *Pennsylvania,* at least by *thirty per Cent.* and that Difference, in Favour of our Farmers, is of itself sufficient to enrich them; while the others find the Disadvantage they are exposed to, so heavy, (especially the remote Inhabitants of their Country) that a bare Subsistence is all they can reasonably hope to obtain. Take this Province throughout, the Expence of transporting a Bushel of Wheat, is but *Two-pence,* for the Distance of one hundred Miles; but the same Quantity at the like Distance in *Pensylvania,* will always exceed us *one Shilling* at least. The Proportion between us, in the Conveyance of every Thing else, is nearly the same. How great, then, are the Incumbrances to which they are exposed! What an immense Charge is saved to us; how sensible must the Embarrassments they are subject to, be to a trading People!

## Richmond

County consists of Staten Island, which lies nine miles South Westward from the city of New-York. It is about 18 miles long, and at a medium six or seven in breadth. On the South side is a considerable tract of good level land, but the island is, in general, rough, and the hills high. The inhabitants are principally Dutch and French. The former have a church, but the latter having been long without a minister, resort to an Episcopal church in Richmond Town, a poor mean village and the only one on the island. The parson of the Parish receives £40 per annum raised by a tax upon the county.

Southward of the main coast of this and the colony of Connecticut, lies Long Island, called by the Indians Matowacs, and named, according to an Act of Assembly in King William's reign, Nassau. Its length is computed at 120 miles, and the mean breadth twelve. The lands on the North and South side are good, but in the middle sandy and barren. The Southern shore is fortified against any invasion from the sea by a beach inaccessible to ships, and rarely to be approached, even by the smallest long-boats, on account of the surge, which breaks upon it with great fury, even when the winds are light. The coast East and West admits of regular soundings far into the ocean, and as the lands are, in general, low for several hundred miles, nothing can be more advantageous to our ships, than the high lands of Neversink near the entrance at the Hook, which are scarce six miles in length, and often seen thirty leagues from the sea. This island affords the finest roads in America, it being very level and but indifferently watered. It is divided into three counties.

## King's

County lies opposite to New-York on the North side of Long Island. The inhabitants are all Dutch, and enjoying a good soil, near our markets, are generally in easy circumstances. The county, which is very small, is settled in every part, and contains several pleasant villages, viz. Bushwick, Breucklin, Bedford, Flat-Bush, Flat-Lands, New-Utrecht, and Gravesend.

## Queen's

County is more extensive, and equally well settled. The principal towns are Jamaica, Hempstead, Flushing, Newtown, and Oysterbay. Hempstead plain is a large, level, dry, champain, heath, about sixteen miles long, and six or seven wide, a common land belonging to the towns of Oysterbay and Hempstead. The inhabitants are divided into Dutch and English Presbyterians, Episcopalians, and Quakers.

There are but two Episcopal missionaries in this county, one settled at Jamaica, and the other at Hempstead; and each of them receives £60 annually levied upon all the inhabitants.

## Suffolk

Includes all the Eastern part of Long Island, Shelter Island, Fisher's Island, Plumb Island, and the Isle of White. This large county has been long settled, and except one small Episcopal congregation, consists entirely of English Presbyterians. Its principal towns are Huntington, Smith Town, Brookhaven, Southampton, Southhold, and Easthampton. The farmers are, for the most part, graziers, and living very remote from New-York, a great part of their produce is carried to markets in Boston and Rhode Island. The Indians, who were formerly numerous on this island, are now become very inconsiderable. Those that remain, generally bind themselves servants to the

English. The whale fishery, on the South side of the island, has declined of late years through the scarcity of whales, and is now almost entirely neglected.

The Elizabeth Islands, Nantucket, Martin's Vineyard, &c. and Pemy Quid, which anciently formed Duke's and the County of Cornwal, are now under the jurisdiction of the Massachuset's Bay. Sir William Phips demanded them of Governour Fletcher in February 1692–3, not long after the new charter to that Province; but the government here was then of opinion, that, that colony was not entitled to any islands Westward of Nantucket.

An estimate of the comparative wealth of our counties, may be formed from any of our assessments. In a £10,000 part of a £45,000 tax laid in 1755, the proportions settled by an Act of Assembly stood thus:

| | |
|---|---:|
| New-York .............................. | £3332 : 0 : 0 |
| Albany ............................... | 1060 : 0 : 0 |
| King's ............................... | 484 : 0 : 0 |
| Queen's .............................. | 1000 : 0 : 0 |
| Suffolk .............................. | 860 : 0 : 0 |
| Richmond ............................. | 304 : 0 : 0 |
| West-Chester ......................... | 1000 : 0 : 0 |
| Ulster ............................... | 860 : 0 : 0 |
| Dutchess ............................. | 800 : 0 : 0 |
| Orange ............................... | 300 : 0 : 0 |
| | £10,000 : 0 : 0 |

# Chapter II   *Of the* Inhabitants

This Province is not so populous as some have imagined. Scarce a third part of it is under cultivation. The colony of Connecticut, which is vastly inferior to this in its extent, contains according to a late authentick enquiry above 133,000 inhabitants, and has a militia of 27,000 Men; but the militia of New-York, according to the general estimate, does not exceed 18,000. The whole number of souls is computed at 100,000.

Many have been the discouragements to the settlement of this colony. The French and Indian irruptions, to which we have always been exposed, have driven many families into

New-Jersey. At home, the British Acts for the transportation of felons, have brought all the American colonies into discredit with the industrious and honest poor, both in the kingdoms of Great-Britain and Ireland. The mischievous tendency of those laws was shewn in a late paper, which it may not be improper to lay before the reader.*

It is too well known that in Pursuance of divers Acts of Parliament, great Numbers of Fellows who have forfeited their Lives to the Public, for the most atrocious Crimes, are annually transported from Home to these Plantations. Very surprizing one would think, that Thieves, Burglars, Pickpockets, and Cut-purses, and a Herd of the most flagitious Banditti upon Earth, should be sent as agreeable Companions to us! That the supreme Legislature did intend a Transportation to *America*, for a Punishment of these Villains, I verily believe: but so great is the Mistake, that confident I am, they are thereby, on the contrary, highly rewarded. For what, in God's Name, can be more agreeable to a penurious Wretch, driven, through Necessity, to seek a Livelihood by breaking of Houses, and robbing upon the King's Highway, than to be saved from the Halter, redeemed from the Stench of a Gaol, and transported, Passage free, into a Country, where, being unknown, no Man can reproach him with his Crimes; where Labour is high, a little of which will maintain him; and where all his Expences will be moderate and low. There is scarce a Thief in *England*, that would not rather be transported than hanged. Life in any Condition, but that of extreme Misery, will be preferred to Death. As long, therefore, as there remains this wide Door of Escape, the Number of Thieves and Robbers at Home, will perpetually multiply, and their Depredations be incessantly reiterated.

But the Acts were intended, *for the better peopling the Colonies*. And will Thieves and Murderers be conducive to that End? What Advantage can we reap from a Colony of unrestrainable Renegadoes? will they exalt the Glory of the Crown? or rather, will not the Dignity of the most illustrious Monarch in the World, be sullied by a Province of Subjects so lawless, detestable, and ignominious? Can Agriculture be promoted, when the *wild Boar of the Forest breaks down our Hedges and pulls up our Vines*? Will Trade flourish, or Manufactures be encouraged, where Property is made the Spoil of such who are too idle to work, and wicked enough to murder and steal?

* The *Independent Reflector*.

Besides, are we not Subjects of the same King, with
the People of *England;* Members of the same Body politic,
and therefore entitled to equal Privileges with them? If so,
how injurious does it seem to free one Part of the Dominions,
from the Plagues of Mankind, and cast them upon
another? Should a Law be proposed to take the Poor of one
Parish, and billet them upon another, would not all the
World, but the Parish to be relieved, exclaim against such a
Project, as iniquitous and absurd? Should the numberless
Villains of *London* and *Westminster* be suffered to escape
from their Prisons, to range at large and depredate any
other Part of the Kingdom, would not every Man join with
the Sufferers, and condemn the Measure as hard and
unreasonable? And though the Hardships upon us, are
indeed not equal to those, yet the Miseries that flow from
Laws, by no Means intended to prejudice us, are too
heavy, not to be felt. *But the Colonies must be peopled.*
Agreed: And will the Transportation Acts ever have that
Tendency? No, they work the contrary Way, and counter-
act their own Design. We want People 'tis true, but
not Villains, ready at any Time, encouraged by Impunity,
and habituated upon the slightest Occasions, to cut a Man's
Throat, for a small Part of his Property. The Delights of
such Company, is a noble Inducement, indeed, to the honest
Poor, to convey themselves into a strange Country. Amidst
all our Plenty, they will have enough to exercise their
Virtues, and stand in no Need of the Association of such,
as will prey upon their Property, and gorge themselves with
the Blood of the Adventurers. They came over in Search
of Happiness; rather than starve will live any where, and
would be glad to be excused from so afflicting an Antepart of
the Torments of Hell. In Reality, Sir, these very Laws,
though otherwise designed, have turned out in the End,
the most effectual Expedients, that the Art of Man could
have contrived, to prevent the Settlement of these remote
Parts of the King's Dominions. They have actually taken
away almost every Encouragement to so laudable a Design.
I appeal to Facts. The Body of the *English* are struck
with Terror at the Thought of coming over to us, not because
they have a vast Ocean to cross, or leave behind them
their Friends; or that the Country is new and uncultivated:
but from the shocking Ideas, the Mind must necessarily
form, of the Company of inhuman Savages, and the more
terrible Herd of exiled Malefactors. There are Thousands of
honest Men, labouring in *Europe*, at four Pence a Day,
starving in Spite of all their Efforts, a dead Weight to the

respective Parishes to which they belong; who, without
any other Qualifications than common Sense, Health, and
Strength, might accumulate Estates among us, as many
have done already. These, and not the others, are the
Men that should be sent over, for the *better peopling the
Plantations. Great-Britain* and *Ireland,* in their present Circumstances, are overstocked with them; and he who
would immortalize himself, for a *Lover of Mankind,* should
concert a Scheme for the Transportation of the industriously honest abroad, and the immediate Punishment
of Rogues and Plunderers at Home. The pale-faced, half-
clad, meagre, and starved Skeletons, that are seen in every
Village of those Kingdoms, call loudly for the Patriot's
generous Aid. The Plantations too would thank him for his
Assistance, in obtaining the Repeal of those Laws which,
though otherwise intended by the Legislature, have so
unhappily proved injurious to his own Country, and ruinous
to us.—It is not long since a Bill passed the Commons, for
the Employment of such Criminals in his Majesty's
Docks, as should merit the Gallows. The Design was good.
It is consistent with sound Policy, that all those, who
have forfeited their Liberty and Lives to their Country,
should be compelled to labour the Residue of their Days in
its Service. But the Scheme was bad, and wisely was the
Bill rejected by the Lords, for this only Reason, That
it had a *natural Tendency to discredit the King's Yards:* the
Consequences of which must have been prejudicial to the
whole Nation. Just so ought we to reason in the present Case,
and we should then soon be brought to conclude, that
though peopling the Colonies, which was the laudable
Motive of the Legislature, be expedient to the Publick;
abrogating the Transportation Laws, must be equally
necessary.

The bigotry and tyranny of some of our governours, together
with the great extent of their grants, may also be considered
among the discouragements against the full settlement of the
Province. Most of these gentlemen coming over with no other
view than to raise their own fortunes, issued extravagant patents, charged with small quit rents, to such as were able to
serve them in the Assembly; and these patentees being generally men of estates, have rated their lands so exorbitantly high,
that very few poor persons could either purchase or lease them.
Add to all these, that the New-England planters have always

been disaffected to the Dutch, nor was there, after the surrender, any foreign accession from the Netherlands. The Province being thus poorly inhabited, the price of labour became so enormously enhanced, that we have been constrained to import Negroes from Africa, who are employed in all kinds of servitude and trades.

English is the most prevailing language amongst us, but not a little corrupted by the Dutch dialect, which is still so much used in some counties, that the sheriffs find it difficult to obtain persons sufficiently acquainted with the English tongue, to serve as jurors in the courts of law.

The manners of the people differ as well as their language. In Suffolk and Queen's County, the first settlers of which were either natives of England, or the immediate descendants of such as begun the plantations in the Eastern colonies, their customs are similar to those prevailing in the English counties, from whence they originally sprang. In the city of New-York, through our intercourse with the Europeans, we follow the London fashions; though by the time we adopt them, they become disused in England. Our affluence, during the late war, introduced a degree of luxury in tables, dress, and furniture, with which we were before unacquainted. But still we are not so gay a people, as our neighbours in Boston and several of the Southern colonies. The Dutch counties, in some measure, follow the example of New-York, but still retain many modes peculiar to the Hollanders.

The city of New-York consists principally of merchants, shopkeepers, and tradesmen, who sustain the reputation of honest, punctual, and fair, dealers. With respect to riches, there is not so great an inequality amongst us, as is common in Boston and some other places. Every man of industry and integrity has it in his power to live well, and many are the instances of persons, who came here distressed by their poverty, who now enjoy easy and plentiful fortunes.[12]

New-York is one of the most social places on the continent. The men collect themselves into weekly evening clubs. The ladies, in winter, are frequently entertained either at concerts of musick or assemblies, and makes a very good appearance. They are comely and dress well, and scarce any of them have distorted shapes. Tinctured with a Dutch education, they manage their families with becoming parsimony, good providence, and singular neatness. The practice of extravagant gaming, common to the fashionable part of the fair sex, in some places, is a vice with which my countrywomen cannot justly be charged. There is nothing they so generally neglect as reading, and indeed all the arts for the improvement of the mind, in which, I confess, we have set them the example. They are modest, temperate, and charitable; naturally sprightly, sensible, and good-humoured; and, by the helps of a more elevated education, would possess all the accomplishments desirable in the sex. Our schools are in the lowest order; the instructors want instruction, and through a long shameful neglect of all the arts and sciences, our common speech is extremely corrupt, and the evidences of a bad taste, both as to thought and language, are visible in all our proceedings, publick and private.[13]

The people, both in town and country, are sober, industrious, and hospitable, though intent upon gain. The richer sort keep very plentiful tables, abounding with great varieties of flesh, fish, fowl, and all kinds of vegetables. The common drinks are beer, cyder, weak punch, and Madeira wine. For desert, we have fruits in vast plenty, of different kinds and various species.

Gentlemen of estates rarely reside in the country, and hence few or no experiments have yet been made in agriculture. The farms being large, our husbandmen, for that reason, have little recourse to art for manuring and improving their lands; but it is said, that nature has furnished us with sufficient helps, whenever necessity calls us to use them. It is much owing to the disproportion between the number of our inhabitants, and the vast tracts remaining still to be settled, that we have not, as yet, entered upon scarce any other manufactures, than such as are indispensibly necessary for our home convenience. Felt-making, which is perhaps the most natural of any we could fall upon, was begun some years ago, and hats were exported to the West-Indies with great success, till lately prohibited by an Act of Parliament.[14]

The inhabitants of this colony are in general healthy and robust, taller but shorter lived than Europeans, and, both with respect to their minds and bodies, arrive sooner to an age of maturity. Breathing a serene, dry, air, they are more sprightly in their natural tempers than the people of England, and hence instances of suicide are here very uncommon. The history of our diseases belongs to a profession with which I am very little acquainted.[15] Few physicians amongst us are eminent for their skill. Quacks abound like locusts in Egypt, and too many have

recommended themselves to a full practice and profitable subsistence. This is the less to be wondered at, as the profession
is under no kind of regulation. Loud as the call is, to our
shame be it remembered, we have no law to protect the lives
of the King's subjects, from the malpractice of pretenders. Any
man at his pleasure sets up for physician, apothecary, and
chirurgeon. No candidates are either examined or licensed, or
even sworn to fair practice.* The natural history of this Province would of itself furnish a small volume, and therefore I
leave this also to such, as have capacity and leisure to make
useful observations, in that curious and entertaining branch of
natural philosophy.

* The necessity of regulating the practice of physick, and a plan
for that purpose, were strongly recommended by the authour of the
*Independent Reflector,* in 1753, when the city of New-York alone
boasted the honour of having above forty gentlemen of that faculty.

## Chapter III   *Of our* Trade

The situation of New-York, with respect to foreign markets,
for reasons elsewhere assigned is to be prefered to any of our
colonies. It lies in the center of the British plantations on the
continent, has at all times a short easy access to the ocean,
and commands almost the whole trade of Connecticut and New-
Jersey, two fertile and well cultivated colonies. The projection
of Cape Codd into the Atlantick, renders the navigation from
the former to Boston, at some seasons, extremely perilous; and
sometimes the coasters are driven off and compelled to winter
in the West-Indies. But the conveyance to New-York, from the
Eastward through the Sound, is short and unexposed to such
dangers. Philadelphia receives as little advantage from New-
Jersey, as Boston from Connecticut, because the only rivers
which roll through that Province, disembogue not many miles
from the very city of New-York. Several attempts have been
made to raise Perth Amboy into a trading port, but hitherto
it has proved to be an unfeasible project. New-York, all things
considered, has a much better situation, and were it otherwise,
the city is become too rich and considerable, to be eclipsed by
any other town in its neighbourhood.

Our merchants are compared to a hive of bees, who industriously gather honey for others–*Non vobis mellificatis Apes.*[16]

The profits of our trade center chiefly in Great-Britain, and for that reason, methinks, among others, we ought always to receive the generous aid and protection of our mother country. In our traffick with other places, the balance is almost constantly in our favour. Our exports to the West-Indies are bread, pease, rie-meal, Indian corn, apples, onions, boards, staves, horses, sheep, butter, cheese, pickled oysters, beef, and pork. Flour is also a main article, of which there is shiped about 80,000 barrels per annum. To preserve the credit of this important branch of our staple, we have a good law, appointing officers to inspect and brand every cask before its exportation. The returns are chiefly rum, sugar, and molasses, except cash from Curacoa, and when mules, from the Spanish Main, are ordered to Jamaica, and the Windward Islands, which are generally exchanged for their natural produce, for we receive but little cash from our own islands. The balance against them would be much more in our favour, if the indulgence to our sugar colonies, did not enable them to sell their produce at a higher rate than either the Dutch or French islands.

The Spaniards commonly contract for provisions, with merchants in this and the colony of Pennsylvania, very much to the advantage both of the contractors and the publick, because the returns are wholly in cash. Our wheat, flour, Indian corn, and lumber shiped to Lisbon and Madeira, balance the Madeira wine imported here.

The logwood trade to the Bay of Honduras is very considerable, and was pushed by our merchants with great boldness in the most dangerous times. The exportation of flax seed to Ireland is of late very much increased. Between the 9th of December 1755, and the 23d of February following, we shiped off 12,528 hogsheads. In return for this article, linens are imported and bills of exchange drawn, in favour of England, to pay for the dry goods we purchase there. Our logwood is remitted to the English merchants for the same purpose.

The fur trade, though very much impaired by the French wiles and encroachments, ought not to be passed over in silence.* The building of Oswego has conduced, more than anything else, to the preservation of this trade. Peltry of all kinds

---

* It is computed that formerly, we exported 150 hogsheads of beaver and other fine furs per annum, and 200 hogheads of Indian-dressed deer-skins, besides those carried from Albany into New-England. Skins undressed are usually shipped to Holland.

is purchased with rum, ammunition, blankets, strouds, and wampum, or conque-shell bugles. The French fur trade, at Albany, was carried on till the summer 1755, by the Caghnuaga proselytes; and in return for their peltry, they received Spanish pieces of eight, and some other articles which the French want to complete their assortment of Indian goods. For the savages prefer the English strouds to theirs, and the French found it their interest to purchase them of us, and transport them to the Western Indians on the Lakes Erie, Huron, and at the Streight of Misilimakinac.

Our importation of dry goods from England is so vastly great, that we are obliged to betake ourselves to all possible arts, to make remittances to the British merchants. It is for this purpose we import cotton from St. Thomas's and Surinam; lime-juice and Nicaragua wood from Curacoa; and logwood from the Bay, &c. and yet it drains us of all the silver and gold we can collect. It is computed, that the annual amount of the goods purchased by this colony in Great-Britain, is in value not less than £100,000 sterling; and the sum would be much greater if a stop was put to all clandestine trade. England is, doubtless, entitled to all our superfluities; because our general interests are closely connected, and her navy is our principal defence. On this account, the trade with Hamburgh and Holland for duck, chequered linen, oznabrigs, cordage, and tea, is certainly, upon the whole, impolitick and unreasonable; how much soever it may conduce to advance the interest of a few merchants, or this particular colony.

By what measures this contraband trade may be effectually obstructed is hard to determine, though it well deserves the attention of a British Parliament. Increasing the number of custom-house officers, will be a remedy worse than the disease. Their salaries would be an additional charge upon the publick; for if we argue from their conduct, we ought not to presume upon their fidelity. The exclusive right of the East-India Company to import tea, while the colonies purchase it of foreigners 30 per cent. cheaper, must be very prejudicial to the nation. Our people, both in town and country, are shamefully gone into the habit of tea-drinking; and it is supposed we consume of this commodity in value near £10,000 sterling per annum.

Some are of opinion that the fishery of sturgeons, which abound in Hudson's River, might be improved to the great advantage of the colony; and that, if proper measures were concerted, much profit would arise from ship-building and naval stores. It is certain we have timber in vast plenty, oak, white and black pines, fir, locust, red and white mulberry, and cedar; and perhaps there is no soil on the globe, fitter for the production of hemp than the low lands in the county of Albany. To what I have already said concerning iron ore, a necessary article, I shall add an extract from the *Independent Reflector.*

It is generally believed, that this Province abounds with a Variety of Minerals. Of Iron in particular we have such Plenty, as to be excelled by no Country in the World of equal Extent. It is a Metal of intrinsick Value beyond any other, and preferable to the purest Gold. The former is converted into numberless Forms, for as many indispensible uses; the latter, for its Portableness and Scarcity, is only fit for a Medium of Trade: but Iron is a Branch of it, and I am persuaded will, one Time or other, be one of the most valuable Articles of our Commerce. Our annual Exports to *Boston, Rhode-Island* and *Connecticut,* and since the late Act of Parliament, to *England,* are far from being inconsiderable. The Bodies of Iron Ore in the Northern Parts of this Province are so many, their Quality so good, and their Situation so convenient, in Respect of Wood, Water, Hearth-stone, proper Fluxes, and Carriage, for Furnaces, Bloomeries, and Forges, that with a little Attention we might very soon rival the *Swedes* in the Produce of this Article. If any *American* Attempts in Iron Works have proved abortive, and disappointed their Undertakers, it is not to be imputed either to the Quality of the Ore, or a Defect of Conveniences. The Want of more Workmen, and the Villainy of those we generally have, are the only Causes to which we must attribute such Miscarriages. No Man, who has been concerned in them, will disagree with me, if I assert, that from the Founder of the Furnace to the meanest Banksman or Jobber, they are usually low, profligate, drunken, and faithless. And yet, under all the innumerable Disadvantages of such Instruments, very large Estates have, in this Way, been raised in some of our Colonies. Our Success, therefore, in the Iron Manufactory, is obstructed and discouraged by the Want of Workmen, and the high Price of Labour, its necessary Consequence, and by these alone: but 'tis our Happiness, that such only being the Cause, the Means of Redress are entirely in our own Hands. Nothing more is wanting to open a vast Fund of Riches to the Province, in the Branch of Trade, than the Importa-

tion of Foreigners. If our Merchants and landed Gentlemen
could be brought to a Coalition in this Design, their
private Interests would not be better advanced by it, than
the public Emolument; the latter in particular, would thereby
vastly improve their Lands, increase the Number, and
raise the Rents of their Tenants. And I cannot but think,
that if those Gentlemen who are too inactive to engage in
such an Enterprise, would only be at the Pains of drawing
up full Representations of their Advantages for Iron
Works, and of publishing them from Time to Time in
*Great-Britain, Ireland, Germany,* and *Sweden;* the Province
would soon be supplied, with a sufficient Number of
capable Workmen in all the Branches of that Manufactory.[17]

The money used in this Province is silver, gold, British halfpence, and bills of credit. To counterfeit either of them is
felony without benefit of clergy; but none except the latter,
and Lyon dollars are a legal tender. Twelve halfpence, till
lately, passed for a shilling; which being much beyond their
value in any of the neighbouring colonies, the Assembly, in
1753, resolved to proceed, at their next meeting, after the 1st
of May ensuing, to the consideration of a method for ascertaining their value. A set of gentlemen, in number seventy-two,
took the advantage of the discredit that resolve put upon cop-
per halfpence, and on the 22d of December, subscribed a paper,
engaging not to receive or pass them, except at the rate of
fourteen coppers to a shilling. This gave rise to a mob, for a
few days, among the lower class of people, but some of them
being imprisoned, the scheme was carried into execution; and
established in every part of the province, without the aid of
a law. Our paper bills, which are issued to serve the exigencies
of the government, were at first equal to an ounce of silver,
then valued at eight shillings. Before the late Spanish War,
silver and gold were in great demand to make remittances for
European goods, and then the bills sunk, an ounce of silver
being worth nine shillings and three pence. During the war,
the credit of our bills was well supported, partly by the number of prizes taken by our privateers, and the high price of our
produce abroad; and partly by the logwood trade and the de-
preciation of the New-England paper money, which gave ours
a free circulation through the Eastern colonies. Since the war,
silver has been valued at about nine shillings and two pence
an ounce, and is doubtless fixed there, till our imports exceed

what we export. To assist his Majesty for removing the late encroachments of the French, we have issued £80,000 to be sunk in short periods, by a tax on estates real and personal; and the whole amount of our paper currency is thought to be about £160,000.[18]

Never was the trade of this Province in so flourishing a condition, as at the latter end of the late French war.[19] Above twenty privateers were often out of this port, at a time; and they were very successful in their captures. Provisions, which are our staple, bore a high price in the West-Indies. The French, distressed through the want of them, gladly received our flags of truce, though sometimes they had but one or two prisoners on board, because they were always loaded with flour, beef, pork, and such like commodities. The danger their own vessels were exposed to, induced them to sell their sugars to us at a very low rate. A trade was, at the same time, carried on between Jamaica and the Spanish Main, which opened a fine market to the northern colonies, and the returns were, principally, in cash. It was generally thought, that if the war had continued, the greatest part of the produce of the Spanish and French settlements in the West-Indies would have been transported to Great-Britain, through some one or other of her colonies; whence we may fairly argue their prodigious importance.

The provincial laws relating to our trade are not very numerous. Those concerned in them, may have recourse to the late edition of our Acts at large, published in 1752; and for this reason, I beg to be excused from exhibiting an unentertaining summary of them in this work.

## Chapter IV  *Of our* Religious State

By the account already given, of the rise and progress of the acts for settling a ministry in four counties, and the observations made concerning our various Christian denominations, I have in a great measure anticipated what I at first intended to have ranged under this head.[20]

The principal distinctions amongst us, are the Episcopalians, and the Dutch and English Presbyterians; the two last together with all the other Protestants in the colony, are sometimes (perhaps here improperly) called by the general name of dissenters; and compared to them, the Episcopalians are, I believe, scarce in the proportion of one to fifteen. Hence partly arises the general discontent on account of the Ministry Acts; not so much that the provision made by them is engrossed by the minor sect, as because the body of the people, are for an equal, universal, toleration of Protestants, and utterly averse to any kind of ecclesiastical establishment. The dissenters, though fearless of each other, are all jealous of the Episcopal party, being apprehensive that the countenance they may have from home, will foment a lust for dominion, and enable them, in process of time, to subjugate and oppress their fellow subjects. The violent measures of some of our governours have given an alarm to their fears, and if ever any other gentleman, who may be honoured with the chief command of the Province, begins to divert himself, by retrenching the privileges and immunities they now enjoy, the confusion of the Province will be the unavoidable consequence of his folly. For though his Majesty has no other subjects upon whose loyalty he can more firmly depend, yet an abhorrence of persecution, under any of its appearances, is so deeply rooted in the people of this plantation; that as long as they continue their numbers and interest in the Assembly, no attempt will probably be made upon the rights of conscience, without endangering the publick repose.

Of the government of the Dutch churches, I have already given an account. As to the Episcopal clergy, they are missionaries of the English Society for Propagating the Gospel, and ordinarily ordained by the Bishop of London, who, having a commission from the King to exercise ecclesiastical jurisdiction, commonly appoints a clergyman here for his commissary. The ministers are called by the particular churches, and maintained by the voluntary contribution of their auditors and the Society's annual allowance, there being no law for tithes.[21]

The English Presbyterians are very numerous. Those inhabiting New-York, New-Jersey, Pennsylvania, and the three Delaware counties, are regularly formed, after the manner of the Church of Scotland, into consistories or kirk sessions, Presbyteries and Synods, and will probably soon join in erecting a general assembly. The clergy are ordained by their fellows, and maintained by their respective congregations. I except those missionaries among the Indians, whose subsistance is paid by the Society in Scotland for Propagating Christian Knowledge. None of the Presbyterian churches in this Province are incorporated, as is the case of many in New-Jersey. Their judicatories are upon a very proper establishment, for they have no authority by legal sanctions to enforce their decrees. Nor indeed is any religious sect, amongst us, legally invested with powers prejudicial to the common privileges of the rest. The dominion of all our clergy is, as it ought to be, merely spiritual. The Episcopalians, however, sometimes pretend, that the ecclesiastical establishment in South Britain extends here; but the whole body of the dissenters are averse to the doctrine. The point has been disputed with great fervour, and the sum of the arguments against it is contained in a late paper, which I shall lay before the reader, at large, without any additional reflections.

It was published in September 1753, under the title of the *Independent Reflector,* and is in these words:

*The Arguments in Support of an ecclesiastical Establishment,*
   *in this Province, impartially considered and refuted.*

—*Eripe turpi*
*Colla jugo: liber, liber sum, dic age.   Hor.*[22]

Whether the Church of England is equally established in the colonies, as in the southern parts of Great-Britain, is a question that has often been controverted. Those who hold the affirmative, have drawn a long train of consequences in favour of the Episcopalians, taking it for granted, that the truth is on their side. The Presbyterians, Independents, Congregationalists, Anabaptists, Quakers, and all those among us, who in England would fall under the general denomination of dissenters, are warm in the negative. I beg leave, therefore, to interpose in the debate; and as I promised, in the introduction to these papers, to vindicate the religious, as well as civil, rights and privileges of my countrymen; I shall devote this paper to a consideration of so important a point: to which I am the more strongly inclined, because such establishment has often been urged against the scheme I have proposed for the constitution of our college. My opinion is, that the notion of a general religious establishment in this Province, is entirely groundless. According to the strict rules of controversy, the *Onus probandi,* or the burden of the proof, lies upon those who affirm the position; and it would therefore be sufficient for me barely to deny it. I shall, nevertheless, wave the advantage of this rule of the schools; and, as becomes an impartial advocate for truth, proceed to state the arguments, which are generally urged in support of an establishment. I shall then shew their insufficiency, and conclude with the particular reasons upon which my opinion is founded.

They who assert, that the Church of England is established in this Province, never, that I have heard of, pretended that it owes its establishment to any provincial law of our own making. Nor, indeed, is there the least ground for such a supposition. The Acts, that establish a ministry in this, and three other counties, do not affect the whole colony; and therefore can by no means, be urged in support of a general establishment. Nor were they originally designed to establish the Episcopalians in preference or exclusion of any other Protestants in those counties to which they are limited. But as the proposition is, that the establishment of the Church of England is equally binding here, as in England; so, agreeable thereto, the arguments they adduce are the following:

*First*, That as we are an English colony, the constitutional laws of our mother country, antecedent to the legislature of our own, are binding upon us; and therefore at the planting of this colony, the English religious establishment immediately took place.

*Secondly,* that the Act which established the Episcopal Church in South-Britain, previous to the Union of England and Scotland, extends to, and equally affects, all the colonies.

These are the only arguments that can be offered with the least plausibility, and if they are shewn to be inconclusive, the position is disproved, and the arguments of consequence must be impertinent and groundless. I shall begin with the examination of the first: And here it must be confessed, for undoubted law, that every new colony, till it has a legislature of its own, is, in general, subject to the laws of the country from which it originally sprang. But that all of them, without distinction, are to be supposed binding upon such planters, is neither agreeable to law nor reason. The laws which they carry with them, and to which they are subject, are such as are absolutely necessary to answer the original intention of our entering into a state of society. Such as are requisite, in their new colony state, for the advancement of their and the general prosperity;

such, without which they will neither be protected in their lives, liberty, or property: and the true reason of their being considered, even subject to such laws, arises from the absolute necessity of their being under some kind of government, their supporting a colony relation and dependence, and the evident fitness of their subjection to the laws of their mother country, with which alone they can be supposed to be acquainted. Even at this day we extend every general Act of Parliament which we think reasonable and fit for us, though it was neither designed to be a law upon us, nor has words to include us, and has even been enacted long since we had a legislature of our own. This is a practice we have introduced for our conveniency;* but that the English laws, so far as I have distinguished them, should be binding upon us, antecedent to our having a legislature of our own, is of absolute unavoidable necessity. But no such necessity can be pretended, in favour of the introduction of any religious establishment whatsoever; because, it is evident that different societies do exist with different ecclesiastical laws, or, which is sufficient to my purpose, without such as the English establishment; and that civil society, as it is antecedent to any ecclesiastical establishments, is in its nature unconnected with them, independent of them, and all social happiness completely attainable without them.

*Secondly,* To suppose all the laws of England, without distinction, obligatory upon every new colony at its implantation, is absurd, and would effectually prevent the subjects from undertaking so hazardous an adventure. Upon such a supposition a thousand laws will be introduced, inconsistent with the state of a new country, and destructive of the planters. To use the words of the late Attorney-General, Sir Dudley Ryder,† "It would be acting the Part of an unskilful Physician, who should prescribe the same Dose to every Patient, without distinguishing the Variety of Distempers and Constitutions." According to this doctrine, we are subject to the payment of tithes, ought to have a spiritual court, and impoverished, as the first settlers of the Province must have been, they were yet liable to the payment of the Land Tax. And had this been the sense of our

* This practice is very dangerous, and is assuming little less than a legislative authority.

† Afterwards Lord Chief Justice of the King's Bench. These were his words, in an opinion against the extent of the Statute of Frauds and Perjuries.

rulers, and their conduct conformable thereto, scarce ever would our colonies have appeared in their present flourishing condition; especially if it be considered, that the first settlers of most of them, sought an Exemption in these American wilds, from the establishment to which they were subject at home.

*Thirdly,* If the planters of every new colony carry with them the established religion of the country from whence they migrate; it follows, that if a colony had been planted when the English nation were pagans, the establishment in such colony must be paganism alone: and, in like manner, had this colony been planted while Popery was established in England, the religion of Papists must have been our established religion; and if it is our duty to conform to the religion established at home, we are equally bound, against conscience and the Bible, to be pagans, Papists, or Protestants, according to the particular religion they shall please to adopt. A doctrine that can never be urged, but with a very ill grace indeed, by any Protestant minister?

*Fourthly,* If the Church of England is established in this colony, it must either be founded on Acts of Parliament, or the common law. That it is not established by the first, I shall prove in the sequel; and that it cannot be established by the common law, appears from the following considerations.

The common law of England, properly defined, consists of those general laws to which the English have been accustomed, from time whereof there is no memory to the contrary; and every law deriving its validity from such immemorial custom, must be carried back as far as to the reign of Richard I whose death happened on the 6th of April 1199. But the present establishment of the Church of England was not till the fifth year of Queen Anne. And hence it is apparent, that the establishment of the Church of England, can never be argued from the common law even in England; nor could be any part of it, since it depends not for its validity upon custom immemorial. And therefore, though it be admited, that every English colony is subject to the common law of the realm, it by no means follows, that the Church of England is established in the colonies; because, the common law knows of no such religious establishment, nor considers any religious establishment whatever, as any part of the English Constitution. It does, indeed, encourage religion; but that, and a particular church government, are things entirely different.

I proceed now to a consideration of the second argument insisted on, to prove an Episcopal establishment in the colonies, founded on the Act which established the Church of England, passed in the fifth year of Queen Anne, recited and ratified in the Act for an Union of the Two Kingdoms of England and Scotland.[23] And that this Act does not establish the Church of England in the colonies, has been so fully shewn by Mr. Hobart,* in his Second Address to the Episcopal separation in New-England, that I shall content myself with an Extract from the works of that ingenious gentleman, which, with very little alteration, is as follows:

The Act we are now disputing about, was made in the fifth Year of Queen *Ann,* and is entitled, *An Act for* securing *the Church of* England, as by Law established. The Occasion of the Statute was this: The Parliament in *Scotland,* when treating of an Union with *England,* were apprehensive of its endangering their ecclesiastical Establishment. *Scotland* was to have but a small Share in the Legislature of *Great-Britain,* but forty-five Members in the House of Commons which consist of above five hundred, and but sixteen in the House of Lords, which then consisted of near an hundred, and might be increased by the Sovereign at Pleasure. The *Scots,* therefore, to prevent having their ecclesiastical Establishment repealed in a *British* Parliament, where they might be so easily out-voted by the *English* Members, passed an Act previous to the Union, establishing the Presbyterian Church within the Kingdom of *Scotland,* in Perpetuity, and made this Act an essential and fundamental Part of the Union which might not be repealed, or altered by any subsequent *British* Parliament; and this put the *English* Parliament upon passing this Act for securing the Church of *England.* Neither of them designed to enlarge the Bounds of their ecclesiastical Constitution, or extend their Establishment farther than it reached before, but only to *secure* and *perpetuate* it in its then present Extent. This is evident, not only from the Occasion of the Act, but from the charitable Temper the *English* Parliament was under the influence of, when they passed it. The Lord *North* and *Grey* offered a Rider to be added to the Bill for an Union, *viz.* That it might not extend to an Approbation or Acknowledgment of the Truth of the Presbyterian Way of Worship, or allowing the Religion of the Church of *Scotland* to be what it is stiled, *the true Protestant Religion.* But this

* A minister of one of the churches at Fairfield in Connecticut.

Clause was rejected.—A Parliament that would acknowledge the Religion of the Church of *Scotland,* to be the true Protestant Religion, and allow their Acts to extend to an Approbation of the Presbyterian Way of Worship, though they might think it best to secure and perpetuate the Church of *England* within those Bounds, wherein it was before established, can hardly be supposed to have designed to extend it beyond them.

The Title of the Act is exactly agreeable to what we have said of the Design of it, and of the Temper of the Parliament that passed it. 'Tis entitled, *An Act* not for enlarging, but *for securing the Church of* England, and that not in the *American* Plantations, but *as it is now by Law established;* which plainly means no more than to perpetuate it within its ancient Boundaries.

The *Provision* made in the Act itself, is well adapted to this Design; for it enacts, That the Act of the 13th of *Elizabeth,* and the Act of Uniformity, passed in the 13th Year of *Charles* II. and all and singular other Acts of Parliament then in Force for the Establishment and Preservation of the Church of *England,* should remain in full Force for ever; and that every succeeding Sovereign should, at his Coronation, take and subscribe an Oath to maintain and preserve inviolably the *said Settlement* of the Church of *England, as by Law established,* within the Kingdoms of *England* and *Ireland,* the Dominion of *Wales,* and Town of *Berwick* upon *Tweed,* and the Territories thereunto belonging. This Act doth not use such Expressions, as would have been proper and even necessary, had the Design been to have made a new Establishment; but only such as are proper to ratify and confirm an old one. The Settlement, which the King is sworn to preserve, is represented as existing previously to the passing this Act, and not as made by it. The Words of the Oath are, *to maintain and preserve inviolably the said Settlement.* If it be asked, *What Settlement?* The Answer must be, a Settlement heretofore made and confirmed by certain Statutes, which for the greater Certainty and Security are enumerated in this Act, and declared to be unalterable. This is the Settlement the King is sworn to preserve, and this Settlement has no Relation to us in *America.* For the Act, which originally made it, did not reach hither; and this Act, which perpetuates them, does not extend them to us.

It is a mistake to imagine, that the word "territories" necessarily means these American colonies. "These Countries are usually in Law, as well as other Writings, stiled Colonies or

Plantations, and not Territories. An Instance of this we have in the Charter to *the Society for propagating the Gospel in foreign Parts."* And it is the invariable practice of the legislature, in every Act of Parliament, both before and after this Act, designed to affect us, to use the words colonies, or plantations. Nor is it to be supposed, that, in so important a matter, words of so direct and broad an intent would have been omitted. "The Islands of *Jersey* and *Guernsey* were properly Territories belonging to the Kingdom of *England,* before the Union took Place; and they stand in the same Relation to the Kingdom of *Great-Britain* since. The Church of *England* was established in these Islands, and the Legislature intended to perpetuate it in them, as well as in *England* itself; so that as these Islands were not particularly named in the Act, there was Occasion to use the Word *Territories,* even upon the Supposition, that they did not design to make the Establishment more extensive than it was before this Law passed." Further, in order to include the plantations in the word "territories," we must suppose it always to mean every other part of the dominions not particularly mentioned in the instrument that uses it, which is a construction that can never be admited: for, hence it will follow, that those commissions which give the government of a colony, and the territories thereon depending in America (and this is the case of every one of them) extend to all the American colonies, and their governours must of consequence have reciprocal superintendencies; and should any commission include the word "territories" generally, unrestricted to America, by the same construction the Governour, therein mentioned, might exercise an authority under it, not only in America, but in Africa and the Indies, and even in the Kingdom of Ireland, and perhaps, in the absence of the King, in Great-Britain itself. Mr. Hobart goes on, and argues against the establishment from the light in which the Act of Union has, ever since it was passed, been considered.

Dr. *Bisse,* Bishop of *Hereford,* [says he] a Member of the Society, preached the annual Sermon, *February* 21, 1717, ten Years after the Act of Union took Place; and he says, it would have well become *the Wisdom wherewith that great Work* (the Reformation or Establishment of the Church of *England*) *was conducted in this Kingdom, that this foreign Enterprise* (the Settlement of Plantations in *America*) *also should have been carried on by the Government in the like regular Way.* But he owns the Government at Home did not interpose in the Case, or establish any Form of Religion for us. *In Truth* (says his Lordship) *the whole was left to the Wisdom of the first Proprietors, and to the Conduct of every private Man.* He observes, that of late Years the civil Interest hath been regarded, and the Dependance of the Colonies, on the Imperial Crown of the Realm, secured: but then, with Regard to the Religion of the Plantations, his *Lordship* acknowledges, that *the Government itself here at Home, sovereign as it is, and invested doubtless with sufficient Authority there,* hath not thought fit to interpose in this Matter, *otherwise than in this charitable Way: it hath enabled us to ask the Benevolence of all good Christians towards the Support of Missionaries to be sent among them.* Thus Bishop *Bisse* thought as I do, and that the Act of Union nor any other Law prior thereto, did extend the Establishment to the Plantations; and if the *Society* had not been of the same Opinion, they would hardly have printed and dispersed his Sermon. Neither did the civil Rulers of the Nation, who may justly be supposed acquainted with its Laws, think the Act of Union, or any other Law, established the Church of *England* in *America.* This is plain from the Letter of the *Lords Justices* to Governor *Dummer,* in the Year 1725, almost twenty Years after the Union, wherein they say, *there is no regular Establishment of any national or provincial Church in these Plantations.*

If it be urged, that the King's Commission to the late Bishop of *London,* proves an ecclesiastical Establishment here, it is sufficient to answer, that his *Lordship* was remarkable for Skill in the Laws, so far as they relate to ecclesiastical Affairs, as appears from his *Codex;* and he was of the contrary Opinion, for in his Letter to Dr. *Colman,* of *May* 24, 1735, he writes thus: *My Opinion has* always *been, that the religious State of* New-England *is founded in an equal Liberty to all Protestants; none of which can claim the Name of a national Establishment, or any Kind of Superiority over the rest.* This Opinion the Bishop gave not only since the Act of Union, but even seven Years after he had received his Commission; and surely it must be admitted, that as he had Time enough to consider it, so he, of all others, best understood it.

Thus far Mr. Hobart. With respect to the Act of Union, I beg leave only to subjoin, that it is highly probable the Scotch

Parliament believed the English intended to establish their church only in England. For in the close of the Act, by which they had established the Presbyterian Church in Scotland, it is declared in these express words, *"That the Parliament of* England *may provide for the Security of the Church of* England, *as they think expedient, to take Place within the Bounds of the said Kingdom of* England." And whatever latitude the word kingdom has in common speech, it, in a legal sense, is limited to England, properly so called, and excludes the plantations.

Nor can we suppose, that the Church of England is established in these colonies, by any acts prior to the Act of Union above considered. For besides the several opinions against such supposition already adduced, it is unreasonable to imagine, that if there was any such establishment, King Charles II in direct repugnancy thereto, should have made the grant of Pennsylvania, and given equal privileges to all religions in that Province, without even excepting the Roman Catholicks; and that the colonies of Rhode-Island, Connecticut, and the Massachusetts Bay, should be permited to make their provincial establishments, in opposition to an antecedent establishment of the Church of England, especially as the laws of the Massachusetts Bay Province, are constantly sent home, and the King has the absolute power of repealing every act he should think improper to be continued as a law. Whoever, therefore, considers this, and that the King is sworn to preserve the Church of England establishment, must necessarily conclude, that whatever sentiments may obtain among the Episcopalians in America, our Kings and their Councils have always conceived that such establishment could by no means be extended to us. As to Connecticut, all the Episcopalians of that colony, and even their ministers, were legally compellable to contribute to an annual tax for the support of the Congregational clergy, till of late they were favoured with a law which grants them a privilege of exemption from that iniquitous and unreasonable burden. But whether they are subject to the like unchristian imposition in the other colonies abovementioned, I am not sufficiently acquainted with their laws to determine.*

The 13th number of the *Watch Tower* published at New-York

---

* I believe there is no just cause for the complaints transmited by the missionaries. Dr. Douglass assigns several instances of gross misrepresentations and falshoods.—*Vid* his *Summary*, 2d vol. p. 139. Boston edit. 1753, and the *Watch Tower*, N° XLI. published at New-York in 1755.

in 1755, espouses the same side with the authour of the *Reflector,* adds several new arguments and the opinions of eminent counsel at law, and considers the force of what is advanced by the late Dr. Douglass, in favour of his position, that the religious state of the American plantations is an universal toleration of Protestants of every denomination.

The clergy of this Province are, in general, but indifferently supported: it is true they live easily, but few of them leave any thing to their children. The Episcopal missionaries, for enlarging the sphere of their secular business, not many years ago attempted, by a petition to the late Governour Clinton, to engross the privilege of solemnizing all marriages. A great clamour ensued and the attempt was abortive. Before that time the ceremony was even performed by justices of the peace, and the judges at law have determined such marriages to be legal. The Governour's licenses now run to "All Protestant Ministers of the Gospel." Whether the justices act still, when the banns are published in our churches, which is customary only with the poor, I have not been informed. Marriage in a new country ought to have the highest encouragements, and it is on this account, perhaps, that we have no provincial law against such as are clandestine, though they often happen, and, in some cases, are attended with consequences equally melancholy and mischievous.

As to the number of our clergymen, it is large enough at present, there being but few settlements unsupplied with a ministry, and some superabound. In matters of religion we are not so intelligent, in general, as the inhabitants of the New-England colonies; but both in this respect and good morals, we certainly have the advantage of the southern provinces. One of the King's instructions to our governours, recommends the investigation of means for the conversion of Negroes and Indians. An attention to both, especially the latter, has been too little regarded. If the missionaries of the English Society for Propagating the Gospel, instead of being seated in opulent christianized towns, had been sent out to preach among the savages, unspeakable, political, advantages would have flowed from such a salutary measure. Dr. Douglass, a sensible, immethodical, writer, often incorrect, expects too much:* besides, he treats the

* "Our young Missionaries may procure a perpetual Alliance and commercial Advantages with the Indians, which the Roman Catholic Clergy cannot do, because they are forbid to marry. I mean our Mis-

missionaries with rudeness and contempt, and lashes their indolence with unmerciful acrimony.[24]

## Chapter V   *The* Political State

This colony, as a part of the King's dominions, is subject to the control of the British Parliament, but its more immediate government is vested in a Governour, Council, and General Assembly.

The Governours in Chief, who are always appointed by the King's Commission under the Great Seal of Great-Britain, enjoy a vast plenitude of power, as may be seen in their Patents, which are nearly the same. The following is a copy of that to the late Sir Danvers Osborn.

> *GEORGE* the Second by the Grace of God of *Great-Britain, France,* and *Ireland,* King, Defender of the Faith and so forth. To our trusty and well beloved Sir *Danvers Osborn,* Baronet, Greeting. Whereas we did by our Letters Patent under our Great Seal of *Great-Britain* bearing Date at *Westminster* the third Day of *July* in the fifteenth Year of our Reign constitute and appoint the honourable *George Clinton* Esq; Captain General and Governor in Chief in and over our Province of *New-York* and the Territories depending thereon in *America* for and during our Will and Pleasure as by the said recited Letters Patent (Relation being thereunto had) may more fully and at large appear Now know you that we have revoked and determined and by these Presents do revoke and determine the said recited Letters Patent and every Clause Article and Thing therein contained And further know you that we reposing especial Trust and Confidence in the Prudence Courage and Loyalty of you the said Sir *Danvers Osborn* of our especial Grace certain Knowledge and meer Motion have thought fit to constitute and appoint you the said Sir *Danvers Osborn* to be our Captain General and Governor in Chief in and over our Province of *New-York* and the Territories depending thereon in *America,* and we do hereby require and command you to do and execute all Things in

---

sionaries may intermarry with the Daughters of the Sachems, and other considerable Indians, and their Progeny will for ever be a certain Cement between us and the Indians." *Dougl. Sum.* &c. vol. II p. 138. Boston edit. 1753.

due Manner that shall belong unto your said Command and
the Trust we have reposed in you according to the several
Powers and Directions granted or appointed you by this
present Commission and the Instructions herewith given you
or by such further Powers, Instructions, and Authorities as
shall at any Time hereafter be granted or appointed you
under our Signet and Sign manual or by our Order in our
Privy Council and according to such reasonable Laws and
Statutes as now are in Force or hereafter shall be made and
agreed upon by you with the Advice and Consent of our
Council and the Assembly of our said Province under your
Government in such Manner and Form as is hereafter ex-
pressed and our Will and Pleasure is that you the said Sir
*Danvers Osborn* after the Publication of these our Letters
Patent do in the first Place take the Oaths appointed to be
taken by an Act passed in the first Year of our late royal
Father's Reign intitled an Act for the further Security of his
Majesty's Person and Government and the Succession of the
Crown in the Heirs of the late Princess *Sophia* being Prot-
estants and for extinguishing the Hopes of the pretended
Prince of *Wales* and his open and secret Abettors as also that
you make and subscribe the Declaration mentioned in an
Act of Parliament made in the twenty-fifth Year of the Reign
of King *Charles* the Second intituled an Act for preventing
Dangers which may happen from Popish Recusants and likewise that you take the usual Oath for the due Execution of
the Office and Trust of our Captain General and Governor
in Chief in and over our said Province of *New-York* and the
Territories depending thereon for the due and impartial Administration of Justice, and further that you take the Oath
required to be taken by Governors of Plantations to do their
utmost that the several Laws relating to Trade and the
Plantations be observed, which said Oaths and Declaration
our Council in our said Province or any three of the Members thereof have hereby full Power and Authority and are
required to tender and administer unto you and in your Absence to our Lieutenant Governor if there be any upon the
Place.[25] All which being duly performed you shall administer unto each of the Members of our said Council as also to
our Lieutenant Governor if there be any upon the Place the
Oaths mentioned in the said Act entituled an Act for the
further Security of his Majesty's Person and Government
and the Succession of the Crown in the Heirs of the late Princess *Sophia* being Protestants and for extinguishing the Hopes
of the pretended Prince of *Wales* and his open and secret
Abettors as also to cause them to make and subscribe the

aforementioned Declaration and to administer to them the Oath for the due Execution of their Places and Trusts. And we do hereby give and grant unto you full Power and Authority to suspend any of the Members of our said Council from siting, voting, and assisting therein if you shall find just Cause for so doing and, if there shall be any Lieutenant Governor, him likewise to suspend from the Execution of his Command and to appoint another in his Stead until our Pleasure be known and if it shall at any Time happen that by the Death, Departure out of our said Province, or Suspension of any of our said Councillors or otherwise there shall be a Vacancy in our said Council (any three whereof we do hereby appoint to be a Quorum) our Will and Pleasure is that you signify the same unto us by the first Opportunity that we may under our Signet and Sign manual constitute and appoint others in their Stead. But that our Affairs may not suffer at that Distance for want of a due Number of Councillors, if ever it should happen that there be less than seven of them residing in our said Province, we do hereby give and grant unto you, the said Sir *Danvers Osborn*, full Power and Authority to chuse as many Persons out of the principal Freeholders Inhabitants thereof as will make up the full Number of our said Council to be seven and no more, which Persons so chosen and appointed by you shall be to all Intents and Purposes Councillors in our said Province until either they shall be confirmed by us or that by the Nomination of others by us under our Sign manual and Signet our said Council shall have seven or more Persons in it. And we do hereby give and grant unto you full Power and Authority, with the Advice and Consent of our said Council from Time to Time as Need shall require, to summon and call general Assemblies of the said Freeholders and Planters within your Government according to the Usage of our Province of *New-York*. And our Will and Pleasure is that the Persons thereupon duly elected by the major Part of the Freeholders of the respective Counties and Places and so returned shall before their Sitting take the Oaths mentioned in the said Act intitled (an Act for the further Security of his Majesty's Person and Government and the Succession of the Crown in the Heirs of the late Princess *Sophia* being Protestants and for extinguishing the Hopes of the pretended Prince of *Wales* and his open and secret Abettors) as also make and subscribe the aforementioned Declaration (which Oaths and Declarations you shall commissionate fit Persons under our Seal of *New-York* to tender and administer unto them) and until the same shall be so taken and subscribed

no Person shall be capable of sitting though elected. And we
do hereby declare that the Persons so elected and qualified
shall be called and deemed the general Assembly of that our
Province and the Territories depending thereon And you the
said Sir *Danvers Osborn* by and with the Consent of our said
Council and Assembly or the major Part of them respectively
shall have full Power and Authority to make constitute and
ordain Laws, Statutes, and Ordinances for the public Peace,
Welfare, and good Government of our said Province and of
the People and Inhabitants thereof and such others as shall
resort thereto and for the Benefit of us, our Heirs and Successors, which said Laws, Statutes, and Ordinances are not
to be repugnant but as near as may be agreeable to the Laws
and Statutes of this our Kingdom of *Great-Britain*, provided
that all such Laws, Statutes, and Ordinances of what Nature
or Duration soever be within three Months or sooner after
the making thereof transmitted unto us under our Seal of
*New-York* for our Approbation or Disallowance of the same
as also Duplicates thereof by the next Conveyance and in
Case any or all of the said Laws, Statutes, and Ordinances
being not before confirmed by us shall at any Time be disallowed and not approved and so signified by us our Heirs or
Successors under our or their Sign manual and Signet or by
Order of our or their Privy Council unto you, the said Sir
*Danvers Osborn* or to the Commander in Chief of our said
Province for the Time being, then such and so many of the
said Laws Statutes and Ordinances as shall be so disallowed
and not approved shall from thenceforth cease determine
and become utterly void and of none Effect, any Thing to
the contrary thereof notwithstanding. And to the End that
nothing may be passed or done by our said Council or Assembly to the Prejudice of us, our Heirs, or Successors, we
will and ordain that you the said Sir *Danvers Osborn* shall
have and enjoy a negative Voice in the making and passing
of all Laws, Statutes, and Ordinances as aforesaid and you
shall and may likewise from Time to Time as you shall judge
it necessary adjourn prorogue and dissolve all general Assemblies as aforesaid. And our further Will and Pleasure is
that you shall and may use and keep the public Seal of our
said Province of *New-York* for sealing all Things whatsoever
that pass the Great Seal of our said Province under your
Government And we do further give and grant unto you the
said Sir *Danvers Osborn* full Power and Authority from Time
to Time and at any Time hereafter by yourself or by any
other to be authorized by you in that Behalf to administer
and give the aforementioned Oaths to all and every such Per-

son and Persons as you shall think fit who shall at any Time
or Times pass into our said Province or shall be resident or
abiding there. And we do further by these Presents give and
grant unto you, the said Sir *Danvers Osborn,* full Power and
Authority with the Advice and Consent of our said Council
to erect constitute and establish such and so many Courts of
Judicature and public Justice within our said Province under
your Government as you and they shall think fit and necessary for the hearing and determining of all Causes as well
criminal as civil according to Law and Equity and for award-
ing Execution thereupon with all reasonable and necessary
Powers, Authorities, Fees, and Privileges belonging thereunto, as also to appoint and commissionate fit Persons in the
several Parts of your Government to administer the Oaths
mentioned in the aforesaid Act intitled an Act for the further
Security of his Majesty's Person and Government and the
Succession of the Crown in the Heirs of the late Princess
*Sophia* being Protestants and for extinguishing the Hopes of
the pretended Prince of *Wales* and his open and secret
Abettors, as also to tender and administer the aforesaid
Declaration unto such Persons belonging to the said Courts
as shall be obliged to take the same. And we do hereby
authorize and impower you to constitute and appoint Judges,
and, in Cases requisite, Commissioners of Oyer and Terminer,
Justices of the Peace, and other necessary Officers and Ministers in our said Province for the better Administration of
Justice and putting the Laws in Execution, and to administer or cause to be administered unto them such Oath or
Oaths as are usually given for the due Execution and Performance of Offices and Places and for the clearing of Truth
in judicial Causes. And we do hereby give and grant unto
you full Power and Authority where you shall see Cause or
shall judge any Offender or Offenders in criminal Matters
or for any Fines or Forfeitures due unto us fit Objects of our
Mercy to pardon all such Offenders and to remit all such
Offences, Fines, and Forfeitures (Treason and wilful Murder
only excepted) in which Cases you shall likewise have Power
upon extraordinary Occasions to grant Reprieves to the Offenders until and to the Intent our royal Pleasure may be
known therein.[26] And we do by these Presents authorize and
impower you to collate any Person or Persons to any
Churches, Chapels, or other ecclesiastical Benefices within
our said Province and Territories aforesaid as often as any
of them shall happen to be void. And we do hereby give and
grant unto you the said Sir *Danvers Osborn* by yourself or by
your Captains and Commanders by you to be authorized, full

Power and Authority to levy, arm, muster, command, and employ all Persons whatsoever residing within our said Province of *New-York* and other the Territories under your Government, and as Occasion shall serve to march from one Place to another to to embark them for the resisting and withstanding of all Enemies, Pirates, and Rebels, both at Sea and Land and to transport such Forces to any of our Plantations in *America* if Necessity shall require for the Defence of the same against the Invasions or Attempts of any of our Enemies and such Enemies Pirates and Rebels if there shall be Occasion to pursue and prosecute in or out of the Limits of our said Province and Plantations or any of them and if it shall so please God, them to vanquish, apprehend, and take, and being taken either according to Law to put to Death or keep and preserve alive at your Discretion and to execute martial Law in Time of Invasion or other Times when by Law it may be executed and to do and execute all and every other Thing and Things which to our Captain General and Governor in Chief doth or ought of Right to belong. And we do hereby give and grant unto you full Power and Authority by and with the Advice and Consent of our said Council to erect raise and build in our said Province of *New-York* and the Territories depending thereon such and so many Forts and Platforms, Castles, Cities, Boroughs, Towns and Fortifications as you by the Advice aforesaid shall judge necessary and the same or any of them to fortify and furnish with Ordnance, Ammunition, and all Sorts of Arms fit and necessary for the Security and Defence of our said Province and by the Advice aforesaid the same again or any of them to demolish or dismantle as may be most convenient. And foreasmuch as divers Mutinies and Disorders may happen by Persons shipped and employed at Sea during the Time of War and to the End that such as shall be shipped and employed at Sea during the Time of War may be better governed and ordered we do hereby give and grant unto you, the said Sir *Danvers Osborn,* full Power and Authority to constitute and appoint Captains, Lieutenants, Masters of Ships, and other Commanders and Officers and to grant to such Captains, Lieutenants, Masters of Ships, and other Commanders and Officers Commissions to execute the Law martial during the Time of War according to the Directions of two Acts, the one passed in the thirteenth Year of the Reign of King *Charles* the Second, entituled an Act for the establishing Articles and Orders for the regulating and better Government of his Majesty's Navies, Ships of War, and Forces by Sea, and the other passed in the eighteenth Year of our Reign

entituled an Act for the further regulating and better Government of his Majesty's Navies Ships of War and Forces by
Sea and for regulating Proceedings upon Courts Martial in
the Sea Service and to use such Proceedings, Authorities,
Punishments, Corrections, and Executions upon any Offender
or Offenders who shall be mutinous seditious disorderly or
any Way unruly either at Sea or during the Time of their
Abode or Residence in any of the Ports, Harbours, or Bays
of our said Province and Territories as the Case shall be
found to require according to the martial Law and the said
Direction during the Time of War as aforesaid, Provided that
nothing herein contained shall be construed to the enabling
you or any by your Authority to hold Plea or have any Jurisdiction of any Offences, Cause, Matter, or Thing committed or done upon the high Sea or within any of the
Havens, Rivers, or Creeks of our said Province and Territories
under your Government by any Captain, Commander, Lieutenant, Master, Officer, Seaman, Soldier, or other Person
whatsoever who shall be in our actual Service and Pay in
or on Board any of our Ships of War or other Vessels acting
by immediate Commission or Warrant from our Commissioners for executing the Office of our High Admiral or from
our High Admiral of *Great-Britain* for the Time being under
the Seal of our Admiralty but that such Captain, Commander, Lieutenant, Master, Officer, Seaman, Soldier, or
other Person so offending shall be left to be proceeded against
and tried as their Offences shall require either by Commission under our Great Seal of *Great-Britain* as the Statute
of the twenty-eighth of *Henry* the Eighth directs, or by Commission from our said Commissioners for executing the Office
of our High Admiral or from our High Admiral of *Great-
Britain* for the Time being according to the aforementioned
Acts. Provided nevertheless that all Disorders and Misdemeanors committed on Shore by any Captain, Commander,
Lieutenant, Master, Officer, Seaman, Soldier, or other Person whatsoever belonging to any of our Ships of War or other
Vessels acting by immediate Commission or Warrant from
our said Commissioners for executing the Office of our High
Admiral or from our High Admiral of *Great-Britain* for the
Time being under the Seal of our Admiralty may be tried
and punished according to the Laws of the Place where any
such Disorders, Offences, and Misdemeanors, shall be committed on Shore notwithstanding such Offenders be in our
actual Service and born in our Pay on Board any such our
Ships of War or other Vessels acting by immediate Commission or Warrant from our said Commissioners for execut-

ing the Office of our High Admiral or from our High Admiral
of *Great-Britain* for the Time being as aforesaid so as he
shall not receive any Protection for the avoiding of Justice
for such Offences committed on Shore from any Pretence of
his being employed in our Service at Sea. And our further
Will and Pleasure is that all public Monies raised or which
shall be raised by any Act to be hereafter made within our
said Province and other the Territories depending thereon be
issued out by Warrant from you by and with the Advice and
Consent of our Council and disposed of by you for the Support of the Government and not otherwise And we do hereby
likewise give and grant unto you full Power and Authority
by and with the Advice and Consent of our said Council to
settle and agree with the Inhabitants of our Province and
Territories aforesaid for such Lands, Tenements, and Heredi-
taments, as now are or hereafter shall be in our Power to
dispose of and them to grant to any Person or Persons upon
such Terms and under such moderate Quitrents, Services,
and Acknowledgments, to be thereupon reserved unto us as
you, by and with the Advice aforesaid shall think fit, which
said Grants are to pass and be sealed by our Seal of *New-
York,* and being entered upon Record by such Officer or
Officers as are or shall be appointed thereunto shall be good
and effectual in the Law against us, our Heirs, and Successors. And we do hereby give you, the said Sir *Danvers Osborn,*
full Power to order and appoint Fairs, Marts, and Markets,
as also such and so many Ports, Harbours, Bays, Havens,
and other Places for the Convenience and Security of Ship-
ping and for the better loading and unloading of Goods and
Merchandizes as by you with the Advice and Consent of our
said Council shall be thought fit and necessary.[27] And we do
hereby require and command all Officers and Ministers,
civil, military, and all other Inhabitants of our said Province
and Territories depending thereon to be obedient, aiding and
assisting unto you the said Sir *Danvers Osborn* in the Execution of this our Commission and the Powers and Authorities
herein contained; and in Case of your Death or Absence out
of our said Province and Territories depending thereon, to be
obedient, aiding and assisting unto such Person as shall be
appointed by us to be our Lieutenant Governor or Commander in Chief of our said Province, to whom we do therefore by these Presents give and grant all and singular the
Powers and Authorities herein granted to be by him executed and enjoyed during our Pleasure or until your Arrival
within our said Province and Territories; and if, upon your
Death or Absence out of our said Province and Territories,

depending thereon there be no Person upon the Place commissioned or appointed by us to be our Lieutenant Governor
or Commander in Chief of our said Province, our Will and
Pleasure is that the eldest Counsellor whose Name is first
placed in our said Instructions to you and who shall at the
Time of your Death or Absence be residing within our said
Province of *New-York* shall take upon him the Administration of the Government and execute our said Commission
and Instructions and the several Powers and Authorities
therein contained in the same Manner and to all Intents and
Purposes as other our Governor and Commander in Chief of
our said Province should or ought to do in Case of your Absence until your Return or in all Cases until our further
Pleasure be known therein and we do hereby declare, ordain, and appoint that you the said Sir *Danvers Osborn* shall
and may hold, execute, and enjoy the Office and Place of our
Captain General and Governor in Chief in and over our Province of *New-York* and the Territories depending thereon, together with all and singular the Powers and Authorities
hereby granted unto you for and during our Will and Pleasure. And whereas there are divers Colonies adjoining to our
Province of *New-York* for the Defence and Security whereof,
it is requisite that due Care be taken in Time of War, we have
therefore thought it necessary for our Service and for the
better Protection and Security of our Subjects inhabiting
those Parts to constitute and appoint and we do by these
Presents constitute and appoint you, the said Sir *Danvers
Osborn,* to be our Captain General and Commander in Chief
of the Militia and of all the Forces by Sea and Land within
our Colony of *Connecticut* and of all our Forts and Places of
Strength within the same and for the better ordering, governing, and ruling our said Militia, and all our Forces, Forts,
and Places of Strength within our said Colony of *Connecticut,*
we do hereby give and grant unto you, the said Sir *Danvers
Osborn* and in your Absence to our Commander in Chief of
our Province of *New-York,* all and every the like Powers as in
these Presents are before granted and recited for the ruling,
governing, and ordering our Militia and all our Forces, Forts,
and Places of Strength within our Province of *New-York,*
to be exercised by you, the said Sir *Danvers Osborn* and in
your Absence from our Territories and Dominion of *New-
York* by our Commander in Chief of our Province of *New-
York* within our said Colony of *Connecticut,* for and during
our Pleasure. In Witness whereof we have caused these our
Letters to be made Patent, witness ourself at *Westminster,*

the first Day of *August* in the twenty-seventh Year of our Reign.

*By Writ of Privy Seal,*
YORKE *and* YORKE

The Instructions, received with the Commission, are explanatory of the Patent, and regulate the Governour's conduct on almost every common contingency.*

The salary generally granted to the Governour by the Instructions is £1200 sterling out of the revenue here; but that being an insufficient fund, the Assembly in lieu of it, give him annually £1560 currency. The perquisites perhaps amount to as much more.

This office was formerly very lucrative, but becomes daily less considerable, because almost all the valuable tracts of land are already taken up.

The Council, when full, consists of twelve members appointed by the King's Mandamus and Sign Manual. All their privileges and powers are contained in the Instructions. They are a Privy Council to the Governour, in acts of civil government; and take the same oath administered to the King's Council in England. The tenure of their places is extremely precarious, and yet their influence upon the publick measures very considerable. In the grant of all patents the Governour is bound to consult them, and regularly they cannot pass the Seal without their advice.

They enjoy a legislative power, as the Lords do in Parliament; and exercise also judicial authority upon writs of errour and appeals. They are convened by the Governour, and he is always present when they sit as a court or Privy Council, which is ordinarily at the fort. In their legislative capacity they meet without the Governour, and always at the City Hall. They sit according to their seniority, and the eldest member present is Speaker of their House. In a committee the chairman has no voice. They cannot vote by proxy, but have the privilege of entering their dissent, and the reasons at large, on their minutes. Their proceedings are very formal, and in many respects they imitate the example of the Lords. Their messages to the Assembly are carried by one of their own members, and the

---

* The Instructions are, in number, above a hundred and never recorded. They are changeable at the King's pleasure, but rarely undergo any very considerable alteration.

House always rises at his entrance and receives them standing. The Council never publish their legislative minutes, but the Assembly always print their own votes, nor do either of these Houses permit strangers to be present at their conventions.[28]

A counsellor's title is *The Honourable*. They serve his Majesty without salaries. The business of the Privy Council Board is of late very much increased, and never had so great weight in the colony as at present; which is much owing to the King's calling lawyers of reputation to the assistance of his Governours. The present members are the honourable

| | |
|---|---|
| Cadwallader Colden, | Joseph Murray, |
| Archibald Kennedy, | John Rutherford, |
| James De Lancey* Lieutenant Governour, | Edward Holland, |
| | Sir William Johnson, Bart. |
| Daniel Horsmanden, | John Chambers, |
| George Clarke, jun. | William Smith. |

The business in Council daily increases, and is now become very burdensome, being entirely transacted by a few members. Mr. Colden resides in the country; Mr. Clarke in England; Mr. Rutherford, being an officer, moves with the army, and Sir William Johnson has his residence, in the Western part of the county of Albany.

The General Assembly consists of twenty-seven representatives chosen by the people, in pursuance of a writ of summons issued by the Governour.[29]

At the day appointed for their appearance, such as are elected convene themselves at the Assembly-Chamber, in the city of New-York; and, by the clerk of the House, inform the Governour of their meeting. If they are above thirteen in number, some persons (generally the judges of the Supreme Court) are sent to the Assembly-Chamber empowered by a commission to take their oaths and subscriptions. They are then called before his Excellency, who recommends their choice of a speaker. For that purpose they again retire, and conduct the person they elect into the Chair, which is seated at the upper end of a long table. After that he is presented to his Excellency, in the Council-Chamber; and upon his approbation of their choice, which is of course, the Speaker addresses himself to the Governour,

---

* The office of Lieutenant Governour requires no service, except on the death or in the absence of a Governour in Chief. It gives no rank in Council, nor is there any salary annexed to it.

and in behalf of the House prays, "That their Words and Actions may have a favourable Construction, that the Members may have free Access to him, and they and their Servants be privileged with a Freedom from Arrests." The Governour, after promising these things on his part, reads his speech to both Houses; and, at the request of the Speaker, delivers a copy for the use of the Assembly.

I need not enlarge upon the customs of the General Assembly, for they take the practice of the British House of Commons for their model, and vary from them in but very few instances. Money bills are not returned to them by the Council Board, as the Lords do to the Commons; and yet the reasons for this practice are much stronger here than at home. When the Governour passes the bills sent up to him, both Houses are present in the Council-Chamber. It is then customary for him to ask the advice of his Council with respect to every bill, and he signs them at the foot after these words, "I assent to this Bill, enacting the same, and order it to be enrolled." After that the acts are published in the open street, near the City Hall; his Excellency and the two Houses being present.

The daily wages of the representatives, as regulated by sundry Acts of Assembly, are annexed to the following list of the present members of the House. [See p. 257; Ed.]

The continuance of our Assemblies was unlimited, till the political struggles, which took rise in Mr. Cosby's administration, forced Mr. Clarke, who succeeded him, to pass the act restricting them to three years; but this was repealed by the King, and a septennial law enacted soon after the arrival of Governour Clinton, which is still in full force.

No colony, upon the continent, has formerly suffered more than ours, in the opinion of the King's ministers. This has been owing to the ill impressions made by our Governours, who are scarce ever disengaged from disputes with the lower House. Our representatives, agreeable to the general sense of their constituents, are tenacious in their opinion, that the inhabitants of this colony are entitled to all the privileges of Englishmen; that they have a right to participate in the legislative power, and that the session of Assemblies here, is wisely substituted instead of a representation in Parliament, which, all things considered, would, at this remote distance, be extremely inconvenient and dangerous. The Governours, on the other hand, in general, entertain political sentiments of a quite different nature. All the immunities we enjoy, according to them, not only

For the City and County of
New-York

Paul Richard,
Henry Cruger,     } Esqrs; each
William Walton,   } 6 s. per
John Watts,       } diem

City and County of Albany

Peter Winne, } Esqrs; 10 s. per
Peter Douw,  } diem

West-Chester County

John Thomas,        } Esqrs; 6 s.
Frederick Philipse, } per diem

Suffolk County

Eleazer Miller,  } Esqrs; 9 s.
William Nicoll,  } per diem

Queen's County

David Jones,    } Esqrs; 6 s.
Thomas Cornel,  } per diem

King's County

Johannes Lott,   } Esqrs; 6 s.
Dominicus        } per diem
  Vanderveer,    }

Ulster County

Johannes Jansen, } Esqrs; 6 s.
Moses De Pew,    } per diem
  jun.           }

Richmond County

William Walton, } Esqrs; 6 s.
Benjamin        } per diem
  Seaman,       }

Dutchess County

Henry Beekman, } Esqrs; 6 s.
Henry Filkin,  } per diem

Orange County

Theodorus      } Esqrs; 6 s.
  Snediker,    } per diem
Samuel Gale,   }

Borough of West-Chester

Peter De Lancey, Esq; 10 s.
per diem

Township of Schenectady

Jacobus Mynderse, Esq; 10 s.
per diem

Manor of Renslaerwyck

John B. V. Renslaer, Esq; 10 s.
per diem

Manor of Livingston

Robert Livingston, jun. Esq;
10 s. per diem

Manor of Courtlandt

Philip Ver Plank, Esq; 6 s.
per diem

flow from, but absolutely depend upon, the mere grace and will
of the Crown.* It is easy to conceive, that contentions must

---

* "We are no more than a little Corporation.—I would advise these
Gentlemen (Assemblies) for the future, to drop those Parliamentary
Airs and Style about Liberty and Property, and keep within their
Sphere, and make the best Use they can of his Majesty's Instructions
and Commission; because it would be high Treason to sit and act
without it.—This is our Charter. If we abuse or make a wicked Use
of his Majesty's Favours, we are, of them, but Tenants at Will; we
only hold them during Pleasure and good Behaviour."—These are the
accurate and bright thoughts of the gentleman [Archibald Kennedy]
who published a pamphlet, entitled, *An Essay on the Government of
the Colonies*, in 1752. Sir William Jones, Attorney-General to James
II. was of a very different opinion. For he told the King, "That he

naturally attend such a contradiction of sentiments. Most of our disputes, however, relate to the support of government. Before Lord Cornbury's embezzlements, the revenue was established for a long period, but afterwards reduced to a few years. The violent measures, in Mr. Cosby's time, led the Assembly to the scheme of an annual provision. These are the words of that much famed address of the House, to Lieutenant Governour Clarke, on the 8th of September 1737, previous to the change.

The true Causes of the Deficiency of the Revenue, we believe are too well known to your Honour, to make it necessary for us to say much on that Head. Had the conspicuous Loyalty of the Inhabitants of this Province, met with a suitable Treatment in Return: it is not unlikely, but we should now be weak enough to act like others before us, in being lavish beyond our Abilities, and raising Sums unnecessary to be given; and continued the Donation, like them, for a longer Time than what was convenient for the Safety of the Inhabitants: but Experience has shewn the Imprudence of such a Conduct, and the miserable Condition to which the Province is reduced, renders the raising of large Sums very difficult if not impracticable. We therefore beg Leave to be plain with your Honour, and hope you will not take it amiss, when we tell you, that you are not to expect, that we either will raise Sums unfit to be raised; or put what we shall raise into the Power of a Governour to misapply, if we can prevent it: nor shall we make up any other Deficiencies, than what we conceive are fit and just to be paid; or continue what Support or Revenue we shall raise, for any longer Time than one Year. Nor do we think it convenient to do even that, until such Laws are passed, as we conceive necessary for the Safety of the Inhabitants of this Colony, who have reposed a Trust in us for that only Purpose; and which we are sure you will think it reasonable we should act agreeable to, and by the Grace of God we will endeavour not to deceive them.

The sentiments of this address still prevail among the people, and therefore the success of the present solicitations, for a permanent, indefinite, support, will probably be in vain.

---

could no more grant a Commission to levy Money on his Subjects in the Plantations, without their Consent by an Assembly, than they could discharge themselves from their Allegiance." *Life of Sir William Phips*, p. 23.

The matter has been often litigated with great fervency on both sides, and the example of the British Parliament urged as a precedent for our imitation. To this it is answered, that the particular state of this Province differs so widely from that of their mother country, that we ought not in this respect to follow the custom of the Commons. Our constitution, as some observe, is so imperfect in numberless instances, that the rights of the people lie, even now, at the mere mercy of their Governours; and granting a perpetual support, it is thought, would be in reality little less, than the loss of every thing dear to them.

It must be confessed that many plausible arguments may be assigned, in support of the jealousy of the House. A Governour has numberless opportunities, not proper to be mentioned, for invading the rights of the people, and insuperable difficulties would necessarily attend all the means of redress.

By gradual advances, at seasonable junctures, we might have introduced such amendments, as would at this day have established a sound and well fortified political frame; but through our utter neglect of education, the ancient Assemblies consisted of plain, illiterate, husbandmen, whose views seldom extended farther than to the regulation of highways, the destruction of wolves, wildcats, and foxes, and the advancement of the other little interests of the particular counties, which they were chosen to represent.[30]

---

## Chapter VI   *Of our Laws and Courts*

The state of our laws opens a door to much controversy. The uncertainty with respect to them renders property precarious, and greatly exposes us to the arbitrary decisions of bad judges. The common law of England is generally received, together with such statutes, as were enacted before we had a legislature of our own. But our courts exercise a sovereign authority, in determining what parts of the common and statute law ought to be extended; for it must be admitted, that the difference of circumstances necessarily requires us, in some cases, to reject the determinations of both. In many instances they have also extended, as I have elsewhere observed, even Acts of Parliament, passed since we have had a distinct legislation, which is adding greatly to our confusion. The practice of our courts is not less uncertain than the law. Some of the English rules are adopted and others rejected.[31] Two things therefore seem to be absolutely necessary for the publick security.

First, the passing an act for settling the extent of the English laws. And,

Secondly, that the courts ordain a general set of rules for the regulation of the practice.

To give a particular account of our laws civil and criminal, cannot be expected in this work. All lands are held of the Crown by socage tenure, as those of East-Greenwich, at home, in the county of Kent; and the manner of obtaining a title to such as are vacant, or in the possession of the Indians, is this:

Formerly the custom was to apply to the Governour in Council, for a license to purchase lands of the natives in his Majesty's name. A deed was then privately obtained from the Indian Proprietors to the King, and annexed to a second petition to the Governour, for a warrant to the Surveyor-General, to make a survey of the quantity purchased. Another warrant, upon the return of the survey, was then issued to the Attorney-General, to prepare a draught of the Patent; which being transmitted to the Secretary's Office, was then engrossed upon parchment, and the Great Seal affixed to it by the Governour.

In these surveys and deeds more lands were often included, than the Indians intended to sell; and these frauds being frequently complained of, an order was made by the Governour and Council, in 1736, that thenceforth no Indian deed should be taken, until the land proposed to be granted, was actually surveyed by the Surveyor-General, or one of his deputies, in the presence of the Indian Proprietors: that the bounds of the tract should be then entered in the deed, and a certificate endorsed, that they are agreeable to the survey, and that he saw the consideration money or goods, *bona fide*, delivered to the vendors.[32]

The patenting of lands, has long been, and still continues to be, very expensive.

Our law judicatories are numerous; I begin with the lowest.

## Of the Justices Court

Justices of the peace are appointed by commission from the Governours, who, to serve their purposes in elections, sometimes grant, as it is called, the Administration to particular favourites in each county, which is the nomination of officers civil and military; and by these means, the justices have been astonishingly multiplied. There are instances of some who can neither write nor read.* These genii,[33] besides their ordinary powers, are by Acts of Assembly enabled to hold courts, for the determination of small causes of five pounds and under; but the parties are privileged, if they choose it, with a jury of six men. The proceedings are in a summary way, and the conduct of the justices has given just cause to innumerable complaints. The justices have also a jurisdiction, with respect to crimes under the degree of grand larceny. For any three of them (one being of the quorum) may try the criminal, without a jury, and inflict punishments not extending to life or limb.

## The Sessions and Court of Common-Pleas

The Court of Common-Pleas takes cognizance of all causes, where the matter in demand is in value above five pounds. It is established by an ordinance of the Governour in Council. The judges are ordinarily three, and hold their offices during pleasure. Through the infancy of the country, few, if any of them, are acquainted with the law. The practice of these courts is similar to that of the Common-Bench at Westminster. They have each a clerk commissioned by the Governour, who issues their writs, enters their minutes, and keeps the records of the county. They are held twice every year. These judges, together with some of the justices, hold, at the same time, a Court of General Sessions of the Peace.

## The Supreme Court

The jurisdiction of this court extends through the whole Province, and its powers are very great. For it takes cognizance of all causes civil and criminal, as fully as the King's-Bench and Common-Pleas at Westminster. In civil controversies, the value of the sum demanded must exceed twenty pounds. This court has four terms in a year, and always sits at New-York.† The judges, for many years past, have been but three. The Chief Justice has ten shillings as a perquisite, upon the first motion

* Lord Bacon's observation, that there are many who count it a credit to be burdened with the office of a justice of the peace, is very applicable to us. *Bacon's Works*, fol. Vol. II. p. 151.—The Statute of 38 Hen. VIII limited the number of justices to eight in a county.

† The terms commence on the third Tuesdays in January, April, and October, and on the last in July. The first and the last continue five days, and the two other terms ten.

in every cause, together with an annual allowance of £300. The second and third justices have also yearly appointments, too inconsiderable to be worth mentioning. They hold their offices by separate commissions under the Great Seal of the Province, which were formerly during pleasure, but of late *quàm diu se bene gesserint.*\*34

The Supreme Court was, at first, established by several laws of the Province; but the terms were, afterwards, directed by an ordinance of the Governour and Council, which is alterable at pleasure.35

Whether this court has a right to determine causes in a course of equity, was a question much litigated, during the troubles in the several administrations of Mr. Cosby and Mr. Clarke. Colonel Morris, afterwards Governour of New-Jersey, sat then as Chief Justice upon the Bench, and delivered a long, argumentative, opinion in the negative.† The people were, in general, on that side, and the Exchequer Court bell scarce ever rung, but the city was all in confusion. Petitions against the Court, from several parts of the Province, came up to the Assembly, who desired to hear Council; and accordingly Mr. Smith36 and Mr. Murray, delivered their opinions at their request, both which were afterwards printed by their order. The former, who spoke first, urged numerous authorities, to prove that no court of equity could be legally established except by prescription or an act of the legislature, and concluded with these words—

> 'Tis with the greatest Submission that I tender my Opinion upon these Points.—I have said nothing with a Design to offend any Man, nor have I omitted saying any Thing, that I thought might tend to the publick Good. *Liberavi Animam meam.* I have endeavoured to discharge the Trust, and support the Character, with which this House has honoured me. You have my sincere and real Sentiments. If I have erred in any Thing, it has been unwillingly. I am heartily a Friend to this Colony, and earnestly wish its Prosperity. I have no In-

---

\* Prosecutions, by information, are often commenced in the Supreme Court by order of the Governour and Council, and criminals sometimes committed by their warrants; for which reason some are of opinion, that the judges ought not to be members of that Board, which is frequently the case.

† See the printed opinion, and the arguments of Messieurs Alexander and Smith for the defendant Van Dam *adsectum* the Attorney-General; in support of a plea to the jurisdiction of the Supreme Court, on a bill filed there for Governour Cosby in a course of equity. *New-York* printed by John P. Zenger, 1733.

terest in the Points in Question, but what are common to all
the Freemen of this Province. I profess the greatest Venera-
tion for the Laws of my Country, and am glad of every Opportunity to do them publick Honour. They place our Liberties
upon the firmest Basis, and put our Properties under the
surest Protection. I rejoice in the Security that we have of a
long Enjoyment of them, by the Settlement of the Succession
in the House of *Hanover.*—'Tis the Excellency of our Constitution, and the Glory of our Princes, that they are sovereign
over Freemen, and not Slaves. 'Tis the Misery of an arbitrary
Government, that a Man can enjoy nothing under it, that he
can call his own. Life, Liberty, and Property, are not his, but
all at the Will and Disposal of his tyrannical Owner. I don't
wonder that our Ancestors have been always so jealous of
their Liberties: How oft have they bravely fought, and nobly
died, in the Defence of them? We have received our Liberties
and our Laws, as an Inheritance transmitted to us in the
Blood of our Fathers. How highly therefore should we prize
and value them! And what Care should we take, that we and
our Posterity may enjoy them in their full Extent? If this be
our happy Case, *we shall sit under our own Vines and our
own Fig-trees, and none will make us afraid.* We shall see our
Country flourish, and ourselves a happy People. But if an
arbitrary Power over our Liberties and Properties be let in
upon us, but at a *back Door*, it will certainly drive many of
us out of our Habitations; and 'tis to be feared, will once
more reduce our Country to a Wilderness, and a Land without Inhabitant: which we doubt not but this *honourable
House* will take Care to prevent.

Mr. Murray laboured to show that the Chancery, King's-Bench,
Common-Pleas and Exchequer, were of original jurisdiction by
the Constitution of England; and was fearful that our establishment of these courts here by an Act of Assembly, would draw
into question our equal rights to all the liberties and privileges
of Englishmen. He closed his opinion in this manner:

And now, Mr. Speaker, I have in the best Manner that I
was capable of, performed what this honourable House desired of me, in giving truly my Sentiments upon the Subject
Matter of these Petitions.

Mr. *Smith*, in delivering his Sentiments last *Friday*, did in
so handsome and elegant a Manner, fully prove that the People of this Colony are undoubtedly entitled to the Customs,
Laws, Liberties, and Privileges of *Englishmen*, that it was
needless for me to attempt the Proof thereof, which otherwise

I should have done. But I do entirely agree with him, in all that he said on that Head; and I hope I have proved that the fundamental Courts, by the Laws of *England,* are as much Part of those Liberties and Privileges, and as much by the Customs and Laws of *England,* as any other of their Liberties and Privileges are; and of Consequence, the People here as much entituled to those fundamental Courts, as to their other Privileges; and have endeavoured to answer all the Objections that I had heard were, or thought could be, made against our being entituled to the same Courts. And upon the whole thereof, as there has been much talked about the Liberties and Privileges of the People, I would beg Leave only to propound this one Question, who is he that argues most in Favour of the Liberties of the People? He who affirms and proves, that they are entituled to those Liberties and Privileges, Laws and Customs of *England,* and the good old original Courts, that are by those Laws, without an Act? or, he who argues and says, we are not entitled to them, until an Act is passed to establish them? I suppose the Answer would be given, without Hesitation, in Favour of the former.

But, Mr. Speaker, if it yet should be said, that there is a Necessity for making Acts relating to those Courts, I would beg Leave to offer to this honourable House, the Imitation of such Laws relating to those Courts, as the wise Legislature of *England* have thought fit to make. I presume, it will not be said, there can be a better Pattern offered for the Assembly to go by. And it is not to be supposed, but that the Parliament at Home has made all the Regulations therein that can be thought necessary; whereas going into new Schemes and new Inventions, may be attended with many Inconveniences, which, when they happen, may not be so easily remedied.

And I beg Leave to conclude, by praying that God Almighty may guide, direct, and influence this honourable House, in their Debates and Consultations upon this momentuous Affair, and that the End thereof may be for the Good of all the Inhabitants of this Colony.

The opposition, to the Exchequer, became now stronger than before the Council were heard. And therefore, under these discouragements, the Court has taken cognizance of no causes since Van Dam's nor has that indeed ever been determined.*

* Sir John Randolph wrote his sentiments concerning these disputes to Captain Pearse. And as he was an eminent lawyer in Virginia I doubt not his letter will be acceptable to the reader.
SIR,
By your Request, I have perused and considered the Arguments of Mr. *Smith* and Mr. *Murray,* before the General Assembly of

The judges of this court, according to an Act of Assembly, are judges of *Nisi Prius* of course; and, agreeable to an ordinance of the Governour and Council, perform a circuit through the counties once every year. They carry with them, at the same

New-York, in Relation to the Court of Equity established there in a new Court of *Exchequer;* which I perceive was done, principally, for determining a Dispute between the Governor and the President of the Council, about their Right to the Salary annexed to the Office of the Commander in Chief, whether he be the Governor or President; and it seems strange to me, that upon such an Occasion, so extraordinary a Step should be taken, as the erecting of a new Court, exempted from the Rules of Proceeding at the Common Law, when the Matter might have been decided in an Action of the Case upon an *Indebitatus assumpsit,*[37] which is the settled Method and most expeditious Remedy, in Cases of that Nature.

Both these Gentlemen seem to have agreed in one Point, that it was necessary to trace the Court of *Chancery* and the Equity Court in the *Exchequer* back to their original Institution, in order to shew whether the Governor of a new Plantation, hath a Power or not to erect Courts, in Imitation of these high and ancient Courts in *England.*—And from their Researches, they seem to have made very different Conclusions. Mr. *Smith* rightly concludes against the Legality of this Court; but Mr. *Murray* is afraid all must be lost, if the four fundamental Courts, as he calls them, can't be obtained in *New-York.*—I own I don't understand the Force of this sort of Reasoning, nor can I conceive, how any Enquiry into the Original of the High Court of *Chancery*, which must after all end in a meer Conjecture, can afford the least Assistance, in forming a right Judgment upon this Question, which must depend upon the particular Constitution of these foreign Colonies.—

The Court of *Chancery* in *England*, has its Being from Custom and Usage, to which it owes its Legality.—If it were to be erected now by the King's Power it could not stand; therefore it is undoubtedly a great Absurdity to suppose, that upon the planting every new Colony by the Subjects of *England*, new Courts must spring up, as it were from the Roots of the ancient Courts, and be established without the Consent of the Legislature, because we can imitate their Methods of Proceeding, though we are very imperfect in Comparison to their Reason and Judgment.—Then I think there is another Impropriety in the Debate of this Question; they would argue from the Power and Prerogative of the King, to entitle a Governor to act in the same Manner. I think before they turn a Governor into a King, they should take Care, to provide for him the same Sufficiency of Wisdom and as able a Council; therefore I must suppose, a mighty Difference between the Power of a King and the Governors abroad.—Their Instructions as to the erecting of Courts, or the Authorities granted in their Patents for that Purpose, are not now, as they were in the Beginning, when there were no Courts; but proper Judicatures being long since established, there is an End of their Power in that Respect, and if any Alteration is found necessary, it must certainly be done by the Consent of the Legislature. The Kings of *England* have always, so far as I am acquainted with the History of the Plantations, used a particular Tenderness in the Business of erecting their Courts of

Time, a Commission of *Oyer* and *Terminer* and General Jail
Delivery, in which some of the county justices are joined.
The judges and practisers in the Supreme, and all other

Judicature, by directing their Governors, to take the Advice of the
General Assemblies in that Matter, and I dare say, that if the
Patents and Instructions of the Governor of *New-York* were to be
inspected, no sufficient Warrant will be found in them, to exercise
this high Power of setting up new Courts. But be that as it will,
this is most manifest, that setting up one or more Men, with
Power to judge Men's Properties, by other Rules than those of the
Common Law, by which alone we of the Plantations must be
governed, must subject the Estates of that People to an arbitrary
Rule, so far as they are restrained from appealing to an higher
Jurisdiction, and may enslave them to the weak, if not corrupt,
Judgments of those Men.—It really seems to be a singular Misfortune to the People of *New-York*, that a Question of this Nature
should be so far countenanced, as to become a Subject of Argument, when I believe, in any other Colony, it would not have been
thought a Matter of any Doubt or the least Difficulty. But above
all, it is most extravagant, that a Court of Equity should be erected,
for the Trial of a Cause, of which, without doing Violence to its
Nature, it cannot have any Jurisdiction; and I have wondered, in
so warm a Debate, that this Point has been passed over.—I think
nothing could entitle the Court of Equity, to proceed in the Cause
between the Governor and *Van Dam*, unless there was a Want of
Proof, of *Van Dam*'s receiving the Money in Dispute, which I
suppose is impossible, since it must have issued out of the publick
Treasury of the Province.—If I had been to have argued this
Point, I should have taken a very different Method from those
Gentlemen. Instead of taking so much Pains, in running through
so many Book Cases, to settle what the Constitution of *England*
is, I would have stated the Constitution of this particular Govern-
ment, as it is grounded either upon Treaties or Grants from the
Crown of *England;* for as *New-York* was a conquered Country, it
is very probable, something may have been stipulated, between the
*States General* and Crown of *England,* in Behalf of the Subjects
of *Holland,* which were left there in Possession of their Estates,
and so became Subjects to *England.*—If there was any such
Treaty, that must be looked upon as the *Fundamental Law of the
Province;* and next to that, the King's Charters must take Place.—
I don't at all doubt, but some Way or other, the Common Law was
established there, and if not, as there is a Legislature, I suppose it
is adopted by the Country; for there is undoubtedly, a great Difference between the People of a conquered Country, and Colonies
reduced by the King's Consent by the Subjects of *England.* The
Common Law follows *them* wherever they go, but as to the *other*,
it must arise either from Treaties or Grants; therefore it is a Pity,
every Thing in Relation to this Matter has been omitted, which
would have been of great Use to those, who are unacquainted with
the Facts, in forming a Judgment in this case.—I can't forbear
observing a mighty Weakness in the Lawyers of *New-York,* in
blindly following a common Error, in Relation to the Statutes of
*England* being in Force there; whereas there is no Foundation in
Sense or Reason for such an Opinion. The Common Law must be

courts, wear no peculiar habits as they do at Westminster-Hall and in some of the West-India islands; nor is there, as yet, any distinction or degrees among the lawyers.

The door of admission into the practice is too open. The usual preparatories are a college or university education, and three years apprenticeship; or, without the former, seven years service under an attorney. In either of these cases, the Chief Justice recommends the candidate to the Governour, who thereupon grants a license to practice under his Hand and Seal at Arms. This being produced to the court, the usual state oaths and subscription are taken, together with an oath for his upright demeanour, and he is then qualified to practice in every court in the Province. Into the county courts, attornies are introduced with still less ceremony. For our Governours have formerly licensed all persons, how indifferently soever recommended; and the profession has been shamefully disgraced, by the admission of men not only of the meanest abilities, but of the lowest employments.[38] The present judges of the Supreme Court are the honourable (for that is their title)

James De Lancey, Esq; Chief Justice.

John Chambers, Esq; second justice.

Daniel Horsmanden, Esq; third justice.

They have but two clerks; one attendant upon the Supreme Court at New-York, and the other on the circuits. The former seals all their process and is Keeper of the Records.

## The Court of Admiralty

The only officers of this court are the judge, or commissary, the register and marshal. The present judge, Lewis Morris, Esq; has, by his commission,* a jurisdiction in all maritime affairs, not only here, but in the colonies of New-Jersey and Connecticut.

---

the only Rule, and if we wade into the Statutes, no Man can tell what the Law is. It is certain all of them can't bind, and to know which do, was always above my Capacity.—Those that are declarative of the Common Law, serve us rather as Evidences, than by any binding Quality as Statutes.

I am, Sir,

Your most obedient Servant, &c.

JOHN RANDOLPH.

* It is under the Seal of the Admiralty, and dated January 16, 1738.

The proceedings before him are in English, and according to the course of the civil law.

## The Prerogative Court

The business of this court relates to the probate of last wills and testaments, and the grants of letters of administration on intestates estates. The powers, relative to these matters, are committed to the Governour, who acts ordinarily by a delegate.

## The Court of the Governour and Council

The authority of this court is best seen in the Instruction on which it depends.

> Our Will and Pleasure is, that you, or the Commander in Chief of our said Province, for the Time being, do all in Civil Causes, on Application being made to you, or the Commander in Chief for the Time being, for that Purpose, permit and allow Appeals, from any of the Courts of Common Law in our said Province, unto you or the Commander in Chief, and the Council of our said Province; and you are, for that Purpose, to issue a Writ, in the Manner which has been usually accustomed, returnable before yourself and the Council of our said Province, who are to proceed to hear and determine such Appeal; wherein such of our said Council, as shall be at that Time Judges of the Court from whence such Appeal shall be so made, to you our Captain General, or to the Commander in Chief for the Time being, and to our said Council, as aforesaid, shall not be admitted to vote upon the said Appeal; but they may, nevertheless, be present at the hearing thereof, to give the Reasons of the Judgment given by them, in the Causes, wherein such Appeals shall be made.
>
> Provided nevertheless, that in all such Appeals, the Sum or Value appealed for, do exceed the Sum of* three hundred Pounds Sterling; and that Security be first duly given by the Appellant, to answer such Charges, as shall be awarded in Case the first Sentence be affirmed; and if either Party shall

---

* Before the arrival of Sir Danvers Osborn, appeals were given to the Governour and Council, in all causes above £100 sterling, and to the King in Council, in all those above £300 sterling. By this instruction, the power of the Supreme Court and of the Governour and Council, is prodigiously augmented. In this infant country few contracts are equal to the sums mentioned in the instruction, and therefore an uncontrolable authority in our courts may be dangerous to the property and liberties of the people. Proper checks upon judges preserve them both from indolence and corruption.

not rest satisfied with the Judgement of you, or the Commander in Chief for the Time being, and Council as aforesaid, our Will and Pleasure is, that they may then appeal unto us in our Privy Council. Provided the Sum or Value so appealed for unto us, exceed five hundred Pounds Sterling, and that such Appeal be made within fourteen Days after Sentence, and good Security given by the Appellant, that he will effectually prosecute the same and answer the Condemnation, and also pay such Costs and Damages, as shall be awarded by us, in Case the Sentence of you, or the Commander in Chief for the Time being, and Council be affirmed. Provided nevertheless, where the Matter in Question relates to the taking or demanding any Duty payable to us, or to any Fee of Office, or annual Rent, or other such like Matter or Thing, where the Rights in future may be bound, in all such Cases, you are to admit an Appeal to us in our Privy Council, though the immediate Sum or Value appealed for, be of a less Value. And it is our further Will and Pleasure, that in all Cases, where, by your Instructions, you are to admit Appeals to us in our Privy Council, Execution be suspended, until the final Determination of such Appeals, unless good and sufficient Security be given by the Appellee, to make ample Restitution of all that the Appellant shall have lost, by Means of such Judgment or Decree, in Case upon the Determination of such Appeal, such Decree or Judgment should be reversed, and Restitution awarded to the Appellant.

## The Court of Chancery

Of all our courts, none has been more obnoxious to the people than this. There have been (as I have already shewn) few administrations since its first erection, in which our Assemblies have not expressed their disapprobation of its constitution by ordinance, and the exercise of the Chancellor's power by the Governour. During the administration of Governour Cosby, a bill was filed by Sir Joseph Eyles and others, to vacate the oblong Patent granted by his immediate predecessor to Hauley and Company. The defendants excepted to the Governour's jurisdiction, but being over-ruled, they resorted to the Assembly with a complaint, and the House, on the 6th of November 1735, resolved, "That a Court of *Chancery* in this Province, in the Hands or under the Exercise of a Governor, without Consent in General Assembly, is contrary to Law, unwarrantable, and of dangerous Consequence to the Liberties and Properties of the People."

The same sentiments obtained among the people in Mr.

Clarke's time, as is very evident in the memorable address of the Assembly, in 1737, a part of which, relative to the Court of Chancery, is too singular to be suppressed.

The settling and establishing of Courts of general Jurisdiction, for the due Administration of Justice, is necessary in every Country, and we conceive they ought to be settled and established, by the Acts of the whole Legislature, and their several Jurisdictions and Powers by that Authority limited and appointed, especially Courts that are to take Cognizance of Matters in a Course of Equity.—This has been the constant Practice in *England,* when new Courts were to be erected, or old ones to be abolished or altered; and the several Kings of *England,* in whose Reigns those Acts were made, never conceived, that the settling, erecting, or abolishing Courts, by Acts of the Legislature, had any Tendency to destroy or in the least to diminish their just and legal Prerogatives.—It was the Method in Use here, both before and since the Revolution, and particularly recommended to the Assembly to be done in that Manner, by a Message from Governor *Sloughter* and Council, on the 15th Day of *April* 1691. He was the first Governor since the Revolution; and the Governors that since that Time assented to those Acts, we suppose, never in the least imagined, they were giving up the Prerogative of their Masters when they gave that Assent; nor did we ever learn that they were censured for doing so.—On the contrary, the constant Instructions, that have from Time to Time been given to the Governors of this Province, seem clearly to point out the doing of it, by Acts of the Legislature, and not otherwise, as may be gathered from the Instruction, for the erecting of a Court for the determining of small Causes, by which there are positive Directions given to the Governors, to recommend it to the Assembly, that a Law should be passed for that Purpose; but notwithstanding these Directions, given in direct and express Terms, the Governors never would apply for such an Act, but erected that Court by an Ordinance of themselves and Council, as they did the Court of *Chancery,* which had before that Time been erected by Acts of the Legislature in another manner.—They could not be ignorant, what Dissatisfaction the erecting of a Court of *Chancery* in that Manner, gave the Generality of the People.—This was very manifest, by the Resolves of the General Assembly, at the Time of its first being so erected, and often since, declaring the illegality of such a Proceeding. And though these Resolves, have been as often as made, treated by the Governors with an unreasonable Disregard and Contempt of them, yet to Men of Prudence, they might have been effectual, to have made them decline persisting in a Procedure, so illegal and so generally dissatisfactory; and which (as they managed it) proved of no Use to the Public or Benefit to themselves. For as few of them had Talents equal to the Task of a Chancellor, which they had undertaken to perform, so it was executed accordingly. Some of them being willing to hold such a Court, others not, according as they happened to be influenced by those about them. So that were it really established in the most legal Manner (as it was not) yet being in the Hands of a Person not compellable to do his Duty, it was so managed, that the extraordinary Delays and fruitless Expence attending it, rendered it not only useless, but a Grievance to the Inhabitants, especially those, who were so unfortunate as to be concerned in it: which we hope you think with us, that it is high Time should be redressed.

Your Honour well knows, that the establishing that Court, in the Manner it has been done, has been a Subject of Contention, between the Governors and the Assembly; and since it is confessed by all, that the establishing both of that, and other Courts, by Act of the Legislature, is indisputably legal, and gives them the most uncontrovertible Authority; and if unquestionably legal, what is so, cannot be destructive of his Majesty's Prerogative.—We therefore hope, you will make no Scruple of assenting to this Bill, to put an End to a Contention, that has not been, nor will be, while it continues, beneficial to his Majesty's Service.—

From this time, the Chancery has been unattacked by the Assembly, but the business transacted in it is very inconsiderable. A court of equity is absolutely necessary, for the due administration of justice; but whether private property ought to be in the hands of the Governours, I leave others to determine.* As the publick business of the colony increases, few of them, I believe, will be ambitious of the Chancellor's office, as they have not the assistance of a Master of the Rolls. The present officers of this court (which is always held in the Council-Chamber at the fort) are, his Excellency Sir Charles Hardy, Knt. Chancellor, two masters, two clerks, one examiner, a register, and a sergeant at arms, and not one of them has a salary. In our proceedings

---

* Some are of opinion, that the Governour's jurisdiction in this, and the Spiritual, or Prerogative, Court are incompatible.

we copy after the Chancery in England, and indeed in all our courts, the practice at home is more nearly imitated in this and New-Jersey, than in any other Province upon the continent. Few of our Assemblies have been capable to concert any new regulations of this kind; and hence the lawyers have had recourse to the English customs and forms, which they have generally adopted. While the New-England colonies, through the superior education of their representatives, have introduced numberless innovations, peculiar to themselves; the laws of our mother country have gradually obtained here, and, in this respect, the publick has perhaps received advantages, even from the ignorance of our ancestors.

FINIS

# Editor's Appendixes

## Notes

# Appendix A. The Reception of Smith's History in England: A Review

*The History of the Province of New York, from the first discovery to the year* 1732. *To which is annexed, A Description of the Country, with a short Account of the Inhabitants, their Trade, religious and political State, and the Constitution of the Courts of Justice in that Colony. By* William Smith, A.M. of New-York.    4to.  6s.   Wilcox.

It must not be supposed, that the present history can furnish out the variety of incidents, which make relations of this kind pleasing to the generality of Readers. We must be contented here with a detail of events, not, in their own nature, very extraordinary;—with a narrative, interesting only from our connections with the country to which it refers. The Author takes the materials of this history from the minutes of the Council of New York, and from the journals of the General Assembly, continued down from the accession of William III. These, with some other assistances, viz. Colden, Alexander, Charlevoix, &c. have enabled him to deliver a series of occurrences, which are, however, lengthened out by laws, letters, grants, &c. to a prolixity that cannot fail of disgusting such as read only for entertainment.

His first part begins with the discovery of the colony; its settlement by the Dutch; and the encroachments of the English; till it was ceded to the latter, in the year 1664.

The remaining four parts are employed in giving an account of the wars of the colony, and their domestic bickerings. A few Frenchmen, from the most feeble beginnings, had art sufficient to take advantage of the dissentions of their neighbours, and though under all the discouragements of a cold climate, and disagreeable country, imperceptibly strengthened themselves, grew formidable to those by whom they were at first despised, and encroached upon their possessions.

[This review is taken from *The Monthly Review; or, Literary Journal*, XVI (London, June 1757), 517–518.]

We see here the treaties made, the alliances formed on either side, the massacres committed, the tortures inflicted, (disclaimed, indeed, yet practised by each) as either party happened to be victorious. But the private feuds of the colony take up the greatest part of the performance. The governors appointed by the crown of England are, in general, described as men of mean parts, or indigent circumstances; either incapable of the task, or too deeply engrossed by the sordid views of private interest, to pursue the good of the public; first, perhaps, accepting the employment to repair a shattered fortune, and using every instance of fraud and oppression to attain that end; proud of a power to which they were unaccustomed, and fond of exercising it upon every occasion, merely to shew its extent. To them are opposed the members of the Assembly; men bred up in all the fierceness of republican opposition; all equally attached to self-interest (as a discerning reader may gather from their conduct) yet averse to any thing that carries the least appearance of oppression; endeavouring to be privately rich, by with-holding the necessary supports from the government, yet giving the name of patriotism to their opposition of any expensive measures taken for public security; losing in debate the opportunity of action, and furnishing the vigilant enemy with the means of growing stronger by their divisions. What wonder then, in a colony composed of men so ill qualified to govern, and subjects so hard to be governed, they should leave an enemy, despised at first for his weakness, an opportunity of growing formidable by pursuing a contrary conduct!

"The French, in Canada," as our Author observes, "have always been jealous of the increasing strength of our colonies; and a motive of fear led them naturally to concert a regular system of conduct for their defence. Confining us to scant limits along the sea coast, is the grand object they have long had in view; and seizing the important passes from Canada to Louisiana, seducing our Indian Allies, engrossing the trade, and fortifying the routes into their country, were all proper expedients toward the execution of their plan."

Thus much will suffice to give the Reader a general idea of the work before us; which, as the Author has not intended to amuse, but to inform, is wrote in a simple, unadorned manner, and his veracity, we doubt not, may be depended upon. In a word, those who desire to be made acquainted with the affairs of New York, will not meet such ample information in any former work on the subject, as our Author's materials seem to be more authentic, and more copious, than those of any other writer concerning the affairs of this Province.

# Appendix B. *The Reception of Smith's History in New York: The Colden-Smith Correspondence and the Jones-Pintard Correspondence*

## 1. Cadwallader Colden to William Smith, Jr.*

FLUSHEN   January 15, 1759[1]

Sir:

I did not see your History of New York till last Week. The account you give (page 179 of that History) of the transactions between the Government of New York & Captain Laughlin Campbel is in every circumstance a misrepresentation of facts. It is in the principal part absolutely false & an egregeous calumny of the persons, who at that time had the administration of Government in their hands.

It is now about 20 years since that affair happened. Many of the circumstances I cannot with sufficient certainty recollect; & it is probable that none who were not immediately concerned in that affair can at this time remember them. I shall content my self therefor with giving you a summary account of that affair, so far as, I doubt not, can be proved by liveing evidence.

It is true that Captain Campbel imported a number of families from Scotland a great part of which (I believe the greatest) had paid their own passages, & were at liberty to dispose of themselves after they arrived in America as they thought fit. The others were bound by indentures to Captain Campbel to serve him or his assigns some certain number of years in consideration of the expence of transporting them to America, or under some other obligation to repay that expence with a profit to him. Soon after their Arival Captain Campbel presented a petition to Lieutenant Governeur Clark in Council setting forth in substance (so far as I can remember) that he had imported some certain number (which I have forgot) of families or persons in order to cultivate or improve some part of the vacant lands of this Province & pray'd the grant of a large tract of land (probably 30,000 acres as you mention) to him his heirs & assigns, in order to settle thereon those families & persons which he had imported for its cultivation & improvement. This petition & the import of it became immediatly subject of common discourse in the town. Whereupon the persons who came with Captain Campbel & had paid their own passages met together in companies in the streets & where they loudly exclaimed against it, saying they had left Scotland to free themselves from the vassalage they were under to their Lords there, & they would not become vassals to Laughlin Campbel in America. The Governor being informed of this ordered these persons to be called together & to be interrogated on this head They jointly & severally to a man declared they would not become tenants to Laughlin Campbel.

It being likewise doubted whether Captain Campbel was in capacity to settle a sufficient number of persons to have so large a tract of land cultivated pursuant to the directions in the King's In-

---

* [These first six letters are from the Colden Papers, New-York Historical Society, box 6, folder 4. They have been published in *Collections of the New-York Historical Society for the Year 1921* (New York, 1923), pp. 283–295, and in abridged form, *ibid.*, series 2, II (New York, 1849), pp. 193–214, with supporting documents.]

structions. He said that as his settling on the frontiers towards Canada would be a considerable additional defence of the Province he expected that the Assembly would bear the charge of supporting the families that were to settle upon it till they could support themselves by their own labour & that he had or would present a petition for that purpose. The assembly knowing the aversion which the people who came over with Captain Campbel had to him, for it was notorious, did not enter on the consideration of his petition & I firmly believe that he gave in no other petition to the Assembly.

These transactions were publick & the subject of common discourse yet I never hear Mr. Clark or any other person in the administration blamed at that time by any indifferent person on account of Captain Campbel's petition that it was not granted.

This being the state of the case I leave it to you to say whether Lieutenant Governer Clark could consistently with the trust reposed in him, grant 30,000 acres of land to Laughlin Campbel; or whether it would not have been a lasting obstruction to the settlement of the frontiers to grant 30,000 acres of land there to any person who was in no capacity to settle & improve so great a tract. I likewise leave it to others who are better acquainted with Captain Campbel's character than you are to say whether it be in the least probable that Captain Campbel would have refused a share in that grant to any person who had influence to procure it for him under colour of the pretensions which he made.

Captain Campbel might have had 2000 acres of land for himself on the frontiers & the others quantities in proportion to their abilities but they chose to settle in the inhabited part of the country. In short Captain Campbel had conceived hopes of erecting a lordship for himself in America. He imagined that the people whom he inticed over with him would have become his tenants on condition of being supported till they could mentain themselves & an easy rent afterwards. His disappointment came from these people obstinately refuseing to become his tenants on any terms & from the Assemblies being unwilling to support them at the expence of the people of this province & not from Mr. Clark's refuseing them land for they might have had it as before mentioned but none of them were willing or in ability to make settlements on the frontiers.

So far as I know this story which you tell was not propogated till since Captain Campbel's death, at a distance of time when these transactions are forgot by people who had no concern in them: & were propogated by his family after they were reduced to distress by his misconduct in order to move the compassion of some persons who had it in their power to advance them & they have succeeded. As these stories were only propogated in private it was not easy to take public notice of them but now that you have published this calumny in Europe & America a public redress is become necessary.

This public defamation being an egregeous injury to the public faith & honour of the Government of New York, you know the proper method for redress that may be taken. But as I think that your writing of this & publishing of it has only arisen from your credulity in some who do not deserve the confidence you placed in their veracity & from a generous indignation at what you thought a base breach of trust in the Lieutenant Governor & others I shall at present leave it to you to propose what you think may be an adequat redress of so public an injury.

No doubt several of the persons who came over with Captain Campbel & were not servants are still alive; from them you may learn the truth of the principal facts which I now affirm. Perhaps some of them may now live in the city. I have forgot all their names except one Montgomerie, brother in law to Captain Campbel, who lately lived at Cackeyat. I shall expect your answer without delay & that thereby the opinion will be confirmed of your sincerity & integrity which has been hitherto intertained by

Sir

Your most humble servant<br>CADWALLADER COLDEN

## 2. Cadwallader Colden to William Smith [Sr.]

FLUSHEN   January 15, 1759

Sir

You may remember that so long since as May last I desired you to write to Nathan Birdsel to pay the remainder of what is due to me & you said you would but I have heard nothing since that time of that affair. If he has not paid I must desire you to proceed but as I am unwilling to increase charges on the poor man I am desirous to be don with as litle as possible & for that purpose please to write to David Akin who is his security & is likewise sued & put him in mind that if Birdsel do not speedily pay execution for that, remainder will go out or what is proper to be wrote on that occasion. I must beg of you that care be taken that the letter be delivered.

I was surprised very lately on receiving the 179th page of your son's history. Tho my name be not mentioned in it it has in the discourse in town occasioned by that publication & I am informed was to my Lord Loudoun. This has occasioned my writing the inclosed to your son which I leave open for your perusal & desire the favour of your delivering it to him. I expect that you on recollection may remember the substance of what I write. I am very desirous that a proper redress be made in a manner the least disagreable to your son & I desire your assistance for that purpose. You know some persons may with some kind of satisfaction suffer this calumny to pass tho' they really know the truth & may likewise be as well pleased to have your son's veracity as an historean called openly in question. Please to let me know your thoughts freely on the subject I expect it from the friendship which has long subsisted between us & you will thereby likewise oblige

Sir

Your most obedient

To the Honorable WILLIAM SMITH, Esq.

## 3. William Smith [Sr.] to Cadwallader Colden

NEW YORK   31 January 1759

Sir:

I have kept your judgment on foot against Nathan Birdsall. On the 25th instant I received yours of the 15th and have wrote to David Akin in a very pressing manner & sent it by John Wing his neighbour, who promised carefully to deliver it and I suppose it may have reached him by this time.

I delivered the letter enclosed to me, as directed. I remember something of that affair, but as not less than four gentlemen were concerned, cannot tell in particular on whom the censure fell. But know that ye common opinion concurred with what is written. Publick acts are allways subject to publick judgment and what every body is concerned in every one thinks he has a right to give this opinion upon. As this case is among friends I chuse to suspend mine. When your letter was read, I perceived it gave offence, I urged an answer and obtained a promise, but suspect from what I observed that it will be with some resentment. I beg that you will consider it as a certain Truth: *Quod Filii mei ex Ephebis excessi togam viritem statim arripuint.*[2] They feel an independence, and I cease to be any longer accountable for their conduct. I foresee a storm.

"Hoc Ithacus velit"[3]

And perhaps it may be *impar Congressus*[4] on the youngest side.

I remember that in the time of Mr. Cosby a gentleman whom we well knew was attacked in what was esteemed a weak part. We that were his friends judged it proper that he should answer it, he smiled and said, I am not named, the censure is not applicable to me and upon considering the matter we judged that he acted wisely in neglecting the censure.

For my part I think according to the Old Oracle, that "the beginning of Strife is as when one letteth out water." The simile is beautifull. A hole peirced in a mill dam by the incumbent pressure will soon grow large. Hence the advice: "Leave of[f] Contention before it be meddled with." These are the best sentiments that I can suggest in an affair which as to me is of so much delicacy. I am

Sir

Your most obedient humble Servant

WILLIAM SMITH

P.S. This haveing been written with frozen
ink, I fear will be scarce legible.

The Honorable CADWALLADER COLDEN, Esq.


## 4. William Smith, Jr., to Cadwallader Colden

NEW YORK, February 5 1759

Sir,

Your letter of the 15 January, which came to me unsealed, contains such a heavy charge of misrepresentation, falsehood and calumny, that I am almost inclined, to think myself relieved from the obligation, which your age, rank, character, and particularly your professed friendship to my father, would otherwise undoubtedly, have laid me under, to take notice of every thing, wherein you might conceive yourself in the least degree concerned. However since your papers, may after your decease, fall into such hands, as may make a bad use of that letter, I thought proper not to leave it to pass intirely unanswered.

In historical accounts it is scarce possible to avoid mistakes. As the memory of them, so the proofs relating to facts, ordinarily decrease in proportion to our removes from the period of action—all therefore that can be done, is to make use of the best lights that offer, and to permit nothing to slide into a work, unsupported by the best evidence, which the nature of the thing will admit. He that writes under these guards, will escape all just censure, even tho' he should happen to err; And yet every man has a right to correct him, if it be done with decency and candour. But an abrupt intrusion upon him, with an angry accusation unhappily defeats the very design of the corrector, by rendering his disinterestedness suspected; the unbiased advocate for truth being generally calm and unruffled. My meaning, Sir, is this, that the first attack ought not to be in such terms as these, "Your Account is in every Circumstance a Misrepresentation, It is in the principal Part absolutely false, and an egregious Calumny of the Persons w[h]o had the Administration of Government in their Hands." Nor ought a Threat to be so much as insinuated, because it presupposes the person reproved, to have no other principle or passion to be wrought upon, than fear, the most dastardly and abject of all passions.

From this recrimination I would not have you understand, Sir, that I believe the passage against which you except, is false and scandalous—If that was the case, free as I am, from the least consciousness of a design, willfully to misrepresent, any gentleman's conduct in Captain Campbel's affair, I should think myself bound by the most sacred ties, to retract what I have written, and make immediate reparation. And tho' the commencement of our correspondence, may incline you to imagine me to be not very much under your influence, I beg you'l take my promise, that I will hear any evidence you are inclined to offer in support of your charge; and if it is sufficient, I will instantly expunge the guilty passage, against which you complain.

In my own vindication give me leave to add, Sir, the occasion of its insertion, the authority upon which it was founded, and my motives for publishing that part of the narrative.

I remember to have seen Captain Campbel when I was a boy, and perhaps his Highland dress, which was then a novelty in the country, might at that age have made the impression the deeper, and attracted my attention to the general conversation about him and his affairs. When I drew near the close of the detail of our public transactions, and observed from the minutes of Council, which I perused, our inattention to the French incroachments at Crown Point, Campbel's project of settling the lands about Saraghtoga on the Wood Creek started into mind, and I became anxious to know, why a design which seemed to me a very proper and salutary remedy to the late misstep, was rendered abortive. I consulted public fame and tradition, and they warrented in the main what you see I have since written; But chusing in a matter of that importance, to found myself on further authority, I sent for one of Captain Campbel's sons, and desired him on the next visit to his mother, who then lived in your neighbourhood in the Highlands, to set down, from her own mouth, in writing, all she could remember about the matter, and to give me a sight of the papers, which her husband had left behind him at his decease. He did so, and I found the vulgar accounts still farther confirmed. This last indeed was the evidence of a party interested, but that no stone might be left unturned to come at the truth, I in the next place took occasion to converse more than once with Mr. Alexander upon this subject, a Gentleman of His Majesty's Council, famed for his good memory, clear judgment and minute attention to the course of our public affairs, and to whose testimony whether we consider his opportunities to know the truth, or integrity in the relation of it, you I am persuaded, will be the last of all men to object. In these conferences, I related to him what I had collected, relating to Campbel's disappointments and their causes, and told him of my design to make a public use of the story. He seemed to know it well, and expressed himself with that ready indignation, which usually accompanies a strong remembrance of an injurious, wrong measure, for he immediately said, the obstructions given to Captain Campbel were scandalous; and then added some further particulars of information on that head.

By these accumulated proofs I had no reason to doubt the main facts, of which for the greater safety, I chose nevertheless to draw up only a general relation. I have since frequently mentioned Campbel's sufferings in accidental companies of the best sort, and as I never, till the receipt of your letter found the account I gave, drawn into question, I am apt to believe that no one has imposed upon my credulity, that the facts are notoriously true, and that the authors of Captain Campbel's misfortunes, whoever they were, sensible of their guilt, hid their heads in silence, not daring to contradict or oppose, what was once generally known, and still is believed to be true.

Among my inducements for publishing that anecdote, which offends you so much, I need only to mention, that it was partly for the sake of historical truth, and partly to call up the public attention to a similar project, should any one be hereafter attempted; But principally to spread the compassionate emotions I felt in my own breast, and to keep up the claim of the widow and children of that loyal, unfortunate adventurer, to the special regards of the public. I am glad to hear that three of his sons are now in His Majesty's service, preferred upon the score of their father's misfortunes and in a condition to support their mother, who, without the help of her children, thro' a train of adversities, would, if I am not very much misinformed, soon be obliged to depend upon the cold charity of mere strangers.

Upon the receipt of your letter, I took some pains to get a second perusal of Captain Campbel's papers, among which I saw Governor Cosby's Proclamation, and I think Mr. Clarke's Advertizement. And when they come to hand, I believe it will be very easy from them, and the examinations which I have now hopes of obtaining, to establish what I have ventured to relate beyond all possible doubt. It affords me one of the greatest pleasures of my life to reflect, that the present ease of that poor lady (for she is a well bred woman) is in some measure owing to me; and since the truth of the paragraph you dislike, may be the next, as she conceives it to have been the first step in the ladder of her sons preferments in the Army, I shall not be very forward to erase it, without full proof of the alligations contain'd in your letter, the burthen of which lies upon you; but when that comes whether by your means, or upon my own discovery, out of a single eye to truth and justice, I shall act such a part, as will confirm the opinion you do me the honour to entertain, of the sincerity and integrity of

Sir,

Your most obedient humble Servant

WILLIAM SMITH, Jr.

## 5. Cadwallader Colden to William Smith, Jr.

FLUSHEN　February 17 1759

Sir:

I shall return no answer to the greatest part of your letter of the first of this month which I receiv'd on the ninth because the doing it would lead me from my purpose. However much the stile of your letter may become you it does not become me to make a return to it. At my time of life it is highly imprudent to enter into any kind of contention. I am only desirous to have my character freed from a vile aspersion privately propogated to which the publication of your History gives great force. I inclosed my letter open to your father in hopes that his friendship would prevent indecent warmth on both sides & with this view I shall inclose this in the same manner.

In a private letter to your self I charged you with too much credulity in believing a misrepresentation of facts & a falshood on the evidence of persons interested & of publishing them to the world. I pointed out to you the means by which you may be informed of the truth. I expected from your candour that you would take some pains to inquire & that if you found it as I represented, you would make what proper redress is in your power to those persons whose characters are injured by that publication.

I affirmed, 1. That the heads of families who came over with Captain Campbel absolutely refused to settle under him on the frontiers & were not in ability to settle by themselves. Several of them are still alive; some of them I am told are in the city. The truth of this may be known from them.

2. That Captain Campbel was in no ability to settle 30,000 acres of land. The truth of this may likewise be known from the same persons who came over with him & appears by the difficulties he was under in settling a small farm in Ulster County.

3. That when Captain Campbel applied to the Assembly for their assistance to support him in settling they would not grant it I expect some who were members at that time may remember.

If these things be as I affirm I leave it to you to say whether Mr. Clark could, consistently with the trust reposed in him, grant 30,000 acres of land to Captain Campbel & whether the granting of it under these circumstances could have been of any additional security to the frontiers.

I repeat these plain simple facts on which the dispute between you & me depends & I shall now add that at that time I wrote only from memory. Since that time the minutes of Council in Captain Campbel's affair and the file have been inspected. There you will find many circumstances which had escaped my memory in confirmation of what I have wrote to you. I believed you had been deceived, otherwise I had never given you the trouble of a single line. You have now living & written evidence pointed out to you for your information. I gave you & I now again give you an opportunity of showing your candour & love of truth, the most distinguishing qualifications of an historian & I again give you an opportunity to make redress where you have undesignedly injured others. By this method I think I act most consistently with the friendship which has subsisted between your father & me & with some regard to your character for with all the strength of evidence which can be produced you know that other methods might have been taken.

As Mr. Alexander's memory is very dear to me, I cannot entirely pass what you write as from him. On recollection you will find that Mr. Alexander was not in the Council at that time After near 20 years distance in time, Mr. Alexander may have intirely forgot the circumstances of an affair in which he was in no manner concerned & he may have unwarily believed, as you & many others have after such a distance of time, on a tale privately propogated to serve a private purpose; but this makes it the more necessary that the truth appear. I willingly receive what you have wrote in excuse. And as I desire nothing of you inconsistent with the strict rules of honour, I remain confident that your answer will shew your resolution to make a proper redress & thereby confirm the opinion intertained of you by

Sir Your

To WILLIAM SMITH Junr, Esq.

## 6. Cadwallader Colden to William Smith [Sr.]

FLUSHEN   February 19 1759

Sir:

I have your favour of the last of January. I receiv'd at the same time a letter from your son the answer to which I inclose & am obliged to you for your advice. You may be assured that I shall

avoid contention of any kind at my time of life & I have that opinion of your son's candour that I cannot apprehend any on this occasion after the first impression is over & he has had time to reflect.
However, he cannot fully excuse the not takeing what information
he could from the Secretaries office before he had published, for if he
had, any trouble which I now give would have been prevented The
pointing out to him the evidence in this affair & where to be found
plainly shews that I have no thoughts of entering into a dispute to
his prejudice.

I find by the Governors speech that the settling the frontiers is to
come under consideration at this time. It is not improbable that this
story may be made use of on this occasion to my prejudice I am
confident you will not permit it where you can prevent it, & I expect
you will be well pleased to make use of the opportunity if it offers
in vindication of

Sir

To the honorable WILLIAM SMITH, Esq.

## 7. Dr. Samuel Johnson to Archbishop Secker, New York, March 20, 1759*

One book indeed, which has, I imagine, been a principal occasion
of the complaints against the Society[5] and Missionaries, is the History of New York lately published in London, which doubtless Your
Grace has seen. This was wrote by one Smith of this Town, upon
which Mr. Barclay[6] has made some very just remarks, which were
sent about two months ago, and I hope are now in the Secretary's
hands. This Smith is a lawyer here of some note, who with two
others of the same profession, Livingstone and Scott, all bitter enemies to our Church and College, were believed to be the Chief writers
of the Reflectors & Watch Towers—And I believe one of the leading
occasions of his writing this history was, that he might abuse the
Church, Society and Missionaries, as it contains a summary of
what they had before published in those papers so far as religion is
concerned. But your Grace will see by our Controversy with Hobart,
and by Mr. Barclay's remarks compared with Smith's history, that
it is indeed fencing against a hail, to hold any controversy with
them, there being nothing they will stick at, however so false and
injurious, in opposing and discrediting the church, and which they
would not cease to repeat and inculcate, over and over again, however so thoroughly it was answered. I could wish Mr. Barclay's
Remarks were printed that both our benefactors and enemies at
home, might see how little regard our adversaries here have for
truth or common honesty, who are so indefatigably laboring, and
with so much success to disaffect our Benefactors both to the

* [These paragraphs are taken from Edmund B. O'Callaghan, ed.,
*Documents Relative to the Colonial History of the State of New
York*, VII (Albany, 1856), p. 371.]

Society and us.—What connections any of these gentlemen may have in England I know not. I am told it is one Dr. Avery with whom our Dissenters here chiefly correspond.

## 8. Cadwallader Colden to Alexander Colden*

Coldengham[7], June 15, 1759

Dear Son,

As I have been conversant in the public transactions in this Province near forty years, and am now by my age become unfit for action and retired I have thought that I could not do better than to employ part of what time I have remaining in writing Memoirs of the public transactions for the use of my children wherein I was privy to or could discover the true motives of action. There is more to be learned from experience than can be by precept, for the first makes a much stronger impression on us than the other and I am desirous that my children if possible may have all the advantages of my experience which perhaps I acquired too late in life for my own advantage.

I designed at first to have wrote only loose memoirs of what passed in my own time; but having lately read Mr. Smith's History of New York I think that as this is the first and only History of this Province, it probably may serve as a foundation for future history and therefor I think it may be of use to you to make some remarks on it. In the first place he has not been informed of some things, of other things he has been misinformed, and I wish I could not add that some things he seems to have willfully misrepresented. When I come to my own times I shall intermix the remarks on that History with the memoirs which I think may be of use to my children.

Truth and sincerity are so essential to history that as an historian would be laught at who should introduce his History with "I will tell you no Lye," I will not deceive you so when History is introduced more solemnly with "The sacred Laws of Truth have been infringed neither by positive Assertions, oblique, insidious Hints, wilful suppressions or corrupt misrepresentations,"† the author with men who know the world puts the reader more upon his guard.

Mr. Smith places the value of his History on his having extracted it from the records of the Province. No doubt this is of great advantage for the ascertaining of facts and chronology, but little can

---

* [The next ten letters were all written by Colden to his son, Alexander (1716–1774), who succeeded his father as Surveyor General of New York and also became Postmaster of New York City. The originals are in The New-York Historical Society and were printed in the Society's *Collections for the Year 1868* (New York, 1868), pp. 177–235. Ostensibly a running commentary on Smith's *History*, each letter treats a separate problem or gubernatorial administration. Together they constitute a kind of episodic provincial history writ small.]

† Preface to Smiths History.

be learned from thence of the motives and springs of action; and the life of history, the great use of it, is in discovering these first motives and springs of action. There are many things in his History of which he could have no information from the records.[8]

Mr. Smith gives the arguments at large which the Dutch Governor made use of to support the pretensions of the Dutch to the New Netherlands. This may be grateful to the descendants of the Dutch who live in New York, but it may be expected by the English that he should have given the answers to these pretensions in which he is silent. The Princes of Europe founded their pretensions in America on the first discovery and in taking possession. It was impossible to take possession of every part at once but by that of part with a publick declaration of the territory they intended to hold by this discovery and actual possession. There is no question that the first discovery of North America was under Commission from the King of England and that the first settlement was made by the English with a publick declaration by the King's Letters Patent that he claimed by that discovery and possession from the 39th to the 45th degree of latitude. After this according to the rules then and there observed among Potentates, no nation in amity with England could settle within these bounds without a breach of the amity between them. It must certainly [have] been on reasoning from these principles and the argument of superior force that the Dutch expelled the Swedes from Delaware. The Dutch took advantage of the intestine disorders and the civil war in England to establish themselves in the country claimed by the Crown of England, and the English certainly were in the right to reclaim this country as soon as the publick tranquility permitted them to do it. The Dutch in a similar case would have done the like. The cautious proceeding of the States General in giving their authority to the settling a colony on Hudson's River shews that that they were sensible of the justice and force of the English claim. It is common on declaration of war to reclaim countries which had been yielded on treaty for on a declaration of war all former treaties become void and in such reclaiming either side is fond of making use of the historeans of the other side to justify their claim.

The Dutch in this Province it is probable think the Articles of Surrender are still in force and that any breach of them is a piece of injustice to them and therefor among other things they may in their own minds justify themselves in carrying on the illicit trade with Holland in opposition to the Laws of Trade which has been carried on from New York for many years. But:

1. It may be justly doubted whether these articles could be construed properly to extend farther than to the persons of the Dutch inhabitants who then submitted.

2. When afterwards the States General by publick treaty quitted all claim to this country, no regard is had of these articles of surrender but the country is absolutely given up without condition.

3. If these very persons who submitted to the English Government voluntarily and without force renounced their allegiance and

submitted anew to the States of Holland, they then forfeited without doubt all the priviledges that they could claim by the articles of surrender.

That this was the case when the Dutch regained in 1673 what they called the New Netherlands I believe is true. I have been told by some of the Dutch inhabitants of New York who remembered the thing well, that the Dutch ships when they came under Staten Island had no thoughts of attempting the conquest of New York, but only to take in wood and water, knowing there was not sufficient force to hinder them; but that while they were there the Dutch inhabitants invited the Dutch commodore to take possession of the place at the same time informing him of the weakness of the English Garrison, the Governor and the greater part of the garrison being then absent at Esopus on an occasion which I shall afterwards mention.

When the Dutch ships came up to the town, the inhabitants all flocked to the shore to welcome them with all the demonstrations of joy which they could make. The inhabitants of Albany, Esopus, and on Delaware River made their submission to the Dutch without the least appearance of force. When the case is thus truly set forth, the surrender without capitulation is not so extraordinary nor the lenity of the sentence against Manning who commanded in the fort so ridiculous as it appears to be according to the account given of it in Mr. Smith's History.

Mr. Smith's account I know is founded on the records of New York; but can any man believe that Manning on his trial would confess absolutely the charge exhibited against him without excusing himself from the disposition in which the Dutch inhabitants were and the weakness of his own garrison or that if he had not greatly extenuated his crime that so mild a sentence could have been pronounced against him and by which he was certainly absolved from all treachery tho' found guilty of cowardice.

While Colonel Lovelace was Governor, the Esopus Indians made war on the Dutch setlers there. The Indians killed several and made many men and women prisoners. The remainder were forced into a small stockaded fort where they defended themselves with great difficulty against the Indians till they were relieved by the English Garrison of New York, the greatest part of which Colonel Lovelace sent with some pieces of cannon for their relief. While the Christians were besieged the Indians burnt some of their prisoners alive in sight of the fort; and while the Dutch of Esopus were in this distress several of their own countrymen from Albany came to a place called Sagartie about 10 miles from the fort and supplied the Indians with all kinds of ammunition. Such are the effects of having no other principle of action but the love of money. The Dutch of Esopus to this day remember this behavior of their countrymen of Albany and speak of them with the greatest indignation.

The Dutch of Esopus were all farmers, those of Albany who supplied the Indians were Handlers (as the Dutch call them), people who live by retailing goods to the Indians.

As soon as the English soldiers arrived the Indians fled into the woods. They were pursued and defeated. Peace was soon after concluded by which the Indians yielded all the land as far as any cannon had been carried which was to the upper end of Marbletown. Colonel Lovelace gave these conquered lands to his soldiers and called it Marbletown. The common men generally sold their shares and dispersed, but the families of the officers remain in that place to this day. They were Broadhead, Garton, Nottingham, and Pawling.

It may be observed to the honour of the English that there is not one instance of their killing and destroying in cold blood merely for their own security where their ennemies may have been thought too numerous. The Spanyards in America and the Dutch in the East Indies have acted otherwise. Many thousand innocent people have been sacrificed to their jealousy. I was told of one instance of the like nature in this country.

On a certain occasion, I walked from the North or Hudson's River to the East River at a little distance from the town in company with the Mayor and several old men who went on purpose to shew me the boundaries of some lands. As we passed over a piece of high ground between the place where Mr. DeLancy the Lieutenant Governor now lives in the Bowery and the East River, I was told by some of them that in the Dutch time a great number of Indians fled from the Eastward and encamped on this rising ground in hopes of the assistance and protection of the Dutch. They were received friendly but a number of the men of the town dressed themselves like Indians in the night, went out and fell upon the Indians while they were a sleep, murdered the greatest number of them, while a few made their escape into the town as to their friends, and the Indians never discovered this piece of treachery. The Dutch historians generally pass over these acts of cruelty in their own countrymen, however necessary they may have been thought for their own security, and the condemning them to oblivion or secreting them from all other nations is certainly most consistant with this kind of policy; but as certainly it is as much for the interest of other nations that they should not be forgot, especially to the English who abhor all such cruelties.

As to Mr. Smith's note at the bottom of page 32 with regard to the law *post liminium,* I would ask this Question: if the Dutch by virtue of this law could reclaim their inheritance after they had reconquered this country, could the English by the same law reclaim their inheritances of the Dutch after the English recovered the country?

While I have freely censured some parts of Mr. Smith's History, I cannot but take notice of an uncommon impartiality in a lawyer of applauding the exact administration of justice by Governors who ruled only by the dictates of their own discretion. He seems to grant that justice may be don under a despotic government, but I doubt whether it be possible that justice can be don where the administration of it is in the hands of lawyers, for tho' the judgment given may be just it is allwise attended with injustice in the expense and delay which attends it.

The Governors of New York took on them the power of granting divorces which has been in disuse at least ever since the Revolution; neither is there any court in this province that can give this remedy tho' in the neighboring colonies a divorce is more easily obtained than perhaps in any other Christian country.[9] Query whether this may not be for the advantage of a new country which wants people. It is certain that the natural increase of people in New England has been very great—perhaps more than in any other of the English colonies.

Now I have taken notice of what has occur'd to my memory and which I think deserves your notice to the time that the States of Holland renounced all claim to this country. If I continue at leisure and in health, you may expect to have more on the same subject from,

## 9. Cadwallader Colden to Alexander Colden

June 25, 1759

Dear Son,

There are only one or two things in Mr. Smith's History before the Revolution, that I shall observe upon, more than what I have taken notice of in my preceeding of the 15th. The first is his character of Sir Edmund Andross which he gives in the following words: "The Historians of New England where he was afterwards Governor *justly* transmit him to posterity under the odious character of a sycophantic tool to the Duke, and an arbitrary Tyrant over the people committed to his care. He Knew no Law, but the Will of his Master, and Kirk and Jeffries were not fitter instruments than he to execute the despotic projects of James II"[10]

The facts which Mr. Smith tells us in support of this character are, that the Duke of York recommended a Dutch clergyman, Nicholas Rensalaer, to Sir Edmund for a living in one of the churches in New York or Albany, *probably to serve the popish cause.* Is not this an *oblique, insidious hint?* Could King James do nothing without a view to serve popery? Sir Edmund Andross was a Protestant as many of the Dukes servants were. Might not they be desirous of a Dutch minister who had received ordination in the Church of England to preach to the Dutch in New York in their own language, where few of them understood English, and might they not do this without any design to promote popery? Mr. Smith's next proof of Sir Edmund's tyrannic disposition is that he summoned *Newenhytt,* the Dutch minister at Albany before the council, treating him with contempt and harassing him with an expensive attendance because *Newenhytt* disputed Rensalaer's right to administer the sacrament, which Mr. Smith tells us he did because Rensalaer had received Episcopal ordination and was not approved of by the classis of Amsterdam. Mr. Smith thinks this a small offence to deny that a person who has received Episcopal ordination can administer the Sacraments in an English colony, and to set up a foreign jurisdiction in ecclesiastic matters, within the dominion of the Crown of England. I say Mr. Smith thinks this a small offence when he complains of an expensive attendance on this account. Whatever he may think as an independent in principle, he knows better as a lawyer. As to my part, according to Mr. Smith's account of this matter, I think Sir Edmund shewd great moderation, in referring it at last to the Dutch consistory at Albany. The third instance of Sir Edmund's tyranny is that he called the Magistrates of Albany before him, because they had imprisoned Rensalaer for *dubious words* delivered in a sermon. Had Sir Edmund imprisoned any person for *dubious words,* I think it would have been a stronger proof of his tyranny, than the punishing the magistrates under him for doing it. Mr. Smith's last proof of Sir Edmund's tyranny is, his seizing and imprisoning the Governor of New Jersey. Mr. Smith does not tell us the reasons of this proceeding, and I know them not. [But Mr. Smith mistakes when he says that Sir Edmund was removed from the Government of New York. His having the Government of New England given him, while he was Governor of New York, if it prove any thing as to this point, shews that his conduct was approved of. Nicholson was only Lieutenant Governor of New York to act in Sir Edmund's absence from New York.]

Mr. Smith is sensible of the weakness of the proofs of Sir Edmund Andross' tyrannical disposition from any thing in his administration in New York and therefor he tells us it *was through want of more opportunities to shew himself in his true light,* another *oblique insidious hint* and positive assertion. Mr. Smith lays the stress of his proofs of Sir Edmund's tyrannic and sycophantic disposition on the New England historians. No doubt their being of the same principles with himself gives them the greater credit with him; but whether his own History will, with people of different principles add any thing to their opinion of the veracity and candour of independent historians, must be left to the judgement of the readers. However this be, it is certain that at the time Sir Edmund Andross governed the people of New England, they were zealous republicans, bigotted independents, having banished all others of different religious principles from among them, and persecuted some of them to death. They were enthusiastic to a degree as appears from their public proceedings in witchcraft. To all which is to be added a stiff formal behavior different from the rest of mankind. Among such a people it must have been very difficult for a Gentleman of Sir Edmund's education, and of his principles, both as to religion and politics, to behave so as to please them; for moderation often gives the greatest offence to bigots. If it be considered likewise, that as Sir Edmund was appointed their Governor, in consequence of their having had their charter vacated, in the court of chancery in England, he by his comeing among them, at that time, must be received with great disgust. He must be a very extraordinary man indeed, who, in his circumstances, could at all times keep his temper among such a people. These things I only observe in general; for I am, in no shape informed of the particulars of Sir Edmund's administration at Boston. The Revolution opened a wide door for the people of New England to make their complaints and to expose

Sir Edmunds character in the strongest colours; yet notwithstanding of this King William and his ministers, soon afterward, appointed Sir Edmund Andross Governor of Virginia, a more lucrative government than New York, and Massachusetts Bay together. Where he distinguished himself by putting the Secretaries Office and the Records in good order which before he came had been in the greatest confusion. This certainly shew'd that he had a regard to the properties of the people whom he governed to have them secured for he had no personal interest in it. On the whole of this character of Sir Edmund Andross, I shall leave it to the reflections of any impartial reader how far *the sacred laws of truth have been infringed neither by positive assertions, oblique insidious hints, willful suppressions, or corrupt misrepresentations.*

When a man of candour finds a gentleman's character aspersed with such odious epithets as "*Arbitrary Tyrant, Sycophantic tool &c,*" without proof to support them, he cannot avoid to have his indignation raised, and thereby a quite contrary effect is produced from what the historian designed. From any thing I can learn in Mr. Smith's History of Sir Edmund's administration in New York (for I disregard "*Positive Assertions*") Sir Edmund was a good Governor. It is a public injury to have a good Governor represented as the worst.

My dear son, take special care, that you be never provoked to asperse any man's character and to represent any man as a bad man without the clearest evidence; for it often happens that the authors of calumny only expose themselves with men of candour, and thereby discover the *badness of their own hearts* in a manner that could not otherwise be don. It is of use to reflect how often we ourselves have don amiss and that under some circumstances good men have don what they ought not to have don. Remember what I now write is only for your own private use, and that at my age, I am unwilling to set dogs a barking. The noise of discords is more than ever disagreable to the ear of

Your Affectionate Father<br>CADWALLADER COLDEN

[a postscript]

There is only one thing more to remark in the History of New York before the Revolution: it is this. Mr. Smith takes notice of the advantageous turn in Colonel Dongan's administration in favour of the liberties of the people by his calling an Assembly of the representatives of the people for enacting of laws. How comes it that these laws are absolutely disregarded since the Revolution? It is certain that the Acts of Parliament under James the Second remain'd as much in force as those under any of his predecessors or successors. How comes it that the Acts of Assembly under his governor are not of the same force as those under any other of the King's Governors? I expected he would have answered this as a lawyer for it is as material as many things he has particularly observed; but he is absolutely silent on this head. The only answer I can give to it is that when laws are made inconsistent with the well being of any community, no authority can keep them in force.

They become *Felo's de se*.* One of them I have been told gave a perpetual revenue and that was thought sufficient to destroy all the rest. If I mistake not such inconsistent with the good of the people are to be found among the English statutes entirely in disuse tho' not repealed, but I question that their malignancy was destructive of all the other statutes however beneficial they might be which were enacted in the same reign.

## 10.  Cadwallader Colden to Alexander Colden†

Coldengham, July 5, 1759

Dear Son:

We may clearly see the the pernicious effects of liberty turned to licentiousness in New York, at the time of the Revolution. All the Governors of New York, even supposing them as bad as Mr. Smith represents them, did not produce half the mischief, in all the time of their government, which was produced in one year by the suppression of legal government. Blood shed, rapine, confiscations, arbitrary & tyrannic acts & animosities, which could not be stifled in many years, were the consequence. It is evident that King William & his ministers thought the Revolution could not be obstructed, by continueing King James his officers in the exercise of their authority. This appears by the orders given for that purpose, & that they thought it most prudent to do so. They must have been very weak indeed, who could imagine, that the power of New York, tho' it had been united, could in the least promote or obstruct the Revolution in Great Brittain: & therefor, in my opinion, none in New York could claim any merit on that occasion. They only pursued their own disorderly passions, without any real concern for the good of their country. This is too generally the case in all popular commotions, under the plausible outcry for liberty. How cautious then ought every one to be in contributing anything towards the weakning of the legal powers of government, or to do any thing which may give power to a disorderly mob. A mob can never be directed by reason; but is hurried into the worst extremes, by prejudice and passion. The consequence generally turns to the destruction of those, who plumed them selves in their ability to incite the mob, which afterwards they are often no more able to govern, than to govern a whirl wind. Every attempt to put power in the mob ought to be crushed in the bud, especially in mixed governments. This was allwise don in the Roman republic, so long as they were able to preserve their liberty.[11]

* The Scotch historians tell us that the heads of clans had by law the first night of their tenants bride and that this law remains unrepealed because of its being so shameful in itself. Mr. Smith tells us Colonel Dongan was a good governor and had the interest of the people at heart; from whence came these bad laws which are to be sunk in oblivion from the representatives of the people?

† [Published as a separate in *Collections of The New York Historical Society for the Year 1869* (New York, 1870), pp. 201–212.]

Our ennemies never fail to take advantage of intestine divisions & confusions. It is probable this induced the French at this time to attempt the conquest of New York. Mr. Smith has given an account of this, from Charlevoix; but he has omitted to inform us of an instruction given to the Count de Frontinac, in case of success, which may be of use to the people to know. Viz: The French King ordered that all the inhabitants should be driven out of the country, Papists only excepted, who would swear allegiance to the King of France.

Mr. Smith tells us that Colonel Slaughter, the first Governor of New York after the Revolution, was *"utterly destitute of every qualification of government, licentious in his Morals, Avaritious & poor."* Who can read this character without thinking that it is greatly exaggerated? If this be true, & characters which you will find afterwards, New York gained little by the Revolution. Colonel Slaughter may well be thought weak, in having been prevailed on, while in liquor, to order the execution of a person whom he had resolved to have reprieved till their Majesty's pleasure should be known, as I have been told he was resolved; but this is no proof of licentiousness of his morals. Nor is there anything in the History of New York to prove his avarice. That he was poor is no proof of it.

By the first Act or Resolve of the first Assembly after the Revolution, a power is assumed of repealing laws without the concurrence of the other branches of the Legislature, or a judicial power of declaring them void. A power which in no wise belonged to them: & which, if countenanced may be highly prejudicial both to the Crown & the subject: & yet this usurped power has, in this instance, taken effect ever since. Do you think if a Governor had but attempted to usurp any such illegal power, that Mr. Smith would have passed it over without a note, as he does this in the Assembly.

As to the claim of the people of New York as an inherent right to be represented in assembly, of which Mr. Smith takes notice page 75 they seem often to forget their subordination, in the manner they make this claim. I shall mention one remarkable difference between the claim of the people of England, and the claim of the people in the colonies. It is impossible that the Supreme Legislature, that the King, Lords, & Commons can be guilty of High Treason; but it cannot be doubted, that a Governor, Council, & Assembly may be guilty. It is an illegal usurpation in a subordinate power to claim the same rights & privileges with the supreme. The admitting of it would at least be a solecism in politicks.

Mr. Smith's character of Colonel Fletcher is that, *"He was by Profession a Soldier, a man of Strong passions, & inconsiderable talents, very active, & very avaricious."* I find several instances in the History of New York, which shew that Colonel Fletcher pursued the interest of his country with zeal & activity: & I discover no want of talents, unless it be, that he seems not to have studied much the art of cajoling an assembly; & this Mr. Smith might have excused, by his being bred a soldier, had Mr. Smith any inclination

to excuse any Governor. But I cannot discover the least instance of
Colonel Fletcher's avarice. Surely his thanking the Assembly & at
the same time refuseing a present of £500 to himself & £500 more
to be distributed among the officers & soldiers is not told as an
instance of his avarice: nor is his contributing largely to the building of Trinity Church another instance.

As the greatest part of the province consisted of Dutch inhabitants,
all our Governors (Mr. Smith says) as well in the Duke's time as
after the Revolution, thought it good policy to incourage English
preachers & school masters in this colony; but he seems to differ in
opinion, by calling Fletcher a bigot, for being bent on such a
*"Project"* as he terms it. There was not one Church of England
nor one English school in the English colony of New York. But
Colonel Fletcher built one church & recommended to the assembly
to provide for ministers & school masters, *ergo* he was a bigot. I
do not think that I trespass on candour when I suppose, that if an
Independent Governor had been bent to bring over the whole colony
to his principles, Mr. Smith would have called it a laudable zeal in
him. The same kind of warmth, which is zeal for Independency, is
bigotry for the Church of England. Popular republican writers know
the use of epithets, with superficial readers, & never neglect the use
of them.

While Colonel Fletcher was Governor, the inhabitants of New
York carried on a trade to Madagascar, while that island was frequented by pirates. Many likewise of the pirates came & dispersed
on Long Island & round Delaware Bay. They brought a great quantity
of gold with them. When I came first to America, in the year 1710,
no payments were made without a considerable part in chickeens
or Arabian pieces, tho scarce one of them be now to be seen.
Several of the now principal families, I have been told, took their
first rise from their commerce with the pirates, some of them by
gaming. However it has been often remarked, that none of the
pirates made any use of their money to any real advantage to themselves, except one Jones, who settled on the South side of Long
Island, whose son made a remarkable figure as Speaker of the Assembly, while Mr. Clinton was Governor:[12] excepting this one, no
remains of the others are to be discovered. That Colonel Fletcher
was really concerned in this commerce no where appears, so far
as I know, or have heard. It would have been very difficult for him
to have put a stop to it with his utmost indeavour, where there are
so many harbours, under the inspection of no officer, & where the
temptations to concealment were so strong.

I intend to remark no farther on Mr. Smith's character of any
Governor, because what I have wrote I think sufficient to shew how
far his characters are to be depended on. Notwithstanding of what
I have observed, it does not follow that he has willfully & maliciously
calumniated them. The force of early prejudice, from a narrow
education, a weak judgment & a stubborn temper of mind are
sufficient to account for these & many more absurdities in such
kind of writers. How differently, at all times, do different sects &

parties think & speak of the same actions. The truth often is hid between them, & neither of them discover it. I shall add a little story of Colonel Fletcher, which I had from Mr. Sharpass, who came to New York with him, & retained the character of a very honest man to his death. It will in part shew Colonel Fletcher's character.

Colonel Fletcher was Lieutenant Colonel of a Regiment, which was ordered to Flanders. King William was scantily supplied with money, & for that reason the soldiers were often unpaid, or paid only in part. This was the case with this regiment, when they were ordered to march for imbarcation. On their march Colonel Fletcher, with some of the officers, had gon forward to an inn, when the regiment mutinied, & refused to march farther, till their arrears were paid them. They formed themselves in good order, with their sergeants only at their head; the commissioned officers being forced to leave them. Colonel Fletcher having notice of this, immediately returned, & after having harangued them & reasoned with them for some time, he ordered them to march; but not a man would stir a foot. On which he rode off to the right of the regiment, & pulling out a pistol said, "You right hand man, march, or I will shoot you through the head." The right hand man immediately moved his legs, and every man marched after him, as the Colonel on horseback took the ground which they left, & came close up to those, who according to their order were to march next, with his pistol in his hand: & thus put an end to the mutiny.

I intend to make no farther remarks on Mr. Smith's History, till I come to the time in which I had opportunity to be well informed of the public transactions; only before I leave the subject I have been upon, I cannot forbear taking notice of that assumeing air which these Independents[13] take upon them, in judgeing & condemning others, & in setting up for Patriots. This they know gives them authority among the gaping mob, allwise pleased to hear their superiors ill spoken of; but it lessens them more with men of sense & discretion, who love order & peace, & detest tumults and confusion. In place of argument, I think, it may be better to set the colony of New York, in its worst state of government, while it was under the despotic rule of the Duke of York, in contrast with the colony of the Massachusets Bay, while it was entirely under the government of genuine independent republicans, that we may see how much reason these modern Independents have to boast.

In New York a general liberty of conscience was allowed; not the least appearance of persecution on religious matters. In the Massachuset Bay none but Independents[14] were allowed the common privileges; all others were persecuted, either driven out of the country or severely whipt, & some put to death.

In New York Mr. Smith allows that justice was speedily administer'd, the people remain'd easy & quiet in their possessions, & very few law suits any where, except in those parts which were peopled from New England. In the Massachusets Bay, on the contrary, it is known, that the people were exceedingly litigious, on every little difference at law. Offences were multiplied by positive laws, restraining the innocent freedom & pleasures or diversions usual among men. A man was whipt at Boston who accidentally meeting his wife in the street, after long absence, kissed her. By this unnecessary restraint of our natural freedom, hypocrisy was unavoidably introduced among all ranks. By these unnatural restraints, a kind of inthusiasm prevailed in Boston, which, if it had not been restrained by the King's authority, had gon near to have unpeopled the country, by the numerous prosecutions & executions on pretense of witch craft.

Lastly, New York generally was at peace & in amity with the Indians and its neighbours; But New England was allmost perpetually at war with the Indians, & at variance with its neighbours.

In short we have instances in history of kingdoms well governed, under absolute monarchy; but it seems to me, that it is impossible that a people can be happy, under a government formed on genuine Independent principles: & this opinion is confirmed by what I have observed in New England, the only country in the world, in which the government was formed on these principles. Every prudent man will, as far as in his power, guard against the illegal usurpations of men in the administration; but at the same time, he will be no less careful that legal authority be not so far depressed, as to introduce licentiousness & public disorder. Tho this maxim be evident to the meanest capacity, it is very little minded by popular declaimers.

I am now come to a period, proper to put an end to this letter; but before I do it I shall mention two problems, which occurr'd to me, on reading Mr. Smith's History, the solution of which have given me some thought.

1. How comes it that the old genuine Independents, & Enthusiasts in general, have so little regard to veracity? I think it not difficult to find the solution of this. Enthusiasts are at perpetual variance with nature; but truth consists in a conformity with nature; & therefor Enthusiasts are at continual variance with truth. Generally, with some exceptions however, they, who have a byass to enthusiasm, have likewise a byass to lyeing. They have still a stronger propensity to believe lyes, & the more absurd or contrary to nature the more greedily they receive them.

2. What is the true definition of a bigot? We find the zealous men of all sects & of all parties freely bestowing this name on each other, it may be of use therefor to discover, if we can, who are really bigots, & who not. I must answer this like a doctor. It is a desease of the brain, which, without distinction, often seizes the zealots of all sects and parties, of whatever denomination they be: and the pathognomonic system, by which it may be distinguished from all other deseases of the mind, is that they think it right to tell any lye, either in defence of or for promoting their sect or party. There are two distinct & very different species of this desease. One arises from a preternatural formation of the brain itself. These when ever they obtain power become tyrants: and all tyrants are bigots. Indeed tyranny & this species of bigotry are essentially the

same, both agree in this general maxim: Every thing is right which is necessary for our purpose, whether it be by calumny or flattery, murder or fawning, robbery or bribery, perjury or praying &c. From what other principles could the prosecutions & executions on witchcraft have arisen in Boston. They think them fools who have any squeemishness of conscience in the use of the necessary means. In the most common acceptation, bigotry is only employed in speculative opinions, & tyranny on our external actions; but, on due reflection, you will find that they both proceed from the same principles, in different persons, according to their different stations in life. The other species of bigotry arises only from some disorder in the fluids of the brain. These seldom go farther than to the free use of any kind of words, which serve their purpose. The first sort is seldom cured, but the other is frequently by accustoming the patient to the use of free air, & change of company.

From what I have said I think a distinction may be easily made, between zeal & bigotry. A proper degree of warmth and spirit is necessary to carry on any great design; but then zeal makes use only of laudable means: bigotry considers nothing farther than that the means are proper for its purpose. It is not however to be supposed that all lyars are bigots or enthusiasts: no only such who lie in a certain & regular system. Irregular lies arise only from sudden fits of disorder in the imagination of weak minds, like hysteric fits in woemen. You see that I continue to write with that freedom which you my son may expect from

Your affectionate father
CADWALLADER COLDEN.

# 11. Cadwallader Colden to Alexander Colden

Coldengham, Sept. 25, 1759.

Dear Son,

You know that since my last to you on the subject of Mr. Smith's history of New York my thoughts have been diverted to other matters. I shall now begin where I proposed in my last in making remarks on that part of it where I had many opportunities of being well informed.[15]

I know not on what authority Mr. Smith says that Mr. Hunter when a boy was put aprentice to an apothecary; it may be on as slender authority as many other things he writes. When I knew Mr. Hunter he was an exceedingly well shaped and well proportioned man, tho' then advanced in years. In his younger years he had been of uncommon strength and activity. He understood the belles lettres well and had an intimacy with the distinguished men of wit at that time in England, among them Dr. Arbuthnot, Queen Anne's favorite physician, was his most intimate and useful friend tho' he and the doctor differed greatly in their political sentiments for Mr. Hunter was a stanch Whig. He wrote some pieces in the *Tatlers*. When he was appointed Governor of New

York a very high compliment was made in one of the *Tatlers* to him under the name of "Eboracensis." He wrote some elegant little pieces in poetry which never appeared in his name. He had an exceeding pretty and entertaining manner of telling a Tale and was a most agreable companion with his intimate friends.[16] He was fond of men of learning and encouraged them whenever he had opportunity. In short he was a gentleman of extraordinary abilities both natural and acquired and had every qualification requisite in a Governor.

The first appearance Mr. Hunter made in the world was at the Revolution as one of the gentlemen who served as a guard under the Bishop of London to the Princess Anne when she retired from her father's court and he soon afterwards received a commission in King William's army. He continued in the army all King William's wars and Queen Anne's till after the battle of Ramillies in which time he gave many proofs of high courage.

One winter when part of the Duke of Marlborough's army was quartered in Holland, Mr. Hunter was Lt Colonel and Commandant of the troops quartered in one of their towns. The magistrates of this town had so far incurred the displeasure of the people of the town that nothing would satisfy them but the deposition of their magistrates by a new election. The magistrates found they could not by their interest prevent this and were become very uneasy and affrayed and therefor applied to Colonel Hunter to hinder the assembling of the people for that purpose, representing to him that they had allwise been zealous in the interest of the confederacy and that if new magistrates should be chosen they would be in an opposite interest. As Colonel Hunter knew that it was dangerous for the soldiery to interfere in the civil government of the Republic, he wrote to the Duke of Marlborough for instructions. The Duke was cautious in his answer, but by it the Colonel understood that the Duke would be well pleased to have the election prevented. Notwithstanding all the efforts of the Magistrates, the towns people at last met in the great Church to proceed to a new election. Colonel Hunter called the Regiment together privately without beat of drum and marched them towards the great church and when he was near it ordered all the drums to beat the granadiers march. This so frightened the people in the church that they rushed out by the doors and windows in the greatest fright and confusion. Many were bruised and lamed and an end thereby put to the attempt for a new election. Colonel Hunter marched the regiment past the church (without taking the least notice of what passed) to the place where the Regiment usually performed their exercise. When after they had gone through their usual exercise he dismissed them.

At the battle of Ramillies, Mr. Hunter was one of the Duke of Marlborough's *aid de camps*. In the time of the battle Mr. Cadogan as from the Duke ordered Colonel Hunter to go to the General of the horse on the right and order him to carry all the horse from the right and join the horse on the left and immediately attack the French horse. This was such an extraordinary order that Mr. Hunter thought proper to repeat it aloud in the hearing of several officers and asked if this was his Grace's order to which Mr. Cadogan answered yes. When Mr. Hunter delivered these orders to the General of the horse on the left he seemed surprised and after a little hesitation swore he would leave one regiment, which he did, and then put the orders he had received in execution. To this it is agreed by all, both English and French, that the victory was principally owing. But what is still more remarkable is that Mr. Hunter believed as he told me that Mr. Cadogan had given the orders as from the Duke without the Duke's privity, and what makes this the more probable is that the Duke about that time was born down dismounted and for some time in great danger so that he was not in a capacity to give orders. Mr. Hunter that day tired out four horses in the execution of his duty.

This was such a signal piece of service in Mr. Cadogan, without takeing the least honour of it to himself, that the Duke remained ever after very sensible of it. He therefore resolved to give Mr. Cadogan the honour of takeing Antwerp, the most considerable city in Flanders, and for that purpose the Duke gave him the command of that part of the army which was to form the siege, and Mr. Hunter had the command of the horse which were to invest the place, while the foot were on their march. When Mr. Hunter came before the town some of the French officers came out to parley. While he was in discourse with them and persuading them to surrender as they could hope for no relief, a merchant of the town came behind Mr. Hunter and pulled him by the sleeve. Mr. Hunter turned and went aside with the merchant. Sir, said the merchant, it is to no purpose to talk with these men, but I believe you may have better success with the Spanish Governor who commands in the citadel. Mr. Hunter asked by what means he could come to treat with the Spanish Governor. The merchant answered that the Spanish Governor is a good natured man and entirely directed by his secretary, and added, "if you will give me leave, I will bring the Secretary to you." The method of doing it was immediately settled. By the Secretary's means Mr. Hunter had a private conference with the Spanish Governor and the terms agreed to, viz: that the Spanish Governor should be continued Governor of Antwerp under King Charles and that the Secretary should have one of the Spanish regiments then in garrison. Mr. Hunter informed the Duke, by express, of these terms and he readily confirmed them. The French having discovered that the Spanish Governor was resolved to admit the English troops into the citadel they likewise capitulated for the town before the army under Mr. Cadogan could come up to form the siege. After everything had been settled, Mr. Hunter, highly pleased with the service he had done, went to wait on the Duke but was surprised to be received very coolly. Sir, said the Duke, I think you might have trusted to me to publish the service you have done. Mr. Hunter protested that he had not either by word or writing mentioned anything of it to any person living, and added as this affair could not be carried on without the privity of several of the officers who were along with him he could not answer for what they may have done. But as the Duke hereby was disapointed in the honour he designed for his favorite, Mr. Cadogan, he resented it on Mr. Hunter. Perhaps the Duke thought that Mr. Hunter was too much in the secret of what gained the victory at Ramillies and was chagrined on that account. Mr. Hunter was highly disgusted on such treatment after so signal service and thereupon left the army in the winter and went over to London.

Here you have some material anecdotes in history which I think are not to be found in any thing which is printed, but they may be depended upon for I had them from Mr. Hunter's mouth with every particular circumstance which attended them which would be too tedious to relate here and I cannot sufficiently depend on my memory.

Mr. Hunter had friends in Queen Anne's court and by their interest he obtained the government of Virginia. Mr. Smith mistakes when he says that he was appointed Lieutenant Governor of Virginia. Mr. Hunter had the commission of Governor in Chief, but it was by a compromise with the Earl of Orkney. He was taken prisoner by a French squadron in his passage to Virginia and carried to France. By his having lost the Duke of Marlborough's favour he could not easily obtain an exchange. He had leave to return to England on his parole to solicit his exchange and at last was exchanged for the Bishop of Quebec after he had returned to Paris.

The Duke of Marlborough's influence over the Queen began about this time to lessen, and Dr. Arbuthnot prevailed with the Queen to name Mr. Hunter for the government of Jamaica which happened to be vacant without consulting her Ministry who had designed that government for another; but Mr. Hunter being apprehensive that if he went to Jamaica against the inclinations of the ministry he would be made uneasy in his government, and the government of New York becoming vacant at this time by the death of Lord Lovelace, the Ministers were willing that he should have the government of New York. Therefor Mr. Hunter desired his friend to inform the Queen that he would rather have the government of New York than Jamaica and it was accordingly granted him.

As Mr. Hunter was without doubt a man of the greatest abilities that ever governed New York, I think the relating these most remarkable incidents in his life previous to his having the government may serve to illustrate his character and this is a proper period to put an end to this letter before I begin an account of his government which if I continue in a humour to write, you may soon expect from,

Your affectionate father.

## 12. Cadwallader Colden to Alexander Colden.

COLDENGHAM   October 15, 1759

I intend now to write most remarkable parts or incidents in Mr. Hunter's administration which at this time occur to my memory.

About the time Mr. Hunter was appointed Governor of New York, a great number of Germans were encouraged to come over to England. The ministry thought it might be of public advantage to send over a number of them with Mr. Hunter to be employed in makeing of pitch and tar. They were transported at the charge of the government and furnished with large iron kettles and other necessaries for that purpose. Mr. Hunter was to subsist them and to draw on the Treasury for all necessary expenses. Mr. Hunter, after his arrival, employed them accordingly and drew bills on the treasury for the expense. But the Queen having changed the ministry, and the new ministry endeavoring to make every measure of their predecessors as far as they could unpopular, this of importing and employing foreigners was exposed to censure and among other things that it contributed to put the church in danger which at that time was the popular cry. The Treasury refused to pay Mr. Hunter's bills and absolutely disapproved of the agreement made with the Germans for their settling the colony of New York. This put Mr. Hunter under great difficulties in the beginning of his administration as all his bills were protested and he became personally liable for the payment and discredited him with the people of the province. The Germans looked to him only for their subsistence and for the performance of the other parts of the agreement made with them. Their clamours were for some time abated by Mr. Hunter's inlisting a considerable number of them into the forces that were raised on the expedition at that time intended against Canada. After this enterprise ended unsuccessfully, these Germans were disbanded and suffered to take their arms with them. Now they not only became more clamorous but became also mutinous.

Mr. Hunter, in his return from Albany, where he met the Five Nations of Indians to compose their minds after their disappointment by their failure of the enterprise against Canada in which they had been engaged, stopt at Mr. Livingston's house near to which these Germans were settled. The principal men among them came to him and demanded the performance of the promises which had been made them. Mr. Hunter for some time reasoned the matter with them by informing them of the reason of their disappointment and how he had suffered more than they had with a promise of using his best endeavors to obtain them satisfaction, but they continued turbulent and he was at the same time informed that a great number of the Germans were together arrived in an adjoining wood. With some difficulty he put them off for two days with a promise to think of some method to give them satisfaction and an answer on the morning of the third. Mr. Hunter immediately sent an express to Albany, which is forty miles distant from the place where he was, with orders to the commanding officer to press sloops to carry down immediately the two independent companies which were posted there. They arrived in the night before the time Mr. Hunter was to meet the Germans. The officer was ordered to land his men and keep them together under the bank of the river near the house without shewing themselves and on a signal to be given to march them up briskly to the house with drums beating. The principal men of the Germans came as appointed and at the same time the other shew'd themselves at a distance in a body armed. Mr. Hunter did not now treat them with all the complaisance he did before, and one of them beginning to bluster with threatening language, the signal was made for the soldiers to march. The Governor with his own hands seized the fellow who had threatened him and some other gentlemen who were with him seized the rest. Upon the appearance of the soldiers, the Germans without doors immediately departed, some of them discharging their pieces as they went off. The soldiers marched directly into the German village and disarmed them.

Mr. Hunter has been much blamed in respect to the Germans, as if he had broke the promise made them, whereas the breach was by the Ministry, and Mr. Hunter was really a fellow sufferer with the Germans. But after this riotous behavior with design to force a compliance by seizing the Governor's person, he thought it imprudent and unbecoming in him to give them encouragement.

Governor Burnet afterwards gave lands to many of the Germans. They in general have proved industrious, useful members in the society and orderly. But when numbers of people think they have injustice done them and have not legal means within their reach for redress they commonly and naturally become mutinous and fly to force. This has been the true reason of the cruel wars with Indians lately and perhaps at all times.

Mr. Smith makes such mention of Colonel Peter Schuyler on several occasions that had you known him as I did you would pay little regard to Mr. Smith's characters whether in panegyric or satyre. Colonel Schuyler was a plain country farmer who had on some occasions given proof of his courage. This with strong connexions between that family and some of the Mohawk tribe gave him a considerable interest with the Mohawks but as to the other tribes it was in no respect such as Mr. Smith represents it. His whole exterior and deportment had much of the Indian mixed with the sullen Dutch manner. He was no way distinguished by abilities either natural or acquired, and you may judge of his sense of honour by his being prevailed on by Mr. Nicholson to join with him in the grossest imposition on the Queen and the British Nation by carrying to England five or six common Indians and making them personate one the Emperor of the Five Nations and the others the kings of each nation. He might have paid dear for such an attempt had it not been that the Ministry were at that time fond of amuseing the people with the eclat of such an appearance at court, for they might easily have been informed if they knew it not that there is no such thing among the Five Nations as either emperor or king. The Five Nations so far resented it that they never afterwards would suffer one of these Indians to appear in their public councils. I saw several years after this one of these Indians standing at a distance among the women and young men while the Five Nations were at a public conference with the Governor of New York.

As I have no thoughts of mentioning any thing particularly of the

Indians dureing Mr. Hunter's administration it may be proper to observe that he had so great a diffidence of all the people at Albany that at the public meetings with the Indians he had allwise a French woman standing by him who had married one of our Indians to inform him whether the interpreters had done their part truely between him and the Indians, notwithstanding that Colonel Schuyler was present at the same time. This woman, commonly called Madame Montour, had a good education in Canada before she went among the Indians and was very useful to Mr. Hunter on many occasions, for which reason she had a pension and was sometimes admitted to his table in her Indian dress. It is certain that the Indians have had at all times great diffidence in the interpreters being allwise taken from among the traders who make a practice in deceiving the Indians.

Queen Anne changed her ministry soon after the time that Mr. Hunter arrived in his government, and he thereby lost the support of his best friends. Mr. Hunter was far from being a high churchman in principle. Mr. Nicholson was a zealous church man in the highest sense of the word, and at that time when "The Church" became the popular cry and was the political ingine of the ministerial faction, he was thought a proper person to be employed and received a commission to command the provincial forces which were to attack Canada by land while the forces from England attacked it by way of St. Laurence River, tho' he had nothing to recommend him for that service besides his zeal for the church, for he was not bred a soldier nor had he seen any military service which deserved the name. He was subject to excessive fits of passion so far as to lose the use of his reason. After he had been in one of these fits while he had the command of the army, an Indian said to one of the officers, "The general is drunk." "No," answered the officers "he never drinks any strong liquor." The Indian replied, "I do not mean that he is drunk with rum. He was born drunk."

The greatest number of the inhabitants of New-York were at that time of republican principles, consisting of Dutch and English Independents.[17] The assemblies are at all times fond of power and to have their Governor dependent on them, tho' they cover this view with different pretences. At this time the Church clergy joined in the design to distress the Governor in hopes of haveing the good churchman, Colonel Nicholson, appointed governor. He had a crowd of clergymen allwise about him who were continually extolling his merits among the people and doing all in their power to lessen Mr. Hunter. Mr. Hunter had then a hard task. His friends in the ministry out of place, his bills to a great value protested. Mr. Nicholson and the clergy who ought to have assisted him endeavoring to undermine him, and the Assembly refusing to grant any support on the terms on which he could accept of it without breach of his instructions. Tho' he was at the same time so sensible of the difficulties he was under as to say to some of his friends that he expected to dye in a jail, he kept up his spirits, never suffered the least dejection or diffidence of his affairs to appear in public. He kept up the dignity of the Governor without lessening the expence which attended it notwithstanding [all] of the difficulties he was under as to money. At this time while Mr. Hunter had the greatest reason to be shagreened and out of humour, he diverted himself in composing a farce with the assistance of Mr. Morris which he called *Androborus* (the man eater). In this the general (Nicholson), the clergy, and the Assembly were so humorously exposed that the laugh was turned upon them in all companies and from this laughing humour the people began to be in good humour with their Governor and to despise the idol of the clergy.[18]

A violent party spirit had been kept up with great animosity between those who joined with Leisler at the Revolution and the others who opposed him. They who were in opposition to Leisler generally had the greatest influence in the Assembly, and were in favour with all the succeeding Governors except the Earl of Bellomont and Lt. Governor Nanfan. In the year 1713 Leisler's party had a majority in the Assembly. There were great complaints from numbers of people by their want of payment for public services. The Leisler party thought they had been unjustly used by preceeding Assemblies and therefor they took this opportunity of doing themselves justice. When the Assembly, after having granted a revenue for five years, resolved to pay all the debts of the government by striking bills of credit for that purpose to the value of 27,680 pounds to be sunk in twenty one years by an excise on strong liquors.

In this bill, payment was made for services don in the year 1687 and for services don in every year from that time downward. Leisler's son had 2,025 pounds allowed him for his father's services and expenses at the time of the Revolution and most of his adherents had allowances made to them. William Smith put in a demand of 356 pounds 17s 10d½ for goods taken by force from Gabriel Minvielle by Leisler, and the assembly gave six pence in full of all demands. From the proceedings at this time, this conclusion, I think, may be fairly drawn, that either former Assemblies had been unjust in refuseing or neglecting to pay just debts so long due or this Assembly acted profusely in giveing away their constituent's money in favour to their friends. Or perhaps the former Assemblies and this, all of them, acted partially and more from favour or resentment than from justice. Governor Hunter had all his demands paid. In the act it was declared that as public notice had been made for every one to make his demands who had any claim on the Government that all the publick debts were paid and that no claim for any past service should after this be allowed. We shall soon see how well this was observed. But by a clause in the act the bills were not to be issued until the act received the royal approbation.

On the Queen's death the Assembly was dissolved and a new Assembly called in which the superiority of the Leisler party was greater than in the former Assembly and resolved to make up for the suffering of their party while the opposite faction had been so long in power. They therefore resolved in contradiction to the former act that many debts and services were left unpaid and rewarded

by that act which were as justly due as those which were paid,
(here they confirm the observation I before made) and passed a bill
which was afterwards enacted for issuing bills to the value of 41,517
ounces and a half of Spanish coined plate or of 16,607 pounds current money of New York at 8s per ounce, as Spanish money at that
time passed for the sinking and paying of which the excise on strong
liquors was continued from 1734 to 1739 and a duty was laid on
wine and spirits for seventeen years from the time of passing the act.

All who had served under Leisler as soldiers or otherwise were
paid for their services and many others for services since the year
1687. Each of the Council had 250 ounces, each of the Assembly
from 183 ounces to 275. The Governor had 2,525 ounces, 17 penny weight and a half for incidents and extraordinary disbursements.
They calculated to half a penny weight in the allowance to the Governor to shew how careful they had been not to allow him a half
penny weight too much. But the leading men in the Council and
Assembly besides the common allowance with some of their friends
had considerable payments made them generally for services don
without mentioning any particular service. Mr. Livingston had 3,710
ounces of plate. I believe he never was exceeded in soliciting for
himself, by any man.

The Assembly was not willing to trust so useful an act to the
royal approbation as the former had been, and therefor it was enacted
to take effect immediately. Indeed it never had the royal approbation.
In the preamble to the first act the Assembly say that the debts of
the government were occasioned by misapplication of the funds and
extravagant expending of the revenue by former governors. Their
saying so would not be a sufficient proof to any man that knew
them. I have known many things asserted in the public resolves
which not one of the leading members would assert to be truth
when singly by himself. There has been a mighty clamour at all
times made in general terms of the misapplication of public money
by governors, but when they were called upon to give particular
instances I never heard of any except of £1500 pounds granted for
fortyfying the Narrows on the river below New York which Lord
Cornbury applied to building a pleasure house on Nutten Island
for himself and succeeding governors to retire to when he inclined
to free himself from business. But I believe it may be safely asserted that all the extravagant expending of the revenue by the
governors of New York put together does not equal the profusion
of the public money by this Assembly. Mr. Smith passes slightly
over this extraordinary act of his favorite part of our Constitution.

Mr. Hunter was seized with a violent rheumatism in the winter
of the year 1718 which ended in an obstinate sciatica which made
him lame. His lady was heir to the estate of Sir Thomas Orby and
he was desirous to secure that estate for his children and he had
hopes of recovering what was due to him from the Treasury on
account of the Germans. But as he foresaw that the leaving his
government if it was known some time before he did, might give
occasion to intrigues, he kept his design absolutely secret from his

friends and domestics. Not a single man was informed of it till he communicated it to the Assembly after they had gone through the business on which they were called. You may see by their address in Mr. Smith's History, on that occasion, that no governor could leave his government with greater reputation than he did. I cannot forbear to tell you what he heard him say not many days before this address with indignation in his countenance. "People think it a fine thing to be a governor. A governor by ——— a Tom Turdman's is a better office than to rake in the dunghill of these people's vile affections." You know that the Assemblies in North America consist generally of a low rank of people who have no generous principles. But it was much worse at that time. Several of the Assembly were Dutch boors, grossly ignorant and rude, who could neither write or read nor speak English. This puts me in mind of what happened to me some years since I was at Newport in Rhode Island at the time of their anniversary election of their magistrates. I was invited to a public entertainment usually given on that occasion. After dinner one of the new elected Council while we sat at table addressed himself to me, saying: "What would you give in New York for the privilege we enjoy this day of electing all our officers from the Governor to the constable?" I begged leave to put a question or two before I answered and then I asked him whether every man had an equal vote. He answered, "Yes, every free man has an equal vote with the richest or best man in the colony." I next asked him whether the election is carried by majority of votes, which being answered in the affirmative, I again asked him whether the greatest number in their colony were wise men or otherwise, which last question produced a general silence.

When Mr. Hunter came to his government he at first thought that an American Assembly might be governed by reason, but experience taught him that it was a vain imagination. It may be a question whether mankind in general can be governed otherwise than by their affections. For that reason wise legislators found means to raise artificial affections to control the natural. But, my dear son, that you may always regulate your affections by reason is earnestly recommended to you by your affectionate Father.

## 13. Cadwallader Colden to Alexander Colden*

Dear Son:

I have for some time been diverted from my Memoirs of the Government of New York. I now return to them. Colonel Peter Schuyler, as president of the Council, succeeded to the administration on General Hunter's going to England. He was so weak a man that he was persuaded by Adolph Philipse to lodge the King's Seal in his hand, to prevent any use to be made of it without his consent.

* [This letter is also printed in *Collections of The New-York Historical Society for the Year 1921* (New York, 1923), pp. 310–319. It was written between November 1759 and February 1760.]

By the King's instructions the President of the Council was, in the absence of the Governor, to receive one half of the sallary & all the perquisites. A dispute arose whether the word *half* did not extend to all the perquesites, as well as to the sallary. In cases where the perquesites were paid into the Secretary's office, on half was retained for the use of the Governor; but when Colonel Schuyler received the perquesites he retained the whole, for his own use.[19]

After Mr. Burnet was apointed Governor he was informed of the dispute relateing to the perquesites, & mentioned it to one of the clerks of the Board of Trade & Plantations, who was to copy the instructions for Mr. Burnet. On looking over the Instruction, he told Mr. Burnet that it was easy to amend it, & without hesitation he wrote in the instructions to Mr. Burnet *"one half of the Sallary & of all the perquesites."* The adding of the word *"of"* before the words *"all the perquesites"* intirely removed the dispute; but at the same time altered the meaning, & I believe is contrary to the intention of the instruction: for by the word perquesite is intended a reasonable reward for a perticular service, & certainly he that performs that service is intituled to the reward. This shows what the clerks of the great offices will sometimes take upon themselves to do. Whether the instructions to the Governors of New York continue to be made out as thus corrected by the Clerk I know not.

As soon as Mr. Burnet arived in his government a dispute arose, whether the Assembly could be continued legally after the commission was determined by the authority of which it was called. To remove this objection it was answered that the writ being in the King's name & under his seal, the death or removal of a governer could not determine it, & the practise since that time has justified this opinion. The very persons, who at that time, insisted on the illegality of continueing an Assembly, after the determination of the Governer's commission, who called them, advised the continuance of the Assembly under the like circumstances, when they could not be assured of having persons in the same interest elected. The argument which prevailed with Mr. Burnet to continue the same Assembly was this. He was assured that the members of that Assembly would readily grant the support of government for five years, & tho the gentlemen who wanted a new Assembly gave the like assurances, he thought the first were more to be depended on; for tho' the principal persons might with confidence expect to be elected for the city, they could not be assured of the generality of the country members, or that they would have a sufficient interest over them, since it was doubted but that some of the principal men in the contrary [country?] would be re-elected.

Mr. Smith mistakes when he says, that Colonel Schuyler & Mr. Philipse were removed from the council, because they had opposed in council the continuance of the Assembly. This would have been too bald a reason, to be offered to the King, for removeing these gentlemen from his Council of New York. The reason given was by proof of Colonel Schuyler's having committed the custody of the King's Seal to Mr. Philipse & of Mr. Philipse's having received it into his custody. This was highly criminal in both & they were gently used in having no farther notice taken of it, than by their removal from the Council. Mr. Burnet's motive to have them removed was to strengthen the interest of those gentlemen who had undertaken to serve him.

I shall add nothing at present to the accounts, which Mr. Smith has given, of the methods taken by Mr. Burnet, to restrain the trade between New York & Canada, in goods fit for the Indian market, & of his indeavours to promote a direct trade with all the Indians to the westward of us; but I cannot pass over an egregious misrepresentation of the case between Mr. Rou & the French congregation in New York. On reading Mr. Smith's account of this affair, one would imagine that Mr. Burnet had set up an high commission court in eclesiastic matters to the jurisdiction of which Mr. Smith's father had pleaded.

The true state of Mr. Rou's case is this. When he came over to New York on the invitation of the French inhabitants there, he & some gentlemen trustees for the French congregation enter'd into a mutual contract in writing, he to perform the duties of pastor of the French Protestant congregation at New York according to the rules which had been used by the Protestants in France, & they in consideration of his services engaged to pay a certain sum of money yearly to him. Of this contract there was only one authentic, which was in the hands of the trustees. Mr. Rou had only a copy without any test of its being authentic. On some disputes which happened between Mr. Rou & some of his congregation, the consistory refused to pay him his sallary. Mr. Rou insisted that he had don his duty, & performed his part of the contract; but as he had no legal evidence of the contract, he was advised to sue in Chancery, in order to oblige the trustees to produce the contract. Accordingly Mr. Rou filed a bill in Chancery, wherein he demanded of the trustees, whether they or any of them knew of a contract entered into between the trustees of the French congregation & him, & if they did to discover the contents thereof. The trustees answered on oath, "We do not know of any such contract." It is to be observed that since the makeing of that contract some of the trustees had been changed. Mr. Rou's council objected to the sufficiency of the answer, alledgeing that they ought to answer, "We nor no one of us know," for tho all of them may not know, one or more of them did. I was at that time a Master in Chancery & it was referred to me to judge whether the answer was sufficient. After a tedious hearing of council on both sides, I said, that on supposition that some of the defendents were ignorant of the contract & that others knew it, I could not conceive how they who knew it could join in the oath that we (meaning all of us) do not know, because in this case they must swear to the ignorance of the others, which I thought a man who had a proper regard to an oath could not do, & all the defendents were men of good reputation. Upon which Mr. Alexander, who was of council for Mr. Rou, replied, "I do not wonder that you should be of this opinion; but," pulling out a paper from his pocket, "here is a copy of the contract in the hand writing of one of these gentlemen, tho' we can not prove it." On which I declared the answer insufficient, & ordered that they should answer more particularly as demanded in the bill. On which they answered, "True it is, we do not know, but (nameing the names) do know, & the contents of the contract are."

This made so strong an impression on me at the time that I could never afterwards forget it, to see men, who had left their native country & their all, from a consciencious scrupulousness in religious matters, prevaricating in this manner on solemn oath in a court of justice. The truth of the facts, which I tell you, will fully appear from the Bill & answers which I suppose still remain among the Chancery papers. After an authentic copy of the contract was thus obtained, Mr. Rou was left in quiet possession of his pulpit, & had his sallary paid him; but as Mr. Smith observes, some of the most considerable persons of his congregation left their church. We may on this reason, likewise observe, that sometimes private resentment is of greater force than that religious zeal, which makes us leave our country & all that is dear to us.

But, before I leave this subject, I cannot with justice to Mr. Rou avoid takeing notice of the character which Mr. Smith gives him. Mr. Rou, he says, was a man of learning, but proud, pleasurable & passionate. He sets Mr. Mulenar's character in contrast: viz, that he was of pacific spirit, dull parts, & unblameable life & conversation. Were it not for the contrast it may be difficult to say what Mr. Smith means by "*a pleasurable man,*" being a phrase seldom or never used in the English language, but as it is set in contrast with "*unblameable life & conversation,*" the reader may readily conceive that Mr. Smith calls Mr. Rou a man of pleasure. I knew Mr. Rou & I never heard him reproached with any immorality. He was bookish & as such men often are, peevish, & had nothing of the courtly polite Frenchman. The game of chess was the only amusement he took & perhaps he was too fond of it. It was said that he had wrote a treatise on that game.

From what has been said it will easily appear how proper & discreet & like a lawyer Mr. Smith's, the father, defence of the trustees was by setting up the jurisdiction of a consistory, a Collogue Synod of the French Protestants in France, a jurisdiction which at that time had no existence, & which if it had existed could have given Mr. Rou no relief & this in opposition to the King's courts. Lest disputes should arise in future ages about the birth place of this distinguished orator as had happened with respect to Homer, Mr. Smith in a note assures us of the place of his birth.

As Mr. Burnet's refuseing to qualify Mr. De Lancey, after he had been elected a member of the Assembly for the city of New York, gave the first rise to the violent party strugles which continued many years afterwards, it may be useful to you to relate that affair more particularly than Mr. Smith has don.

At that time the members of the Assembly had been allwise qualified by the state oaths being administred by the Governor; but lately they are qualified by a *Dedimus potestatem*[20] to the judges of the Supreme Court jointly or severally for that purpose. Mr. De Lancey being chosen, in place of one of the members for the city of New York, who was dead, was sent by the house to the Governor to be qualified, as usual. Mr. Burnet by Mr. Morris's advice, I make no doubt, refused to qualify him, as being a foreigner not naturalized. This gave a very general dissatisfaction, not only on Mr. De Lancey's private account, who was generally esteemed in the place; but likewise on account of the great numbers, who were in the like circumstances: for the greatest number of the inhabitants were foreigners, Dutch & French, or their descendants, & this objection, they were affray'd, might be extended to their real estates & inheritances. I had been for some time from home, & did not return till the evening after this had happened. The next morning Mr. Livingstone, the Speaker, came to my house, & began to talk with great concern on what had happened the day before. I was absolutely ignorant of it so far that I did not understand him, till he told me the particulars. In the afternoon I went to wait on Mr. Burnet; while I was with him, Colonel Hicks, who was much in the Governor's interest, & a leading member in the House, came there, & desired to speak with me in private. He told me that the House was in a ferment, that they looked on the matter as a breach of their principal privilege of being sole judges of the qualification of their own members, & that the Governor's friends would oppose him in it. I informed Mr. Burnet of what Colonel Hicks had told me & likewise the conversation I had with the Speaker in the morning. He was staggered, & immediately sat down to write a message to the Assembly, in which he yielded by halves, & with apparent reluctancy. On reading what he had wrote, I told him that I was convinced he must either yield or break with the assembly, & that if he did break, it would be on a very unpopular subject, the privilege of the House, & on a subject in which great numbers would think themselves and their families greatly interested. The Governor then wrote a message, wherein he said, that he had thought it proper to inform the House of the objection made to Mr. De Lancey's qualification, but at the same time he left it intirely to the judgment of the House. Mr. Burnet was certainly in the wrong in entering on a thing of such consequences, without being assured that his friends would support him in it. Perhaps it was thought, that the objection would be a perpetual check on Mr. De Lancey's conduct; but it had a contrary effect. Mr. De Lancey was a man of strong & lasting resentment, & his family seem to have taken a resolution from that time, to have Mr. Morris removed from the office of Chief Justice, if by any means it could be don.

I come now to the remarkable resolves of the Assembly, in the year 1727, against the court of Chancery, which Mr. Smith sets down at large in his history. It may be safely affirmed, that every fact set forth in the preamble to the resolves is false, or greatly exaggerated, except the exorbitant fees & charges of the lawyers attending the court, without which Mr. Smith tells us, the present lawyers despise the practice. It is certain, however, that the unreasonable length of the bills & answers & the dilatory pleas put in by them were real grievances & which it is not in the power of the Chancellor to prevent; but without these, in Mr. Smith's opinion, the business of the Chancery must rest, & the people of this province be deprived of relief in equity.

Strangers to the men who compose our Assembly, to their manner of proceeding, & to what has passed in that House, may be apt to give the greatest credit to what they solemnly assert, whereas in truth it deserves less than that of private persons. No one man in the House thinks himself answerable for what passes there, & as a body they think themselves not accountable to any other authority: & for that reason often act very unaccountably. It has been too frequent, that angry party men take this method, to spread slander & calumny with impunity. I shall therefor relate the circumstances which attended these famous resolves.

Mr. Philipse, Speaker of the Assembly at the time these resolves were made, had been in partnership with one Codringtone in some mercantile business. At the conclusion of the partnership, which was several years before that time, Mr. Philipse gave Mr. Codringtone his bond for a considerable sum of money, if I remember right, fifteen hundred pounds. Codringtone was some years dead. Mr. Philipse neglected to pay either principal or interest, & at last refused payment. Codringtone's widow sued the bond at common law, in the Supreme Court of New York. Mr. Philipse pleaded that the bond was paid before it was given. The oddness of the plea became the discourse of the coffee house. One day while I was there, I asked Mr. Philipse's attorney, who happened to be present, what he meant by such a plea? He answered it was none of his, he knew better, that he was obliged to put it in by his client. The plea was overruled & judgement given. Mr. Philipse made this plea with resolution to remove the suit into Chancery. You know the Governor is Chancellor in this Province. Mr. Philipse, some time before this suit was brought, but while he expected it, paid unusual court to Mr. Burnet. His visits were remarkably frequent, & as he was Speaker of the Assembly, Mr. Burnet received him very graciously. Mr. Philipse in his bill set forth, that at the time he gave this bond Mr. Codringtone was indebted to him by accounts in a much larger sum. Codringtone had been dead several years, & perhaps none liveing who had been privy to the transactions between them. All the evidence which Mr. Philipse could produce was not sufficient to convince Mr. Burnet, that a man of Mr. Philipse's sense & experience in business would give his bond for 500 pounds to an other, who owed him a greater sum at the same time. Mr. Burnet dismissed his bill, & left the matter to the common law as it stood before. This happened a small time before these resolves, the method Mr. Philipse took to obtain them is no less remarkable.

The Assembly haveing finished their business, it was generally known that the Governor intended to put an end to the sessions next day at 12 o'clock, by giveing his assent to the bills then ready, at which time the Governor calls the Assembly to be present as witnesses of his assent. The Assembly had adjourned to the usual time of their daily meeting; but, as the business was over, the members, on such occasions, seldom attend till near the time that they expect to be called up. Mr. Philipse having prepared his friends, they with some others met at eleven, & immediately ordered the committee of grievances to sit. Colonel Hicks, who was the Governor's friend, was put in the Chair, & having the resolves ready drawn up in writing they immediately voted them, without suffering any argument, & the Speaker takeing the chair immediately after, they were reported & confirmed; but the Clerk had not time to enter them in the minutes, before the house was called up by the Governor, & the clerk was left in the house to enter them. Few of the Governor's friends were present & they so surprised, that they knew not how to act. Mr. Burnet gave his assent to the bills, & while the acts were as usual published, he was informed of what had passed by one of the members: & therefor instead of prorogueing the Assembly as he intended, he dissolved them with some marks of resentment. A feeble resentment which only served to increase the popularity of the opposite party, & to increase their strength in the next election.

I have allread[y] extended this letter beyond the length I had confined my self to, in writing to you on this subject & therefor shall delay what I have farther to tell you of Mr. Burnet's administration to another opportunity.

Perhaps you may think that I write with resentment to Mr. Smith the historian. He is so assuming in his manner, especially in giving characters, often unfair, allwise partial, whether his characters be favourable or otherwise, continually biassed by his connections, either as to family, political party or religeous sect, that some resentment is unavoidable. It is not fit that Mr. Smith's History should pass for a chronicle of the province of New York.

Your affectionate father
CADWALLADER COLDEN

## 14. Cadwallader Colden to Alexander Colden.

Coldengham, December 31, 1759.

Dear Son

Mr. Burnet after he had been some years at New York applied himself to the study of scripture prophecy on principles which he told me he had received from Sir Isaac Newton. The prophets, he said, have a language peculiar to themselves and that if their language be understood, the prophecy becomes as easy to be understood as other writings. He had a very extraordinary memory and he had read the prophecies so often over that he could at once point out the chapter and verse in which any subject was treated or any prophetical word was to be found. For some time this study so intirely engrossed his thoughts that upon all occasions he introduced it into discourse even so far that his conversation became disagreable to his best friends. He was zealous to convince them for he said the evidence of Christianity stands on miracles and the prophecies are perpetual miracles renewed every time any prophecy is accomplished. The evidence of the miracles done by Christ grows daily weaker by the length of time and therefor there is a necessity of a perpetual renewal of miracles. But notwithstanding of all the pains he was at and his publishing his thoughts in print I know not that he at any time made one convert, tho' perhaps he has wrote better on that subject than any else has don.

Studious men are apt to fall into some kind of enthusiasm or other which surprises the rest of mankind to see men fall into who on all other occasions discover an uncommon force of reason and yet on some particular subjects to be uncorrigeably whimsical and unreasonable. The great Sir Isaac Newton in some instances is thought to have fallen into this misfortune. How comes this about? Is it not that they become somehow fond of some peculiar notions and by continually insisting on them and presenting them to their imaginations, they strike their minds with as much force as realities. A man that often repeats a lie of his own may at least believe it to be true. It is thought several instances can be given to prove that this really happens.

Tho Mr. Burnet was a zealous Christian, he was not in all points orthodox. If I mistake not, he was Arian. I heard him tell that after his father's death he found among his papers a letter from Archbishop Tillotson in which the Archbishop wished the church could get fairly rid of that Athanasian creed. He used often to say that many Orthodox are knaves but he never knew a heretick that was not an honest man.

Mr. Smith is injurious to Mr. Burnet's memory where he insinuates that some thought his removal necessary for the public tranquility. There was not the least ground for this insinuation. The generality of the people were not so insensible of Mr. Burnet's merit tho' a faction had the artifice to make some noise at the close of the last session of Assembly in the manner before mentioned. Mr. Smith has given a pretty full account, how much Mr. Burnet studied the true interest of the province more than any before him or any since. No instance can be given of oppression in any shape. No man was more free from avarice. He was generous to a degree so far that if he erred it was not in takeing sufficient care of his private interest. He expended yearly considerable sums in private charitie, which he managed so that none knew of them more than what could not be avoided and thereby in some degree doubled the charitie to many who received it. That which excited the malice of a faction was merely the effect of his great merit. The stopping the trade which a few merchants had with Canada carried on to the prejudice of Great Britain and of all the American colonies and his giveing relief in Chancery against the frauds of artful and rich men. Neither the ministry nor the people of Great Britain at that time saw the consequences of the Indian trade and of the ascendency over the Indians which was thereby to be gained, tho had they considered that matter with the same attention which Mr. Burnet did it is probable the present war might have been prevented No discovery of any kind can be properly valued by those who do not understand it, and for that reason new discoveries are never at first valued as they are at some distance of time afterwards, because few take the trouble necessary to understand them till they have obtained a reputation by being espoused by men of known and distinguished knowledge. There is something in the English Constitution which renders their ministry short sighted  They are so much employed in expedients for the present time that they are unwilling to think of things at a distance.

The true reason of Mr. Burnet's removal I had from Colonel Montgomerie, his successor. There had been a remarkable misunderstanding between the present King when Prince of Wales and his father King George the 1st, dureing which all the Princes' servants who had offices under the King were removed from their offices. Colonel Montgomerie was one of these. When the Prince became King the offices under him as Prince of Wales of course fell, and the officers were to be otherwise provided, and the King likewise thought it proper to recompense those servants more particularly who had suffered by adhering to him. For these reasons Colonel Montgomerie had his choice of several offices both at home and abroad. He made choice of the government of New York as the most lucrative and attended with the least trouble. New York being a more healthy climate made him prefer it to Jamaica which was likewise in his option.

When Mr. Burnet heard that he was to be removed he could not avoid entertaining some resentment. He knew that he had executed his office faithfully and with a view to serve his King and Country. The present royal family had acknowledeged some obligations to Bishop Burnet, the Governor's father, on his being the first person that had named the house of Hanover to King William as the next Protestant family in the succession to the Crown of Great Britain and King William had given the Bishop leave to make the first mention of it to that family some years before the Act of Succession was passed. The Princess Sophia, in acknowledgement of this, had sent a present of a handsom silver gilt tea equipage to the Bishop which Governor Burnet had with him at New York. No man in Great Britain had been more zealous for the succession in the house of Hanover than the Bishop had been. Of which the royal family had often declared themselves sensible. It is no wonder then that Mr. Burnet entertained some resentment on being turned out to make room for one who had only private merit in personal services to give him a preference.

Mr. Burnet's friends at court obtained an audience of the Queen in hopes by her influence to divert the King from removing of Mr. Burnet.  The Queen answered them with courtly politeness that the King was very sensible of Mr. Burnet's merit, that the people of New England were a troublesome people, and therefor the King thought it necessary to appoint a gentleman of Mr. Burnet's abilities governor of that colony of Massachusetts Bay. She knew, she said, that the government of Massachusetts Bay is not so lucrative as New York, but that the King's service required Mr. Burnet's accepting of it at present and that afterwards any loss he had thereby in his private fortune should be made up. Notwithstanding of this, his friends were apprehensive that he would refuse to accept of that government and they were therefor very earnest with him to accept of it.

The people of the Massachusetts government had for sometime past continually quarrelled with their governors and had refused to give them a reasonable support. One of their Governors deserted his government and no gentleman of any character was willing to accept of it. When Mr. Burnet arrived in his government, he was received with all the respect that they could show; but he carried with him royal instruction which he foresaw would be the source of dispute: viz, that he should insist on their Assembly's granting a thousand pounds sterling yearly salary to the Governor for an indetermined time. Mr. Burnet advised with his friends in New York before he went to his government as to the part he was to act, in inforceing this instruction. He then resolved to take care that it might not become a personal quarrel between him and the people, but he did not observe this rule afterwards. Whether it was by any advice which he received there or from some thing in his natural temper I know not, for he loved an argument. The Assembly in their reasoning did not think it proper to declare the true republican principles which swayed them and it was not difficult for Mr. Burnet to shew the fallacy and weakness of the arguments which they used. He charged them with disingenuity which he made appear from their manner of arguing. This produced angry replies and the dispute became personal. The thing which by all means he was to avoid because it served their purposes to make it such. These disputes continued all the time of his administration and made it vexatious and disagreable to himself. Before they were ended he died of a fever without receiving any sallary.

Similar instructions have been since that time given to the governors of New York. It has seemed very odd to me that the ministry has insisted in giving such instructions without having it in their power to enforce them and putting their governors under the necessity of either breaking the instruction or of starveing, at least of loosing the purpose for which they desire their Governments. It is easy to guess which of these two all of them have chosen. Nothing has so much lessened the King's authority in the colonies as this impolitic step has don.

Now you have everything relating to Mr. Burnet which I think may be of use to you to know so far as has occurred to the memory of your affectionate father, C.C.

## 15. Cadwallader Colden to Alexander Colden

Coldengham    January 31, 1760

Mr. Burnet had been acquainted with Col. Montgomerie in England, and from the confidence he had in their former friendship he continued in the Governor's house with a resolution to write Colonel Montgomerie to lodge with him till he left New York; but some of the party who were in opposition to Mr. Burnet went on board the ship before Colonel Montgomerie came on shoar, told him of Mr. Burnet's design'd invitation and dissuaded him from it so effectually that he afterwards absolutely refused Mr. Burnet's invitation and went into private lodgings, on which Mr. Burnet removed from the Governor's house before night and carried away every thing of his next day notwithstanding of which Col. Montgomerie did not go into the Governor's house till after Mr. Burnet left New York.

As we were walking in formality to publish Colonel Montgomerie's commission, I overheard him say to Mr. Clark that he would absolutely trust to his advice and he kept his promise to his death. Mr. Clark by his having been a considerable time Secretary to the Province had experience in the public affairs and understood men and business. Mr. Clark was likewise Deputy to Mr. Horace Walpole as Auditor of the Revenue in America and probably it was by Mr. Walpole's advice that Colonel Montgomerie placed his confidence in Mr. Clark.

Colonel Montgomerie did not want natural abilities nor any part of the education proper for a gentleman, but he had given himself up to his pleasures, especially to his bottle and had an aversion to business. He was likewise the most diffident of himself of any man I ever knew. He was much in debt and wanted to recover his fortune by the profits of his government with as little trouble to himself as possible. Mr. Clark served him well for these purposes.

Mr. DeLancey was at the head of the party in the assembly which had been in opposition to Mr. Burnet and which had now the ascendant in that house. Mr. DeLancey was to be gratified in his resentment against Chief Justice Morris and the Governor was to use his interest to have the acts repealed which had been passed in Governor Burnet's Administration prohibiting the direct trade to Canada with Indian goods. In consideration of these the Governor had his salary secured for five years and all the perquisites which any Governor before him ever had. Both sides punctually performed their ingagements to each other. But it was surprising to me how easily the Board of Trade and Plantations were induced to recommend to the King the repealing of the laws in favor of the direct trade with the Indians and which prohibited the furnishing the French with goods to enable them to carry on that trade to the prejudice to Great Britain and of the colonies after all that had been laid before them by Mr. Burnet on that head. They probably thought that the people of New York were only interested in the Indian trade and that it did not concern Great Britain. They seem to have had nothing in view at that time but to serve the private purposes of a Governor. Mr. DeLancey had the advantages of his own private trade in view which were very considerable. But as the resentment against Chief Justice Morris was productive afterwards of violent party struggles, it may be of use to know all the circumstances attending it.

The fixing of the salaries of the officers of goverment had been for some time a matter of dispute between the Governors and Assembly. The Assembly thought that since they gave the money they have likewise the right of applying it to the several uses of government and of determining what the officers sallaries shall be. The Governors insisted that it is the right of the Crown to determine the rewards due to the servants of the Crown. The matter was compromised in the administrations of Brigadier Hunter and Mr. Burnet. The Assembly yielded to leave out of the support bill the specifying the particular salaries to be paid to each officer on the Governor's giving his word of honor that he would not grant warrants for a larger sum than what was specified in a list privately presented to the Governor by the Assembly before they passed the support bill. After the Assembly at this time had agreed to grant the usual support for five years in making up the list of the officers' salaries to be presented to the Governor, they lessened Mr. Morris's salary as Chief Justice by fifty pounds a year. Mr. Morris was a member. He moved to know whether he had been guilty of any neglect or misdemeanor in his office that made them punish him by lessening his salary. They declared that it was not for that reason but from the poverty of the colony, and if I mistake not he obtained an entry to be made on their minutes accordingly, tho Mr. Morris and his friends used a good deal of argument with the Governor to prevent his agreeing to the lessening of the salary and he did do it. It was certainly allowing private persons to have too great influence on the courts of justice since it was only don to gratify private resentment. I remember that I used this argument with Colonel Montgomerie on this occasion in Council. When an assembly act merely from humor they act like children, and like children, the more they are humored the more humorsome they grow. This was verified in subsequent times, but at that time Colonel Montgomerie thought it best to keep them in good humour who had the purse in their hands. However, he was desirous, if possible, to prevent all dispute and therefore desired Mr. Alexander and myself to propose to Mr. Morris from him that if Mr. Morris would forbear makeing any dispute with him upon the head he would join his interest to any representation which Mr. Morris should make to the King's ministers in order to have an instruction not to suffer the lessening of the Chief Justice's salary by any vote of the Assembly or something to this purpose. We did so but could not prevail on Mr. Morris.

Mr. Morris's eldest son was of the Council. When the warrant for his father's salary was proposed with the abatement of £50 he opposed the change from the usual salary and in a premeditated speech, and among other things said that the doing it was illegal, unwarrantable and arbitrary. These were hard words which shocked the Governor. However, he had till next Council day to explain himself when still insisting on what he had said before, he was suspended with the consent of the Council from his seat at the board till the King's pleasure should be known for useing such harsh expressions against what was done with the consent of every branch of the legislature of the Province. I was not in Council at the time, being in the country. When I came to town Colonel Montgomerie shewed me copies of all that passed and declared Mr. Morris had forced him to do a thing much against his inclination. On a hearing before the Board of Trade, the suspension was confirmed and Mr. Morris the younger removed from the Council.

Colonel Montgomerie's view was to live as much as possible at ease and at the same time retrieve his fortune and for that purpose his administration was intirely directed to the humours of those men who at that time had the Assembly under their influence, except where he apprehended any measure might lead him into public dispute. Had he lived, these condescensions to the humours of others would have in time intirely defeated his other view of living at ease, for after these gentlemen had got all the offices in the hands of their friends and dependants he became sensible of their neglect before he died. His yielding to lessen the Chief Justice's salary merely to gratify a private resentment gave the Assembly such a sense of their influence on a Governor that all his successors found the effects of it. For afterwards Assemblies did not so much as ask the Governor's consent to the officers salaries, but put them in their bill which he must accept in the manner they offered it or loose his own salary, and in this case they suffer no amendment to the bill by the Council, no not so much as a conference on the subject. Hereby the Assembly claim the sole power of rewarding all the officers of government and of judging of the reward due for their services.

Mr. Smith has in his history given a good general account of the agreement for a partition line between New York and Connecticut. I think it may be of use to you to know some particulars which probably Mr. Smith did not know. In 1725 commissioners were appointed in New York, of whom I was one, to meet commissioners from Connecticut in order to run out and settle the boundaries pursuant to the agreement between the two colonies in 1683 as recited in Mr. Smith's History. The first thing we entered upon was the method to be pursued in the survey for running the lines. The difficulty chiefly consisted how to run a line parallel to Hudson's River everywhere twenty miles distant from it which will be found difficult to do if it be not impracticable where a river has many turnings and windings so as precisely to comply with the words of the agreement. The commissioners from Connecticut took every method to perplex the matter and to evade the agreeing to any method of survey. After many fruitless meetings and some adjournments to different times and places, we gave them notice that we intended to run the lines *ex parte* and desired them to be present at our work and witnesses of what we did. As I was sensible that everything don in this case *ex parte* would be subject to endless disputes and thereby the settling of the frontiers would be obstructed, when we had met to take a parting glass I took one of their commissioners aside. I told him that I suspected they had something at heart which they were affrayed to discover. I promised that if he would be free with me I would make no bad use of what he should tell me, and perhaps we might fall on some method to make them easy. He told me their whole concern was for the people of Ridgefield, and that if we could make them easy as to that part of the line adjoining to Ridgefield we should have no dispute as to any other part. After informing my fellow commissioners of what had passed and some discourse among ourselves we resolved to renew the conferences. After which the method for running the partition lines was agreed to without much dispute. From this you will know the reason of the lines being run in the manner they are. By the expense of these frequent meetings and adjournments the money given by the Assembly for running the lines was expended before they could be actually marked out upon the land or the survey be made for that purpose.

In the year 1730 several of the inhabitants of Ridgefield made proposals to some gentlemen in New York for running the partition lines on private expense on condition of having a quantity certain of the equivalent lands from Connecticut granted to them. An agreement was accordingly made between the Governor and Council of New York on one part and several persons of New York and Connecticut on the other part who were to be at the charge of running the lines on condition of having 50,000 acres of the equivalent lands granted to them on the usual quitrents and fees for obtaining the patent.

The gentlemen in New York who had the principal management of this affair had been Mr. Burnet's friends in whom he confided in the time of his administration. Mr. Harison had been of their number, but after he knew that Mr. Burnet was to be removed he left Mr. Burnet and joined with those who had been in opposition to him in such manner that Mr. Burnet said openly that Mr. Harison's ungratitude to him would not recommend him to his successor for he had received many favours from Mr. Burnet. For this reason Mr. Harison was not invited to join in takeing a share of the Patent. He complained to the Governor of this neglect and at the Governor's desire he had the offer of a small share which he accepted of with seeming thankful acknowlegement but at the same time he was highly disgusted by his discovery that he was despised by the gentlemen whose friendship he had forfeited and by the others whose friendship he had courted. He had somehow found access by letter to the Duke of Chandos. He represented these lands to the Duke not only as of great value by the extraordinary goodness of the soil but by their containing valuable mines and by their being convenient for carrying on an extensive fur trade and thereby persuaded the Duke to solicit a grant of them from the King for himself and some other gentlemen in England, the names of the other gentlemen being only used in trust for themselves and the Duke whose name did not appear in the grant. In this the Duke was exceedingly deceived, because there were no mines in that land and no fur trade could be carried on from that part of the country and the soil of the lands was nothing better than the generality of the country. The grantees in New York could not obtain their patent till they had completed the partition lines between the colonies of New York and Connecticut and near twelve months passed before this could be done. In the mean time, the grant in England passed and the gentlemen in New York were at all the expense of running the lines and of obtaining a patent without knowing that any application had been made in England for a grant of the same lands.

As this affair had a great influence on the publick transactions during the administration of the succeeding governor, it is proper that you should know this affair more particularly than as it is told by Mr. Smith in his history.

I have only one thing more to mention which may serve for a little amusement. Colonel Montgomerie designed to have been in New York in the fall of the year, but the ships were driven off by hard gales of wind to Barbadoes where they continued till next spring. I heard Colonel Montgomerie tell that while he was at Barbadoes a very old man died who on his deathbed confessed that he was the person who cut off King Charles' head. That as soon as he had performed the execution he was carried on board a ship bound to Barbadoes where he had lived in good reputation to the time of his death.

Now you have all that you can learn of Colonel Montgomerie's administration from

Your affectionate father

## 16. Cadwallader Colden to Alexander Colden.

Coldengham   February 21, 1760

My Dear Son:

In my last I finished all that I intended to write of the History of New York, within the period to which Mr. Smith confines his History: and I should have concluded with what I have already wrote had not Mr. Smith, at the conclusion of his history made a large stride to reach a matter of posterior date relating to one Laughlin Campbell. Mr. Smith has so grossly misrepresented this whole affair, by giving a false account of every material circumstance, and what he has published is so egregious a calumny of Mr. Clark, Lieutenant Governor of New York, and of other persons interested in the grant of lands in New York, that I cannot pass it over, without giving you the true account of that affair; in doing of which I have had my memory much assisted by the papers relating to it which remain on the Council file.

After great numbers of families had transported themselves from the North of Ireland to Pennsylvania, Laughlin Campbel in the year 1737 went over from the island of Ila [Isla] in Scotland to Pennsylvania to learn on what [terms] he could procure lands there, for a number of families which he proposed to bring over to settle there. While he was at Philadelphia, he was informed of a proclamation published by Colonel Cosby, the late Governor of New York,

promising 100,000 acres of land free of all charges excepting the
survey and quitrents, to be granted in quantities in proportion to
the numbers of persons who should import themselves into this
province in order to settle and improve lands. Mr. Campbell came
to New York from Philadelphia to inform himself of the truth of
this. But before I proceed farther it is necessary to inform you
that Colonel Cosby before his death had found means to have a grant
of this land for himself in the name of other persons in trust for
him. However iniquitously this may have been don, it had put it
out of Mr. Clark's power to grant that land, and Mr. Campbell in
a conference with Governor Clark and the Surveyor General of Lands
confessed that he could not obtain lands in Pennsylvania otherwise
than at the rate of £15 for each hundred acres, besides the quitrent
and charges of survey. He was then informed that the 100,000 acres
was already granted, but that he could have other lands on much
easier terms than he can in Pennsylvania or anywhere else and
they undertook that he should have lands granted in proportion to
the number of families imported at the rate of £3 sterling for every
hundred acres free of the charge of Indian purchase survey and
other expense of any kind except the quitrent with which he declared
himself well contented. However before he returned to Scotland he
went to Maryland to learn on what terms he could obtain lands
there.

The next year Mr. Campbell brought over 30 families and he
was offered a grant of 19,000 acres for himself free of all charges
except the survey, being all the lands which remained of those
which had been purchased which he neglected to take for reasons
which you will discover from what follows afterwards. In August
1739 he brought over 41 families more, but it is false that he
brought any of them over on his own expense in such manner that
he or his family suffered thereby; for all of them either paid him
for their passages and freight of goods or bound themselves as
servants as usual in such cases for the payment, and he disposed of
these servants with profit to himself as is usually don in America
in like cases.

When he came over the second time, he was again offered a
sufficient quantity of land on the terms promised him before he
imported any one person and with which he had declared himself
contented, and the place the land was to be set out for him was
named to him near where Fort Edward now stands; but he insisted
on having the 100,000 acres promised by Colonel Cosby's proclamation on the terms in that proclamation and put in a petition to the
Governor and Council to that purpose which occasioned an inquiry
and examination into the transactions previous to that petition as
will appear by the reports of Committee of Council appointed for
that purpose and made the 18th and 22d of April 1741, still remaining on the file of the Council.

The true reason of Mr. Campbell's declining the terms to which
he had agreed before these families were imported was that he and
the persons that he had brought over with him were in no ability

to comply with these easy terms and much less in ability of settling and improveing new lands till such times as they could maintain themselves by their own labor. This inability was well known at the time and may still [be] proved by persons living who came over with Mr. Campbell. As this inability was an unanswerable objection to their having lands on any terms, Campbell was advised to apply to the Assembly for their assistance to support his people till such time as they should be able to support themselves, which he did but without effect. For the Assembly, after inquiry, found that the people he had brought over with him were unwilling to settle under him as he proposed and Mr. Campbell's behavior after he came into the country gave the Assembly a prejudice so far to his disadvantage that they disliked his settling on the frontiers.

This being the case and it being at the same time well known that no part of the 100,000 acres promised by Colonel Cosby's proclamation had been settled pursuant to that proclamation, he had nothing to say or no game to play but to insist on the benefit of that proclamation as a matter which the government was absolutely obliged to perform. Suppose the case to be so, yet certainly the intention of that proclamation was not to give land to persons who were in no ability to settle and cultivate the same. But as the case then stood it cannot be supposed that Governor Clark was under any personal obligation to be at the charge of making the Indian purchase and to be at all other necessary expenses out of his own pocket. If the settling of the frontiers at that time by these people had been of public benefit it ought to have been at the public expense. Which the assembly refused to do for the reasons before mentioned.

As most of the people who came over with Mr. Campbell were unwilling to settle on the frontiers, they met with no disappointment. They dispersed themselves among the inhabitants and provided for their families as others had usually don in like cases. You knew that several of those who came servants with Mr. Campbell are now possessed of valuable farms in their own right in fee simple. Mr. Campbell only was disapointed of an unreasonable expectation by his not obtaining lands at other people's expense in order to make merchandise of them. Mr. Smith can never be excused in making this publication without makeing use of all the means which were in his power for a true information. The minutes of Council he tells us were open to him for his perusal. They would have shown him that the account he had received of that matter cannot be true. He was a boy at the time these things happened and he could have no knowledge of them, and therefor I cannot pass over the concluding sentence in his narrative without particular notice, viz: *"But it unfortunately drop't through the sordid views of some persons in power who aimed at a share in the intended grant to which Campbell, who was a man of spirit, would not consent."* It was impossible for Mr. Smith to have such evidence of this fact as to induce any man of the least candor to publish so great a calumny on any gentleman, because of my own knowledge it is false and none who knew Mr. Campbell can believe it. From this and many other parts of his history, Mr. Smith appears to be fond of calumny otherwise he would have made use of the means of information which he owns were in his power.

Mr. Smith's History has been of use to me in the chronology and in bringing things to my memory which otherwise might have escaped me. The remarks which I have made have helpt at times to fill up a vacant hour and I flatter myself they may be usefull to any who intend to write the hystory of New York when personal prejudices are removed and posterity can judge impartially. However this be, I hope they may be of use to you and that you will receive them as an instance of love from

Your affectionate father

## 17. Cadwallader Colden to Alexander Colden[21]

Dear Son: February 21, 1760

I finished in my last all that I intended to write on that period of time to which Mr. Smith confines his History of New York, and I should have concluded with what I have already wrote had not Mr. Smith at the conclusion of his book made a large stride to reach a matter of posterior date relating to Captain Laughlin Campbel. Mr. Smith has so grossly misrepresented this whole affair by giveing a false account of every material circumstance and so egregious a calumny of Mr. Clark and of other persons entrusted with the grant of lands that I can not pass it over without giveing you the true account of this matter.

Laughlin Campbell in the year 1737 arrived in Pennsylvania from Scotland in order to find what incouragement he could have to settle lands in that colony. The only terms on which he could obtain lands there, as he himself afterwards related, were at the rate of £15 for each hundred acres besides the quitrent and charges of survey and other officers' fees. While he was in Pennsylvania he heard of an encouragement from Colonel Cosby which had been offered for settling of 100,000 acres of land on the frontiers of New York and therefor came to New York to learn on what terms he could obtain lands there. Colonel Cosby had published a proclamation with consent of Council inviting Protestants to transport themselves to the Province of New York with a promise of 100,000 acres already purchased of the Indians to be granted to them at a certain rate or number of acres to each family, free of all charges. The particular account of this may come properly in the history of Colonel Cosby's administration. It is sufficient in the present case to tell that by sinister means this land was granted by Colonel Cosby in trust for himself, and therefore at the time Mr. Campbel came to New York it was not in Mr. Clark's power to grant that land. Mr. Campbel was told that the 100,000 acres of land mentioned in the publication made by Governor Cosby had been already granted. He was informed of the usual method of obtaining lands in this province: viz, by

first purchasing the lands of the Indians, haveing the same surveyed
and afterwards a patent under the King's Seal for this Province.
He objecting to the difficulties which a stranger might have in making the purchase and the other expenses which might attend the
procuring a patent for the same in order to incourage the settling
of the frontiers, the Governor and Surveyor General of Lands undertook to make the purchase of the lands from the Indians and to be
at the charge of survey and the fees of the officers in obtaining a
patent at the rate of £3 sterling for every hundred acres. He was
pleased with this proposal, and promised to bring over a number of
families to settle lands on these conditions. Notwithstanding of
this, after he had left New York he went to Maryland and finding
that he could obtain lands no where on so easy terms as in New
York, he the next year brought over 30 families. On the importation
of these families he was offered a grant of 19,000 acres of land free
of all charges except that of the survey which he neglected to take
for reasons which you will perceive by what follows afterwards. In
August 1739 he brought over 41 families more but it is false that
he brought them over or any of them on his own expense for all
of them either paid him for their passages and freight of their
goods or bound themselves as servants for the payment. He was
so far from being a sufferer that he made a considerable profit
by the importation of these people. After his arrival the 2d time
he was offered land on the conditions offered to him at his first
coming to New York with which he did not comply and probably
was not in any capacity to comply. But what principally obstructed
the grant was that Captain Campbel (as Mr. Smith calls him) was
in no ability to settle these families either by himself or with the
assistance of those that came over with them. This inability was
notorious to all who knew Mr. Campbel and the persons who came
over with them. He was advised to apply to the Assembly for their
assistance to make that settlement for security of the frontiers; but
the Assembly declined giving any assistance because many of
those he had brought over with him refused to settle under him,
saying that they had left their own country to free themselves from
the vassalage they were under to their lords there and would not
become vassals to Laughlin Campbel in America, and few or none
of them were willing to settle on the frontiers towards Canada.
The Assembly at the same time entertained a bad opinion of Mr.
Campbell as one not proper to be trusted. Mr. Smith says that the
execution of this project so beneficial to the Province failed by a
breach of private faith and public honour through the sordid views
of some persons in power who aimed at a share in the intended
grant to which Mr. Campbel who was a man of spirit would not
consent. This assertion to my own knowledge is absolutely false.
When these things happened Mr. Smith was a boy and could have
no knowledge of them and it is impossible that he could have any
evidence of what he asserts such as could induce a man of the least
candour to publish such vile reflections of any other person.
It is true that Mr. Campbell insisted on his pretensions for a

grant of land pursuant to Colonel Cosby's advertisement tho he had been told before he imported any person that the lands mentioned in that advertisement had been already granted by Colonel Cosby because he had nothing else to found his pretensions on. There were then no lands to be granted which had been purchased of the Indians and the government was persuaded that Mr. Campbel sued for a grant with a view only to make merchandise of the same as he was incapable of settling a large tract. This they thought entirely opposite to the view they had of incouraging the settling of the frontiers. No man will easily believe that Mr. Campbel would have refused any person a share with him who had power or influence enough to obtain a grant of so large a tract for him. What I now write I not only assert on my own knowledge, but I may refer to many still living and particularly to the persons that Mr. Campbel brought over with him for confirmation of the same. But the whole may be more easily cleared up by a report of a Committee of Council the 18th and 22d of April 1741 which was appointed to inquire and examine into Mr. Campbel's pretensions. Mr. Smith vouches his having had the minutes of Council under his perusal as vouchers for the truth of what he writes in his History. In the report of the Committee many particulars appear to Mr. Campbel's prejudice which now he is dead I choose not to repeat. But in this case the Council and Mr. Smith are in direct contradiction. When it is considered that the minutes of Council are transmitted to the Board of Trade and Plantations it is not likely that Mr. Campbel could meet with what Mr. Smith calls redress there.

As Mr. Campbel in his petition allwise refers to a publication by Colonel Cosby of 100,000 acres of land allready purchased of the Indians which he promised such as should transport themselves into this province, I do not pretend to justify what was don by Colonel Cosby with respect to those lands. All I say is that they were granted before Mr. Campbel came first to New York and he knew that they were not then in the power of the Government.

It appears by the remarks which I have made on several parts of Mr. Smith's History that his republican and independent principles have so far prejudiced him against Governors that in many instances he slanders their administration without any foundation and in none more than this, for it appears evidently when the truth is known that the Governor and Surveyor General were at that time zealous in promoting the settlement of the frontiers by the families which Mr. Campbel imported, had it been in their power to do it and had not he by his bad conduct and private sinister views prevented the assistance which the assembly otherwise might have given towards makeing that settlement. The agreement made with Mr. Campbel by the Governor and Surveyor General shews it was on much easier terms than lands could be at that time obtained— so easy that they could not thereby propose any private advantage to themselves—and yet he never mentioned this agreement in any petition he made on this occasion. Tho' he confessed it before the committee because he was not in a capacity to comply, it was inconsistent with the real view he had of obtaining these lands for merchandise. Mr. Smith, by makeing the least reflection, if he had inclined to have considered the matter impartially, might easily see that it could not be expected that the Governor or other officers intrusted with the grant of lands could make the purchase at their own expense and the necessary surveys of such a large tract and far less at their own expense go through all the charges necessary for making the settlements and maintaining the people till they could maintain themselves by their own labour, for it is most certain that Mr. Campbel and his company were in no capacity of settling themselves even supposing the land had been given them free of all charges. He might on the least reflection see that their private fortunes were not sufficient for such an undertaking, and unless this expense could be some way provided for it was impossible to make the proposed settlement, and that without this were previously taken care of, the granting of such a large tract of land could only serve private and sinister purposes. Never was a laudable zeal for the public benefit more grossly and injuriously misrepresented than this has been don.

## 18. Samuel Jones[22] to John Pintard

Oyster Bay, West Neck, November 24, 1817*

In page 28, speaking of Governor Nicolls, Smith says, "he erected no courts of justice, but took upon himself the sole decision of all controversies whatsoever." This must be a mistake; for the orders and regulations made during his administration, for the government of the Province, and which formed a part of the book called the Duke's Laws, appear to have been passed "at a Court of General Assizes, in New-York": which is conclusive evidence that the court was erected by him. The former inferior judicatures were probably continued, as it was agreed by the sixteenth article of the capitulation, that "all inferior officers and magistrates should continue till the customary time of new elections, and then new ones to be chosen," for it is not to be supposed that the inhabitants of Albany were to attend before the governor at New-York, a distance of one hundred and sixty miles, for the decision of causes to the value of forty shillings, and under.

In page 31, speaking of Governor Lovelace, Mr. Smith says, "instead of taking upon himself the sole determination of judicial controversies, after the example of his predecessor, he called to his assistance a few justices of the peace;" and adds, "this was called the Court of Assizes." But the Court of Assizes was erected by his predecessor Governor Nicolls. It was held before the Governor and Council, in whom the legislative power, under the Duke, was vested;

* [These next four letters from Samuel Jones to John Pintard, are found in The New-York Historical Society. They were printed in the Society's *Collections for the Year 1821* (New York, 1821), III, 350–367.]

and, therefore, the court from time to time, issued orders and regulations which were considered as laws of the Province. It is not improbable that some other persons besides the Council were occasionally called to assist as judges in the court. What is said in the note in the same page, respecting the town courts, is certainly exceptionable. No mention is made when or by whom such Courts were erected. The word "overseers," wants explanation; and the word "seven," seems to be a mistake; for it cannot be supposed that so many judges would be required for such a court, and of such characters, as would make it difficult, if not impracticable, to assemble the requisite number. Perhaps the word *seven* should be *even*. To give an accurate account of all the provincial judicatures, from the conquest, in 1664, would require considerable research. Mr. Smith, when he compiled his History, was extensively engaged in business as a lawyer; and had little, or no leisure, to make the necessary examinations; and, therefore, relied in a great measure, on the information he had got in revising the laws of the colony. But as the revisers were directed to commence the work with the session of the Legislature, in 1691, it is not probable they paid much attention to previous transactions.

When Governor Andros quitted the administration of the government of New-York, is not mentioned. The reader is left to suppose, either that he continued to administer the government until the arrival of Dongan, or that the Province was some time without any governor. But the truth is, that Anthony Brockholst was commander in chief in that interval. When the administration of Brockholst commenced or ended, I am not informed; but he certainly acted as commander in chief in July, 1681, and in April, 1683. The precise time of his administration may probably be ascertained by the minutes of Council.

The assertion in page 34, that Andros was "immediately" preferred to be Governor of Boston, is incorrect. That appointment did not take place till the year 1686.

In page 44, Mr. Smith mentions Governor Dongan's issuing orders for choosing representatives to meet him in Assembly; but says nothing of their meeting. It appears by the records, that a session of the Assembly was held pursuant to the summons; at which several important laws were passed. Another session was held in 1684, but, it is believed, that there was not any other session of the Assembly until the Revolution. The cause of the omission requires investigation. It has been alleged, and, it is not improbable, that the Duke, upon becoming King, refused to confirm the privileges he had before granted, and determined to govern the Province by his absolute power. It is, therefore, reasonable to suppose, that in the new commission or orders to Governor Dongan, the authority respecting the Assembly was omitted, or revoked.

The word "Nuromand," in the second note in page 46, is a typographical error. It should be "Huron and."

In page 58, Mr. Smith mentions the seizing the fort; and in the beginning of page 59, is the following sentence: "Colonel Dongan, who was about to leave the Province, then lay embarked in the bay, having a little before resigned the government to Francis Nicholson, the Lieutenant Governor." The latter part of this representation is believed to be a mistake. The fort was seized the 31st of May, 1689; and it appears by a minute of Council, of the 28th of July, 1688, that the King's order to his Excellency Colonel Thomas Dongan, to deliver up the seal of the Province unto his Excellency Sir Edmund Andros, was then read, and ordered to be recorded amongst the records of the Province of New-York; and, in another minute of the Council of the 30th of the same month, it is mentioned that it was his Majesty's pleasure, that this Province should be annexed to his government of New England. The last patent issued by Dongan, is dated the 2d of August, 1688. It is said there are no minutes of Council in the Secretary's office, from the 2d of August, 1688, until the 19th of March, 1691. What is become of them is uncertain. But without doubt, Dongan resigned his authority pursuant to the order he had received; and Sir Edmund Andros must have been in New-York the 24th of August, 1688, for he issued a proclamation, dated that day at New-York, reciting that he had received certain information of her Majesty's being safely delivered of a prince; and, therefore, with the advice of the Council, ordering a general thanksgiving for the same, "to be observed in the city of New-York, and dependencies, on Sunday, the second day of September, next coming; and fourteen days after in all other parts of this dominion." (*See Hutchinson's History of Massachusetts Bay, printed at Boston, 1764, page* 372.) Sir Edmund Andros, and other officers of government, were seized and imprisoned by the inhabitants at Boston, the 18th of April, 1689. Upon the news reaching New-York, a letter was sent to some of the principal inhabitants of Boston, dated at New-York, the 1st of May, 1689, and signed by Francis Nicholson, Frederick Philips, Nicholas Bayard, and Stephen Courtland, (who were all members of the Council,) in which they express their surprise to hear of the confusion the inhabitants of Boston had occasioned, by taking "that part of the government" to themselves; and their hope that his Excellency, and the rest of the officers, might be restored to their former stations, or, at least, have liberty to come "hither." And then add: "for this part of the government we find the people in general inclined to peace and quietness, and doubt not the people will remain in their duties." (*See Hutchinson's History of Massachusetts Bay, page* 383.) From these facts it is manifest that Dongan resigned his authority, as Governor, at least nine months before Leisler seized the fort; but that he remained here until that time is not improbable, as he possessed a large and valuable estate in the Province. Mr. Smith seems not to have known any thing of Sir Edmund's having received a new commission which included New-York, and, therefore, supposed that Dongan must have resigned the government to Nicholson; but there is reason to believe that he resigned it to Sir Edmund himself. It is said that Leisler convened two sessions of Assembly, at which various laws were passed; and it is certain that he, in some measure, aided in the expedition against Canada, in 1690. Mr. Smith, in his History, takes no notice of either of those circumstances; and, in the account he gives of the expedition, in page 68, he differs materially from the account given by the commander of the land forces. Mr. Smith says, "Sir William made two attempts to land below the town, but was repulsed by the enemy with considerable loss of men, cannon, and baggage." The commander of the land forces, in his account, given to the Council of Massachusetts, says, the army landed the 8th of October, and continued ashore until the night of the 11th, and then re-embarked. And from his account, it does not appear that there was any considerable loss of men or baggage by the enemy. Five field pieces, by some neglect, were left a-shore when the troops embarked, and were lost for want of due care. (*See Hutchinson's Account of Massachusetts Bay, page 401, and Appendix, No. 21.*)

In page 73, there is the following sentence: "those acts which were made in 1683, and after the Duke's accession to the throne, when the people were admitted to a participation of the legislative power, are, for the most part, rotten, defaced, or lost." From this assertion it might be supposed, that some acts were passed by the representatives of the people, after the Duke's accession to the throne, and while he was King; but we meet with no evidence of any session of an Assembly being held during his reign: on the contrary, there is abundant evidence of the wish of James the Second, to rule by arbitrary power.

In page 103, after mentioning the trials of Bayard and Hutchins, it is added, "after these trials, Nanfan erected a Court of Exchequer." The correctness of this assertion is, at least, doubtful. No Court of Exchequer was ever erected under the colonial government, any otherwise than by the ordinances establishing the Supreme Court, authorizing it to have cognizance of all pleas, civil, criminal, and mixt, as fully and amply to all intents and purposes as the Courts of King's Bench, Common Pleas, and Exchequer, in England, have, or ought to have. And it is worthy of remark, that the Court of Exchequer is not mentioned in any other part of this History, except in the account given of the Supreme Court, in page 246; and from the account there given, it is manifest that the question was, whether the Supreme Court had authority to hear and determine causes in a course of equity, according to the practice of the Court of Exchequer, in England? The trials of Bayard and Hutchins were in March, 1702; and in the minutes of Council, the 6th of April, 1702, is the following entry: "whereas there are several matters depending in the Court of Exchequer, which cannot be finished or put an end to by the time limited in the ordinance for establishing Courts of Judicature, &c. It is hereby ordered, that the Clerk of the Council prepare an ordinance impowering and requiring the said Court of Exchequer, to meet and sit, and as near as may be, according to the course of the Court of Exchequer, in England, to hear, try, and determine, all such matters and things as now are, or shall from time to time be hereafter commenced, or depending before the said Court of Exchequer, until the same shall be fully and perfectly finished and ended." This order was probably the ground of Mr. Smith's assertion, that "Nanfan erected a Court of Exchequer." Whether any ordinance was prepared or issued pursuant to the order I have not been able to discover. But it appears from the terms of the order, that instead of erecting a court of exchequer, the court of exchequer therein mentioned was a court then in existence, and was erected by the "ordinance for establishing courts of judicature." The only ordinance then existing for establishing courts of judicature bears date the 15th of May, 1699. That ordinance erected courts for trial of causes to the value of forty shillings and under; courts of sessions and common pleas; and a Supreme Court; which Supreme Court is thereby fully impowered to have cognizance of all pleas, civil, criminal, and mixt, as fully and amply to all intents and purposes whatsoever as the Courts of King's Bench, Common Pleas, and Exchequer in England have or ought to have; but erects no court by the name of the court of exchequer. By that ordinance the Supreme Court could hold only two terms in a year, each to continue five days and no longer. But by an ordinance dated the 2d of April, 1704, reciting that the times limited by the ordinance of the 15th of May, 1699, for the meeting and sitting of the Supreme Court, were so sheldom and so short, that the suits therein could not be finished but at great expense both of money and time; the Supreme Court was authorized to hold four terms in a year. It is therefore probable if any ordinance was issued pursuant to the order of council of the 6th of April, 1702, it was only to authorize the Supreme Court to sit and hear exchequer causes in the vacation.

In page 134 it is said, "when the Dutch began the settlement of this country, all the Indians on Long Island were in subjection to the five nations." This is at least doubtful. An early historian asserts that the Narragansets held dominion over part of Long Island. (See 1 vol. Mass. Historical Society, page 144, &c. Daniel Gookins;) and the Montauk sachem at the east end of the island paid tribute to the united colonies of New England several years previous to 1656. —(See 2d vol. of Hazard's collections of state papers, page 361.) Long Island is at least 120 miles in length; the possessions of the Dutch on the island never extended above thirty miles eastward of New-York. The eastern part of the island, and extending to the town plot of Oysterbay inclusive, was settled by people from New England. The Dutch finding all the Indians within and adjoining their settlements on Long Island tributary to the Mohawks or five nations, probably concluded from that circumstance that all the Indians on the island were so: but I doubt there being any evidence that such was the fact; on the contrary, there is a tradition among the Montauk Indians that their ancestors had wars with the Indians on the main, who conquered and compelled them to pay tribute. This tradition is corroborated by the historian who asserts that the Narragansets held dominion over part of Long Island; and by the fact that the Montauk sachem paid tribute to the four New England colonies.

The description of Hudson's river in pages 201 and 202 is erroneous in several particulars. The Saucondaga river which in this description is supposed to be the Hudson, may be considered as a distinct river or a branch of the Hudson. Its course from its source is first southerly and then northerly and easterly, until it falls into the Hudson 12 or 15 miles southwesterly from the south end of Lake George. From this junction the course of the Hudson is first south somewhat east 6 or 8 miles; then northerly and easterly 8 or 10 miles; and then generally south about 12 or 15° west to the bay at New-York. About 15 or 20 miles north of where it receives the Saucondaga, the Hudson is divided into two nearly equal branches; the one called the north-east, and the other the north branch. The assertion that the Hudson is navigable for batteaux from Albany to Lake George, except two portages of half a mile each, is incorrect, and contrary to the note on the same sentence, in which it is said, "in the passage from Albany to Fort Edward, the whole land carriage is about 12 or 13 miles." The Hudson passes 8 to 10 miles west of the south end of Lake George. The north-east branch in its course approaches nearer to the lake, perhaps within 5 or 6 miles. The notion that a summer's passage to Albany is on account of the fish in the river diverting to such as are fond of angling, is without foundation. I have many times passed up and down the river by water between New-York and Albany, and although I have made frequent trials upon such occasions, I never took a single fish by angling.

In page 244 it is asserted, that "justices are by act of assembly enabled to hold courts for the determination of small causes of five pounds and under." The first act giving them jurisdiction to five pounds was passed the 16th of December, 1758—The book (Smith's) was printed in 1757.

It is remarkable that the words *governor* and *error* wherever they occur in this History have the letter *u* in the last syllable. This however is not to be attributed to Mr. Smith. In the original manuscript those words were written *governor* and *error*. The person in London to whom the copy was sent to get it printed there made the alteration. And I well remember, that on receiving the books and discovering the alteration, Mr. Smith expressed his disapprobation of it.

This History has often been charged with partiality in respect to the episcopalians and presbyterians. But I have never heard any particular of such supposed partiality mentioned; nor am I acquainted with any circumstance that would warrant the supposition. It has also been charged, particularly by Lieutenant Governor Colden, with misrepresentation respecting the conduct of the government towards Captain Lauglin Campbell. Mr. Smith says, "the project of Captain Campbel unfortunately dropped, through the sordid views of some persons in power, who aimed at a share in the intended grant; to which Campbel, who was a man of spirit, would not consent." But from what I have been able to learn upon the subject, it is at least doubtful whether Campbel's failure was owing to the cause mentioned by Smith. It seems his expectation was to obtain a grant of the land to himself, and to settle the families he brought from Scotland on it under him in the manner of the clans in the highlands of Scotland; and when he found that could not be effected, he dropped the project in disgust.

I have lately met with what is called a Continuation of the History of New-York, printed at the end of a new edition of Smith's History by Ryer Schermerhorn.[23] The author, whoever he was, does not seem to possess all the requisites for such a work. Some of his observations are pertinent and judicious; but the production is exceptionable in various respects and in many particulars. To enumerate its errors and defects would require more time and labour than I feel disposed to bestow upon it. I will however mention a few; Rip Van Dam had administered the government as president of the Council from the death of Governor Montgomerie to the arrival of Governor Cosby, who soon after his arrival laid before the Council an instruction, dated the 31st of May, 1732, by which half the salary and perquisites was ordered to the President for the time being, and the other half was ordered to be paid to Governor Cosby; and the council immediately made an order for Van Dam to pay into the hands of the treasurer half the money he had received for salary and perquisites since the death of Governor Montgomerie. Van Dam refused to pay the money; and the Attorney General thereupon exhibited a bill of complaint to the justices of the Supreme Court against Van Dam, charging that he had, as President of the Council, received the whole salary and perquisites accruing by the administration of the government from the death of Governor Montgomerie, on the 1st July, 1731, to the arrival of his present excellency Colonel William Cosby on the 1st of August, 1732; and that his Majesty by an instruction, dated the 31st of May, 1732, had ordered to the President for that time half the salary and perquisites; and praying a discovery upon oath of the salary and perquisites; and that the defendant may be decreed to pay half into the treasurer's hands for the use of his Majesty. Van Dam by way of plea set forth three exceptions to the power of the court. The question therefore was, whether the justices of the Supreme Court were authorized to hear and determine causes in equity according to the course of the court of exchequer in England. The judges of the court were then Lewis Morris, Chief Justice; James De Lancey, second justice; and Frederick Philips, third justice. The Chief Justice gave his opinion in the negative; but the other two judges being of opinion that the court could hear and determine matters on the equity side of the exchequer, overruled the exceptions. And it was upon that question that Smith and Murray were heard before the Assembly. The author of the continuation makes no mention of the controversy respecting the half salary or the exchequer, but supposes the question respected the establishment of the Court of Chancery, which is a mistake.

Speaking of the address of the Assembly to Lieutenant Governor Clarke in 1737, the author of the continuation says it complained of the Court of Chancery not being regulated by law; and "that under Governor Sloughter in 1691, that court was established by an act of the General Assembly." This is not correct; the Assembly in that address, after declaring their opinion that courts of general jurisdiction ought to be settled and established by the acts of the whole legislature, add, "it was the method in use here both before and since the revolution, and particularly recommended to the Assembly to be done in that manner by a message from Governor Sloughter and council on the 15th of April, 1691." The phrase "court party," does not seem to be properly applied. There were generally, if not always, parties in the colony during the colonial government. But they were rather personal than political; and it is not believed that any of them ever were, or could with propriety be called the *court party.*

The words *governor* and *error,* where they occur in this continuation, have *u* in the last syllable. This probably is because they are so in the quarto edition of Smith's History; but if the author had known how that happened, it is not likely he would have continued it.

SAMUEL JONES

Oysterbay, West Neck, Queen's County,
    State of New-York, 24th November, 1817.

## 19. Samuel Jones to John Pintard,

*Oysterbay South, 24th November, 1817.*

Sir,

Your letter of the 12th instant was duly received; and I now enclose some remarks on Smith's History of New-York, and what is called a continuation of it. To elucidate the history of the province during the reign of James the Second, and until the arrival of Governor Sloughter, it will be necessary to examine the commission or orders given by the Duke of York, after he became King, to Governor Dongan; and the tenour and extent of the new commission to Sir Edmund Andros in 1688; and the provincial records during the time that Leisler acted as commander in chief.

I have part of a pamphlet entitled *A Letter to a Noble Lord,* printed in London, if I recollect right, in 1757; several pages at the beginning and end being lost. This pamphlet was written in New-York; and it is believed from circumstances that William Smith, afterwards Chief Justice of Canada, was the author; that he copied it himself, never permitting either of his clerks to see a word of it; that the manuscript was carefully nailed up in a box prepared for the purpose and sent to London to be printed.[24] The pamphlets when received from London were not publicly distributed; and only a few of them were given to particular individuals. But it soon became known in the city that such a pamphlet existed. I was then a clerk in Smith's office, and wished to procure one of the pamphlets, but all my endeavours for the purpose were fruitless; and I never got one until some time during the revolutionary war, when I met with one at an auction in New-York and purchased it. The Society ought to possess the pamphlet, and if a complete one cannot be procured, I will send them what remains of mine. I also have a pamphlet entitled *An Impartial Account of Lieut. Col. Bradstreet's Expedition to Fort Frontenac,* printed in London in 1759, which I will send to the Society if they have no copy of it. I formerly had several other pamphlets which would be useful to the Society; one containing the trial of Zenger; another relating to the case of Forsey and Cunningham, in which case Lieutenant Governor Colden laboured to introduce an appeal from the verdict of a jury; and a copy of the journal of the proceedings of the convention of New-York that adopted the Constitution of the United States. These are either mislaid or left in New-York; but as they were extensively circulated, I suppose copies can be procured in the city.

It is said that but few of the acts of the legislature passed previous to the Revolution of 1689 are to be found in the Secretary's office. It was the practice at that time to enrol the acts of the legislature on parchment; and I recollect to have seen at Boston in 1785, on the floor in an upper room of a public building, among a parcel of loose papers, several parchment rolls containing copies of acts of the legislature of New-York, which I suppose were carried to Boston by Sir Edmund Andros after he received his new commission including New-York in his government.

I wish to be informed whether the Society include recent publications in their collection; such as gazetteers and tracts of that sort? I make the inquiry because all those I have seen contain errors and mistakes which will have a tendency to mislead the future historian.

The old recorder has not forgotten his friend the common councilman; nor the many agreeable hours we passed with the former members of the corporation. But, as you well observe, we must all look for another and better world: that we may all be truly thankful for the many blessings bestowed upon us in this life; and well prepared for the change, is the sincere wish of

Your old friend,<br>Samuel Jones

JOHN PINTARD, ESQ.
Recording Secretary of the New-York Historical Society.

[1818]

## 20. Samuel Jones to John Pintard

1. In the 2d page, Smith says, the Dutch erected Fort Good Hope, on Connecticut river in 1623; but Trumbull, in his History of Connecticut, says it was not erected until 1633.—(See Trumbull's History of Connecticut, page 21.)

2. After mentioning the meeting of the New England colonies upon a design of extirpating the Dutch; and that Massachusetts Bay

declined the enterprise; Smith says, in the 5th page, "which occasioned a letter to Oliver Cromwell from William Hooke, dated at New-Haven, November 3, 1653, in which he complains of the Dutch for supplying the natives with arms and ammunition, begs his assistance with two or three frigates, and that letters might be sent to the eastern colonies commanding them to join in an expedition against the Dutch colony;" and then adds, "Oliver's affairs would not admit of so distant an attempt." But Trumbull, in his History of Connecticut, says, the application to Cromwell was in the name of both the general courts of Connecticut and New-Haven; and that in answer to their petitions, Oliver sent an armament for the reduction of the Dutch, which arrived at Boston early in June, 1654; that the colonies immediately commenced preparations for the expedition: but while these were making with vigour and despatch, the news of peace between England and Holland prevented all further proceedings relative to the affair.—(See Trumbull's History of Connecticut, pages 219, 220, and 227, 228.)

3. In the beginning of the 10th page, Smith says, "while the Dutch were contending with their European neighbours, they had the art always to maintain a friendship with the natives until the war which broke out this year (meaning 1663) with the Indians at Esopus, now Ulster county. It continued, however, but a short season." But it appears from Trumbull's History of Connecticut, that in or about 1643, a war broke out between the Dutch and the Indians, on the main and on Long Island, which continued several years; and that the Dutch governor applied to New-Haven for assistance.—(Pages 138, 139 and 164.)

4. In the 9th line of the 11th page ,between the word "latitude" and the word "which," the words, "and crosseth over thence in a straight line to Hudson's river in forty-one degrees of latitude," are omitted.

5. In speaking of the commissioners appointed by King Charles the Second, the 26th of April, 1664, to visit the New England colonies and settle disputes, Mr. Smith, where their names occur, mentions Sir George Carteret as one of them; but George Cartwright, Esquire, was the commissioner, and not Sir George Carteret. In the commission, the commissioners are thus designated: "Colonel Richard Nichols, Sir Robert Carr, Knight; George Cartwright, Esq. and Samuel Maverick, Esq."

6. Between the word "and," at the end of the 10th line, and the word "why," in the 11th line of the 26th page, the words "by Mr. Howell and Capt. Young of Long Island," are omitted; and the words "to agree upon the bounds of the said colony," substituted in their stead. It is remarkable that the words substituted do not comport with what precedes or follows them. Instead of a comma, there should be a period at the end of the word "respectively," in the 16th line of the same page; and instead of a period, there should be a comma at the end of the word "above-named," in the 18th line; and the word "governors," part of which is at the end of the 17th and part at the beginning of the 18th line, should be "governor." Query,

whether the word "thirteen," at the beginning of the 20th line, should not be "twelve."

7. The date, 1698, in the beginning of the 28th line of the 77th page, should be 1691. This is probably a typographical error.

8. Speaking of the judges of the Supreme Court, Mr. Smith in page 245 says, "they hold their offices by separate commissions under the great seal of the province, which were formerly during pleasure, but of late quamdiu se bene gesserint."[25] The correctness of the latter part of this sentence is much doubted. Mr. De Lancey obtained from the colonial Governor Clinton, the commission of Chief Justice during good behaviour; but I have always understood that the commissions to all the other judges during the colonial government were during pleasure; and the Assembly, in their petition to the King in 1775, pray that he would be graciously pleased to remove the distinction between his subjects in England and those in America, by commissioning his judges here to hold their offices during good behaviour. The truth may be ascertained by the records in the Secretary's office.

Samuel Jones.

Oysterbay South, 1818.

## 21. Samuel Jones to John Pintard

*Oysterbay South, 30th January,* 1818.

Sir,

Your letter of the 23d of December last was duly received, together with the two volumes of the collections of the New-York Historical Society, for which I return them my thanks.

I possess no traditionary knowledge of Leisler or the transactions of his government. Doubtless there must be some record of public affairs during the time he acted as lieutenant governor or commander in chief of the colony. Trumbull, in his History of Connecticut, mentions that there was a meeting of commissioners from Massachusetts, Rhode Island, and Connecticut, with Leisler at New-York the first of May, 1690, to consult the common defence; and says that at this meeting the commissioners conceived the plan of an expedition against Canada; that it was proposed with about eight or nine hundred Englishmen and five or six hundred Indians to make an attack upon Montreal, while a fleet and army of eighteen hundred or two thousand men were to proceed up the St. Lawrence, and at the same time make an attack upon Quebec; and gives an account of the proceedings of both armies, which seems to have been taken from authentic documents. From this account it appears that the agreement of the commissioners at New-York was signed by Leisler; and that a copy of it remains among the records of Connecticut.—(See Trumbull's History of Connecticut, pages 402–405.) It is presumable that Leisler upon that occasion must have convened an assembly of the colony to enable him to perform his part of the agreement.

It appears by the Society's catalogue that they possess the papers called the Independent Reflector. It was supposed that William Livingston, afterwards governor of New-Jersey, William Smith, jun. afterwards chief justice of Canada, John Morin Scott, William P. Smith, and William Alexander, afterwards Lord Stirling, were the authors of those papers. How long the publication continued I do not recollect; but I cannot believe that it was, or could have been, tyrannically suppressed as mentioned in the catalogue. My impression is that the printer refused to continue the publication: perhaps his refusal may have been attributed to the influence of some persons in power. Livingston, Smith, and Scott, not long after commenced a periodical production under the title of the Watch Tower. It was published in Hugh Gaine's newspaper; he having agreed with the authors, in consideration of fifty pounds a year, to appropriate the front page of his paper to their use. This contract ended in the autumn of 1755; and the printer refused to continue or renew it. Whether the authors wished it, I do not know; but I heard Mr. Gaine tell Mr. Smith he should not continue it. Mr. Livingston, some years afterwards, published periodical papers for a considerable time. These I preserved and had bound in a volume which I gave to his son William near twenty years ago, and I suppose it yet remains in his possession, and probably many other of his father's publications, as he informed me he intended to collect and republish them.

The Society ought to possess a copy of the proceedings of the Provincial Congress and Convention of the colony; but there is reason to believe their proceedings were not all regularly entered into books: for when the revisers of the laws of the state applied to John McKesson, who was secretary both to the Congress and Convention, for a copy of the constitution of the state, in order to have it printed with the revised laws, he informed them that no copy had ever been made or entered; and it appeared that some parts of the constitution then remained on separate and unconnected papers; so that it would have been impracticable to make a correct copy of it without the information and assistance of Mr. McKesson. What has become of those papers I do not know. The last account I have had of them, they remained in the possession of Mr. McKesson, thrown indiscriminately into a barrel. If they are yet in that state, there is reason to fear they will soon be lost or destroyed, unless some care is taken to preserve them: I therefore suppose the legislature would upon application order them to be delivered to the Historical Society.

In the list of the members of the Society I see my name. When, how, or by what means I became a member is unknown to me; your information upon the subject will therefore oblige,

Your friend,<br>Samuel Jones.

JOHN PINTARD, ESQ.
Recording Secretary of the N. Y. Historical Society.

# Notes

(The editor's annotations are set in square brackets. All other notes are William Smith, Jr's., marginalia from his own interleaved copy of the *History,* located in The Philip H. and A. S. W. Rosenbach Foundation in Philadelphia.)

## Part I. From the Discovery of the Colony to the Surrender in 1664

1. [William Burnet, Governor of New York, 1720–1728, whom Smith very much admired.]

2. It was thought to be a demonstration of a discovery of the country *before* this period, that the marks of a hatchet were found in the body of a tree in the spring 1775, which had been made in *1590*. The block was brought to town and shewn to me; but the discoverer abated of the value he had set upon this curiosity, when I observed upon the authority of Stith's *History* that the Indians might have got the instrument from (according to De Laet, Cascade, where Jacques Cartier, the discoverer, had wintered in 1536 at St. Croix a little above Quebec and afterwards revisited the St. Lawrence in 1540 with 5 ships, and continued the crew at Charlebourgh, above St. Croix, to 1542, or from) the English, who came first to Wococon or Ocacock to the southward of Cape Hatteras on the 2 July 1582, and a few days after entered Albemarle Sound. That they returned to it under Sir Richard Greenvil on the 26th May 1585, and on his return that summer to England, left above 100 persons at Roanoke, who expanded themselves southward and northward, and had dealings with the Indians above 130 miles NW into the country. That Sir Francis Drake visited the new colony in 1586, after burning St. Anthony and St. Helena in Florida, where he found the Spaniards had commenced settlements. That Sir Richard Greenvil revisited that country the same year, and Capt. White with his company the next;

and that in 1588 Sir Walter Raleigh had then expended forty thousand pounds sterling upon the enterprises for planting a colony under the name of Virginia.

Sir Thomas Smith's company, after Raleigh's assignment, arrived 3d August 1590, the year designated by the circles on the block. Mr. Robert Yates, the surveyor who brought it to town, gave me the following certificate of the Discovery in a letter of 3 May 1775.

> Sir:
> In the course of the survey of the Patent granted in the year 1672 to Jan Hendrickse Van Baale, in the County of Albany, as claimed by the Proprietors thereof, the surveyors were particularly directed by the arbitrators appointed for the determination of its contested Boundaries, to box the marked trees standing on, and at some distance from the lines. In consequence of it a number of trees were boxed—several whereof appeared to have been cut or marked, whose respective ages upon ascertaining the streaks grown over such marks, counted from 110 to 140 years: But what more particularly struck my attention, and to which I can find no satisfactory solution, is, that at the distance of about one mile S.W. from a hill called Kuyck-uyt, in a pine wilderness, remote from any settlement, one of the axmen for the sake of keeping him in employ, was ordered on the 7th March 1775, to cut a pink pine tree of about two foot diameter, whereupon there was little of any appearance of a mark—about six inches in the tree a cut or mark was discovered, and the block taken out. In splitting it with the grain, it opened to our view several cuts of an ax or other sharp iron tool, the dents whereof appeared as fresh and new, as if the mark had been made within a year. In counting of the rings or streaks grown over this mark it amounted to one hundred and eighty-five, so that the cut was made in the year 1590; at least 17 years before Hudson's discovery of this country. It is well known that the natives had no *iron* tools before their acquaintance and intercourse with the Europeans; and it is this circumstance, that involves me in the difficulty of accounting for its mark at that early period. Proof of the number of streaks grown over marks, has often in our coasts been allowed to ascertain its age. I have therefore been at some pains to discover its certainty; and can from my own experience declare, that it amounts to demonstration. Amongst a variety of instances the two following are the most remarkable. . . . [recites cases from 1772 and 1768] /s/ Roberts Yates. New York May 3d 1775.

On inspecting the block, I observed that the rings of growth differed in their distance from each other, probably according to the variety of the years as more or less favorable to its increase. But if the age of the tree is to be computed by the 4th part of its diameter acquired in 185 years, and was consequently for 24 inches over 740 years old, how venerable our forests of pines! in which there are many trees of 3 & 4 feet diameter, which must *then* be from one thousand to near fifteen hundred years old; and how many more they continue at a stand and on the decline before they fall, none can determine. The land most abounding with firs is light, dry and sandy; and where the trunks have rotten away, they leave knotts which no weather seems to affect, from the repletion of the interstices with resin, or an unctuous substance that is very inflamable, and which the country people collect & use for lights to work by in long winter's evenings. These are found where there is not the least appearance of a hillock for the trunk to which they originally belonged; and this leads to as remote antiquity for their first formation, as for rocks and other permanent substances. Pliny says "Vita arborum querundam immensa credi potest" [the life of trees can be considered as immense. Pliny the Elder, *Natural History*]; but he mentions no species of trees with certainty, of an age equal to what we conjecture of the American firs, commonly called *Pitch Pine*. There is a white pine tree on the banks of Batten Creek in the Township of Cambridge in this Province, of the diameter of 7 feet. No fir as yet discovered exceeds four.

3. [See Thomas J. Condon, *New York Beginnings. The Commercial Origins of New Netherland* (New York, New York University Press, 1968); and Van Cleaf Bachman, *Peltries or Plantations: The Economic Policies of the Dutch West India Company in New Netherlands, 1623–1639* (Baltimore, Johns Hopkins University Press, 1969).]

4. [Conditions offered by the Lord Director General of the Government of New Netherland, to the Masters Weyting (Whiting) and Hill, delegates from the noble Council of Hartford: on behalf of our Hartford Plantation, they will pay as an annual stipend to the most powerful orders, the Directors General of the States General of the Federated Provinces of Belgium or their deputies, a tenth part of the income of the fields, not only from the plow, the hoe, and other means of cultivation (but also) fruit orchards, gardens, vegetables that have been set apart, with the exception of those not exceeding a Dutch juger (a measure of land 240′ x 120′); or in the place of the ten parts, a generous price to be determined later as long as they shall be the possessors of the said plantation. Done in the Citadel of Amsterdam in New Netherland on July 9, 1642.]

5. [Among Smith's associates in 1756, when he wrote this, was William Alexander, who claimed the controversial title "Earl of Stirling" and extensive lands on the basis of the Dowager's earlier claim.]

6. [See Ronald D. Cohen, "The Hartford Treaty of 1650: Anglo-Dutch Cooperation in the Seventeenth Century," *New-York Historical Society Quarterly*, LIII (1969), 311–332.]

7. [William Beekman, then Lieutenant-Governor of "South River," the Delaware area captured by the Dutch from the Swedes.]

8. [The chief magistrates of Dutch towns.]

9. [John Winthrop, Jr., 1606–1676; see *DAB*.]

10. [See Albert E. McKinley, "The Transition from Dutch to English Rule in New York," *American Historical Review*, VI (1900), 693–724.]

11. Sir Robert Carr arrived at Bristol, 1 June 1667, and died the

next day. Cartwright went home in 1664, leaving Maverick at Boston (vid *N England's memorial* by Nath: Morton Secretary for New Plimouth p. 219 Edit 12° 1721).

## Part II. From the Surrender in 1664, to the Settlement at the Revolution

1. The Duke's Commissioners in their Narrative express themselves thus. "The bounds between the Dukes Province and Conecticote were mistaken by wrong information, for it was not intended that they should come nearer to Hudson's River than Twenty miles, yet the Line was set down by the Commissioners to go from such a poynt NNW whereas it ought to go just N otherwise the line will goe into Hudson's River." Hutch col: 412.

2. He published an instrument to encourage sellers under the title of; "The Conditions for New Planters in the Territories of his Royal Highness the Duke of York." I have met with three printed copies of it. The remainder is in these words;

The purchases are to be made from the Indian sachems, and to be recorded before the Governour.

The purchasers are not to pay for the Liberty of purchasing to the Governour.

The purchasers are to set out a town & inhabit together.

No purchaser shall at any time contract for himself with any sachem, without consent of his associates or special warrant from the Governour.

The purchasers are free from all manner of assessments or rates for five years after their town plot is set out, and when the five years are expired, they shall only be liable to the publick rates and payments, according to the Custome of other inhabitants, both English and Dutch.

All lands thus purchased and possesst shall remain to the purchasers and their heirs as free lands to dispose of as they please.

In all territories of his Royal Highness, Liberty of Conscience is allowed, provided such Liberty is not converted to Licentiousness or the disturbance of others in the exercise of the Protestant Religion.

The several townships have liberty to make their peculiar laws, and deciding all small cases within themselves.

The lands which I intend shall be first planted, are those upon the west side of Hudson's River, or adjoyning to the *Sopes:* (The Governour hath purchast all the *Sopes* Land which now is ready for Planters to put the Plough into, it being clear ground.) But if any number of men sufficient for two or three or more towns, shall desire to plant any other lands, they shall have all due encouragement, proportionable to their quality and undertakings.

Every township is obliged to pay their minister, according to such agreement as they shall make with him: and no man to refuse his proportion, the minister being elected by the major part of the householders, inhabitants of the town.

Every township hath the free choice of all their officers, both civil and military; and all men who shall take the oath of allegiance to His Majesty, and are not servants or day labourers, but are admitted to injoy town-lots, are esteemed freemen of the jurisdiction; and cannot forfeit the same, without due process in law.

R. Nicolls

[The hundred-word bibliographical note which follows is crossed out by Smith.]

3. [A schout was a Dutch municipal administrative officer; a schepen was a Dutch alderman or petty magistrate.]

4. [See Charles H. Wilson, *Profit and Power. A Study of England and the Dutch Wars* (London, Longmans Green, 1957), pp. 111–142.]

5. It was this Governor who introduced the Prohibition by Proclamation in 1671, against Masters of Vessels carrying persons off, without a pass from the Secretary's Office and a dispatch for his vessel; and it laid the foundation for fees to that office, which were refused by the merchants, but not until near a hundred years afterwards. See the Minutes of Council on the 19th & 23rd of June 1766. Sir Henry Moore made the legality of the Let-passes a question, and upon a diversity of opinion between Mr. Chief Justice Horsmanden and Mr. Justice Smith, the Council advised an Establishment by Act of Assembly, which was never obtained as might have been foreseen from the jealous temper of that day, when all the Provinces were alarmed by the Stamp Act and the Statute for quartering troops etc.

6. [Captain John Manning, Commander-in-Chief at Fort James in July 1673. For his court martial and trial, see E. B. O'Callaghan, ed., *The Documentary History of the State of New-York* (Albany, 1849–1851), III, 80–99 *passim*.]

7. [Percy Kirke (1646?–1691), brigadier general present at Sedgmoor in 1685, and notorious for his cruelty to the rebels; Judge George Jeffreys (1648–1689), as recorder of London (1678–1680) gained notoriety for his severity in the "Popish Plot" cases, and held the "bloody assize" in the west after Monmouth's Rebellion was suppressed in 1685.]

8. Rémy, Seigneur de Courcelles—His Commission dated at Paris, 23 March 1665, published in Council as from Quebec, 23 Sept. 1665. He was appointed Governor and Lt. General in Canada, Acadie, & Newfoundland and other Northern Countries of France in the Place and Stead of the Sieur De Mézy recalled but dead before he knew of the supersedens. In 1663, 19 Nov., Viscount Prouville de Tracy was created Viceroy in North and South America with authority over all governors. May 1664 this edict passed constituting the West India Company—It was given to them to appoint governors and all officers in North and South America & Africa but they requested that the Crown would nominate the officers for Canada. De Tracy returned to France in 1666. The West India Company grant continued to 1674 and was then extinguished and the Crown reseized.

9. [Arent Van Corlaer. See the letter from Governor Nicolls of New York to Governor Tracy of New France, May 28, 1667, in Edmund B. O'Callaghan, ed., *Documents Relating to the Colonial His-*

*tory of the State of New-York* (Albany, 1853), III, 156–157. See also *ibid.*, pp. 128, 132, 143–145, 147, 151, 162, 324, 326, 327, 559, 815, 817.]

10. Talons the Intendant of that day was a man of abilities and enterprise. [Jean Talon, Intendant of New France, 1665–1668 and 1670–1672.] It was he that excited to the western excursion of Pere Marquet, a Jesuit, and Joliet, a Citizen of Quebec, who in 1673 made the firm discovery of the Mississippi in 42 4/2 [?] north latit. Talons had been Intendant in [Nainant?]. He was recalled after Frontenac's arrival at his own request, but desired to postpone the voyage till the Province could not suffer by his absence. He took Acadie in his way home in 1673.

11. [It may be of some consequence that in these last nineteen paragraphs discussing the history and manners of the Five Indian Nations, Smith never mentions or acknowledges Cadwallader Colden's *The History of the Five Indian Nations Depending on the Province of New-York in America* (1727 and 1747). He did, in fact, rely considerably upon Colden's material.]

12. [See John H. Kennedy, *Thomas Dongan, Governor of New York (1682–1688)*, (Washington, Catholic University of America Press, 1930); and Thomas P. Phelan, *Thomas Dongan, Colonial Governor of New York, 1683–1688* (New York, P. J. Kenedy and Sons, 1933).]

13. This is a copy of it intitled. The Humble Address of the Sheriffs. . . . [The transcribed document, dated Oct. 9, 1683, is omitted here.]

14. De la Barre was considered of too advanced an age. Denonville's Commission is of 1 January 1685 & was registered at Quebec 3d August following.

15. [Bateaux were long, tapering river-boats with flat bottoms, used especially in New France.]

16. [Jerome R. Reich, *Leisler's Rebellion. A Study of Democracy in New York, 1664–1720* (Chicago, University of Chicago Press, 1953) is the fullest modern account. Reich's interpretation, however, must be read with caution.]

17. [See Lawrence H. Leder, *Robert Livingston, 1654–1728, and the Politics of Colonial New York* (Chapel Hill, University of North Carolina Press, 1961), pp. 65–69.]

18. [See Allen W. Trelease, *Indian Affairs in Colonial New York: The Seventeenth Century* (Ithaca, Cornell University Press, 1960), ch. 11, for the Iroquois as English allies at this time.]

19. Where he landed 1500 men, commanded the town, & having expended all his ammunition he was obliged to set sail on the 23 of that month.

## Part III. From the Revolution to the Second Expedition against Canada

1. [The Law of New York; or, the laws instituted under the illustrious Prince James, Duke of York and Albany, for observance in

the territories of America, transcribed in the Year of our Lord 1674.]

2. This note was on the 24th April 1691 and preceded by an entry in these words: "Upon an information brought into this House by several members of the House declaring that the several laws made formerly by the General Assembly and his late Royal Highness James Duke of York &c and also the several ordinances or the reputed laws made by the preceding governors and councils for the rule of their Majesty's subjects within this Province are reported among the people to be still in force."

The reader who will find no law to repeal the acts passed before the Revolution, may perhaps misquote in ignorance what ought to be ascribed to art, unless he is informed that one of those acts gave a perpetual revenue to the Crown, and that every subsequent Assembly wished to conceal what a bill to repeal it would draw from under the veil which this Resolve had concealed from the eye of a weak Governor or concerning which they made it his interest to be silent by the new temporary act for establishing a revenue.

3. The sufferers under their government stated their oppressions to this Assembly, who unanimously resolved on the 17th April 1691 that their services were tumultuous, illegal and against the rights of the new King and Queen; that they had illegally and arbitrarily thrown divers Protestant subjects into doleful and nauseous prisons, proscribed and forced others out of the colony; that the depredations upon Schenectady were imputable to their usurpations; that they had ruined merchants and others by seizures of their effects; levied money and rebelliously raised forces, and that their refusal to surrender this Fort was rebellion. The Council concurred with these Resolves the next day. The Assembly at first waved an answer to the Governor's question respecting the propriety of reprieving the convicts. He urged them again 3 weeks afterwards (11 May) for an explicit answer, whether they ought or ought not to be executed, & within 5 days after this the Council consented to the execution, & the Assembly declared their approbation.

4. [Ingoldesby.]

5. [See Lawrence H. Leder, ed., "The Missing New York Assembly Journal of April 1692," *New-York Historical Society Quarterly*, XLIX (1965), 5–27.]

6. [This man, also mentioned earlier, was not related to the author. See Appendix III.]

7. [See James S. Leamon, "War, Finance, and Faction in Colonial New York: The Administration of Governor Benjamin Fletcher, 1692–1698" (unpublished PhD dissertation, Brown University, 1961).]

8. [For Father Millet's mission among the Oneidas, and his retirement, see E. B. O'Callaghan, ed., *The Documentary History of the State of New York* (Albany, 1849–1851), I, 112, 131, 200, 276.]

9. [William Blathwayt (1649?–1717), secretary at war, 1683–1704; commissioner of trade, 1696–1706.]

10. [See Edward P. Lilly, *The Colonial Agents of New York and*

*New Jersey* (Washington, Catholic University of America Press, 1936), pp. 38–40, 42–43, 144n.]

11. [See Lawrence H. Leder, *Robert Livingston, 1654–1728, and the Politics of Colonial New York* (Chapel Hill, University of North Carolina Press, 1961), pp. 109–10, 125, 141–50.]

12. ["cursed greed for gold": see Vergil, *Aeneid*, book III, line 57.]

13. The Earl assigned [as] reasons for [Mr.] Bayard's suspension, a copy of which and of the answers I have in my custody. I give an abstract of both. (1) That he advised Governor Fletcher to issue a Proclamation for the currency of Dog-Dollars contrary to his oath and the King's Instructions. (2) That he connived at an illegal commerce with foreign ships at New York. (3) That he connived at Fletcher's granting commissions to pirates manned here for the Red Sea, procured protections from the Governor & received a reward, advised to a piratical ship's being admitted into port with her spoils & connived at Fletcher's receipt of presents from pirates. (4) That he advised to Fletcher's frequent misapplications & embezlements of the King's Revenue, and other money appropriated by the Assembly to special and public uses. (5) That he advised to extravagant grants & took one to himself of land belonging to the Mohawks, as large as one of the middle counties in England, without reserving a reasonable quitrent. (6) That he advised the Governor's going into the field at elections, where he named members for the Assembly with threatening and abusive language to the Electors. (7) That he connived at Fletcher's neglect of the frontiers in the late war endangering the defection of the Five Nations of Indians and the loss of the Garrisons on that side. (8) That he advised the printing of a scandalous & malicious pamphlet intitled "A Letter from a Gent. of the City of New York to Another Concerning the Troubles which Happened in this Province in the Time of the Late Happy Revolution" to rise up sedition and inflame the colony, in compliance with Fletcher's wicked Designs, & to gratify his own implacable malice against those who were most active in the Revolution. (9) That a few days after his (Lord Bellomont's) arrival, he confederated with several persons disaffected to His Majesty's Government, in an address to Governor Fletcher applauding his justice in countenancing illicit trade, and at the same time upbraided the Earl as discouraging commerce, by issuing his warrant for seizing the ship Fortune and goods unlawfully imported in that bottom, & (10) That contrary to his duty and oath, he conspired against the King's Government by raising scandalous reports to misrepresent his Lordship's Governors, and assisted in forging several false and groundless articles against his Lordship and without his knowledge.

Mr. Bayard gave a written answer from New Jersey on 17 October 1698, 13 days after he had a copy of the charges against him, and intended as appears from his letter to his Lordship to sail for England. This defence follows the order of the impeachments;

1. The Proclamation he alledges was issued with the advice of the Attorney General, as well as the rest of the Council Board, and fixed a Dog Dollar at 5 shillings and 6 pence, tho' current in other colo-

nies at 6 shillings—That this money had & retained a currency, before and after the Proclamation; and if the Treasury had lost by the receipt of them, he offered to exchange them out of his own purse. The 2d article he absolutely denies; and to account for the 3d, he says that several years before he had by a letter to Governor Fletcher then at Philadelphia, requested his favor in behalf of one Thomas Lewis, who had been abroad in a privateer, some of the crew of which had killed the Master, & of Barent Ryndersen, a comrade of Lewis. That the letter was written at the request of his neighbor [Leenders?] Lewis and Samuel Staats; the former a brother to Thomas Lewis, and the other brother-in-law to Barent Ryndersen, & one of his Lordship's new Councillors and very solicitous to procure Governor Fletcher's license for the return of their relations (who were two sons in law to the widow Leisler) and their settlement in New York. That the Governors granted the favors desired, & inclosed the licenses to him which he delivered to Leenders Lewis & Samuel Staats, who unrequested offered him a bag of 100 pieces of 8 for the Governor & 18 or 20 ducats for himself; both which he refused to accept, until he was importuned to gratify their desire of testifying their acknowledgment of the great favor they had received: and for the confirmation of this narrative, he urges an examination of the four persons above named, all of them in town. He adds that the licenses were upon condition of continuing in the Province, & being of to good behavior, and at that day were commonly called protections.

4. He denies this charge; declaring that he advised the borrowing money of the Receiver General about 6 years before, to repel the French who had advanced near to Schenectady, out of any funds in his hands—and had himself made loans to the public during the war, and bound himself to indempnify Mr. Livingston & other lenders, not disposed to rely on the justice of the country for their disbursments.

5. He owns his grant for scholars—thinks it no crime to accept the patent—asserts that others who had Governor Dongan's leave to purchase it, refused the price demanded, & that then he petitioned for it, and drove the bargain with the Indians who never complained (except a few of the meanest) of the sale. He applauds the patent to Colonel Schuyler and Domine Dellius—the clamors against it he imputes to the envy of the Indian traders at Albany—Thinks our approaches to the Indians conducive to the spread of Christianity—assigns the desertion of the Caghnuagas to the thirst of the Mohawks after instruction, and the aid given to them by the French for obtaining it—conceives the settlement of the interior lands, consistant with policy as well as piety in better watching the intrigues of the French.

6. He admits the allegation that the Governor had attended Elections, but he denies that it was by his advice; and he exculpates him from the charge of menacing the people, to whom he heard him recommend a peaceable agreement which was slighted, & the Governor gone before the election.

7. Acquitting the Governor of any neglect of the frontiers, he refutes the accusation of his own connivance at this default; and observes that the advice of Council on these subjects was *nemine contradicente,* & would expose persons still retained at that Board to as much censure as himself, who are nevertheless not blamed.

8. He avers that the pamphlet excepted to contains nothing but the truth. With respect to the Revolution, he informs his lordship that Lt. Governor Nicholson & the Council changed the Government by a Convention of all the civil and military officers, for executing measures by them concerted, 'till orders arrived from England. That this was communicated by express to the Secretary of State and the Lords of the Plantation office, long before others applauded by his lordship thrust themselves into power for private ends, imposing reports upon the public of Jacobites and Papists, of whom there were then not ten in the Colony. He avows his own zeal for the Revolution, but that he thought the operations here ought to have been conducted, according to inclinations from Home, and according to the examples of Virginia, Barbadoes, & Jamaica, without altering the model of the colony constitution, until orders were received for that purpose from England.

—He capitulates his sufferings under the Ruling Party—driven into exile—imprisoned afterwards 14 months—bail refused—fettered with irons, been robbed, & that he remains still unredressed. And to the

9th & 10th articles, he opposed a flat and peremptory denial of their truth.

14. [See John C. Rainbolt, "A 'great and usefull designe': Bellomont's Proposal for New York, 1698–1701," *New-York Historical Society Quarterly,* LIII (1969), 333–351; John D. Runcie, "The Problem of Anglo-American Politics in Bellomont's New York," *William and Mary Quarterly,* 3d series, XXVI (1969), 191–217.]

15. [This is William Smith, the councilor, who became Chief Justice of New York in 1702. He was not related to the historian.]

16. Provision has been since made by the Royal Instructions, to devolve the powers of government on the eldest councillor, on the death or absence of a Lieut. Governor.

17. That County, now so numerous and opulent, was assessed in the year 1702 [less than] any other, contributing but £18 to a general tax of £2,000. The quotas of the rest were these—New York £423, Kings £296, Queens £370, Richmond £90, Westchester £124, Albany £120, Ulster £144, Orange £45.

18. The preamble of this Act, suggested without doubt by the Parties interested in its success, gives a History which no person in England was concerned to contradict in the [year 1710?]. Mrs. Farmer, a descendant from Leisler, sent me a copy of the statute in July 1759. It may serve to shew the propriety of calling for a report of facts which have happened at a distance, before final resolutions are taken upon them.

An Act for Reversing the Attainder of Jacob Leisler & Others.... [the entire Act is printed in the 1829 edition of Smith's *History,* p. 140n.]

19. Atwood the Chief Justice stimulated these prosecutions. I quote Lord Cornbury's speech of 13 April 1704 to prove this. [I have omitted the excerpt, 12 lines long. It is printed in the *History* (1829), p. 144.]

20. Prior to the passing of that act Mr. Bayard preferred what he intitled his petition and appeal to Queen Anne; in which he alledges that the indictment against him was found but by 11 jurors, several of whom were aliens. That the addresses charged to be treasonable were not read at the trial. That the petty jury were aliens, unduly returned & ignorant of the English language. His request is, for a day to be heard, & that copies of records & minutes & depositions attested by Lord Cornbury, may be received as evidence at the hearing. That the Attorney General may be ordered to attend with Atwood and Weaver, who are both fled to London. It is some confirmation of the petitioner's allegations, that the minute of the Privy Council of 21 January 1702, recites that the Queen had that day heard Council for the petitioner, and Alderman Hutchins, and Atwood the Chief Judge, and Weaver, the Solicitor General, by themselves and their Counsel; and that her Majesty having considered this matter, was sensible of the undue and illegal prosecution against them: and in consequence of this Lord Cornbury was ordered to direct the Attorney General of the Province "to consent to the reversal of the sentences against them [Bayard and Hutchins]. . . ." [Smith here quotes at length from the document; it is printed in the *History* (1829), pp. 145–146.]

21. He was at the same time Judge of the Vice Admiralty, & published his case in England, of which the Assembly in May 1703, assert that it contained scandalous, malicious, notorious untruths and unjust reflections on persons then in the Administration of the Province: and it was in the spirit of revenge, that they observed in an address to Lord Cornbury "that the practice in the Admiralty must in time deter all mankind from coming amongst us. . . ." His Lordship ordered a salary in future in lieu of the 7½ per cent, but Mr. Mompesson receiving but ¾ of that allowance for a single year, he became one of the many supplicant creditors in May 1714.

22. ["for hearth and home."]

23. It had been made a question in King William's reign, whether the keeping of schools was not by the antient laws of England prior to the Reformation of Ecclesiastical cognizance. It was thought by some that a schoolmaster might be prosecuted in the Ecclesiastical Court for not bringing his scholars to Church according to the 79th Canon in 1603. Treby, Chief Justice, and Powel, Justice, were of opinion that being a layman he was not bound by the Canons. [Here Smith discusses an English libel case in 1700; see *History* (1829), p. 149n.]

The Royal Instructions required the Governors of the plantations to give all countenance and encouragement to the exercise of the Ecclesiastical Jurisdiction of the Bishop of London as far as conveniently might be in their respective Provinces and particularly directed "that no school master be henceforward permitted to come from this Kingdom and to keep school in that our said Province without the license of the said Lord Bishop of London and that no other person now there or that shall come from other parts shall be admitted to keep school in your Province without your license first obtained." I have reason to think this Instruction has been continued from the Revolution to the present time to the Governors of all the Royal Provinces.

24. The vote on the ways and means to raise this sum is singular —Every member of the Council to pay a Poll Tax of 4%, an Assembly man 2%, a lawyer in practice 2%, every man wearing a perriwig 5/6, a batchelor of 25 years & upwards 2/3, every freeman between 16 & 60 9d, the owners of slaves for each 1/. The project of creating these batteries is a proof either of his Lordship's want of skill in his own profession, or that he discredited the report of the design to attack the capital. The passage of his speech in these words: "I think the best way to [?] that design will be to [?] two batteries of guns at the Narrows, one on each side which I believe is the only way to make this port safe." Many engineers have since informed me that no works there could have that effect. So late as the year 1730, a Poll Tax was ordered toward supporting the Indian trade at Oswego. On every inhabitant (say the sagacious committee who resolved it) "resident or sojourner, young or old, within this colony, that wears a whig or peruke made of human or horse hair, or mixed, by whatsoever denomination the same may be distinguished, the sum of three shillings." The Treasurer returned an account of the number of wigs in August 1731 and the produce being trifling, more effectual funds were provided for the Post and Commerce driven at Oswego.

25. But tho they avowed it to be their endeavor to conform to the letter and interest of the Governour's Commission, and denied the charge of a design to assume any of the powers of government, their address contained a clause which discovered a high and firm spirit. [An 18-line quotation follows; see *History* (1829), p. 155.] His Lordship could expect only a general answer, from the moderate principles of the people of that day, did he dread intimations inconsistant with their loyalty to the Queen or their disaffection to the parent kingdom. The colony politicians of early days contented themselves with general declarations, owning a subordination and yet claiming English privileges; leaving it to their posterity to ascertain the boundary, between the supremacy of England and the submission of her colonies. Happy, if both countries had adopted that poet's rule—sunt certi denique fines/Quos ultra citraque nequit consistere rectum [There are definite limits beyond which and on this side of which the right cannot take a stand.] The Council and Assembly spoke the general sense of the colony, in the following passage of their joint representation, in favor of the post of Oswego, 29 October 1730. "We are truly sensible of and as truly grateful for the many principal favors, by which his Majesty and his Royal Predecessors have distinguished this Colony, and loyalty and fidelity to his illustrious House, our unfeigned love and affection for our Mother Country, & the *happy Dependance* which we have upon the

*Crown and Kingdom* of Great Britain, lay us under all natural and civil obligations, so to act in humble station, as may render us useful and serviceable." Our ancestors claimed every social benefit not injurious to the Mother Country, nor inconsistant with their loyalty to the Crown or their dependance upon Great Britain.

26. It remained nevertheless to be the unparliamentary practice of that day (1704) not only to send reasons in writing for and against amendments proposed to bills, but on conferences for the Speaker to go up with the whole House to a dialogue with the Council where, the Governor taking the chair, he became a party in all disputes between the Council & Assembly.

The Lords of Trade approved of the dissolution and added "We conceive no reason why the Council should not have a right to amend all bills sent up by the Assembly even those relating to money."

27. "and all persons concerned in the issuing and disposing such monies must be made accountable to the Governor, Council and Assembly." The vote to appoint a Treasurer for the public money they raised, passed on the 20th of June 1705, The Assembly soon after took occasion in framing a bill to defray the charge of Fuzileers, spies and outscouts for the defence of the Frontiers, to render the sums due payable by their Treasurer. The Council called them to a conference upon it the 4th of October. The Assembly desired their objections in writing. These were (1) That it gave a sum to her Majesty, & not her *Heirs and Successors* (2) That the Treasurer is compelled to give security to account to the General Assembly, instead of the Crown, the High Treasurer or Commissioners of the Treasury. (3) That the monies are made issuable upon private Certificates of Services. The Council proceeded upon the Royal Instructions, which they recite. The Assembly answer to the first, that it is plain from the bill, that no money to be raised is for the use of the Crown, & no bill in this respect similar to others passed by the Governor and approved at home. To the second, that tho' he is made accountable to the General Assembly, there is nothing in the bill to prevent his accounting also to the Queen and the Treasury. Relative to the third they observe that the "Instruction had been generally taken as a restriction on the Governors" against the disposition of public money, without the approbation of the *Council,* and they insist upon the clauses, (1) because Governors & Receivers General have always quarreled, and the latter been suspended, & all accounting eluded, (2) because the Receivers on the loss of their offices, have generally left the Province, & (3) because money raised for the defense of Albany, had never been applied to that use. The conferences closed by the revival of the objection to the Council's interfering in the amendment of money bills; and sudden prorogation followed to such a distant day, as his Lordship was afterwards compelled to retract it for a speedier meeting, not without exciting doubts concerning the legality of their next convention, some months before the day to which they had been in a passion prorogued. (*Vid* the Journals of 13th October 1705 & 30th

May 1706.) Tho' there was then reason to apprehend an attack from the French, and several bills were passed to raise money for the defence of the colony, his Lordship could not prevail upon the Assembly to wave their objections, so that the services remained unprovided for, until the Assembly carried their point, of having a Treasurer of their own, with the Queen's consent, as above expressed in his Lordship's speech of 27 Sept. 1706. By a clause in an Act for raising a fund for the defence of the frontier etc. passed 5th Anne; the Treasurer was to give such security as *Wm Nicoll*, the then speaker, should approve, but no recognizance or bond could ever be found—(*vid* Assembly Journal, 21 July 1721).

28. Mompesson succeeded Atwood, and fled from a profitable practice in England, for striking a Peer. He had a vote in 1709, for a salary of £130. He died poor, and I remember his widow in deep indigence, as to depend upon the charitable contributions of the Bar, when I first came to it in October 1752.

29. [For a concise modern treatment of the Makemie episode, see Carl Bridenbaugh, *Mitre and Sceptre: Transatlantic Faiths, Ideas, Personalities, and Politics, 1689–1775* (New York, Oxford University Press, (1962), pp. 122–125.]

30. [See Arthur D. Pierce, "A Governor in Skirts," *Proceedings of the New Jersey Historical Society,* LXXXVIII (1965), 1–9.]

31. His Lordship several years afterwards endeavored to obstruct the royal assent to an Act procured in Mr. Hunter's time for payment of the public debts. The Governor informed the Assembly of it in a speech (4 May 1715), adding "what his reasons are, or what effect they may have I know not. I shall only say, that in my opinion, he of all men, ought to have been [?] in this [?], but I cannot think that we can be so." When the Lords of Trade objected in 1718 to two Revenue Acts as affecting the Navigation of the Mother Country, the Assembly presented a long justificatory address with free censures upon the misapplication of public money in the Earl of Clarendon's Administration; [a 4-line quotation omitted]. It was in the same address they made the unpromising attempt to prevail upon the Lords of Trade to forbear reporting an Act for the Royal Disallowance until they had communicated their objections to the Governor of the Colony, and received the answer of the Assembly. Certainly the projection of it was not aware of the consequences of so unparliamentary an innovation. The objections to argumentative altercations in such cases were obvious and unanswerable. They are strengthened by the distances between lawgivers, who have the vast Atlantic between them. We see proofs of our infancy in almost every page of our public transactions. There is no mention of a motion to amend the address, which might have been expected from Mr. Morris. Perhaps he was the draftsman of the whole. He certainly was the Nestor of the day & had the confidence of the Assembly. It was the same House who in 1720 voted a salary of £300 to the Chief Justice for 5 years, with the unconstitutional addition "while Mr. Morris continues and for any person else put into that office, but 200," and gave him other money "for particular services" without specifying what they were.

## Part IV.  From the Canada Expedition in 1709, to the Arrival of Governour Burnet

1. [See George M. Waller, *Samuel Vetch, Colonial Enterpriser* (Chapel Hill, University of North Carolina Press, 1960), esp. ch. 7.]

2. The history of an infant country must consist of many events comparatively trivial. They are nevertheless often characteristic. Some of *our* levies for the expedition were Dutchmen. General Nicholson applied to Mr. Dubois, a City minister, for a person to read prayers to the Dutch soldiery. Dubois, who (if one may speak) was a Presbyterian Bishop among the Dutch churches, then supplied with pastors from Holland and other parts of the United Provinces, and under the care of the Classis of Amsterdam, informed the Assembly of this request. The House named a serious layman, of the name of Paulus Van Vleck, for this service, and ordered Mr. Dubois and two other Dutch ministers, to examine him before two of the Council & as many assembly men, "and if he was found orthodox, to ordain and qualify him for the ministerial function accordingly." Van Vleck urged their compliance, and had a second command upon the ministers. Two of them, DuBois and Antonides, signified by a memorial, "That they were not empowered to ordain any person to the ministerial function in the Dutch churches, by the directions of the Classis of Amsterdam; and therefore prayed they may not be ordered to do anything inconsistent with the constitution of the church to which they belong." Colonel Livingston presented this memorial, upon which no other step was taken. The Legislature was, at that time, chiefly composed of members of the Dutch churches, in which the ministers had great sway; and therefore the clergy were puzzled with the questions, respecting the divine right of ordination, claimed by all Presbyterian ministers; nor a doubt started concerning the authority of the Classis of Amsterdam under the capitulatory Articles of 1664.

3. The address to the Queen contains this illpenned but interesting Information [the 23-line quote which follows concerns the threat of the French subverting the Indian nations; see *History* (1829), pp. 174–175.]

4. [See Richmond P. Bond, *Queen Anne's American Kings* (Oxford, Oxford University Press, 1952); John G. Garratt, "The Four Indian Kings," *History Today*, XVIII (1968), 93–101.]

5. Several extracts from his speeches may show his political creed to be free from the suspicions entertained concerning some of his friends in power at the latter end of Queen Anne's reign. In 1715 on the occasion of George I. [An 8-line quotation follows] and after the suppression of the rebellion in that year [an 18-line quotation follows].

6. Mr. Livingston, the Proprietor of the Manor of that name, set 6,000 acres apart for the German camp and surrendered it to the Crown to enable the Governor to parcel it out to the Palatine emigrants. Mr. Hunter promised but never paid the £600 he was to have for this copious [. . . ]. It was nevertheless one of the debits in his account against the Government for disbursements, in the

demand of which he found various ministerial embarrassments until he bargained it away to one of the ministers for the Government of Jamaica. Mr. Livingston's compensation was a new patent confirming his former grants with a clause enabling his tenants to send a representative to the Assembly. I had this anecdote from his grandson, the present Lord of the Manor in 1777, who then being in the 69th year of his age well remembered his grandfather from whom he heard it and who lived to 1729 and was too intimate with Colonel Hunter & that Governor's friend and successor to make a public use of what might be injurious to Mr. Hunter's reputation. The House hesitated on Mr. Livingston's demanding a seat in May 1717, but Colonel Morris's friendship secured it by carrying a motion to give the [City?] privilege to all who *then* erected manors, & the Village of Islip, & that no other member should afterwards be admitted without the consent of the Governor and the two other branches of the Legislature. The majority imagined the House would thus gain a new fight & lessen the prerogative of the Crown. Mr. Morris's demure face could practice such arts without a smile. Mr. Livingston became Speaker of that House in the ensuing year when Mr. Nicol's attendance for ill health, signified in a letter to the Governor, was excused.

7. [See Walter A. Knittle, *Early Eighteenth Century Palatine Emigration* (Philadelphia, Dorrance, 1937); H. T. Dickinson, "The Poor Palatines and the Parties," *English Historical Review*, LXXXII (1967), 464–485.]

8. [See G. M. Waller, "New York's Role in Queen Anne's War 1702–1713," *New York History*, XXXIII (1952), 40–53.]

9. [See generally Beverly McAnear, *The Income of the Colonial Governors of British North America* (New York, Pageant, 1967).]

10. [See Kenneth Scott, "The Slave Insurrection in New York in 1712," *New-York Historical Society Quarterly*, XLV (1961), 43–74.]

11. [Everywhere we find the Iroquois who, like an importunate ghost, harry us on all sides.]

12. [Where their fear of the Iroquois has made them seek asylum. . . . The most sedentary nation and the one most suitable for the implanting of the faith.]

13. [Jacques N. Bellin (1703–1772) was an engineer and geographer with the French Navy. His map of New England and Nova Scotia appeared in Charlevoix's *Histoire de la Nouvelle France* in 1744. Dr. John Mitchell's "A Map of the British and French Dominions in North America" was published in London in 1755. See Lawrence H. Gipson, *Lewis Evans* (Philadelphia, University of Pennsylvania, 1939), pp. 60–63.]

14. [except keeping them in check.]

15. [having everywhere the compass at hand.]

16. [Of the dead speak nothing but the good. See Diogenes Laertius, *Lives of Eminent Philosophers*, ed. R. D. Hicks (Cambridge, Mass., Harvard University Press, 1959), I, 71 (Chilon, I, 70).]

17. [See Richard A. Lester, "Currency Issues to Overcome Depres-

sions in Delaware, New Jersey, New York and Maryland, 1715–
1737," *Journal of Political Economy*, XLVII (1939), 182–217.]

18. A young gentleman from Scotland, who arrived here from
London 17 August 1715, & figured afterwards in this and the
Province of New Jersey, as one of the most eminent lawyers of his
day. His son was served, as the Scotch express it, Earl of Stirling,
on a Writ of [?], by a jury at Edinburgh, in 1760.

19. These debts had been long since contracted, and the project
for discharging them was a new emission of bills of credit, to be
sunk by continuing the excize, which gave offence to the merchants,
tho' some of them were on the list of the public creditors for considerable sums. The grand jury, composed of some of the most
opulent inhabitants, unawed by the Assembly or Mr. Morris, the
then Chief Justice and a leading member of the House, boldly
addressed Mr. Hunter deprecating his assent to the bill, then in his
hands, as injurious to the commerce of the colony until his Majesty's
pleasure could be known and alledging that the fund was insufficient for sinking the bills of credit proposed to be issued. The
Assembly took fire at this attack, sent to the Governor for the
petition, and ordered the grand jurors into custody. They were
brought to the bar and questioned for their reasons. They answered
that they were expressed in the representation, that they conceived
it lawful to petition one of the branches of the legislature, & that
this implied no reflection upon the other two. They were instantly
dismissed, paying their fees. There were no acrimonious expressions
in the address, but 'tis probable that the Assembly were fearful
of proceeding to extremities, with so many citizens of the first
rank. The subscribers were Stephen DeLancey, Henry Lane, Philip
Van Cortlandt, William Smith (a merchant from the Island of
Jamaica, but a native of Newport Pagnol in the County of Bucks.),
Barent Rynders, Francis Robinson, George [Emmet?], John Reade,
Samuel Provoost, John Moore, Junr., Philip Schuyler, Augustus
Jay, John Rolland, William Walton, Robert Lurting, Henry Vander-
spiegel, & Robert Watts. The prisoners repressed their resentment till
the dissolution of the Assembly; and the dread of it, rendered the
members more easily devoted to the humour and influence of the
Governor, and more obnoxious to the multitude, who discovered
an indecent joy, as often as there was a casual election by the
death of a representative. They sat from 1716 to 1727.

20. [See Daniel J. Pratt, *Report of the Regents of the University
on the Boundaries of the State of New York* (Albany, 1874–1884),
I, 23–25; II, 225–801.]

## Part V. From the Year 1720, to the Commencement of the Administration of Colonel Cosby

1. [Gilbert Burnet (1643–1715), Bishop of Salisbury, wrote a
*History of His Own Times* (published in London, 1723–1734), as
well as sermons, controversial treatises, and political pamphlets.]

2. [See Basil Williams, *The Whig Supremacy, 1714–1760* (Ox-

ford, Oxford University Press, 1952), pp. 169–171, 197–199, 296–298.]

3. [See Arthur H. Buffinton, "The Policy of Albany and English Western Expansion," *Mississippi Valley Historical Review*, VIII (1922), 327–366.]

4. [James Craggs, the younger (1686–1721), friend of George I and of Alexander Pope; secretary of state, 1718.]

5. The order of the House required security in £10,000; and it was reduced by a second vote, on the improbability "that [?] can [?] so much money of the support of government in his hands at one time." Those who thought thus, did not take care to present it; [?] died as [?] for vast sums in 1767.

6. [See Johnson G. Cooper, "Oswego in the French-English Struggle in North America, 1720–1760" (unpublished dissertation, Syracuse University, 1961.]

7. [A stroud was a blanket manufactured for barter or sale in trading with the Indians.]

8. This was the period when that article gained a place among the Royal Instructions, which proved a strong curb upon the vindictive spirit of predominating factions. I mean that which respects such bills as may properly be called *private* ones. It was so well received that the Assembly entered it at large upon their Journals on a motion of one of their own members. It was agreed upon in Privy Council at Whitehall 23 July 1723 by the Lords Justices as an additional Instruction, and has been continued ever since. It restrains the Governor from assenting to any private act [8 lines of direct quotation follow]. It would tend to subvert the laudable policy of this regulation, if Governors suffer themselves to be so hurried at the end of a session, as to slight the question whether the bill [exercises?] the character of a private one or not, or the proofs respecting the notification; and more especially when there is a suspicious party-harmony between the Council and Assembly. I have known bills assented to by one Governor, who had never perused them; and by more than one, who did not read the affidavits sent up with the private bills.

9. [James Alexander and William Smith, father of the historian.]

10. Mr. Smith was a nephew of that Wm. Smith who was one of the grand jury committed by the Assembly in 1717. He had suffered by the memorable earthquake of Port Royal in Jamaica, at the close of the last century, but having repaired his losses by a successful commerce and marriage, removed to New York; & at his instance several branches of his family were induced to leave Buckinghamshire, & become inhabitants of this colony. His uncle came here early in Queen Anne's reign.

11. Mr. Livingston was in the country and so indisposed as to be unable to write but attended 13 Sept. and approved their choice of a new speaker. After the MSS of this History was sent to England for the press, I procured the draft of Chief Justice Morris's opinion, which the reader may peruse in the printed journal of the Assembly for Sept. 1725. It is material to add, that King William made an

order in Council, 18 January 1699, prohibiting the Provincial Governors from granting Letters of Denization, except according to an opinion of the Attorney and Solicitor General set forth in their Report inserted in the order; who after citing several instances of naturalization or denization in the Colonies, particularly letters of denization granted in Nov. 1697 by Colonel Fletcher, and observing that they did not find he had any express powers by his Commission to grant any Letters of Denization, concluded their report in these words [the 7 lines of quotation and source citations which followed have been omitted.]

12. [Louis Joncaire was a French agent who helped win over many of the Senecas.]

13, [There was no other way to keep the colony than for us to become masters of New York; and that this conquest be legal because of necessity.]

14. Beauharnois, who was a natural son to Lewis the 14th and bred at Court, derided the language of this letter which Mr. Burnet had with a scholastic negligence transmitted in the French tongue. The other told Mr. James Livingston, who was then in Canada for his education and noticed by the French Governor, that Mr. Burnet's letter should have maintained the honor as well as the rights of his nation. Perhaps the conveniences of a French parson at his elbow (for Rou & the Governor were inseparable) led him into this uncourtly mistake.

15. It began to totter in the last House. His friend, Mr. Morris, was not able to prevent a reduction of his salary as Chief Justice from £300 to £250 per annum, but he carried a vote that it was only owing to the public necessities that they thought proper to confine him to the pittance allowed to his predecessors. He succeeded Mompesson, and in 1730 told the House as a motive for raising his salary that he was the first native advanced to that honor; but it had no effect. Mr. DeLancey's interest predominating in the House, [?] to mention [?], that the Bar as well as the Bench, had for several years been falling into disrepute, the lawyers naturally sliding into the politics of the Chief Justice, whose adherence to the interests of Hunter and Burnet exposed him to the resentment of Philipse and DeLancey, as well as to a jealous populace, who were swayed not only by their wealth but their connections. Philipse was a native, & the son of Frederic [Flipse?], one of the old Dutch settlers; and DeLancey had married a daughter of Stephanus Von Kortlandt, whose numerous progeny gave him an affinity to many of the most opulent inhabitants. The professors of the law in that day were not numerous, nor had they any support from family or fortune. Alexander, Smith, Murray and Chambers ingrossed the chief business of the bar, and were all batchelors and, except Chambers, strangers and foreigners as the Dutch then affected to call even the natives of Great Britain and Ireland. Richard Bradley, the Attorney General, who had been undersheriff of London, & was promoted for rescuing Dr. Sacheverell from the mob, was of an unguarded, irascible temper, and most of all con-

tributed to that odium, which fell upon the profession at large. The Assembly attacked him in May 1724, for a Breach of Privilege in prosecuting [Hicks & Willet], two colonels of the militia, and members for Queen's County with other justices, for the insufficiency of the County jail. He produced an order of the Supreme Court for the information, & declared his ignorance of their being members of the House, and was dismissed. But he was attacked again on the 2 November 1727. The Committee of Grievances charged that informations were filed for trivial matters against Justices of the Peace and others, with design to frighten them into extortionate compositions [3 lines of quotation have been omitted as well as 11 lines of detail on this legal problem, notably a petition from Albany on the insufficiency of the local jail.]

In the wrath of the first Assembly which met Mr. Montgomerie, and before they came to resolves expressive of great resentment against Mr. Burnet, they brought in a bill to regulate the practice of the lawyers; and on the 20th of June 1729, declared it as their opinion, that some of Mr. Bradley's prosecutions seemed to be intended, rather to "squeeze money" than promote justice, and that if not checked, no good man would either continue in or accept the office of a justice of the peace, & a few days after they resolved to prevent not only the multiplicity of law suits, but *of lawyers*. These things throw some light, upon the reduction of £50 from the Chief Justice's salary of £300 by Mr. Burnet's last Assembly, & the inattention to his memorial for augmenting it in 1730. It is characteristic of the parcimony of that day, to find a man of fortune, in that elevated station, supplicating the House in such terms as these. Speaking of the Assembly, which had made the pitiful deduction of £50, the memorialist "conceived they had rather too low an opinion of the circumstances of the county. That being not now in such necessitous circumstances," he hoped they would establish his salary at 300, & pay the arrears. [The next 6 detailed lines of this plea have been omitted.] He that censures the cajoling of this [contracted?], provincial prejudice, will hardly acquit those, who rendered such condescentions requisite, for the honorable support of an office, essential to the due administration of justice, to private security and the public weal. If other judges have not ventured thus to express themselves upon paper, they have perhaps been obliged to submit to more exceptionable meanesses, in case private submissions to the members & the demagogues of the day. There have been judges, who have assented to bills from the Assembly, to secure votes for more contemptible salaries. To give the proofs, would be an invidious task. Let it suffice in the sequel to find assemblies lavish to the judge of *their* party, and retrenching the allowances of others in the *opposite* connection. He that conceals this, may be a cautious, but he cannot deserve the character of a *faithful* historian.

16. [Perhaps Thomas Jefferson had once noted or recently read this sentence before making his famous observation "that a little rebellion now and then is a good thing, and as necessary in the

political world as storms in the physical." Jefferson to James Madison, January 30, 1787, in Paul L. Ford, ed., *The Works of Thomas Jefferson* (New York, Putnam, 1904), V, 256.

17. Mr. [Bruyn?], a Captain of the Militia in Ulster County, speaking of this Act to Mr. Livingston, charged that he had betrayed his country; the House voted it a presumptious reflection, and took him into custody.

18. [See Stanley M. Pargellis, "The Four Independent Companies of New York," in *Essays Presented to Charles McLean Andrews* (New Haven, Yale University Press, 1931), pp. 96–123.]

19. [with all his might.]

20. [See Daniel J. Pratt, *Report of the Regents of the University on the Boundaries of the State of New York* (Albany, 1874–1884), II, 225–351.]

21. [Thomas Hawley, *et al.*; see Irving Mark, *Agrarian Conflicts in Colonial New York, 1711–1775* (New York, Columbia University Press, 1940), pp. 30n.53, 162n.149.]

22. Beauharnois was a man of activity and had an attachment to Canada by long service in it from 1702 to 1746 when he gave place to a man of still more elevated talents. This was the Count de la Galissoniere who was appointed 10 June 1747, De la Jonquiere, who succeeded Beauharnois being made a prisoner on his passage to Quebec [I have omitted the 17 lines with which this note concludes, treating largely Canadian administrative history of the middle eighteenth century and touching a little upon the French and Indian War. This note and others like it may have been added by Smith in the 1780's when he had settled in Canada. The note has almost nothing to do with New York history.]

23. [See Nellis M. Crouse, "The French in Colonial New York" in Alexander C. Flick, ed., *History of the State of New York* (New York, Columbia University Press, 1933–1937), II, 139–148.]

24. [Inclusion and interpretation of this Campbell episode caused a heated controversy between Smith and Cadwallader Colden. See Volume Two.]

25. [His father.]

# *Appendixes*

## *Chapter I*

1. [See Ferenc M. Szasz, "The New York Slave Revolt of 1741: A Re-examination," *New York History* XLVIII (1967), 215–230.]

2. [A merlon is the part of an embattled parapet between two embrasures.]

3. [See John P. Luidens, "The Americanization of the Dutch Reformed Church" (unpublished dissertation, University of Oklahoma, 1969.]

4. [This Temple of the Trinity was founded in the eighth year of the reign of our illustrious supreme master, William III, by the

grace of God King of England, Scotland, France, and Ireland, Defender of the Faith, and so on, and in the year of our Lord 1696. It was further built by the voluntary contribution and gifts of certain people, especially of the beloved Benjamin Fletcher, the King's commander and representative in this Province, given birth and expanded with his generosity in the time of whose government the inhabitants of this City, professing the Protestant religion of the Anglican Church, as according to the law now established, with a certain certificate of privilege, have been incorporated under the Seal of the Province; and he has given other very numerous, notable donations to the same from his own private estate.]

5. It was penned by the late Mr. Justice Smith one of the first founders of that Church.

6. [With God's Consecration, This Shrine, Sacred to Divine Worship, to be Celebrated for ever, First Founded in the Year of Our Lord 1719; Restored Anew within and constructed in More Ample Form and with More Splendid Adornment in the Year of Our Lord 1748: The Presbyterians of New York, Who Founded it for their Use and for their Fellows, Dedicate it with this Votive Tablet, Supported with Concord, Love, and also Purity of Faith, Worship, and Morality, and More Brilliantly Adorned with Christ's Approval, May It Endure for All Time.]

7. [Holy Shrine of the French Reformed Protestants. Founded in 1704. Interior Restored 1741.]

8. [See Austin B. Keep, *The Library in Colonial New York* (New York, De Vinne Press, 1909), pp. 64–79.]

9. [See Austin B. Keep, *History of the New York Society Library* (New York, De Vinne Press, 1908), pp. 123–178.]

10. [See Arthur E. Peterson, *New York as an Eighteenth Century Municipality Prior to 1731* (New York, Columbia University Press, 1917), especially pp. 1–39; and George W. Edwards, *New York as an Eighteenth Century Municipality, 1731–1776* (New York, Columbia University Press, 1917), especially pp. 13–39.]

11. [See Sung Bok Kim, "The Manor of Cortlandt and Its Tenants, 1697–1783," (unpublished dissertation, Michigan State University, 1966).]

*Chapter II*

12. [See Milton M. Klein, "Democracy and Politics in Colonial New York," *New York History*, XL (1959), 221–246; and George W. Edwards, "New York City Politics Before the American Revolution," *Political Science Quarterly*, XXXVI (1921), 586–602.]

13. [See Esther Singleton, *Social New York Under the Georges, 1714–1776* (New York, D. Appleton, 1902).]

14. [For the Hat Act of 1732, see Charles M. Andrews, *The Colonial Period of American History* (New Haven, Yale University Press, 1934–1938) IV, 349.]

15. [See John Duffy, *A History of Public Health in New York City, 1625–1866* (New York, Russell Sage Foundation, 1968), pp. 40–72.]

*Chapter III*

16. ["you bees don't make honey for yourselves" (Donatus, *Life of Vergil*).]
17. [See Irene D. Neu, "The Iron Plantations of Colonial New York," *New York History*, XXXIII (1952), 3–24.]
18. [See John H. Hickcox, *A History of the Bills of Credit or Paper Money Issued by New York, from 1709 to 1789* . . . (Albany, 1866).]
19. [1748.]

*Chapter IV*

20. [See John Webb Pratt, *Religion, Politics, and Diversity. The Church-State Theme in New York History* (Ithaca, Cornell University Press, 1967), pp. 37–46, 51–58.]
21. [See Frank J. Klingberg, *Anglican Humanitarianism in Colonial New York* (Philadelphia, The Church Historical Society, 1940), pp. 3–48.]
22. [Rescue your neck from the yoke of shame; come, say, "I am free, am free." Horace, *Satires*, book II, vii, 91–92. See Horace, *Satires, Epistles and Ars Poetica*. ed. H. Rushton Fairclough (London, W. Heinemann (1932), pp. 232–233.]
23. [See Arthur Lyon Cross, *The Anglican Episcopate and the American Colonies* (Cambridge, Mass., Harvard University Press, 1902).]
24. [See Klingberg, *Anglican Humanitarianism in Colonial New York*, pp. 121–186.]

*Chapter V*

25. It was not till the year 1772 that a clause was thought of as proper in the Governor's Commission respecting idiots and lunatics. Mr. Tryon had the following one sent to him which was read in Council, 5 October 1772, & referred to Chief Justice Horsmanden for a report as to the propriety of its being inserted in the future commissions. [I have omitted 31 lines of the quoted document.]
Mr. Horsmanden reported on the 10th October 1772 that the Chancellors of this Province had exercised that jurisdiction, supposing it included in the Chancellorship or from the necessity of the case. But that as the Chancellor he now had a special Commission from the Crown for it, he thought the clause expedient in the Governor's Commissions to exclude all exceptions in future. Vid. Min. Council 12 Oct. 1772.
26. Monday   17 June 1782. There was a Court of Commissioners under the Statute of 11 & 12 William III held at the City Hall for the trial of pirates. We sentenced two criminals to be hanged and acquitted a third prisoner. It was agreed that one of the criminals deserved to be pardoned and a doubt was raised whether the pardon could be granted by the Governor or ought to come from England. Lt. General Robertson nor Governor Franklin nor either of the Com-

missioners chose hastily to determine, and the Commission was not at hand. The course taken was to fix the day of execution to the first Monday in June next year, that sufficient time might if it should appear necessary be had for the application to the Crown.

27. With the Commission under the *Great Seal of Great Britain,* the Governor has another under the *Seal of the High Court of Admiralty;* which also runs in the name of the King, and it constitutes him during pleasure [I omit 11 lines of quotation.] By the several clauses of the Commission, he is impowered to take cognizance of all causes, civil & criminal, and to hear and determine according to the rights, statutes, laws, ordinances & customs antiently observed. [Smith goes on at great length, summarizing and quoting verbatim from the governors' commissioned responsibilities; 58 lines have been omitted.]

This abstract is taken from the Admiralty Commission to Major General James Robertson ending thus [I omit 3 quoted lines. Smith here continues a long discussion of the governors' admiralty commissions. I omit 12 lines.]

The Governors have made no use of their Admiralty Commissions [22 more lines have been omitted, all discussing this point, and the status of judges of vice admiralty. This seems important to Smith; and judging by his citations to English law, and so on, he has researched the subject thoroughly. He is especially concerned with overlapping authority and the use made—proper and improper—of authority.]

28. [See Nicholas Varga, "New York Government and Politics during the Mid-18th Century" (unpublished dissertation, Fordham University, 1960), which has three chapters on the Governor, and one each on the Council, Assembly, and county government.]

29. [See Nicholas Varga, "Election Procedures and Practices in Colonial New York," *New York History,* XLI (1960), 249–277.]

30. [See Charles W. Spencer, "The Rise of the Assembly, 1691–1760," in Alexander C. Flick, ed., *History of the State of New York* (New York, Columbia University Press, 1933–1937), II, 153–198.]

*Chapter VI*

31. [See Julius Goebel, Jr., "The Courts and the Law in Colonial New York," in Flick, ed., *History of New York,* III, 3–42; and Herbert A. Johnson, "The Advent of Common Law in Colonial New York," in George A. Billias, ed., *Law and Authority in Colonial America* (Barre, Mass., Barre, 1965), pp. 74–91.]

32. [See Charles W. Spencer, "The Land System of Colonial New York," *Proceedings of the New York State Historical Association,* XVI (1917), 150–164; Edward P. Alexander, "The Provincial Aristocracy and the Land," in Flick, ed., *History of New York,* III, 147–163.]

33. [Plural of genius.]

34. [As long as they conduct themselves well.]

35. [See Paul M. Hamlin and Charles E. Baker, eds., *Supreme*

*Court of Judicature of the Province of New York, 1691–1704,* in *Collections of the New-York Historical Society for the Years 1945–47,* vols. LXXVIII–LXXX (New York, 1952–1959).]

36. [The author's father.]

37. [He assumed it without responsibility.]

38. [See John R. Aiken, "Utopianism and the Emergence of the Colonial Legal Profession: New York, 1664–1710, A Test Case" (unpublished dissertation, University of Rochester, 1967); Milton M. Klein, "The Rise of the New York Bar: The Legal Career of William Livingston," *William and Mary Quarterly,* 3d series, XV (1958), 334–358.]

## Appendix B

1. [Spring Hill, Flushing, N.Y.]

2. [That my sons, immediately upon coming of age, take on the toga of manhood. Cf. Terence, *The Lady of Andros,* act I, line 51: "As soon as my son was grown up and could take his own line in life."]

3. [This the Ithacan (Ulysses) would wish. See Vergil, *Aeneid,* II, 102–104: "If ye hold all Achaeans in one rank, and if it is enough to hear that, take your vengeance at once; this the Ithacan would wish and the sons of Atreus buy at a great price!"]

4. [An unequal gathering. Cf. Julius Caesar, *The Civil Wars,* I, xl, 6: "So going into action with unequal numbers, he sustains impetuous charges of the legions and cavalry."]

5. [The Society for the Propagation of the Gospel, a missionary arm of the Church of England.]

6. [The Reverend Henry Barclay. See Appendix B in Volume Two. I have not been able to locate Barclay's letter.]

7. [In 1728 Colden moved his family to a tract of land a few miles west of Newburgh, N.Y., where he built a house and farm which he named Coldengham.]

8. [The first letter is essentially Colden's commentary upon Part I of Smith's *History.*]

9. [See Matteo Spalletta, "Divorce in Colonial New York," *New-York Historical Society Quarterly,* XXXIX (1955), 422–440.]

10. [The second letter is essentially Colden's commentary upon Part II of Smith's *History.*]

11. [The third letter is essentially Colden's commentary upon Part III of Smith's *History.*]

12. [See David Jones in Volume Two, Appendix B.]

13. [I.e., Presbyterians.]

14. [Here referring to the Congregationalists.]

15. [This letter and the next essentially comprise Colden's commentary on Part IV of Smith's *History.*]

16. [See Lawrence H. Leder, ed., "Robert Hunter's *Androboros*," *Bulletin of the New York Public Library,* LXVIII (1964), 153–190.]

17. [Presbyterian and Dutch Reformed.]

18. [See note 16 above.]

19. [This letter and the next two are congruent with Part V of Smith's *History*.]

20. [A writ empowering one who is not a judge to perform some act in place of a judge.]

21. [This letter appears to be a revised draft of the previous one. Although they are similar, there are sufficient differences to justify publishing them both.]

22. [Samuel Jones (1734–1819), author of these next four letters, was born into a New York family of Welsh and Irish background. He studied law with William Smith, Jr., in the 1750's, and practiced as an attorney throughout his long lifetime. A neutralist in the War of Independence, he became a strong Federalist afterward. He always maintained a lively interest in the history of New York. See the *National Cyclopaedia of American Biography* (New York, 1901), XI, 489. John Pintard was then recording secretary of the New-York Historical Society.]

23. [William Smith, *History of New-York from the First Discovery to the Year 1732 . . . With a Continuation from the Year 1732, to the Commencement of the Year 1814* (Albany: Ryer Schermerhorn, 1814). The continuation (pp. 391–505) was assembled by John Van Ness Yates.]

24. [*A Review of the Military Operations in North America, from the Commencement of the French hostilities on the Frontiers of Virginia in 1753, to the Surrender of Oswego, on the 14th of August 1756; in a Letter to a Nobleman* (London, 1757; New Haven, 1758). There is no certain evidence to demonstrate conclusively whether this long essay was written by William Livingston, or William Smith, Jr., or the two in collaboration.]

25. [During good behavior.]